acts

on art and motherhood

of

creation

hettie judah

acts

on art and motherhood

of

creation

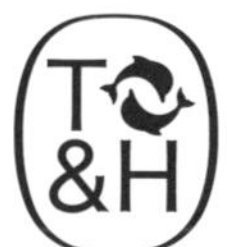

hettie judah

I dedicate this book with so much love to Jacob and Isaac.
You made me the mother I am.

First published in the United Kingdom in 2024 by
Thames & Hudson Ltd, 181A High Holborn, London WC1V 7QX

First published in the United States of America in 2024 by
Thames & Hudson Inc., 500 Fifth Avenue, New York,
New York 10110

Published in association with Hayward Gallery Touring

Acts of Creation: On Art and Motherhood © 2024
Thames & Hudson Ltd, London

Foreword by Brian Cass © 2024 Hayward Gallery Touring
Text © 2024 Hettie Judah

Designed by Carol Montpart

British Library Cataloguing-in-Publication Data
A catalogue record for this book is available from the
British Library

Library of Congress Control Number 2024934196

ISBN 978-0-500-02786-8

Printed and bound in Bosnia and Herzegovina by GPS Group

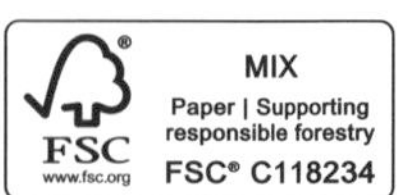

6   **foreword**

8   **introduction:
       the monstrous child**

18   **1 mothers divine**

46   **2 the mother in western art:
       a history in fragments**

82   **3 the artist as mother**

116   **4 creation**

158   **5 maintenance**

198   **6 loss**

224   **7 mothering:
       the family reborn**

252   **notes**
257   **bibliography**
259   **illustration credits**
264   **author's acknowledgments**
266   **acknowledgments**
267   **index**

Acts of Creation: On Art and Motherhood considers how the figure of the mother has been constructed and imagined in art, its meaning shifting according to social, political and religious contexts. But while there is a long history of imagining motherhood – the Madonna and Child is one of the great iconic themes of European culture – these images often reflect abstract ideals or cultural taboos, rather than everyday realities. Art rooted in the lived experience of motherhood is rarely seen.

There are many reasons for this. For much of art history, the reality of motherhood and the domestic realm was considered unimportant or unsuitable for public display. The twin dynamics of mothering and making art were also held to be in opposition. To be successful in one meant failing at the other. For women artists, who often already had to struggle for recognition, motherhood represented an extra burden to overcome.

Acts of Creation tells the story differently. Expanding on the nature and meaning of motherhood, it foregrounds the growing presence of artists – from the feminist avant-garde to the present day – who have reconciled the complexities of motherhood with the demands of art, and while not shying away from struggle, pain and ambivalence, found ways to explore it as a creative act.

Through a range of different approaches and a wide variety of media, including painting, sculpture, drawing, performance, photography, film, print and textiles, the artists discussed address the life-altering nature of pregnancy, childbirth, and childrearing, as well as navigating issues around domesticity, freedom, desire, invisibility, care and the transformations of identity that motherhood entails. Some use the kitchen table as a site of art-making. Others include their children in their work, document their vulnerability, or explore motherhood's radical dissenting potential, as well as its capacity to enrich our imaginations. By looking at how the image of motherhood changes when it is derived from lived experience, it highlights pioneering and imaginative artworks that challenge conventional thinking and redefine motherhood and our visual culture. In doing so, author and curator Hettie

Judah proposes the artist mother as a significant cultural figure that has been overlooked for too long.

This narrative and the related exhibition follow a similar thematic structure, although the former covers a broader chronology and international spectrum. The exploration of the mother begins with the mother as subject. It stretches across time and culture, travelling from the goddess artefacts of various traditions, through the politicization of childbearing in nationalist propaganda, to the pop cultural reimagining of the pregnant body as pin-up. It shifts to explore how a new generation of artists have responded to their experiences of motherhood, from conception, pregnancy and birth to the work of caregiving, to experiences of loss, involuntary childlessness, the ongoing struggles around reproductive rights and alternative family models. At the heart is a series of revelatory self-portraits – a celebration of the artist as mother.

Acts of Creation: On Art and Motherhood continues a long tradition of Hayward Gallery Touring exhibitions illuminating and challenging established art historical narratives. All of us at Hayward Gallery Touring are indebted to Hettie Judah. *Acts of Creation* is a true passion project: the result of many years of researching and writing about art and motherhood. That Judah has created such a compelling book and related exhibition is testament to her passion, insight, and keen sensitivity to the subject and the work of the artists involved.

This project would not have been possible without the support of many individuals and organizations. And while it isn't possible to name everybody here – a more detailed list appears in the acknowledgments – I would in particular like to thank the curatorial team at Hayward Gallery Touring, everyone at Southbank Centre who contributed to this project, as well as our exhibition partners. As always, I am extremely grateful for the unwavering commitment and support from Hayward Gallery Director Ralph Rugoff, Southbank Centre Chief Executive Elaine Bedell and Arts Council England.

Finally, our greatest thanks go to all the artists featured in *Acts of Creation*, whose urgent, compelling and imaginative works open up new ways of seeing and thinking around this important subject.

Brian Cass,
Senior Curator, Hayward Gallery Touring,
Southbank Centre

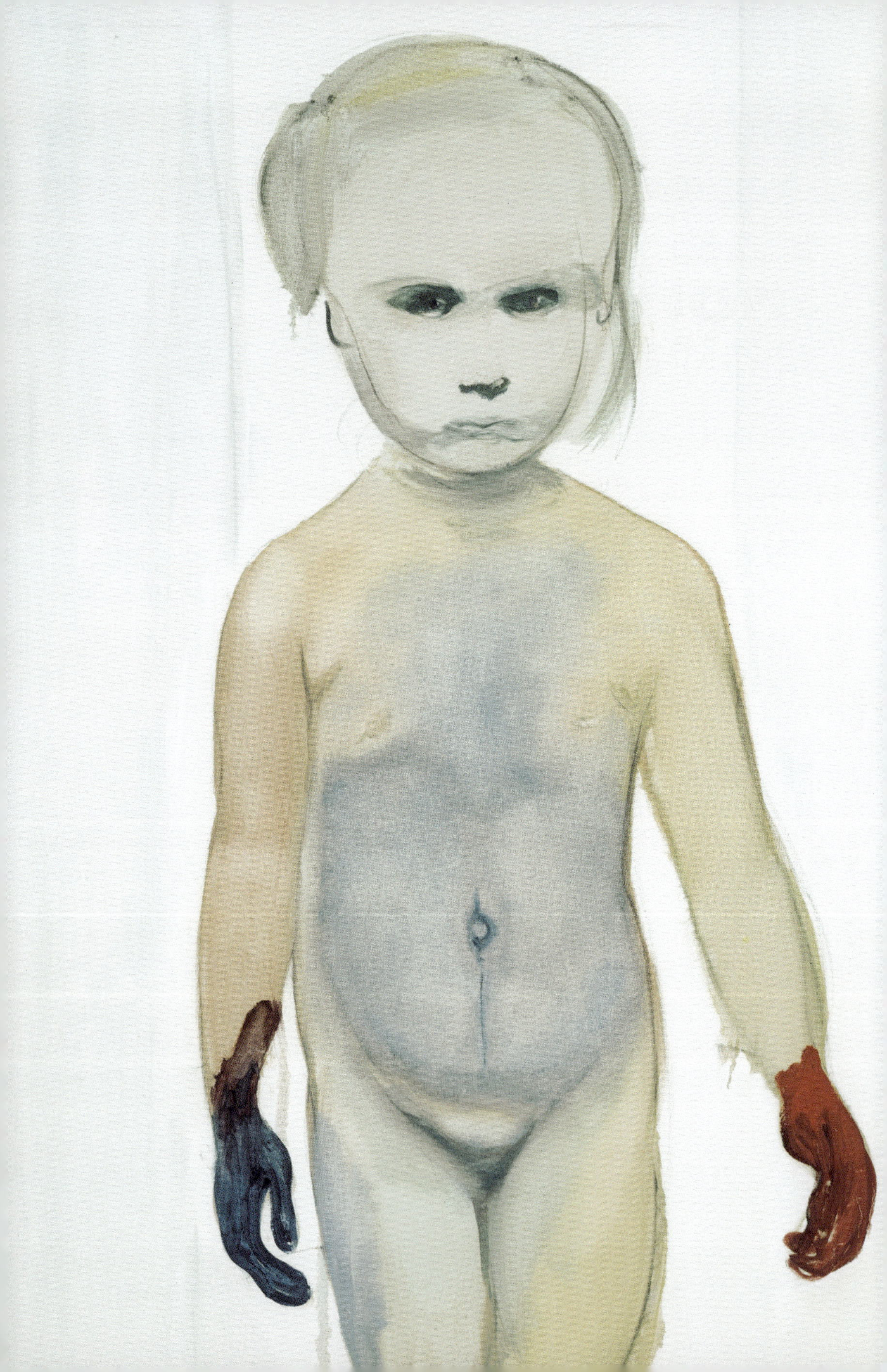

introduction

the monstrous child

A monstrous child is blocking my view and has carved a nest in the soft darkness of my head. It eats the hours, this child, leaving me only crumbs. It eats the night and claims the sleep within it. I am likewise consumed. Who can expect me to see or to think of anything else when the monstrous child has conquered me so completely?

In Marlene Dumas's *The Painter* (1994) **1**, the artist's five-year-old daughter Helena stands naked with her hands dunked in red and blue paint. This is not a portrait of vulnerability. The child fixes the viewer with a serious gaze. Like her mother, she is engaged in the important business of painting. Standing over two metres high, the child looms. There is something a little monstrous about her. *The Painter* is commonly discussed by critics and curators in terms of gender – here the female figure is both painter and muse. Attention is also drawn to the elegant way Dumas constructs the child using the deep colours on her hands: *The Painter* painted from her own paint. To me, *The Painter* speaks of the conditions of making art as a mother, of having another being standing between you and your work.

The monstrous child is not always physically present. They might be a lost child, a longed-for child, an uninvited child, a possible child you are unsure you will ever want, or didn't realize you wanted until it was too late. All of these children worry at our waking thoughts and make bruised territory of our bodies. They stand between us and the world beyond.

•

Throughout histories of art we see motherhood represented in dynastic portraits and carved tombs, as sacred or mythic figures,

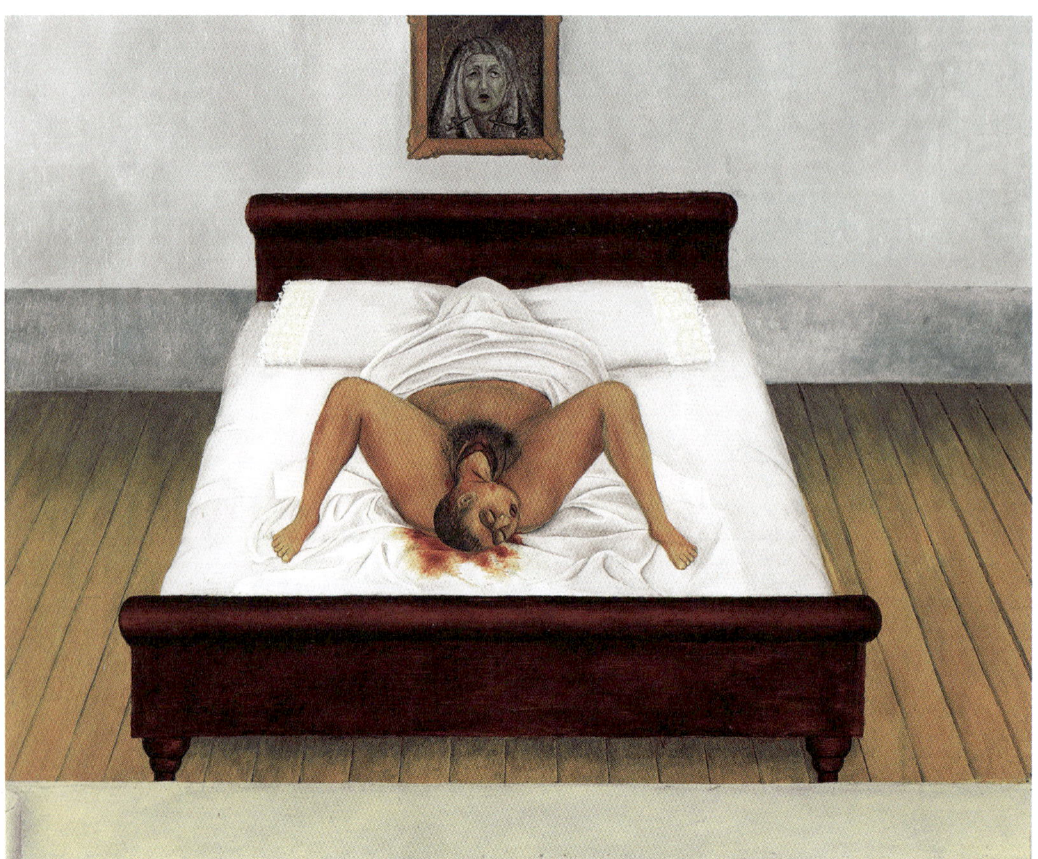

2

and in paintings of everyday life, but until the twentieth century the subject was rarely addressed by artists who drew on first-hand experience. *Acts of Creation* looks at how the figure of the mother has been constructed and reimagined over the last 500 years, as a medical subject, a spiritual ideal and social construct. How might we see the mother differently when motherhood is not only the subject of an artwork, but the circumstance of its creation?

The great feminist artist Judy Chicago engaged in her monumental *Birth Project* (1980–85, see page 31) under the impression no woman artist had properly addressed the subject before. She was not aware of Frida Kahlo's graphic and brutal painting *My Birth* (1932) **2**, made half a century earlier. This was 1980, and Kahlo was still a little-known artist. Neglected, her work was effectively obscured from view. Until we write our own history, Chicago told me, we are condemned to repeat it.[1]

Over the years of my research, I have spent a lot of time looking at art about motherhood, and Chicago's words often spring to mind. It seems to me that the same works are made over and over

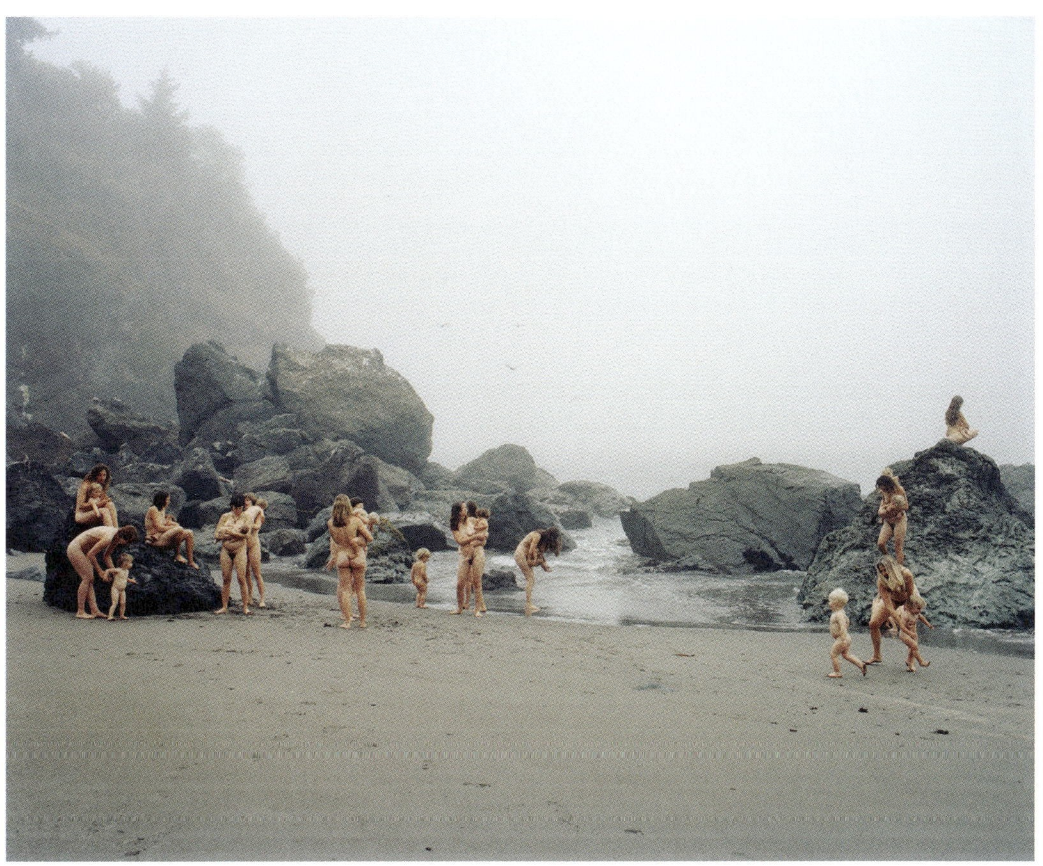

3

again because part of our art history remains unwritten. At the
same time, much art addressing motherhood is at risk of being
forgotten because it has been overlooked in feminist histories
of art. The task of bringing some of these works back into view
seems urgent.

•

In 2016, photographer Justine Kurland wrote an account of her six
years on the road with a small child. It is a story of flying blindly
into the realms of motherhood, and the kingdom of compromises,
negotiations and refusals she found herself in. The *Mama Babies*
series (2004–7) **3** was made when Casper was one, travelling with
Kurland in her old van, criss-crossing the US and photographing
women and children they met along the way. Kurland positions
them naked, seated on mountain top ledges, straggling along a
misty beach, or wading through swamp water. The series is part
Edenic, part post-apocalyptic. As a young mother, Kurland's son

2.
Frida Kahlo,
My Birth, 1932

3.
Justine Kurland,
Mama Baby,
Ocean View, 2006

Introduction

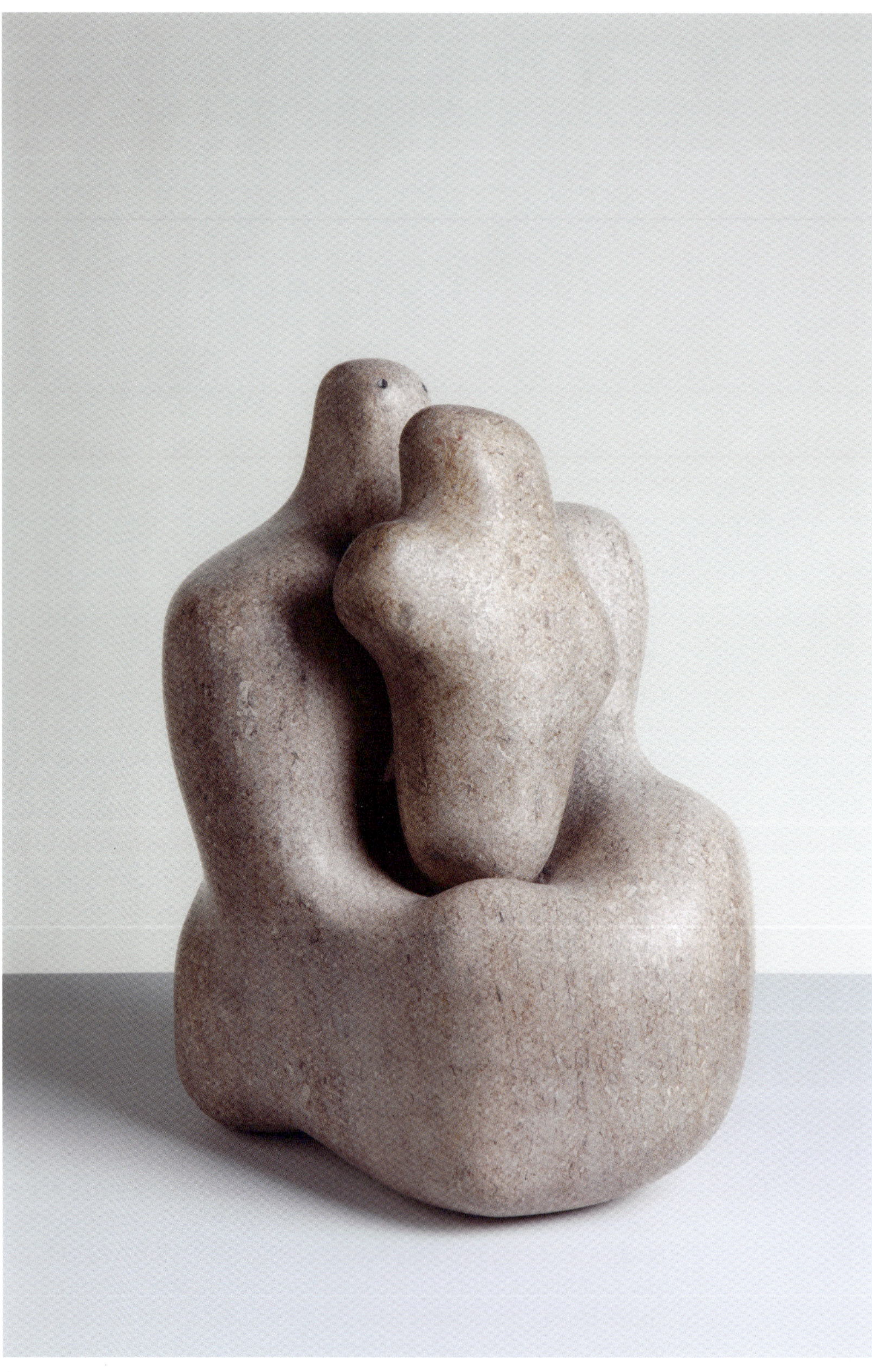

4

4.
Barbara Hepworth,
Mother and Child,
1934

Casper became the focus of her attention, and she struggled to fit photography into the space that remained. 'It was as if each picture took me away from him, and he was forever pulling me back,' she writes. 'I remember complaining to him once, "Jeff Wall doesn't have to make peanut butter and jelly sandwiches in the middle of his photo shoots!" And he, age four, replying, "Oh yeah? What else does Jeff Wall not have to do?"'[2]

Reading Kurland reminds me of my own naïveté, assuming that as a mother, I could continue as I had before, albeit with a baby on my hip as I arted about. I imagined I would conduct interviews, and people would be charmed by my cute and compliant offspring. I'd write as the baby slept. Such happy fantasies. Heavily pregnant, I was poised to accept a book deal. An older cousin read me the riot act, asking what made me think I was different from every other mother in the history of the world? Where was I going to find the time and thinking space to research and write a book to deadline after giving birth?

•

Children are people and people are unpredictable. So, too, is pregnancy, and birth. British sculptor Barbara Hepworth carved her *Mother and Child* 4 in 1934 while pregnant for the second time. Maternity was an important subject for sculptors in this period, with gestation and labour taken as metaphors for the creative act in works by Jacob Epstein and Henry Moore. Hepworth's *Mother and Child* instead imagines a human relationship as well as a formal one. Rather than carving the figures as a single unit, Hepworth created two separate but interlocking forms derived from the same material. Her interpretation reflected emergent ideas in psychology about the importance of early development. As is the way of things, this serene picture was not reflected in her own experience. Unbeknownst to her, Hepworth was pregnant with triplets.

That so many new mothers (artists among them) are shocked by the all-consuming routine of feeding and changing, the repetition, the relentlessness, is testament to the cultural invisibility of real motherhood. In the accelerated life of our modern cities, mothering and other forms of care take place largely out of sight. The family is increasingly a tight private unit rather than an interdependent multigenerational sprawl. When young children make themselves evident in the adult sphere they are often regarded as an unwelcome intrusion.

When I started researching the impact of motherhood on artists' careers in 2019, many of the artists interviewed for my study[3] complained that there was no archetype of the artist mother to help them contextualize themselves. Women who paused art-making to raise children or take salaried employment were seen as hobbyists. They were not considered an interesting proposition by galleries, or capable of producing exciting, experimental work. Where were the artist mother heroes for them to look up to, they asked? The artist mother sits at the heart of this book, with Barbara Hepworth as its figurehead. Hepworth raised four children during the Second World War, fitting art around cooking meals, growing vegetables and the general labour of mothering. Yet as a mother she has been remembered, if at all, for the few months she placed her triplets in a nursing college while struggling as a single parent. Hepworth reminds us of how reflexively society judges mothers for all they do and do not do.

•

In Paris, in the febrile atmosphere of May 1968, the Polish-Argentine artist Lea Lublin committed a discreet act of revolution. Invited to submit work for the important contemporary art annual, the Salon de Mai, Lublin presented *Mon Fils* (*My Son*) **5** a month-long durational piece for which she installed a crib for her seven-month-old son, Nicholas, in front of her painting and undertook his care in view of visitors. Lublin described *Mon Fils* as the simple displacement of her day-to-day activity into a public gallery. She said that she wished 'to produce a work which confronted the real with its representation.'[4] What was being displayed was not Lublin's son, but her acts of motherhood: elements of the visible realm that were present but overlooked. Lublin calmly confronted the audience of an otherwise quite traditional exhibition with aspects of life few were otherwise inclined to dwell on.

I have written *Acts of Creation* alongside work on a touring exhibition of the same title. While I am convinced that this is an important and timely subject, mine is not the first to address it. Since the 1960s, if not beyond, the theme of motherhood has emerged periodically, spawning exhibitions, texts and discussions before being put neatly back in its niche having done little to change opinions within the wider art world. British artist Su Richardson, who participated in Feministo's touring exhibition 'Portrait of the Artist as a Housewife' in 1977, told me she felt quite upset to be invited back into an exhibition on motherhood

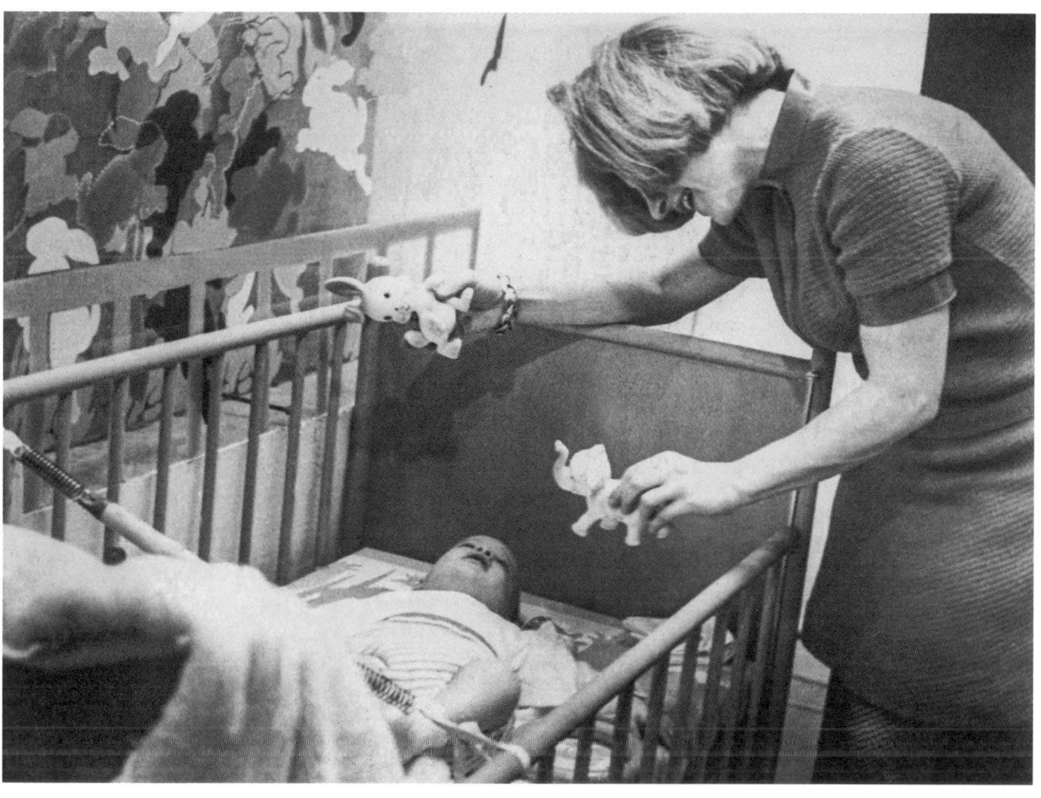

5

5.
Lea Lublin,
Mon Fils
(*My Son*), 1968

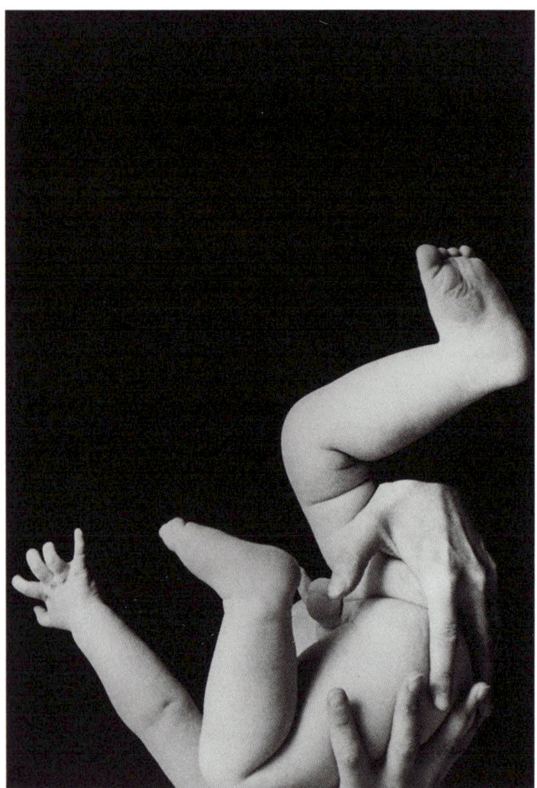

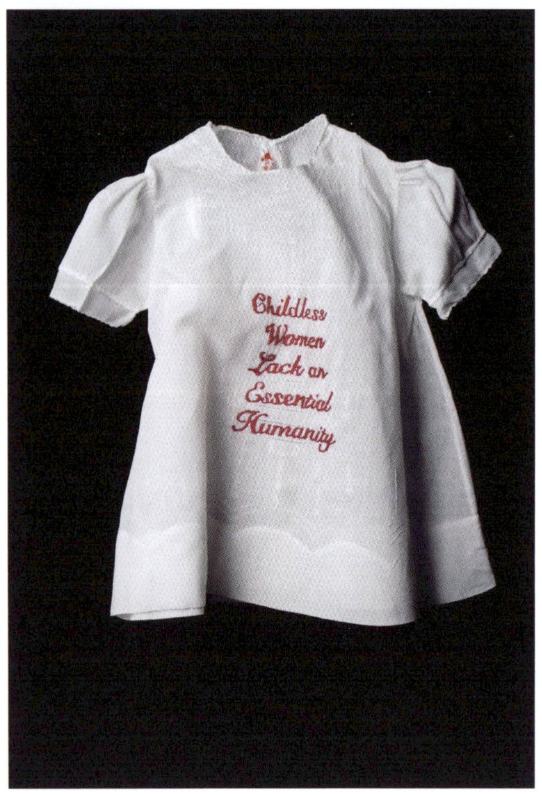

6.
Felicity Allen,
Baby II, 1989

7.
Miriam Schaer,
*Babies (Not) On
Board, The Last
Prejudice? Number 2:
Childless Women
Lack an Essential
Humanity*, 2013

almost half a century later. 'In another 50 years, will we be doing it again?' she asked.[5]

At times this book and the counterpart exhibition consciously tread in the paths of earlier enterprises in the hope of keeping them present in memory and introducing artists to the work of their forebears. In 1990 Felicity Allen's vulnerable and curiously disturbing photograph of a woman's hands cupping a naked boy baby's bottom – *Baby II* **6** – caused a stir in 'Mothers' at the Ikon Gallery in Birmingham. In a catalogue essay for the exhibition, feminist academic Hilary Robinson noted 'an absence at the heart of contemporary representation, a taboo even; this absence is precisely, the body of the mother.'[6] It is only since the turn of the 2020s that this absence has been addressed in any meaningful way in our public galleries and collections.

Regarding reproduction, women's bodies can feel like public property. Women themselves can also be swift to judge those who have chosen different life paths. Researching *Babies (Not) on Board: The Last Prejudice?* (2013) **7** New York artist Miriam Schaer gathered testimonies from other women who had, for various reasons, chosen not to have children. Using red thread, she embroidered vintage children's clothes with unsolicited comments offered by family, friends and even strangers. 'You better hurry up!' scolds a tiny smock. 'Your child is the best artwork you have ever made/ You don't need to make any other art' reads a smug white short suit. A buttermilk yellow dress chides: 'Selfish irresponsible immature unfulfilled materialistic uptight deviant'. All were terms that had been used to describe Schaer's decision not to have children.

I use the terms 'mother' and 'motherhood' in this book, because I address social and cultural constructs. In the final chapter I propose 'mothering' as an activity available to all, regardless of gender identity and parental status, and look at ways in which artists have reimagined the family. When I write of art and motherhood I do so expansively. As well as celebrating motherhood as a subject, this book addresses many areas that are upsetting or uncomfortable. It takes us to places we might otherwise prefer not to go. Nevertheless, we must gaze at the monstrous child, eye to eye. Where words fail us, there is art.

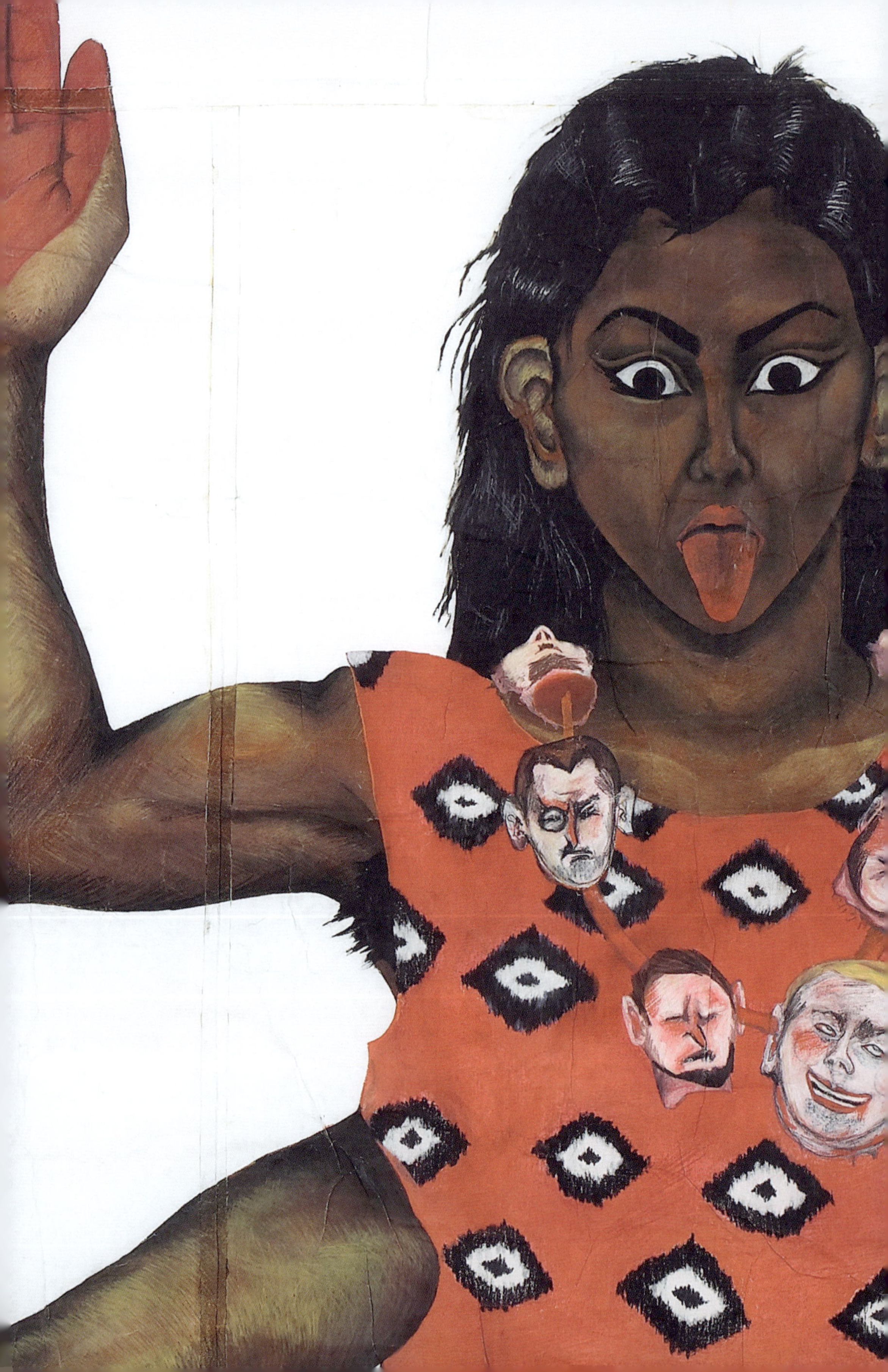

mothers divine

Let us step together onto the cool marble floor of an imaginary museum where we shall start our visit in the European galleries. The existing display opens with 13th-century devotional art. In wooden carvings and gilded panels we meet the Madonna sitting stiff as a throne – the Queen of heaven with her curiously adult-shaped child on her knee. Moving in chronological sequence (for this is a museum of a traditional sort) we meet her again, and again. We find her nursing Jesus from an implausibly positioned 'symbolic' breast, an act of nourishment that gives human substance to the son of God **8**. She appears again as an idealized young woman gazing at a flower communicated in his pudgy hand or playing serenely with the holy infant and his cousin John. We meet Mary as a middle-aged woman, howling as she cradles the stripped and lifeless body of her son, now gaunt and spindly in her lap. Later she performs as an intermediary, presenting the case of the mortal devout to her son in heaven.

Our walk through these galleries reveals the mother as a subject of central importance in Medieval and Renaissance art, albeit one incarnated, with a very few exceptions, by a single figure.[1] For centuries, paintings and sculptures of the Virgin Mary promoted a maternal ideal to which no flesh-and-blood woman could measure up: devoted; self-sacrificing; a virgin before, during and even after giving birth; incorruptible even in death.

If we leave the European galleries and walk to the department of modern art, we can see how this iconography has maintained a hold on the collective imagination. In New York in 1925, Winold Reiss paints her as a coolly elegant figure in devotional blue, whose plucked eyebrows echo the stylized contours of an early Christian icon **9**. Commissioned by the philosopher and patron of the arts, Alain Locke, to open his volume on important Black

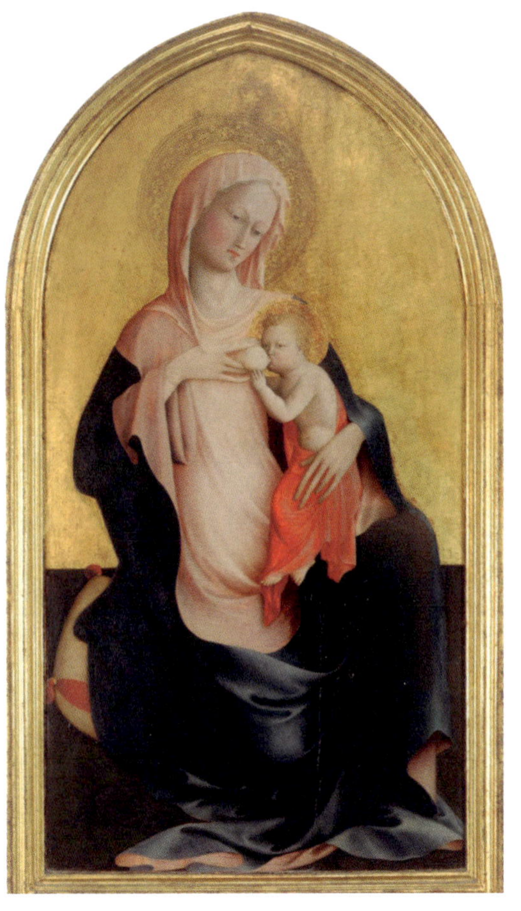

8

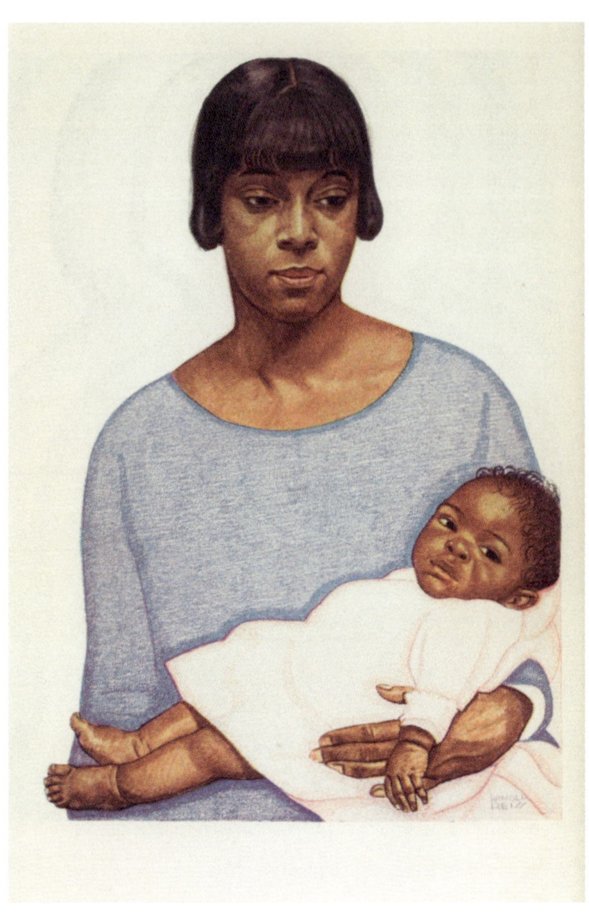

9

8.
Tommaso di
Cristoforo Fini,
known as Masolino,
*Madonna of
Humility*, *c.* 1415

9.
Winold Reiss,
*The Brown
Madonna*, 1925

10.
Dorothea Lange,
*Migrant Mother,
Nipomo, California*,
March, 1936

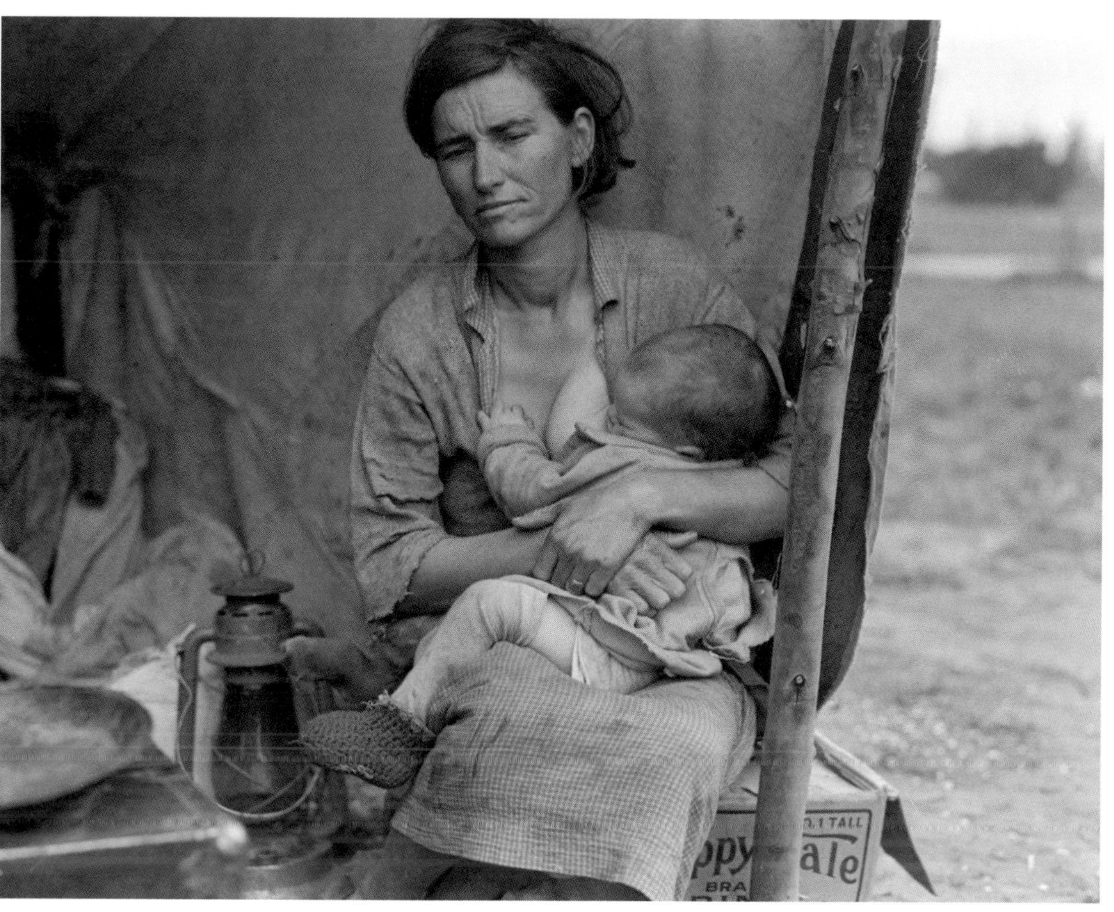

10

cultural figures – *The New Negro: An Interpretation* (1925) – Reiss's *The Brown Madonna* is the idealized mother reimagined for the Harlem Renaissance.

Photographer Dorothea Lange, documenting families in the Dust Bowl of the American South during the Great Depression found a modern-day Madonna in Florence Owens Thompson, a member of the Cherokee nation travelling with four of her children.[2] The six photographs in the celebrated (if subsequently controversial) *Migrant Mother* sequence (1936) include an image of Owens Thompson nursing her baby **10**, a composition knowingly deployed for its associations of noble self-sacrifice and devotion.

We find the subject reborn again in Frida Kahlo's self-portrait with her monkey Fulang Chang, the pink ribbon linking their necks describing the familial tie between artist and animal companion. Painted in 1937, five years after Kahlo was traumatized by a late-stage miscarriage, *Fulang Chang and I* is part of

the artist's continuous process of self-invention – here posed
maternally with her extended animal family.

Staging *Self Portrait/Nursing* (2004, p. 107) the California-
based photographer Catherine Opie looked to the visual drama of
the Baroque. Her body, framed by swags of heavy red drapery, is
thoroughly contemporary – short-haired, full-breasted, tattooed
and still carrying the faint scars of the word 'Pervert' cut across
her chest. As she sits feeding her infant son Oliver, Opie reminds
us of the enduring and pernicious hold the impossible ideal of
the Madonna retains. Even today there are strong preconcep-
tions about what a 'good' mother looks like, about her sexuality
and lifestyle. The mother body remains open to public scrutiny.

This chapter explores how maternal ideals have been constructed alongside our conception of the divine, and how artists
have engaged with and subverted them. For the Madonna is not
the only divine mother in our museum. Beyond the fustily curated
galleries of European art, we will encounter a great maternal pan-
theon of devotional figures – goddesses, icons, nymphs, saints,
monster and even animals – each offering an alternative vision of
what or who a mother might be. While the curators of our imaginary museum might have displayed these artefacts according to
their place and time of origin, we will arrange them differently,
into four galleries, grouped around the cultural roles these figures
perform to reveal affinities that transcend geography and history.

Our first gallery is dedicated to:

11.
Anna Halprin in
Planetary Dance,
c. 1980s

the department of mothers nature

Here we will place great Earth Mother creator figures. Not all
have a material culture that will fit into our gallery: the Earth, as
mother, is often honoured through ritual, her spirit evoked in situ.
The flowing lava body of Pele the volcano goddess formed, and
continuously re-forms, Hawai'i. Our museum, and all within and
around it, are part of Pachamama, the mountainous world-mother
of the Andes. We shall represent these expansive Mothers Nature
through offerings and documentation of ceremonies performed
in their honour.

New rituals emerge to meet the needs of the times. In
California on 10 April 1981 the experimental choreographer and
conjuror of situations Anna Halprin staged *Planetary Dance* **11** as
a rite of cleansing, peace and reconnection after a series of brutal
murders on Mount Tamalpais, which sits within the indigenous
lands of the Coast Miwok people.

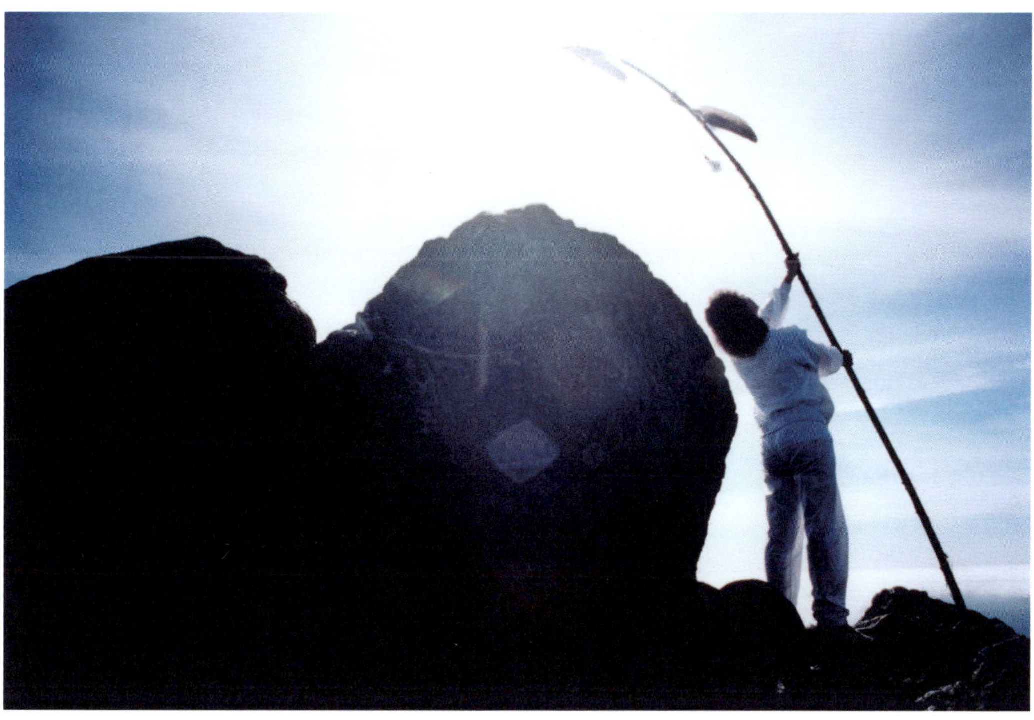

11

The performance began with a dedication to the spirit of Mount Tamalpais, 'for those who consider her a Holy Place', and a dance performed in view of the mountain.[3] On the second day, performers and witnesses walked the trail on which the murders had taken place in the previous twenty-one months. By divine coincidence (or perhaps not, depending on your view of these things) a few days after the ritual, the police received an anonymous tip and the killer was finally captured. The ritual became an annual event, expanding to become an inclusive *Planetary Dance*. On 19 April 1987 it was performed by seventy-five groups in thirty-five countries and continued to grow and change up to and beyond Halprin's death in 2021.

•

Among those expressions of Mother Nature bestowed humanoid form we find Nut, the ancient Egyptian goddess of the sky whose body arches protectively over Geb, the Earth, her husband and brother. Known as 'the one who bears the gods', Nut was mother to Osiris, Seth, Isis and Nephthys, and grandmother (or, by alternative accounts, mother) to Horus.[4] Her body studded with the stars of the night sky, Nut's head is turned westwards, for every

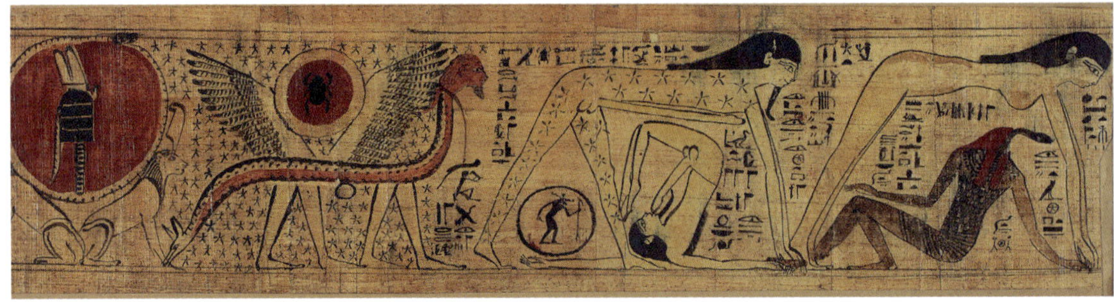

12

evening she consumes the sun god Ra, who travels through her body to be reborn in the east each morning.

The dynamic body of Nut, as pictured in the Egyptian *Book of the Dead* **12**, became a key character in Nancy Spero's vocabulary of female figures, first appearing in 1971 in the furious *Codex Artaud* – a complex and fragile work on paper responding to the violence of the Vietnam War. Nut's body arched across this New York-based artist's works for decades. From 1974 until her death in 2009, Spero depicted only women in her art – a deliberate inversion of the patriarchal convention of 'man' being the representative body for humankind.

As a maternal goddess of the sky rather than the Earth, Nut is unconventional. Supporting, rather than sheltering, humankind, the primordial deity of ancient Greece – Gaia, born of Chaos – personified the Earth. Her offspring were legion: the gods of the heavens and the seas, the Titans, the giants and sundry monsters, the first kings and human tribes. As we are born from this Mother Earth, so will we be returned to her, enfolded into her greater body after death.

Ana Mendieta, who was sent from Cuba to the US in 1961, aged twelve, expressed connection to her mother earth in a poem written in 1981: 'In Cuba when you die...the earth that covers us/ speaks.' Exiled for over twenty years, she feared interment in foreign soil, 'being covered by the earth whose prisoner I am'.[5] Having been made abundantly aware of her outsider status while growing up in the US, as a young woman Mendieta became interested in the Afro-Cuban religion Santería. The religion of enslaved African peoples transported to Cuba, in Santería she felt the kinship of the displaced. Many of her early performances and public actions made reference to ceremonial sacrifice and the life force residing in blood. In her *Siluetas* (1973–80) – body forms outlined or cut into the landscape – Mendieta engaged in ritual immersion within the sheltering body of the Earth.[6]

12.
Nut, from the
*Book of the Dead
of Henuttawy*, Third
Intermediate Period
(*c.* 1070–664 BCE)

13.
Ana Mendieta,
*Untitled
(Esculturas
Rupestres)
[Rupestrian
Sculptures]*, 1981

In 1980, with the exceptional support of the Cuban government, Mendieta returned for the first time. There she invoked the gods of the Taino – indigenous peoples of the Caribbean islands whose culture was virtually eradicated by the arrival of Europeans – in relief works carved and daubed into the cave walls of Jaruco State Park. These *Esculturas Rupestres* (Cave Sculptures) **13** had an ancient appearance that connected them with the island's former inhabitants, but are now largely lost to erosion. Their names are those of the nature deities of the Taino, among them *Iyare* the Mother, *Guanaroca* the First Woman, and *Atabey*, Mother of the Waters.

Wangechi Mutu's roving sentinel deities sculpted from tormented wood, red clay and other found materials, speak of the earth from which they came, but also of being in between, neither one thing (or of one place) nor the other. From the mid-1990s until 2012, Mutu was unable to travel from the US to visit Kenya, the country of her birth – a period that overlapped with her first pregnancy. The alien hybridity of becoming one body composed of two beings informs the monumental bronze sculpture *Water*

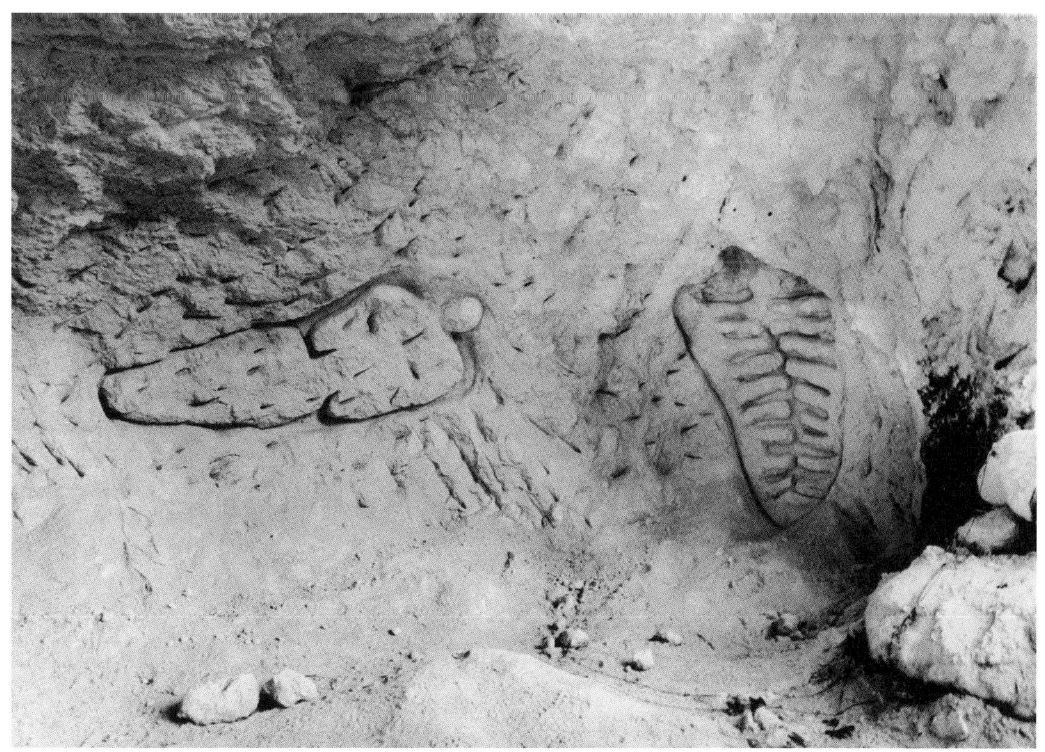

13

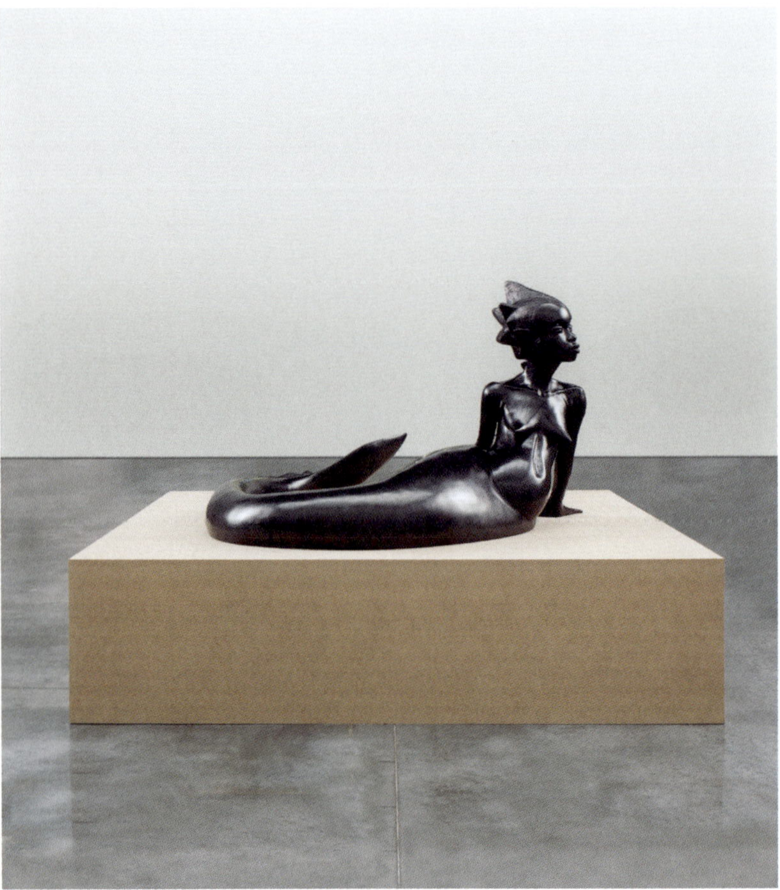

14

Woman (2017) **14**. With the sleek curves and dynamic tail of a siren, *Water Woman*'s belly is distended as though by early pregnancy. The stylized incisions that pattern her spiky hairdo, as well as her tapered breasts, evoke the feminine power figures carved by Luba sculptors of central Africa. *Water Woman* recalls the spirit of the pan-African deity Mami Wata: a personification of the vital living spirit of water and associated voyages, trade and encounters. Mami Wata is plural – composed of many Mami and Papi Wata spirits – and represented either as a siren or as a snake charmer.[7] A mutable and cosmopolitan nature deity, Mami Wata emerged after encounters between European and African mariners in the 15th century. Her likeness derives from sailors' tales of mermaids, ships' figureheads and, in the late 19th century, a popular German print of a Samoan snake charmer.

Let us step into our second gallery:

14.
Wangechi Mutu,
Water Woman, 2017

15.
Louise Bourgeois
in 1975, wearing her
sculpture *Avenza*,
1968–69

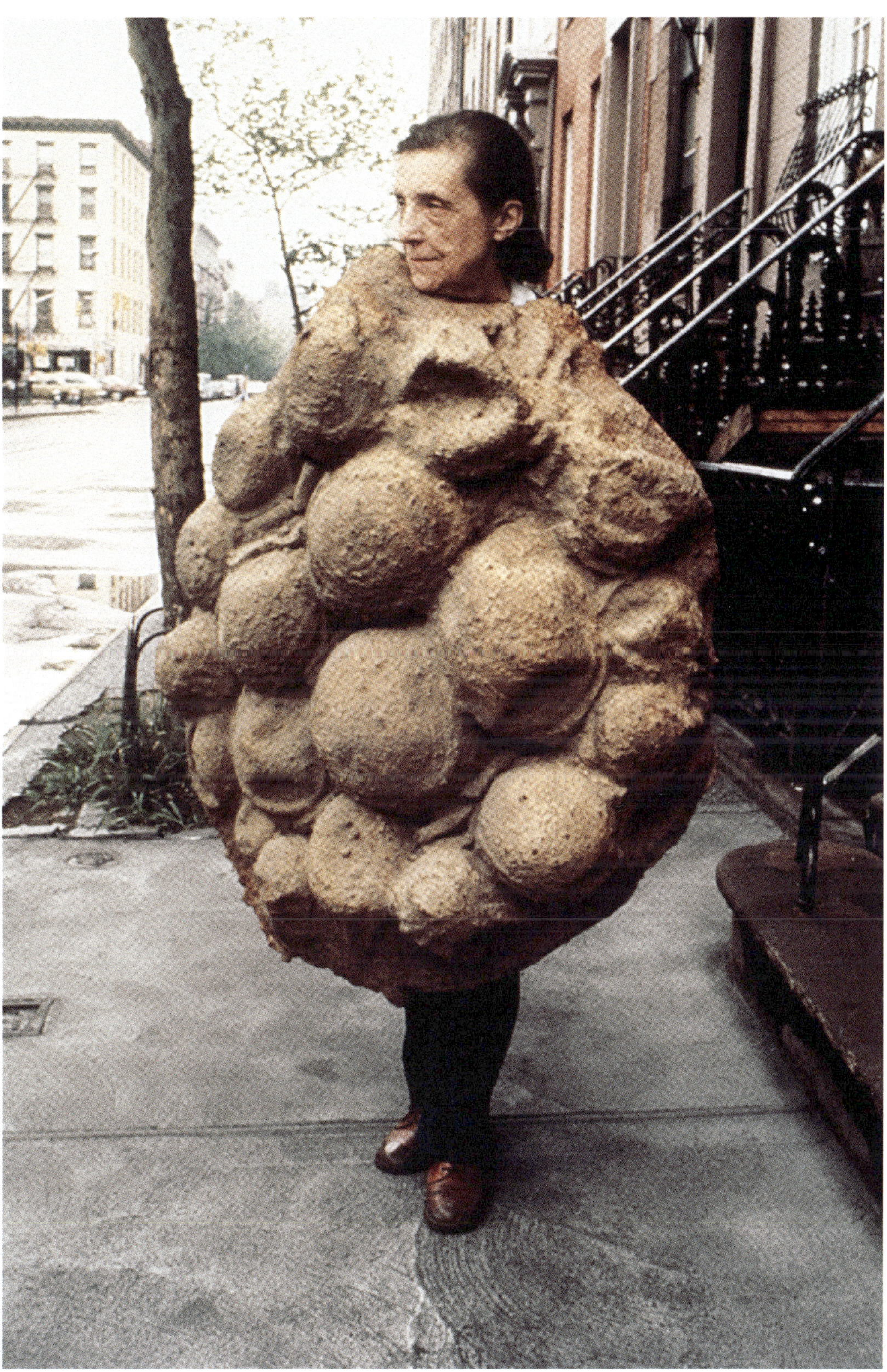

the department of fertility

Here we gather diverse emblems of plenty. We might borrow the ancient Mediterranean deity known as the Diana of Ephesus, whose sculpted torso is covered in breast or perhaps ball-like protuberances. Her modern echo can be found in the many sculptures bristling with bosoms created by Louise Bourgeois, among them *Avenza* **15**, which she wore like a cascading dun latex breastplate for a photograph on a New York street in 1975.

Demeter, the Greek Goddess of fertility and the harvest, casts the world into unyielding darkness and cold every year while she mourns her daughter Persephone. We shall borrow the sculpture of her Roman incarnation Ceres that usually stands in the Uffizi museum, Florence, cloaked in black marble, caught between the worlds of the living and the dead.

The category of 'fertility figures' is a loose one – the term has become a catch-all for corpulent figurines, and artworks with an assumed female form. Perhaps the most pronounced defining characteristic of the more ancient objects within this category is an absence of record through which their character or purpose might be understood. Among them are the anachronistically named 'Venus' figures: portable objects made of bone, horn, stone, and perhaps once wood, carved during the Upper Palaeolithic. The celebrated Aurignacian 'Venus' found at the Hohle Fels cave in Germany is 35–40,000 years old **16**. The earliest known sculpted objects in the human form, she and her kin share exaggerated breasts, stomachs and thighs; legs which taper to points; and small, or sometimes entirely absent heads. They are bulbous female forms that look comforting to hold.

In 1996 art historian LeRoy McDermott proposed that these were self-portraits, modelled by women based on what they could see of their own bodies from a standing position. Comparing women's views over their breasts and bellies at various stages of pregnancy with comparable perspectives of the Gravettian 'Venus of Willendorf', McDermott proposes that the particularity of the form 'lies in what all humans and especially expectant mothers can and cannot see when they look down at their own bodies.'[8]

Alongside these portable sculptures from the Upper Palaeolithic, we will place the heavy-breasted figurines in clay and stone found at Çatalhöyük in modern-day Turkey, the site of one of the earliest agricultural settlements. Made 8,000 years ago, the most elaborate of these Neolithic figures – a woman seated with her arms resting on a pair of leopards **17** – was positioned near a grain store, leading to speculation that these small sculptures

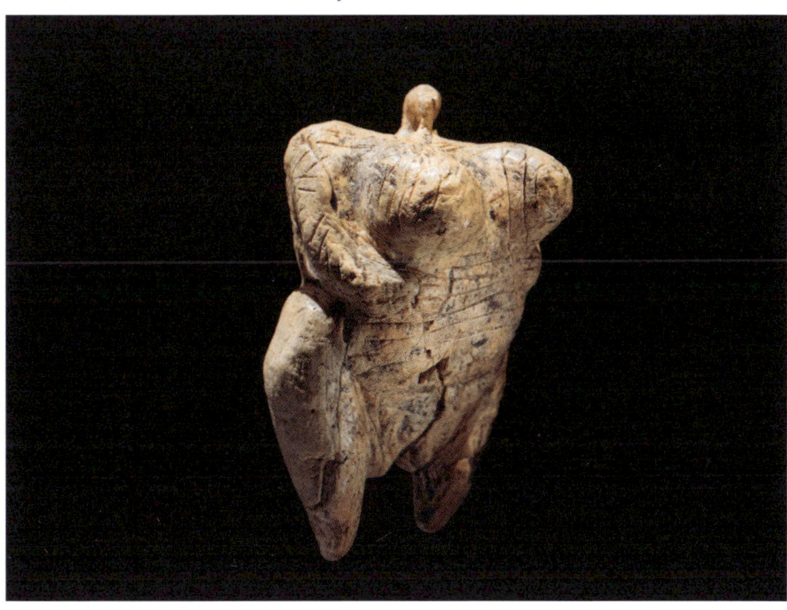

16.
Venus of Hohle Fels,
c. 35,000 BCE

were associated with the harvest, emblems of plenty for one of the first societies of settled farmers.[9]

Devotees of the Goddess Movement, which emerged in the 1960s and 1970s in North America, Western Europe, Australia and New Zealand, viewed such figurines as evidence of a mythic European matriarchal era. This was imagined as a peaceable time of fruitfulness, creativity and tolerance, in which power was derived from the creation of life, rather than the threat of violence. A series of (rather speculative) books written between 1974 and 1991 by archaeologist Marija Gimbutas popularized the idea that these early matriarchal societies venerated a 'great goddess' figure held in common (with some variations) by different peoples of the wider Mediterranean region. From the mid-1960s, Gimbutas was a professor at the University of California, Los Angeles, and her theories influenced feminist artists, in particular those associated with The Women's Building. This radical institution, established in 1973 by artist Judy Chicago, designer Sheila Levrant de Bretteville, and art historian Arlene Raven, was home, among other things, to the first independent art school for women (see page 33).

Chicago's interest in creation myths dates to this period. In 1975, while working on her landmark installation *The Dinner Party* (1974–79), Chicago also collaborated with a radical nun in rewriting Genesis from a female perspective. Chicago was at first interested in childbirth as metaphor – honouring the female

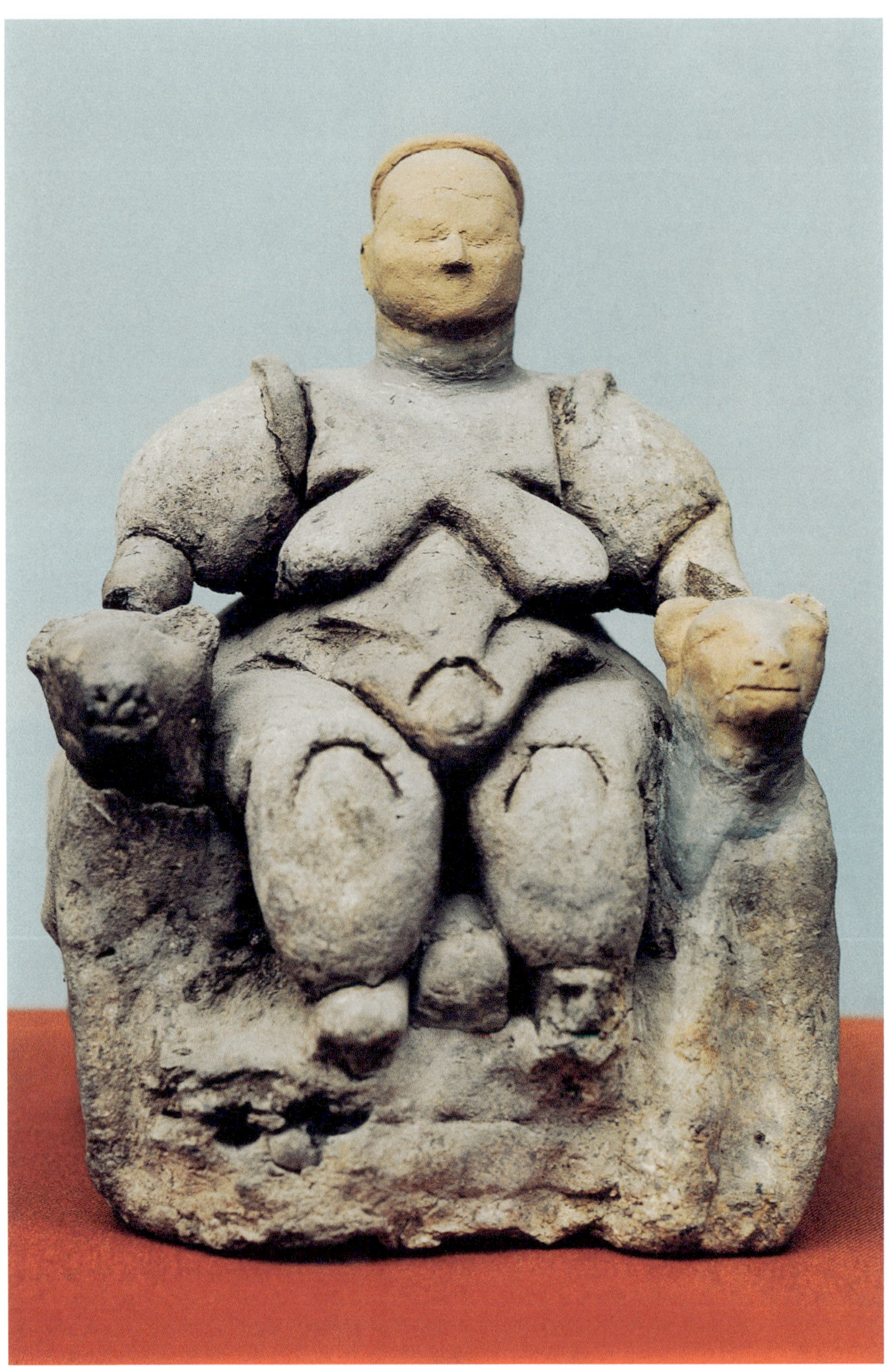

17

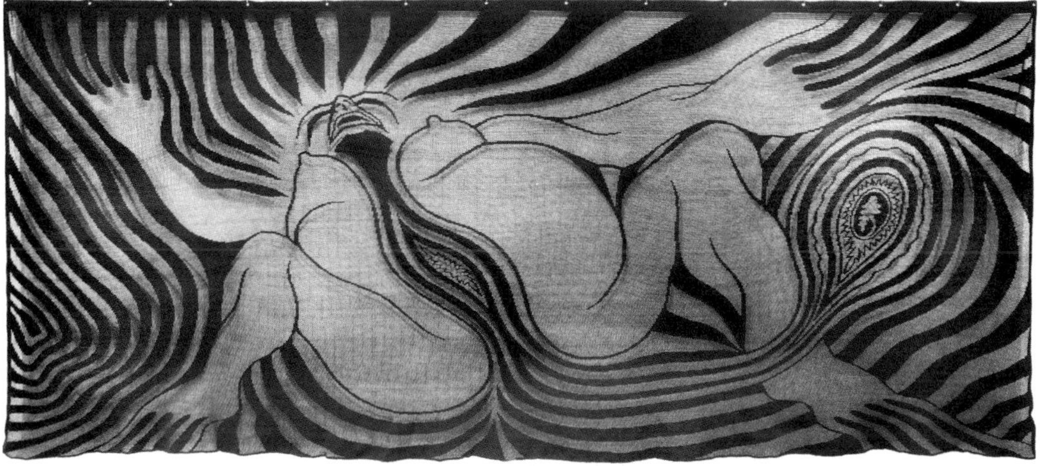

18

body as a site of creation – but after searching for birth imagery
to work from and finding very little, she realized there was a
separate imperative to create images reflecting women's lived
experiences. Her *Birth Project* (1980–85) **18** blended accounts
of parturition with goddess imagery. The landscape-like figure
of the woman becomes a cypher for fertility and generative
power, creating a new symbolic vocabulary for the pain, labour
and everyday miracle of birth. Made in collaboration with 150
skilled needleworkers, Chicago's suite of works was realized in
paint, weaving, crochet, embroidery. These media were significant, Chicago explained: 'Birth, the essential female experience
[was] fused with needlework, a traditional form of women's art.'[10]

The *Birth Project* toured to 100 venues and was seen by
more than quarter of a million people. The central work, the
10-metre-long scroll *In The Beginning* (1982) offers a 're-creation'
myth in which the universe is birthed from chaos, and the fertile
Earth from a mighty mother body.

In the accompanying publication Chicago writes of how the
Birth Project had brought her 'face-to-face with the fundamen-
tal cause of women's oppression; as soon as one gives birth to a
child, one is no longer free. And, tragically, that lack of freedom
is reinforced and institutionalized by the very nature of society.'
Chicago outlines the precariousness that motherhood can bring,
whether for a teenager losing out on her high school education, a
suburban mother of three reduced to poverty when her husband
leaves, or an artist torn between her own needs and those of her
child. Motherhood is a double bind, she concludes: 'Every woman
who has a child is punished for having done the very thing which
society tells her is her womanly goal.'[11]

17.
Seated Woman
of Çatalhöyük,
c. 6,000 BCE

18.
Judy Chicago,
Birth, from the
Birth Project, 1984

•

On the US East Coast, editors of the feminist art and poetry magazine *Heresies* dedicated the Spring 1978 issue to the 'Great Goddess'. Art critic Lucy Lippard wrote about standing stones, there were notes towards an art performance inspired by the mikvah (Jewish ritual bath) by Mierle Laderman Ukeles (*Mikva Dreams*, 1977) and interdisciplinary artist Mary Beth Edelson gave an account of improvised rites she had conducted in a remote cave in Yugoslavia. For these and other feminists, the possible existence of early matriarchal societies offered the intoxicating idea that patriarchy was not the natural and automatic order of human society – that it was in fact violently imposed.

There has been abundant criticism of the Goddess Movement, and not without cause. Even in its own time the tendency to locate childbirth – as per Chicago – as 'the essential female experience' was considered regressive by many feminists. The Goddess Movement was dominated by middle class white women, who located their mythic matriarchal cultures largely in the territory of modern Europe.

Our early forebears did not necessarily think in terms of gender binaries and not all voluptuous 'fertility figures' were necessarily female. Few of the so called 'fat ladies' of Malta feature specific gender characteristics. The androgynous Hapi, an ancient Egyptian deity who personified the annual flooding of the Nile River, was portrayed with a swelling belly, full breasts and a beard. Many structures identified with the mother goddess by Gimbutas have since been exposed as the fruit of overeager pattern recognition.[12] Detractors have noted that the foundational research into early matriarchal societies was conducted by two men at the turn of the 20th century: the German historian Johann Jakob Bachofen and the French social anthropologist Robert Briffault. For Bachofen, evidence of early matriarchal cultures contributed to the picture of social evolution, from primitivism to modern sophistication. Transition from a matriarchal to a patriarchal society was by that rationale the appointed order of things: a progressive transition.

Nevertheless, as even the staunchest critic of the Goddess Movement, Cynthia Eller, concedes: 'A myth does not need to be true – or even necessarily be *believed* to be true – to be powerful, to make a difference in how people think and live, and in what people value.'[13] Such I believe is the case here: adherents were not necessarily working with their eyes shut. In her widely read and influential book on motherhood *Of Woman Born* (1976) Adrienne Rich analyses Bachofen and Briffault's work and makes a clear distinction between the conclusions derived by the original authors and the interpretation she *chose* to apply to their research.[14]

In 2009, art historian Jennie Klein described the Goddess Movement and feminist spirituality in general as 'the un-acknowledged white elephant in the room of feminist body art', untouchable even to those writing about 1970s women's art decades later. While acknowledging criticism, Klein places the Movement in context, pointing out that the consciousness-raising sessions held at The Women's Building made apparent 'the pervasiveness of violence and sexual exploitation experienced by the young women students. Feminist/Goddess spirituality, with its emphasis on the sacredness and beauty of the female body, was taught as a way of countering the unrelenting misogyny experienced by faculty and students alike.'[15]

Gimbutas's popular books and the wider Goddess Movement can be viewed not so much as a catalyst as a lightning rod. Several artists linked to the Movement – notably Nancy Spero and Betye Saar (see page 85) – were already exploring alternative belief systems, symbol languages and the iconography of mythic motherhood more than a decade earlier.

•

Like the Moderna Museet in Stockholm, our Department of Fertility will welcome Niki de Saint Phalle's *She – A Cathedral* **19**. Made for the progressive Swedish museum in 1966, this towering and heavily pregnant incarnation of the French-American artist's *Nana* sculptures lay on her back and was entered through the vagina. Inspired by a pregnant friend, Saint Phalle's *She – A Cathedral* playfully proposed the female body as a house of worship, albeit one that featured a slide, an exhibition full of fake 'masterpieces,' and a working bar housed in one of her breasts.

Not all public venues were comfortable with full-bodied celebrations of female fertility – much of this work was considered shocking at the time. Monica Sjöö's *God Giving Birth* (1968) **20** was inspired by a transcendent sense of connection to the Great Goddess experienced by the artist while delivering her second son at home. (For this, significantly, was an era in which women began to take back agency in childbirth as well.)[16] The painting shows a baby's head emerging between the legs of a monumental mask-faced deity and has endured a long history of censorship. Exhibited at the Guildhall in St Ives, Cornwall, in 1970 the local mayor judged the work blasphemous and ordered its removal.

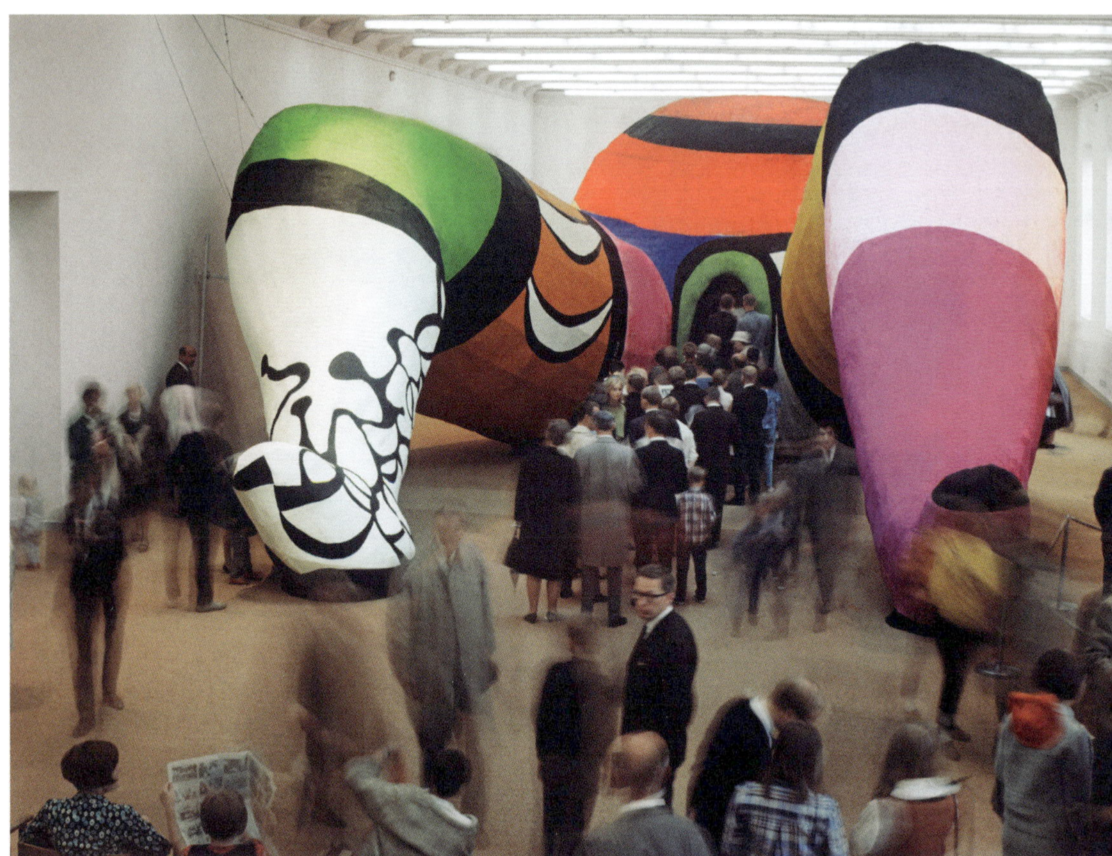

19

When it was shown in 'Images of Womanpower' in London in 1973, Sjöö was threatened with obscenity charges.[17] Years later Sjöö selected the offending image for a gesture of retaliation, brandished by members of her spiritual group Ama Mawu as they entered Bristol Cathedral during Sunday service on 9 May 1993. Protesting the misogyny of organised religion, Sjöö reminded the congregation that between the 15th and 18th centuries, women's knowledge and spirituality had been violently suppressed and that the church had issued no apology for the tens of thousands of women killed in witch hunts across Europe.

　　Before we leave the Department of Fertility, we will make space for a charismatic genre of grotesques found in Ireland and Great Britain. Sheela-na-gigs were carved (some into the outer walls of churches) between the 12th and 16th centuries **21**, though a handful date back much further.[18] Most appear to be bald older women with protruding ribs or withered breasts. Their most pronounced feature is an outsized vulva, prominently displayed, and often pulled to form a wide opening by the sheela's own hands.

19.
Niki de Saint Phalle,
She – A Cathedral,
Moderna Museet, 1966

20.
Monica Sjöö, *God Giving Birth*, 1968

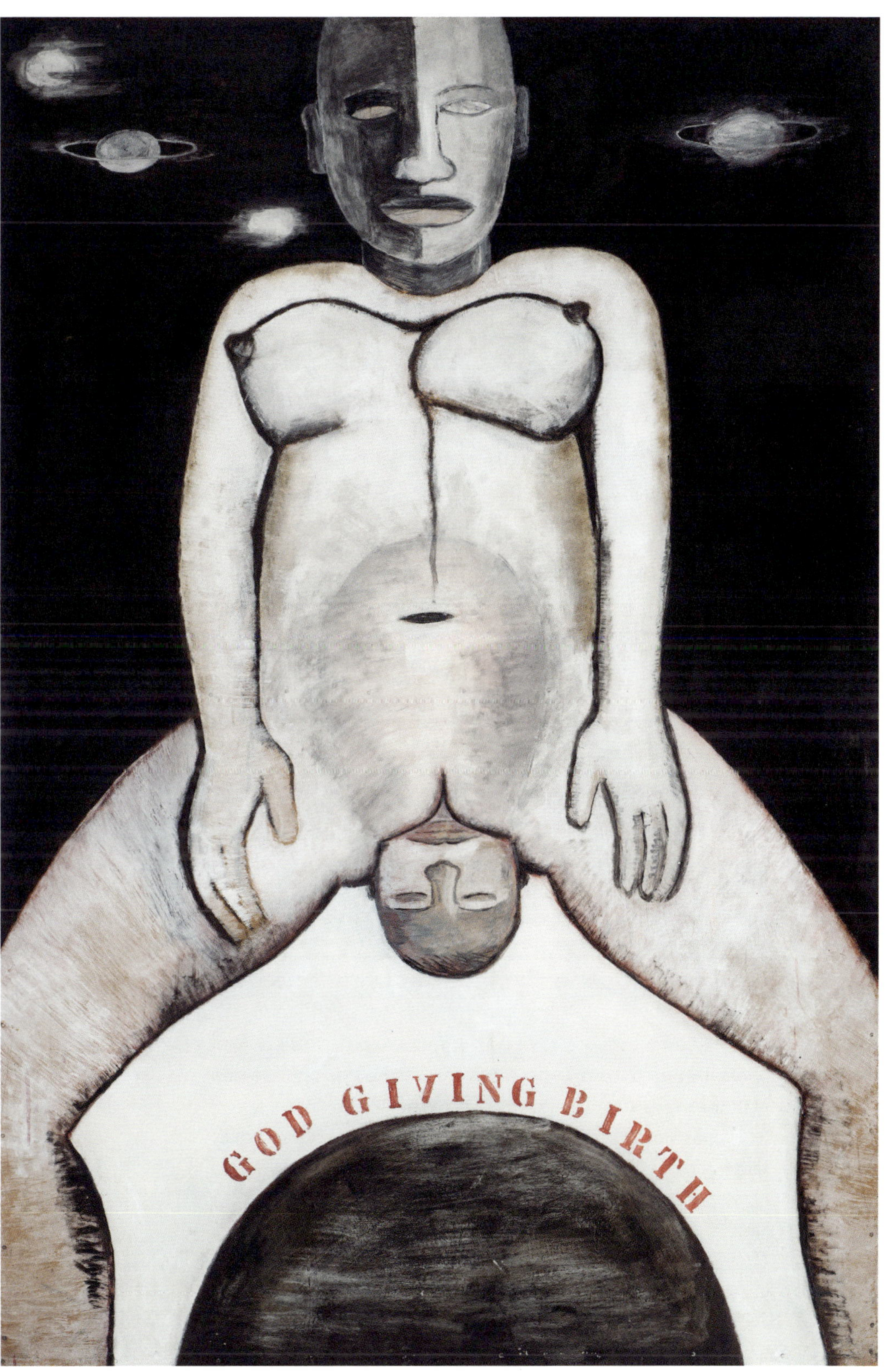
GOD GIVING BIRTH

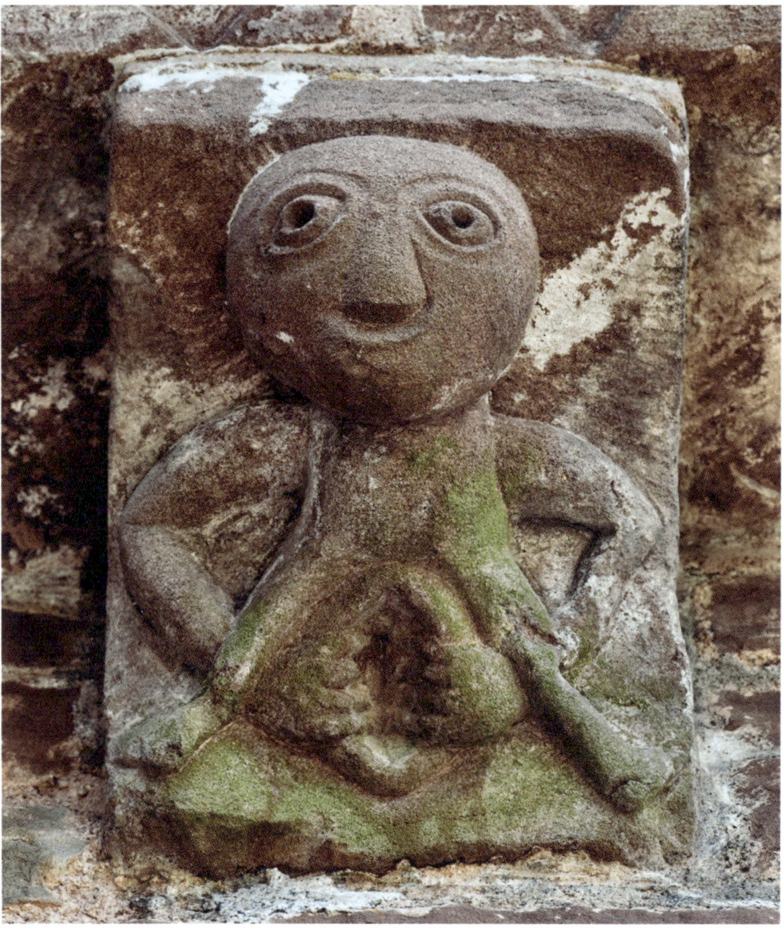

21

While the sheelas are emphatically (and sometimes gymnastically) communicating something, quite what is unclear: they could just as well be an invitation to sex as a deterrent, an insult or a protective talisman. Some have acquired the status of fertility charms in the present day, left food offerings by childless couples.[19] The blunt audacity of the sheelas earned them a starring role in art rooted in feminist spirituality. They make an early appearance in Mary Beth Edelson's uproarious *Trickster* series (1973), for which the artist used photographs of her naked body in a powerful goddess stance in the wild landscape. In the collage *Zipper Sheela Stepping Out* **22** Edelson gives herself a sheela's head and draws a vulva the length of her torso secured with a zipper – a modern and indeed practical variant on the voracious *vagina dentata*.

    With our third gallery we create:

21.
Sheela-na-Gig,
The Church of
St Mary and
St David, Kilpeck,
built *c.* 1140

22.
Mary Beth Edelson,
*Zipper Sheela
Stepping Out*, 1973

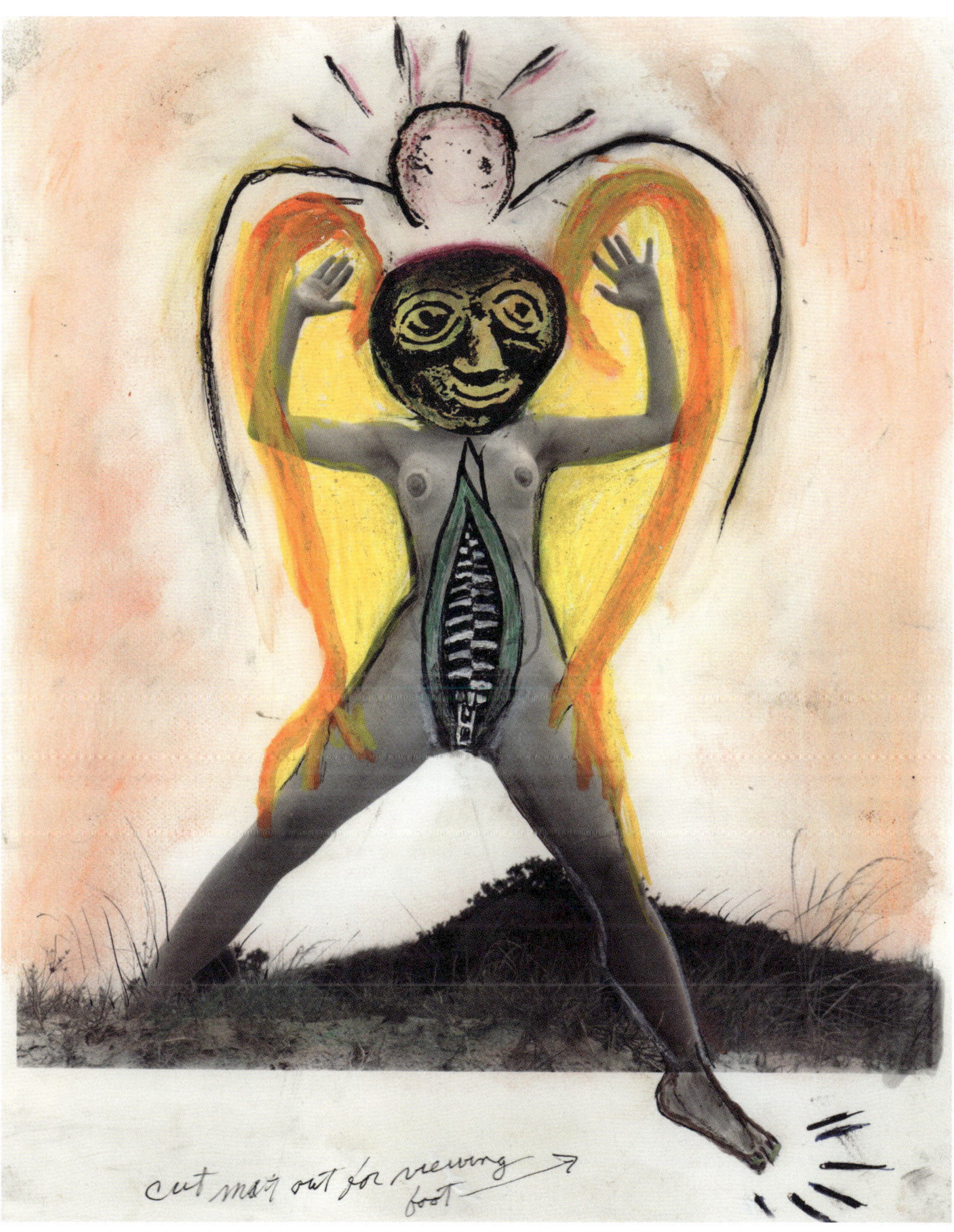

22

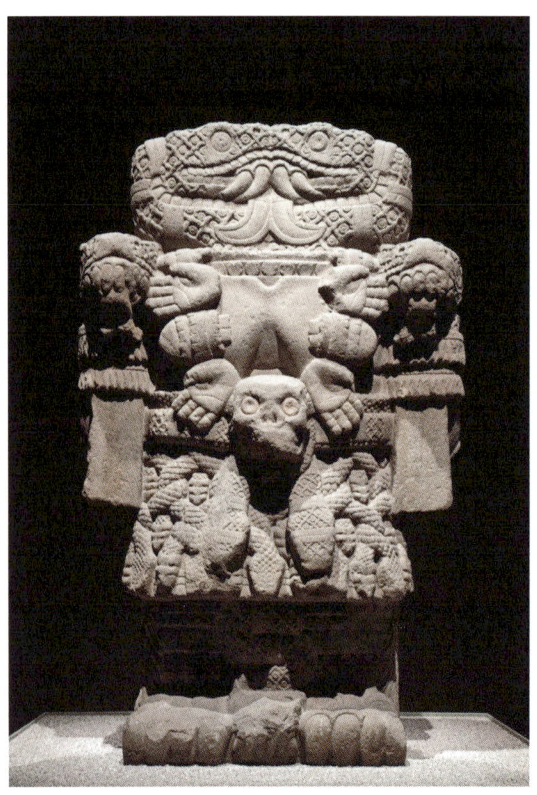

23

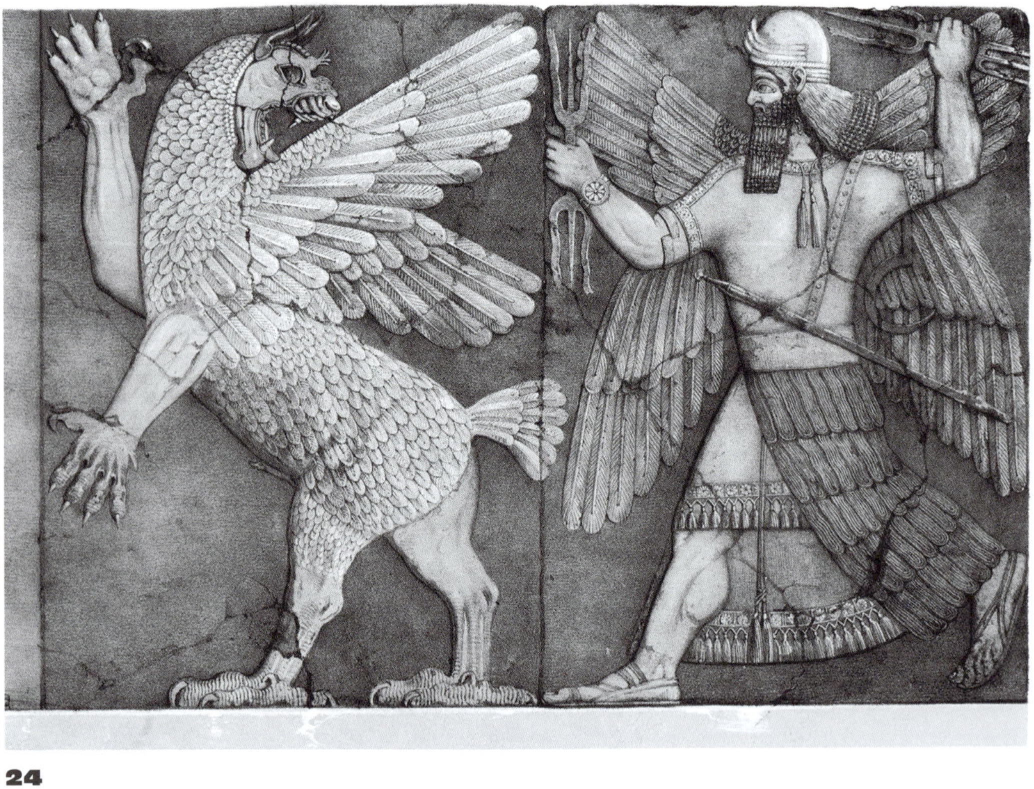

24

the department of ferocity

Here we will position spirited correctives to the self-sacrificing Madonna. There is a duality common to mother goddesses of many cultures – the power not only to give but to take life, maintaining equilibrium. Thanks to its unlimited budget, our imaginary museum has borrowed one of the stars of Mexico's National Museum of Anthropology and History – a 2.5-metre-tall statue of Coatlicue carved in volcanic rock **23**. Identified by her skirt of snakes, Coatlicue the Earth Goddess of the Mexica wears a necklace of hands and hearts, and a human skull for a belt buckle. The coral snakes that rear up head-to-head to form her face symbolize blood streaming from the stump of her neck. Very little of the goddess's own body is visible, but that little portion that is – the inverted 'v' of her drooping breasts and a fold of flesh on her belly – suggest a mature woman. She is the mother of Huitzilopochtli – Aztec god of sun and war – said to have leapt from Coatlicue's womb fully armed and battle ready, to defend her against his jealous older sister. In her role as creator deity, she was one of five primordial women who sacrificed themselves to 'birth' the sun and usher in the present era: 'a grand creatrix, the mother of all beings and objects that inhabited the Aztec universe.'[20]

It does not do to disturb a mother's sleep by dancing and carousing. The rowdy behaviour of young gods sparks the great battle between the goddess Tiamat and the young upstart Marduk in the Babylonian creation epic the *Enuma Elish* **24**. Clay story tablets recovered from ancient sites including the library at Nineveh describe Tiamat as one of two primal deities. After she and her consort Abzu create the first gods, a conflict flares up between the sleep-deprived elders and their hard-partying offspring. When Abzu is killed, Tiamat rises up and transforms from gentle matriarch into the embodiment of chaos and war, creating eleven monsters with poison instead of blood: 'The Hydra, the Dragon, the Hairy Hero, the Great Demon, the Savage Dog, and the Scorpion-man, Fierce demons, the Fish-man, and the Bull-man, Carriers of merciless weapons, fearless in the face of battle.'[21] All who stand against Tiamat cower in terror and retreat, until Marduk offers his services in return for absolute power. Preparing to do battle with Tiamat and her monsters, Marduk crafts seven winds. After disarming her with his evil wind (a relatable fate for many mothers with teenagers), Marduk kills Tiamat by shooting her in the eyes, then slits this formidable goddess in half top to bottom, forming the Earth from one half and the heavens with the other.

23.
Statue of Coatlicue, Mexico (Aztec), fifteenth-century

24.
Battle between Marduk (Bel) and Tiamat. Drawn from a bas-relief from the Palace of Ashurbanipal, King of Assyria, 885–860 BCE, Nimrûd

•

Within Hindu Shaktism the great mother goddess Mahadevi personifies Shakti, the energy animating the world.[22] The plural manifestations of Mahadevi include the radiant warrior Durga, the sublime Parvati, the ferocious embodiment of wrath Kali and Chamunda, the fierce and wraithlike ascetic. In *Housewives with Steak-knives* (1983–85) the British-Indian artist Sutapa Biswas portrays herself as Kali with her traditional markers – wild eyes, a blood-reddened tongue, loose hair, and a garland of human heads **25**. Artist and writer Eddie Chambers later recalled how *Housewives with Steak-knives* challenged 'stereotypes of Indian women as demure and submissive'.[23]

Biswas, who grew up with a picture of eight-armed Durga riding her tiger above her bed, summoned the spirit of Kali for two works made in the graduating year of her BA in Fine Art at Leeds University. This self-portrait is a forceful statement of intent, from her hairy armpits – a declaration of feminist iden-tity – to the severed heads of white dictators and colonialists. Hung tilted forward, Biswas-as-Kali looms over the viewer with machete raised. Clutched in her lower right hand, together with the Tudor rose, is a flag carrying Artemisia Gentileschi's *Judith Beheading Holofernes*. The painting was photocopied from her tutor Griselda Pollock's recently published book *Old Mistresses* – a gesture of fandom that also positions Biswas in a lineage of uncompromising women artists.[24]

Our fourth and final gallery is:

the department of other mothers

Here we will house mythic figures who remind us that mothering is more than a matter of biology. Among them are paintings of Amalthea, saviour and foster mother of Zeus, by Jacob Jordaens and Nicolas Poussin. The Greek mother goddess Rhea feared Zeus's father Cronos would devour her baby son and imprison him in his stomach, as he had their five previous children. Rhea birthed Zeus in secret and Amalthea tended him in a cave on Mount Dicte on Crete, raising him on goat milk. Some versions of the story have Amalthea as a nymph, others as a nanny-goat who suckles Zeus directly from her udders. One of goat Amalthea's horns became the cornucopia and her hide was used to make Zeus's thundering shield the *aegis*.

We shall also include Marina the Monk, a 5th-century saint from what is now Lebanon, who appears as an androgynous

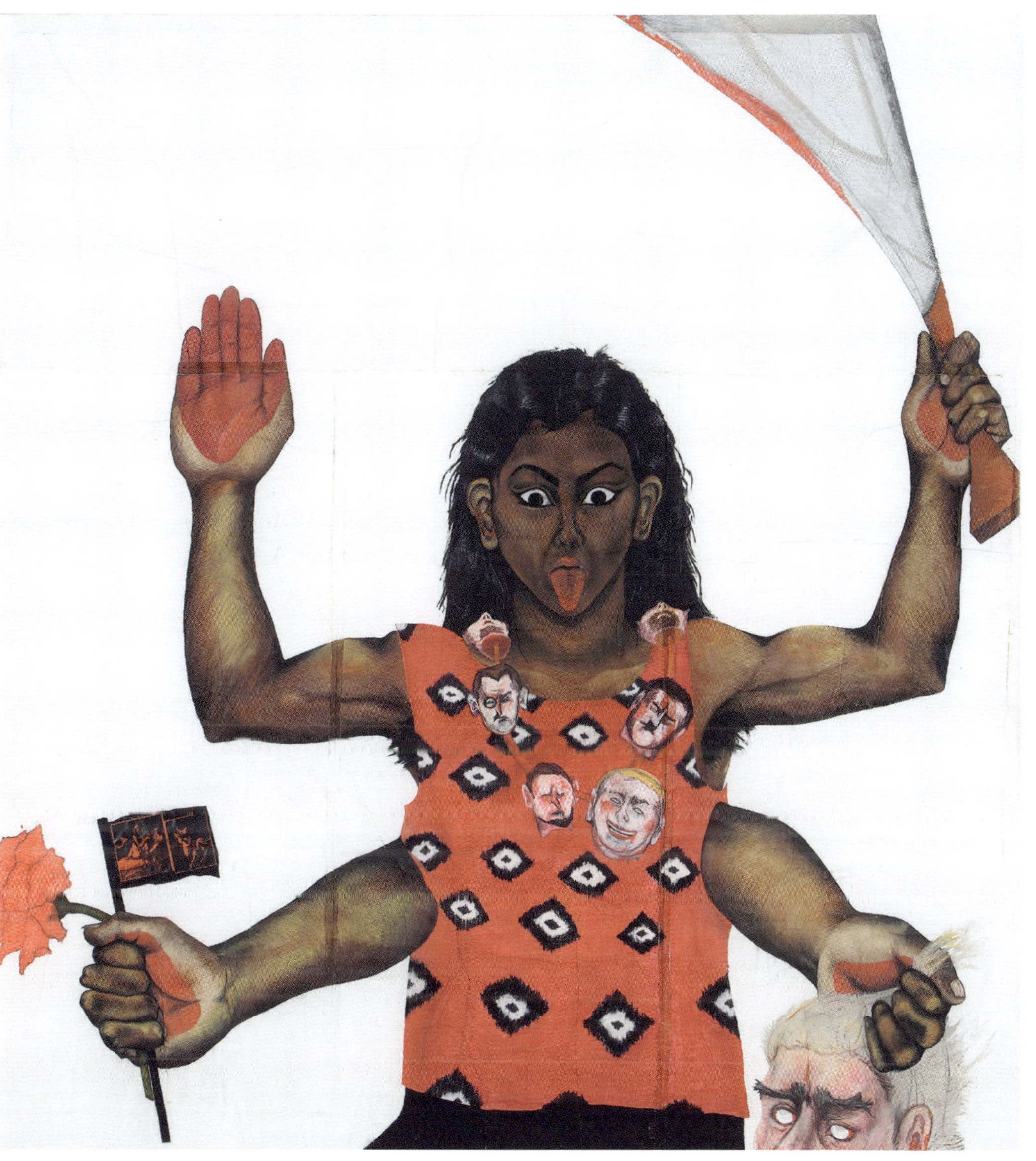

25

25.
Sutapa Biswas,
*Housewives with
Steak-knives*,
1983–85

cowled figure flanking the Madonna on a 16th-century panel by Pietro di Niccolò Duia. Rather than marry, Marina disguised herself as a boy and entered a monastery with her father. Many years after her father's death, when travelling with a group of monks who stayed overnight at an inn, a soldier raped the innkeeper's daughter and told the girl to accuse a monk. Marina was accused but refused to protest her innocence, preferring to face expulsion from the monastery rather than reveal her gender. The innkeeper's daughter delivered a child, which was passed into Marina's care and raised as her own.

The bronze sculpture known as the Capitoline Wolf commemorates the lupine foster mother of Romulus and Remus, the warring twin brothers of Roman myth. Born to the Vestal Virgin Rhea Silvia after she was raped by the god Mars, the infant boys were suckled by a she-wolf after being cast into the River Tiber by their jealous uncle. The bronze sculpture (long thought Etruscan but now considered to be medieval), was originally only the she-wolf, gaunt and protective, eight full teats hanging from taut ribcage and belly. The twin babies that now complete this emblem of Rome were a Renaissance addition.

It is in the guise of the she-wolf that Nancy Spero imagines herself in *The Great Mother* (1960) **26**. Reflecting a fascination with Etruscan and Roman art acquired during a residency in Florence, the work coincided with Spero's early years of motherhood. Slinking on her hands and knees as if to exit the canvas, four protuberances with faces dangle from her trunk – the heads, perhaps, of her three children and, a little apart, that of her husband the artist Leon Golub.

An early 12th-century Chola bronze that we shall borrow from New York's Metropolitan Museum of Art shows the divine infant Krishna being nursed by his foster mother Yashoda **27**. In a beautifully relatable detail, his free hand is twiddling her right nipple while he suckles from the left. Krishna was swapped at birth with Yashoda's daughter to protect him from Kamsa the king of Mathura, who would have killed a boy child. Yashoda is held as an ideal mother – selfless, devoted, delighting in the infant Krishna's playfulness. Examining commercial surrogacy in India in the early 21st century, sociologist Amrita Pande notes the unexpected role Yashoda's story has played in encouraging devout women to become submissive gestatory bodies ready to yield up the children they carry and birth for others. According to Pande, surrogacy became 'a survival strategy and a temporary occupation for some poor rural women...recruited systematically by fertility clinics

26.
Nancy Spero,
The Great Mother,
1960

27.
Yashoda with
the Infant Krishna,
early 12th century

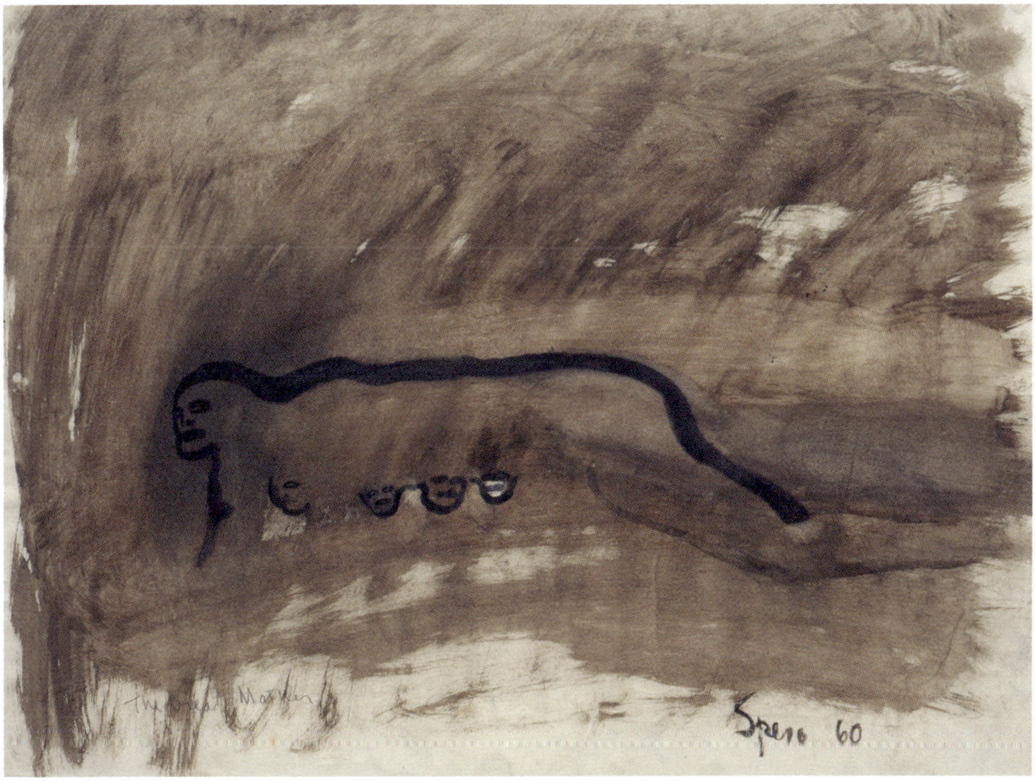

26

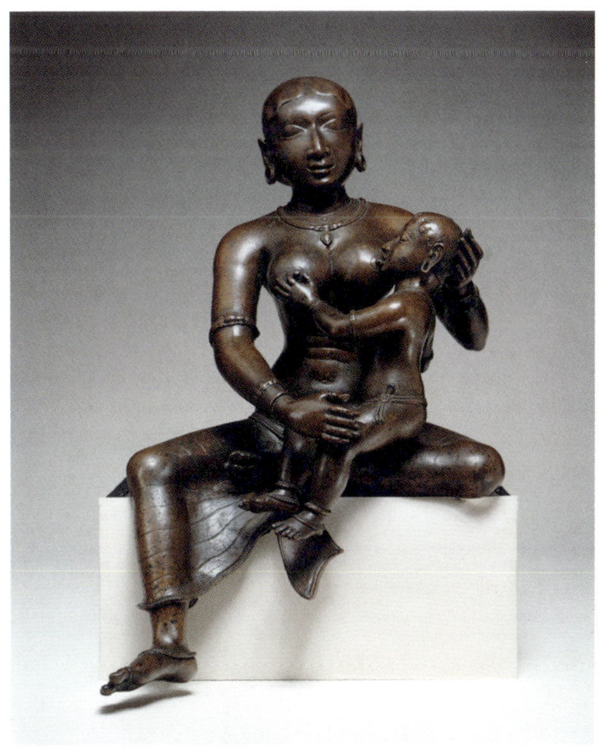

27

and matched with clients from India and abroad.'[25] The figure of
Yashoda enabled these women sequestered in surrogacy hostels
to create an alternative, devotional meaning for a practice that
otherwise carried considerable stigma. Surrogates were encouraged by recruiters to see the process as God's gift, with Yashoda's
selfless nurture of Krishna as an example.

The London-born, New Delhi-based artist Bharti Kher made
her photocollage *Angel* in 2004 **28**, two years after India legalized commercial surrogacy (a practice that was banned by the
government in 2022). Part of Kher's *Hybrid* series, *Angel* shows an
expectant mother with a distended belly, her face anonymized by
a motorbike helmet. Held aloft between her hands is a bat-winged
baby with skin the radiant blue of Krishna. At the mother's feet
is a vacuum cleaner with a dog's head and hairy belly, hinting at
a wild soul pushing to escape from domestic confines. Here is a
contemporary Yashoda for a brave new era, in which the status
and relationships between the various parties is uncertain. We
seem to have come full circle, for as with the devotional images
of Mary we encountered at the start of our walk through this
museum, the child is again the object of worship, and the mother
relegated to a subsidiary role as vessel and attendant. The *Angel* of
the title might be the winged baby, the mother herself, or Gabriel
the divine emissary of the Abrahamic God. Two thousand years
after Gabriel announced Christ's divine conception, reproduction
without sexual intercourse has become a more everyday miracle.

28.
Bharti Kher,
Angel, 2004

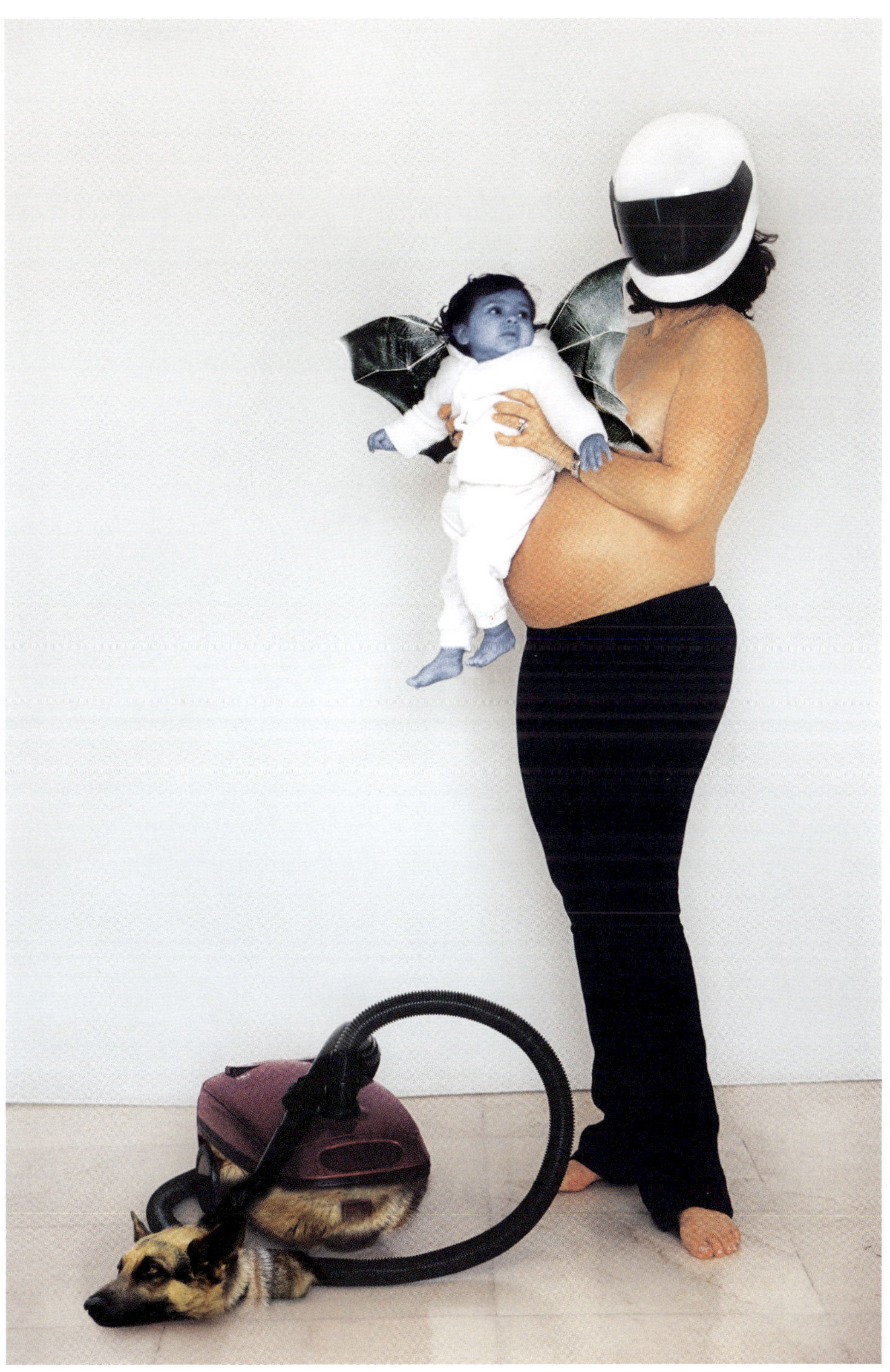

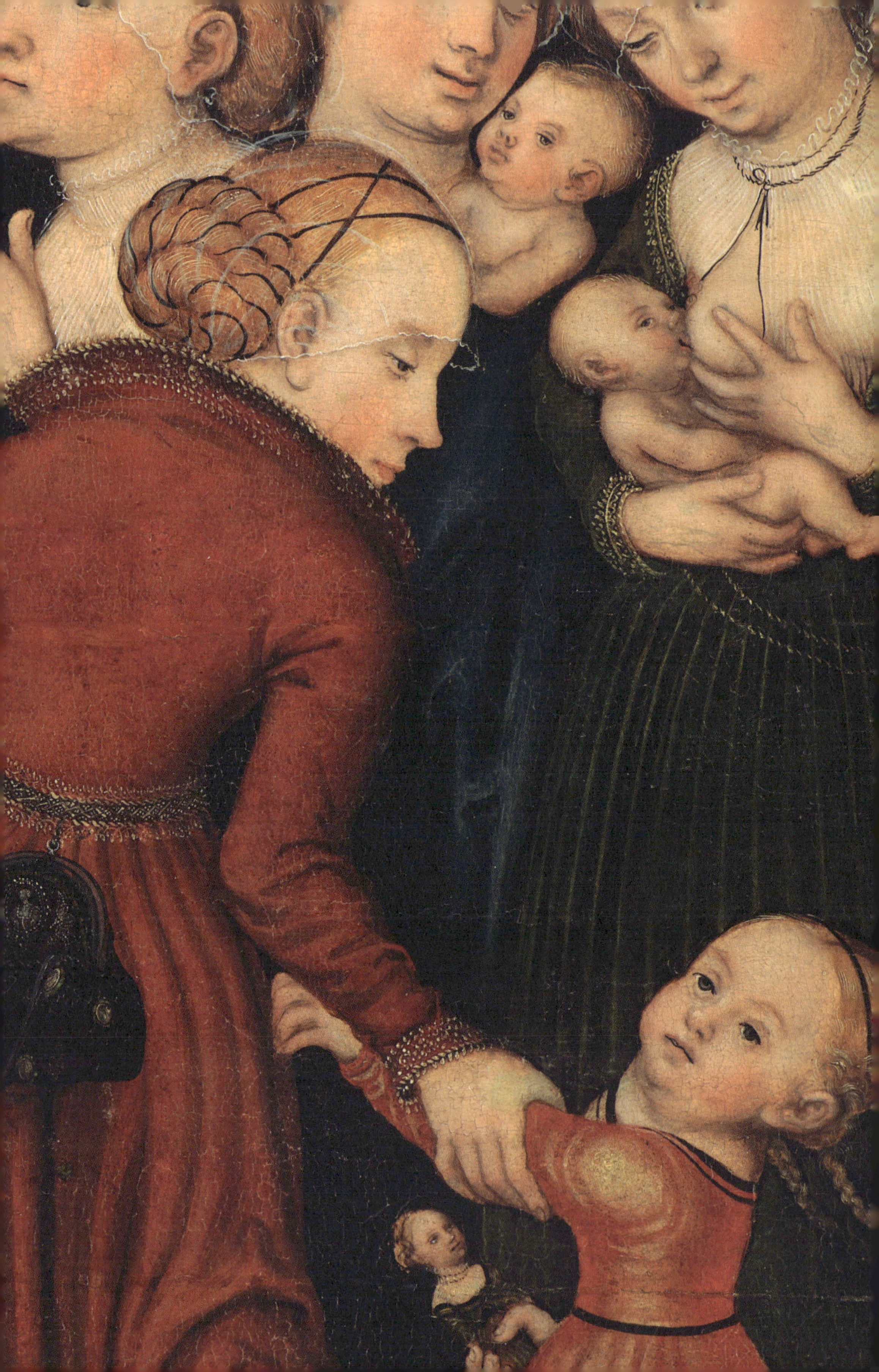

the mother in western art: a history in fragments

The imaginary museum of the previous chapter echoes a game I play in the real world, setting out to meet 'mothers' in museums. Exploring an institution through portrayals of motherhood is enlightening. It reveals social anxieties. British art galleries with roots in the Victorian era have a fetishistic preponderance of 'fallen women'. There are local peculiarities. Mothers in 19th-century Danish paintings are depicted knitting as a sign of diligence and maternal love. We find supposedly ancient mother goddesses resurrected as symbols of new independent nationhood and can observe how the mother body is politically instrumentalized. The search for mothers also reveals the kinds of artists and life experiences valued by that institution, often through acts of omission. This is more than a cute game of 'Where's Mummy?' Over the last five centuries, art has been used both to promote and satirize fashionable ideas around the maternal. Here we shall look at how the mother has been pictured, imagined and constructed through Western visual culture.[1]

the penetrating gaze

The maternal body during gestation was historically both resistant and highly vulnerable to the act of looking. The formation of a baby took place out of sight and was thrillingly (or perhaps terrifyingly) mysterious. In medieval and early modern Europe pregnant women were also considered peculiarly sensitive to visual stimuli. Things witnessed by the mother were believed to influence the baby in utero. Strawberries might produce a red birthmark, while a disturbing sight could cause injury.[2] Women wishing to have a perfectly formed (and by implication, male) child were encouraged to view wholesome and heroic imagery.

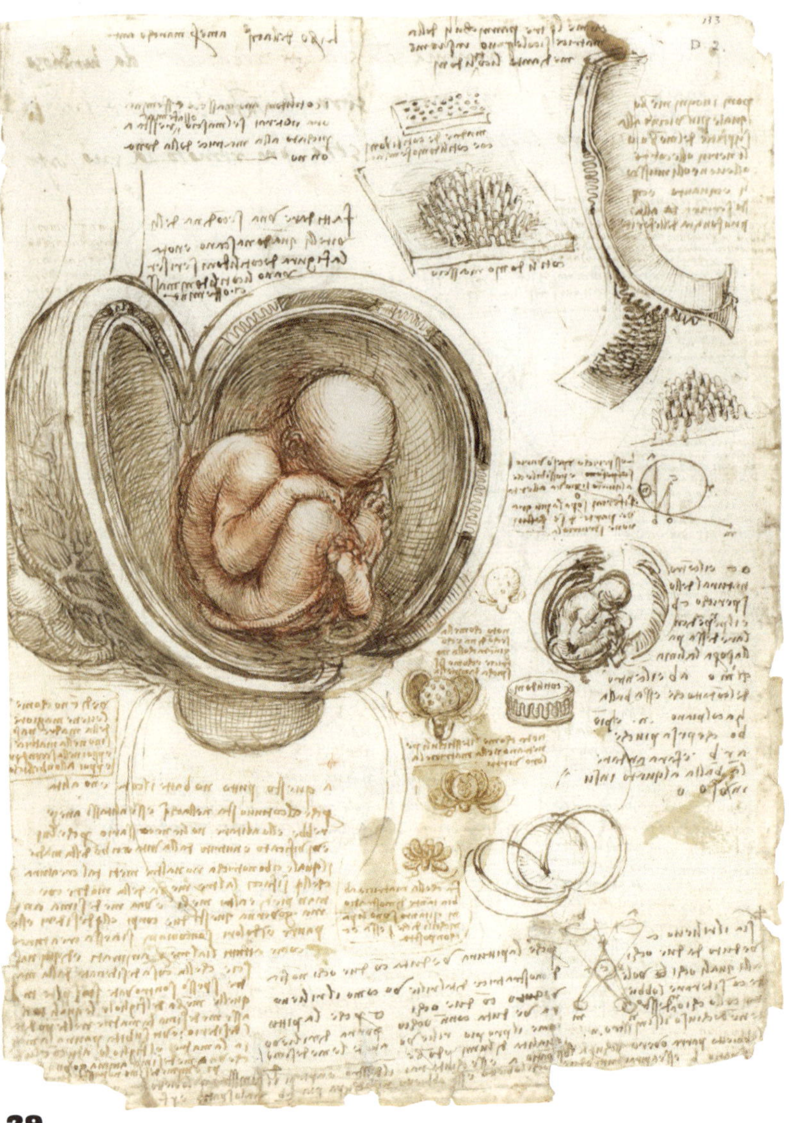

29

Through meticulous anatomical drawings of a human foetus and of the organs of reproduction, Leonardo da Vinci attempted to comprehend and make visible the marvels of conception and gestation. Between 1498 and 1513, defying the prohibition of the Church and often working under cover of night, he dissected over thirty cadavers of men, women and children of various ages. With the physician-anatomist Marcantonio della Torre, Leonardo planned a comprehensive treatise on the human figure. In his notebooks he outlined his intention to follow human development from the moment of conception, describing 'the nature of the womb and how the foetus lives in it', charting its various stages of growth, the systems sustaining it, the process of labour and causes of miscarriage.[3]

In 1511, Leonardo drew the foetus in utero, curled upright in the breech position, giving its skin a rosy tenderness with touches of red chalk **29**. In an adjacent sketch, he speculates that the weight of the head will cause the baby to pitch forward and turn ahead of birth. An enumerated diagram of the membranes of the uterus shows them opening out like flower petals. Leonardo bolstered his understanding of foetal development through the dissection of avian and bovine specimens – motivated by curiosity but also, no doubt, the exceeding unlikeliness of procuring another dead pregnant woman for this clandestine project.

Torre died young and the book was never completed. Leonardo's anatomical drawings were little known until their publication some 400 years after his death. By this time detailed anatomical studies of the pregnant body had been available for over a century. Or more specifically, detailed anatomical studies of the womb. The medical illustrations made for midwifery and obstetrics manuals by Jan van Rymsdyk in the mid-18th century show the relevant body parts in graphically amputated isolation, the modesty of this segmented female body sometimes protected by a sheet or artfully positioned book.

I wonder how different the history of pregnancy and childbirth in Europe might have been had Leonardo's treatise been completed and published in his lifetime. His drawings made before this great project of dissection reinforced erroneous beliefs relating to conception. In a – necessarily speculative – anatomical sketch of human coition made in around 1490, he drew channels into the penis from the lumbar and heart as well as the testes, and from the uterus to the breasts so that menses accumulated in the womb during pregnancy could be converted into milk after birth. His later dissection studies led him to question and challenge such received medical 'truths'.[4]

Through observation of inherited characteristics, Leonardo also proposed that 'the seed of the mother has power in the embryo equally with that of the father.'[5] This was a radical departure from the theory propounded by Aristotle and still popular in early modern Europe, that semen planted the baby in the womb like a grain of wheat in fertile soil, ready to be nourished by a woman's menstrual blood. Such was the power attributed to male seed that in 1537 the German-Swiss alchemist Paracelsus outlined the process by which a homunculus could be grown from semen in a glass flask – bypassing the mother body altogether – first through

29.
Leonardo da Vinci,
*The Fetus in
the Womb: Sketches
and Notes on
Reproduction,*
c. 1511

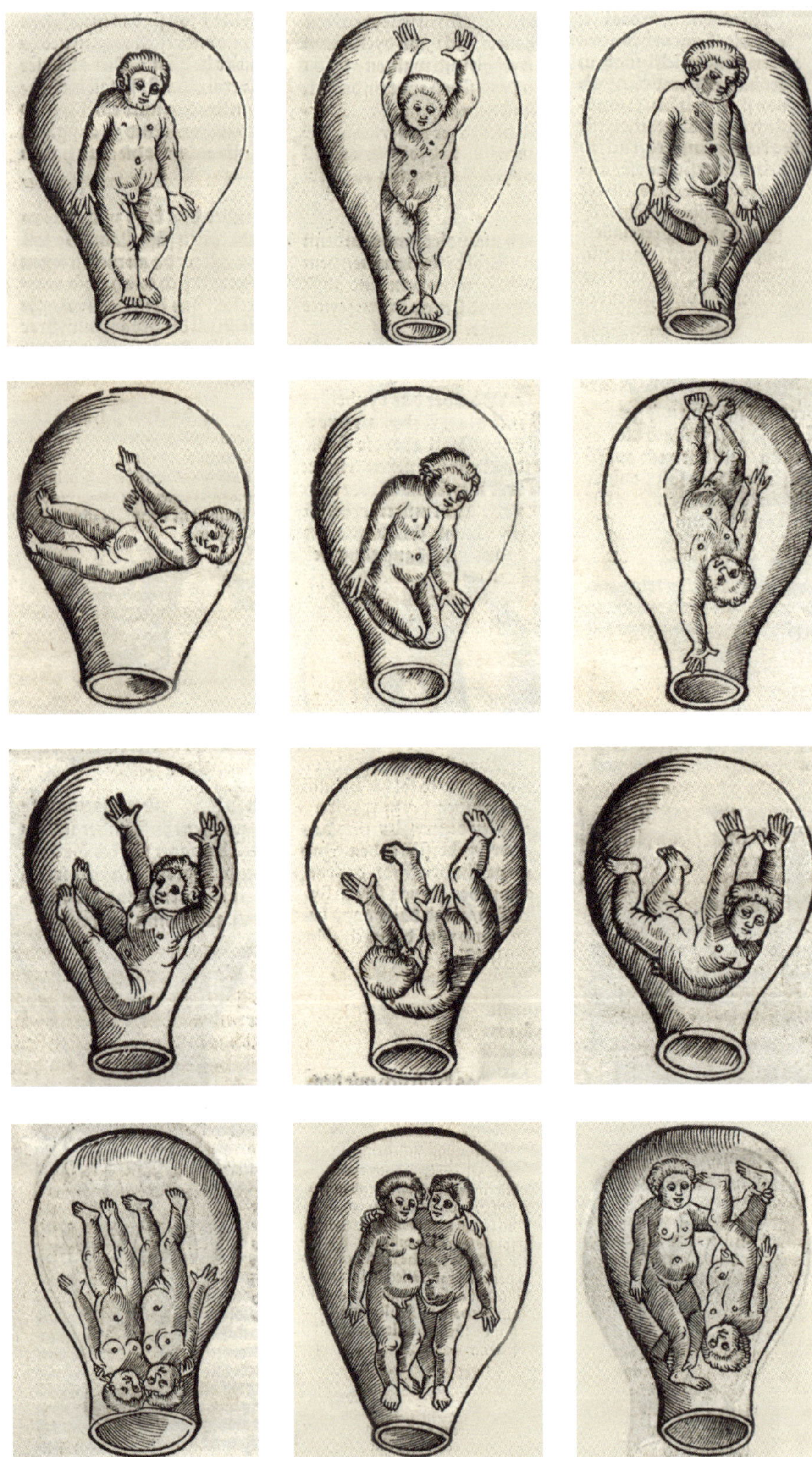

30.
Martin Caldenbach,
woodcut illustrations
for Eucharius
Rösslin, *Der
schwangeren Frauen
und Hebammen
Rosengarten
(The Rose Garden
of Pregnant Women
and Midwives)*, 1528

the application of magnetism and the steady warmth of horse manure and later nurtured with a mysterious blood referred to as *Arcanum sanguinis hominis*.[6]

The alchemist's flask comes to mind when viewing the birth figures drawn by Martin Caldenbach **30** for Eucharius Rösslin's popular 1528 midwifery manual, *Der schwangeren Frauen und Hebammen Rosengarten (The Rose Garden of Pregnant Women and Midwives)*. Caldenbach was a student of Albrecht Dürer – the master polymath of the German Renaissance – but his illustrations of the foetus in utero occupy a very different aesthetic universe to Leonardo's dissection studies. Indeed, foetus is the wrong term here, for Caldenbach's boy babies have the sturdy limbs and tousled mops of toddlers, and occasionally cast one a knowing look as if to apologize for the inconvenient position they have adopted in the womb.

Medical historian Rebecca Whiteley argues that we should not dismiss these birth figures as naïve or merely whimsical. They played a different and very distinct role from drawings of the dissected body. Indeed in 1545, the second English language edition included radical new anatomical diagrams by Andreas Vesalius alongside the birth figures. Whiteley also cautions that it is reductive to see the disembodied, flask-like uterus in which Caldenbach's babies float as a form of 'maternal erasure'.[7]

Birth figures were produced for and consumed by women – among them midwives, mothers and the curious minded – as well as men. Unlike anatomical illustrations, they showed the foetus alive and whole. In an era in which a pregnant woman's gaze was believed to affect her unborn child, and in which talismans and prayers were applied to her body during pregnancy and labour, the cherubic birth figures offered a lively and uplifting visual stimulus, in a way that an image of a dissected cadaver very much did not. While the texts of these manuals could only reach the literate, the diagrams were accessible to all. The illustrations offered something unseeable before the advent of the sonogram: the living foetus inside the living womb.

In the 16th century, the technique of podalic version (the turning of an awkwardly positioned baby) was reintroduced to midwifery. 'Where it was practiced well, it allowed midwives to deliver foetuses that would otherwise have been delivered using dismemberment or craniotomy,' writes Whiteley. 'But podalic version was not simply an innovation, it necessitated a completely new way of visualizing the body.'[8] Rather than assisting a labouring woman through an instinctive natural process, podalic version required that a midwife intervene. Midwives likely learned the technique directly from an experienced practitioner, but the birth figures would also have given them a visual key for the positions they might be working with. While childbirth was progressively to pass into the medical arena, these early midwifery manuals worked not to replace the millennia-old experience of the female midwives with the male physician's 'knowledge' (then still derived from classical sources) but were used as a complement to it.

the sensual body

Based on an episode from Ovid's 1st-century narrative poem the *Metamorphoses*, Titian's *Diana and Callisto* (1556–59) **31** is animated by currents of shame and horror provoked by the spectacle of a transgressive maternal body. Diana, Roman goddess of the hunt and fierce defender of chastity, has stopped with her entourage to bathe in a spring. The nymph Callisto is reluctant, but her companions undress her, revealing her to be pregnant. Months earlier, Jupiter had spotted Callisto napping in a forest glade and, disguising himself as Diana, approached her with a sisterly embrace before revealing his identity and raping her. It was not until the moment pictured by Titian that Callisto's condition is exposed. Diana will not allow this unchaste body to defile the sacred stream, and exiles Callisto who collapses back onto her companions, her body all ungovernable weight. Surrounded by the fresh pallor of white bathing bodies, her face is clouded with horror – bruised and swollen, livid pink around the eyes – a testament to months of private torment. Diana's imperious response to Callisto's rape and pregnancy are shocking (today we might call it 'slut-shaming'), but it was in keeping with treatment of unmarried mothers in Titian's time. Over the following centuries, tragic narratives of unwanted pregnancy would become a dramatic mainstay from opera to theatre, poetry to fiction, cinema to television.

To my knowledge, the earliest extant European painting of a naked pregnant woman, Titian's maternal drama occupies a very different register to contemporaneous depictions of the Madonna. Callisto is all fleshy abundance, an exploited object of desire. There is an interesting parallel here between the two virgins impregnated by a supreme deity. But unlike Mary, Callisto's pregnancy is explicitly the result of intercourse – a pregnancy of the sensual rather than the symbolic body, a revelatory phenomenon as a subject for art. Rediscovered Roman statuary and literature had

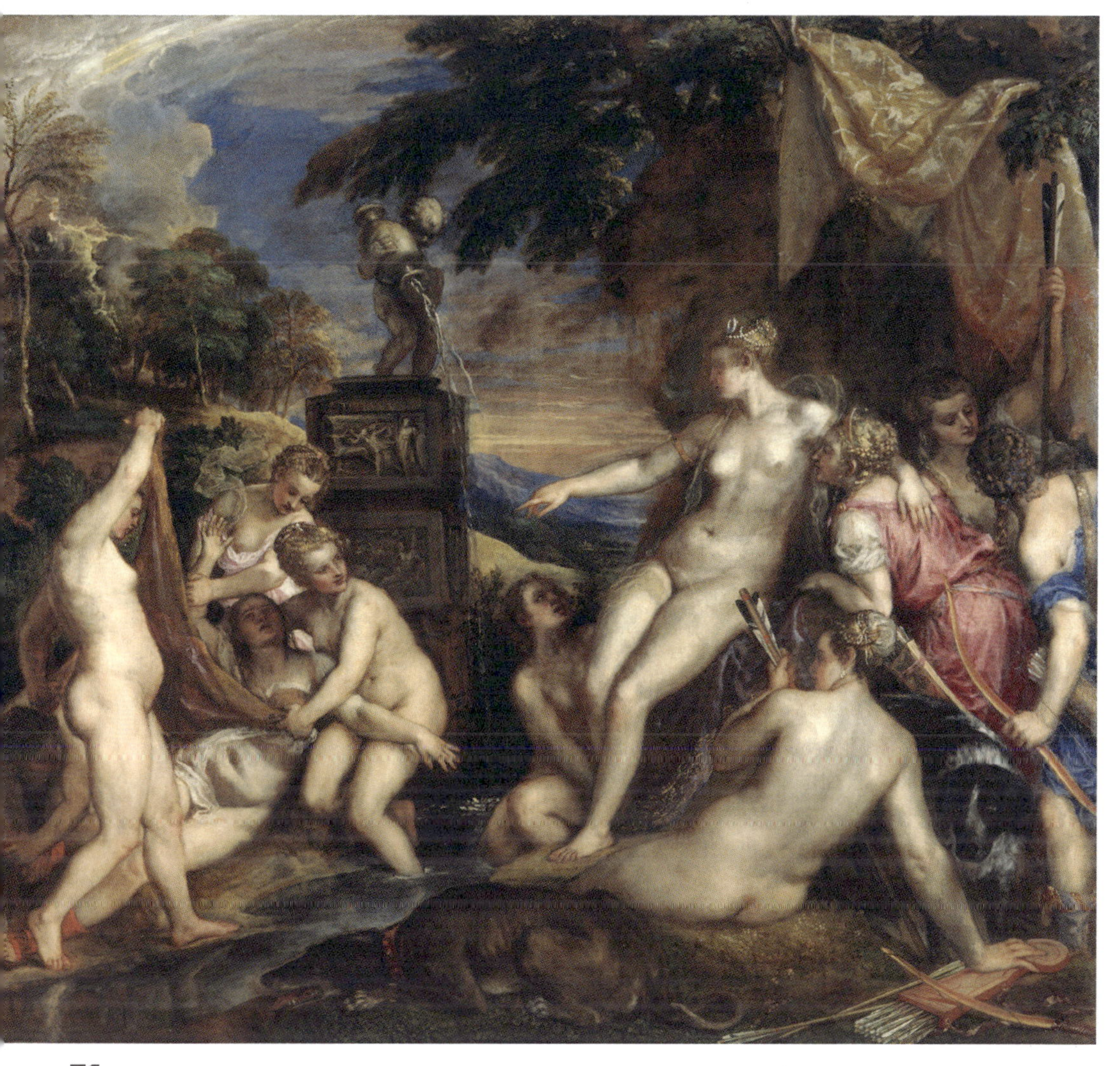

31.

31.
Titian, *Diana and Callisto*, c. 1556–59

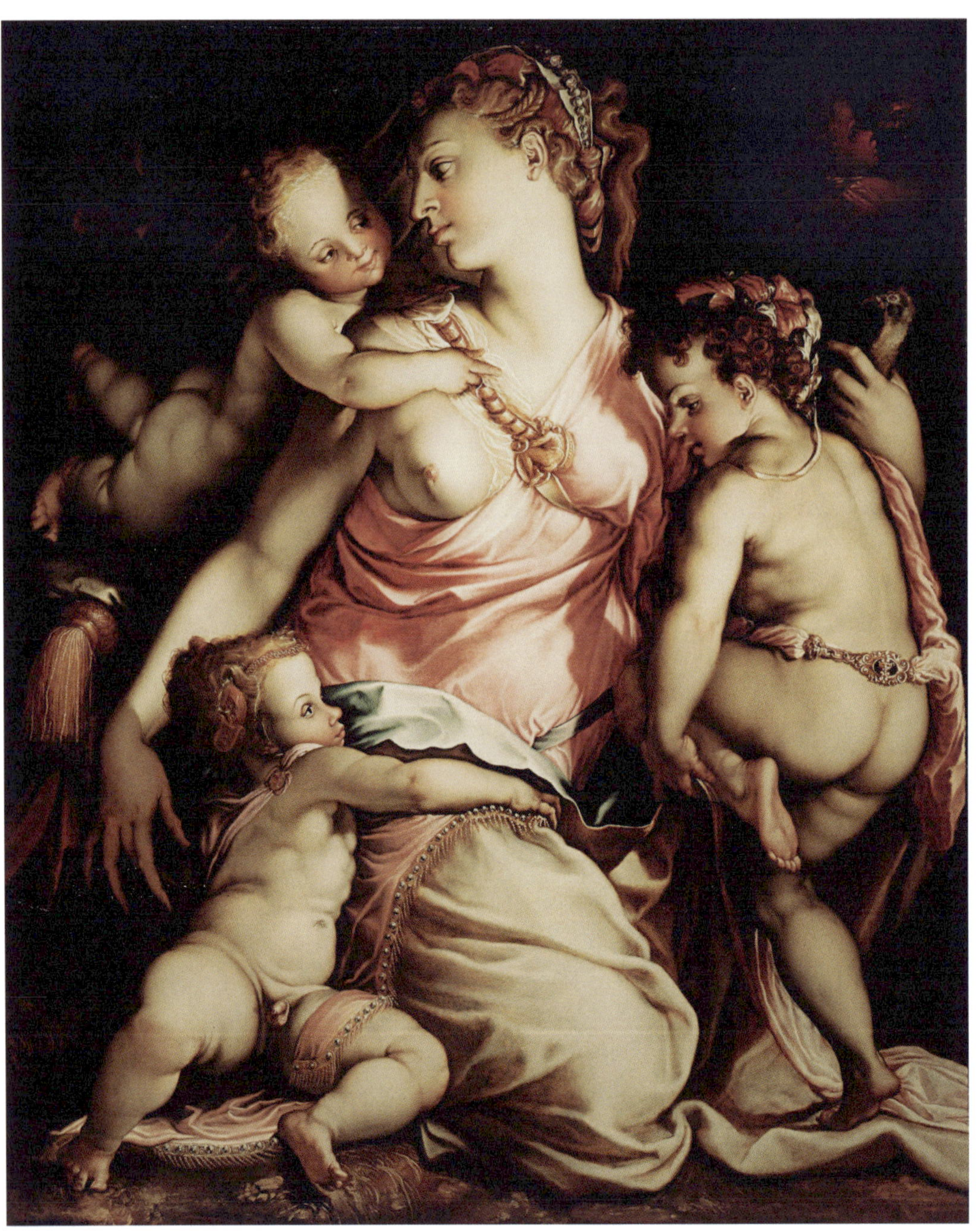

32

32.
Francesco de Rossi,
known as Salviati,
Charity, *c.* 1545

fired up artists' interest in the weighty body in dramatic motion. From the late 15th to mid-16th century, Christian and classical figures alike were rendered with invitingly fleshy verisimilitude.

Titian's great suite of *Metamorphoses* paintings – known as the *poesie* – was created between 1551 and 1562, coinciding with the Council of Trent, an ecclesiastical gathering in Northern Italy tasked with deciding the Catholic Church's response to the Protestant Reformation. Among the many declarations was a decree relating to propriety in religious art. This outlawed elements that might distract from meditative communion with a venerated figure. By then a shift was already underway, since the Renaissance nude had transformed the erotic associations of exposed flesh, the maternal breast included. By implication, sultry Saint Sebastians, jacked Jesuses and voluptuous nursing Madonnas were no longer welcome in the Church (though some were still commissioned by patrons for 'private contemplation'.)

The nursing breast did not disappear but shifted territory to become the preserve of Charity – a Christian virtue embodied by a woman whose most recognisable attribute was her exposed bosom. At the court of Saxony at the turn of the 1540s, Lucas Cranach the Elder painted Charity as a young mother, sinuous and small breasted, naked but for lavish court jewelry and a gossamer veil. A tiny baby nurses from her breast while two playful children clamour at her feet. In the same period in Florence, the painter known as Salviati imagined her in luscious abandon, flooded with light against the drama of a dark background **32**. His Charity is a fantasy in rosy silk, her russet hair braided with pearls and one ivory breast fully exposed. Three cherubs cling to her soft expanses with intoxicated expressions.

A saucier variation known as Roman Charity became popular in the 17th century after featuring in Caravaggio's altarpiece *The Seven Acts of Mercy* (c. 1606). Roman Charity is based on an 'exemplary story' presented by historian Valerius Maximus, who describes the woman Pero saving her incarcerated father Cimon from starvation by breastfeeding him. A version exists by Artemisia Gentileschi, but for full kinky thrills I defer to the Flemish painter Peter Paul Rubens, not known for his moderation in matters of painterly flesh. Rubens's *Roman Charity* (c. 1612) **33** is set in the dim light of a stone-walled jail cell. A spider weaving its way between the window bars marks the length of incarceration, while Cimon himself, grey of flesh and beard, lies shackled to the wall on a bed of straw. Against the father's aged yet still muscular body is pressed his devoted daughter Pero, swathed in

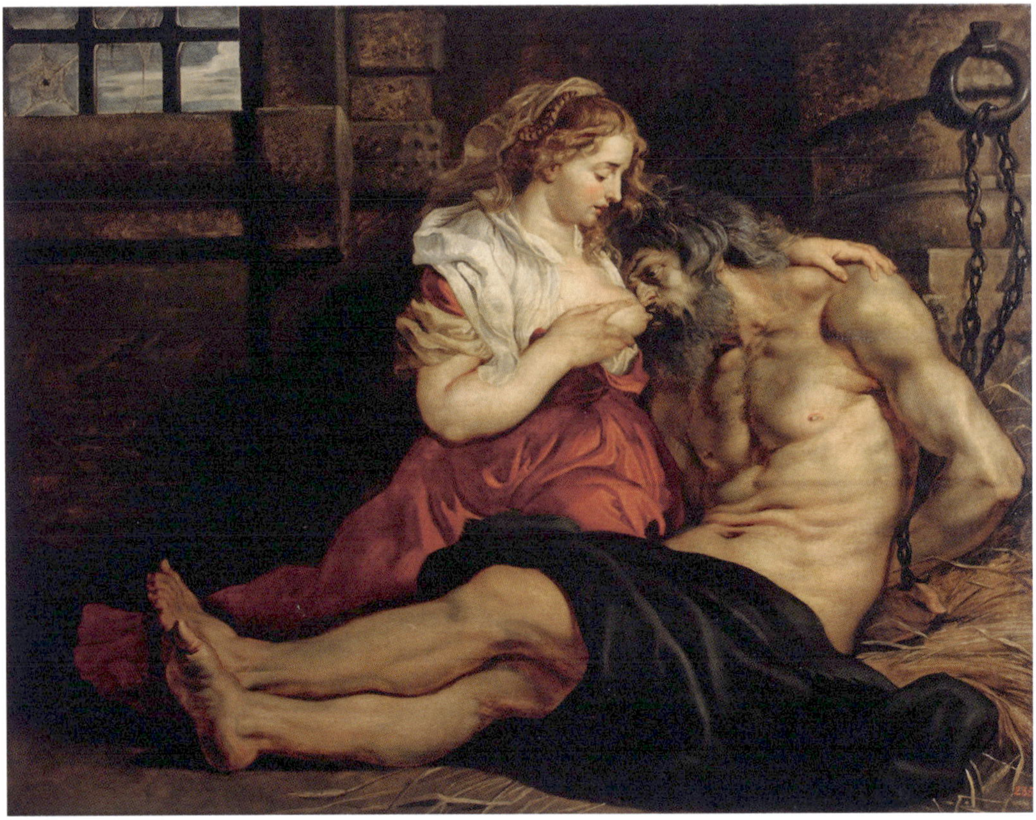

33

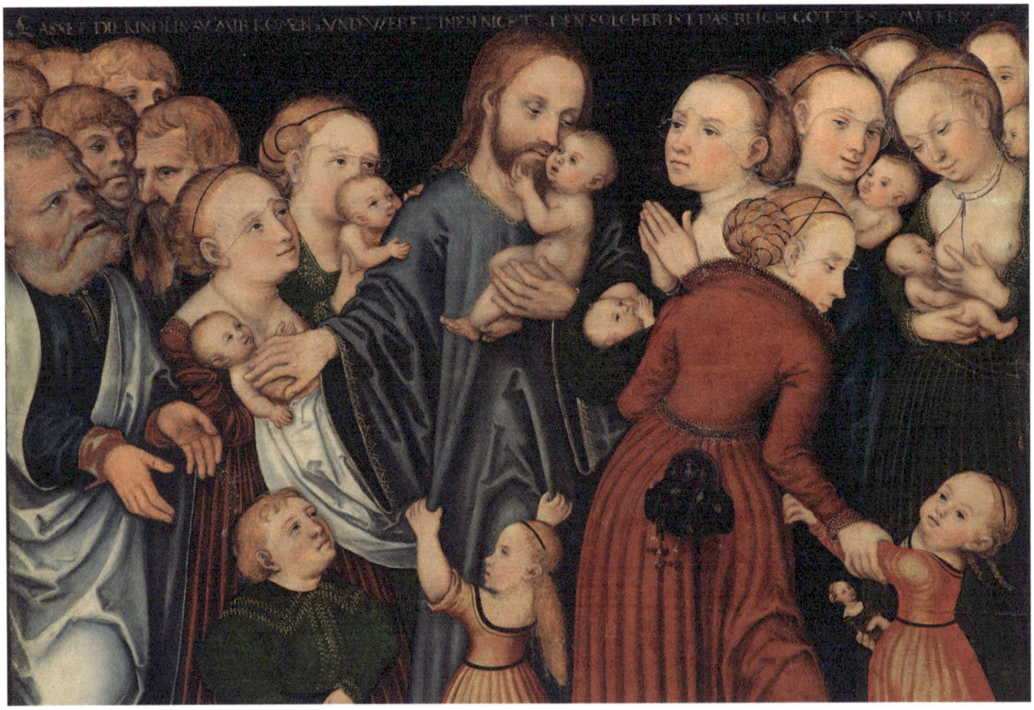

LASSET DIE KINDLIN ZV MIR KOMEN, VND WERET INEN NICHT, DEN SOLCHER IST DAS REICH GOTTES. MAT.EL.X

34

33.
Peter Paul Rubens,
Roman Charity,
c. 1612

34.
Lucas Cranach
the Elder,
*Christ Blessing
the Children*,
c. 1537–53

silk, one ripe breast exposed, squeezed between her fingers as she directs the nipple, shining with a droplet of moisture, toward the old man's mouth. Beneath trailing blonde curls, with tears resting on her flushed cheeks and rosy lips parted, her face assumes an expression that is almost ecstatic.

defenders of the pure hearth

Lucas Cranach was a friend and early supporter of the Protestant reformer Martin Luther who became chair of theology at the University of Wittenburg in 1512. While the great Biblical crowd scenes of the Catholic south tended to be populated by adult characters – monks, apostles, soldiers, shepherds, magi et al. – Cranach's narrative tableaux teem with mothers and children. There is a whole gang of them in the foreground of *The Feeding of the Five Thousand* (*c.* 1535–40) chatting merrily with babies on their laps and at their breasts. They also take centre stage in one of Cranach's most popular subjects – Christ Blessing the Children – a theme addressed by his workshop in at least twenty-five different paintings.

My favourite is held by the Statens Museum for Kunst in Copenhagen **34**. Christ stands at the centre in blue, cuddling a sleepy naked baby. Other babes lean in from their mothers' arms on all sides, one with its tiny hands on his shoulders. Another lies blissfully in its mother's arms while the Saviour lays his hand across its chest and stomach. A little girl tugs impatiently at his robes, while a sturdy boy reaches into his tunic as though he were about to show Jesus his pea shooter. Fashionably dressed mothers with elaborate hairdos and wasp-waisted robes crowd around him, with jolly infants pressed to their faces. One nurses a baby through a peephole in her gauzy bodice. The central mother figure, in pleated crimson with a fine black purse hanging from her waistband, coolly carries a baby in her left arm and steers her infant daughter with her right. In a beautiful piece of symmetry, the red-robed daughter also clutches a doll in her spare hand. Behind the women to Christ's right his disciples look on disapprovingly. It is the little girl with the doll who turns and catches our eye, evidencing a child's quick intelligence and comprehension. For there is nothing random about the popularity of this scene, which illustrates an episode from the Gospel of Matthew: 'Then were there brought unto him little children, that he should put his hands on them, and pray: and the disciples rebuked them./ But Jesus said, Suffer little children, and forbid them not to come unto me: for of such is the kingdom of heaven.'[9] The verses were frequently quoted by Martin Luther in his arguments in support of infant baptism. At the time of the Reformation, dissenting Anabaptist factions argued that baptism should be delayed until a subject could acquire faith. Luther countered that while one could not prove that an infant had faith, one could likewise not disprove it, and quoted Matthew. *Christ Blessing the Children* made clear the role afforded children in a church rooted in simple faith rather than the public performance of good work.[10]

In the Protestant Netherlands in the following century, women expressed faith through their control over the private sphere of the home and application of hygiene within it. The country's merchants had grown wealthy from international trade monopolies, market speculation and colonial exploitation in the Americas. The Dutch were followers of the reformer John Calvin, who preached against religious art as a gateway to idolatry, comparing those who had become accustomed to it to sewage workers who could no longer detect the scent of excrement. Calvin proscribed showy display, commending instead the everyday pleasures of food, drink and nature's beauty. The new wealth of the merchant classes thus went into unflashy but luxurious black garb and the tasteful refinement of the home. In art they looked to quotidian subjects: land and seascapes, foodstuffs, portraiture, genre paintings and floral arrangements that expressed the distant reach of Dutch traders.

In Dutch art of the 17th century, domestic interiors sparkle from the vigorous application of polish and soap. The immaculate surfaces of glazed jars, pewter jugs and glassware scintillate with cool, northern light. Tiled floors are worn smooth from scrubbing. In place of the lush clutter, tumbling throng and Baroque sensuality of art from Catholic Europe comes fresh simplicity, linear order and clear space. As keepers of the home, women maintained a realm of purity boundaried by the doorstep from the corruptions of body and soul threatened by the street beyond: gaming, prostitution, drunkenness and disease. The Pieter de Hooch painting known as *A Mother's Duty* (1660–1) **35** is illuminated by light from an open window looking onto an expanse studded with trees. The brass bedwarmer hanging beside a small box bed is glossy as a pearl. In front of it, a mother in a simple cap is seated with her young daughter kneeling before her, head lowered, as though in prayer. This, however, is an act of devotion of a different kind, for this godly mother's duty is one familiar to most parents of young children: she is combing her daughter's hair for lice.

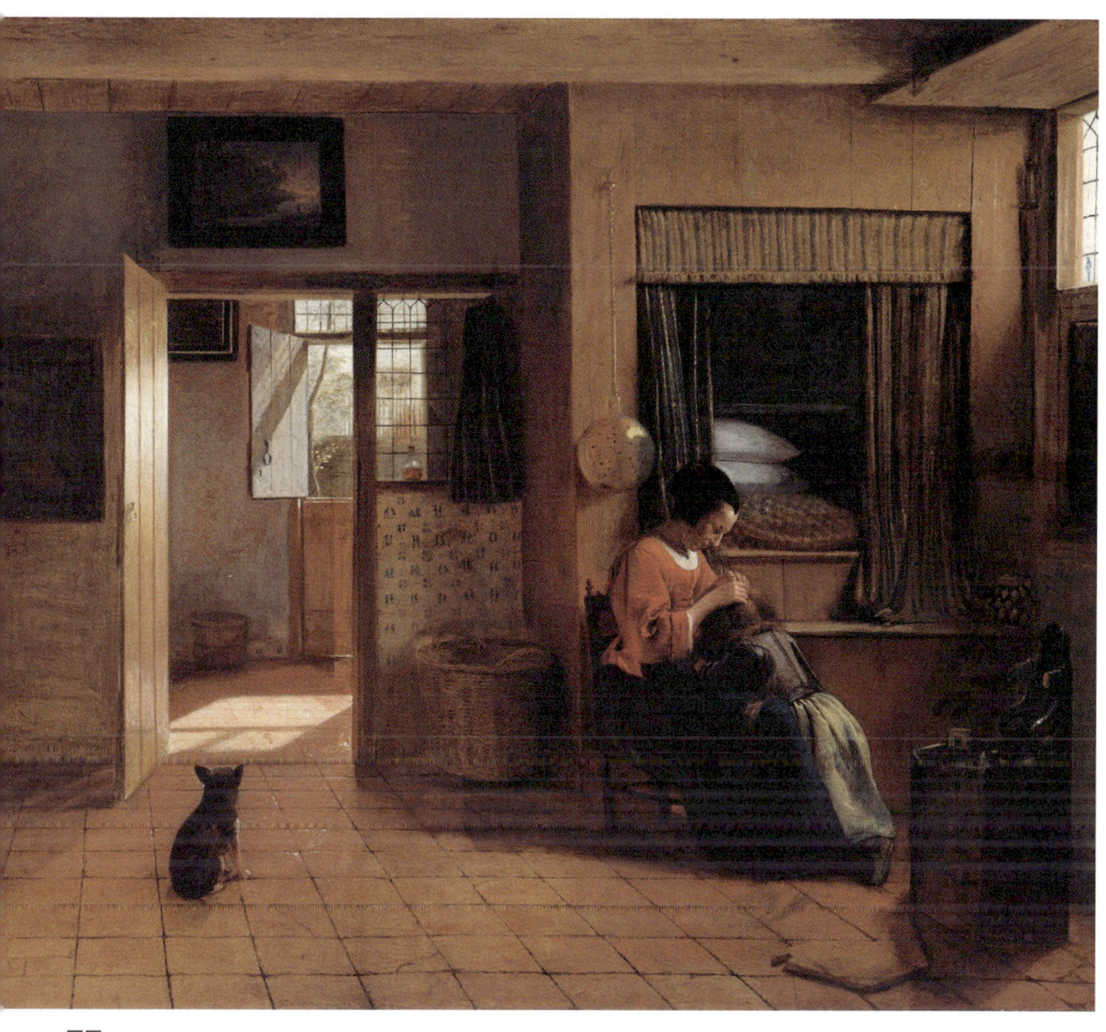

35.

35.
Pieter de Hooch,
A Mother's Duty,
c. 1660–1

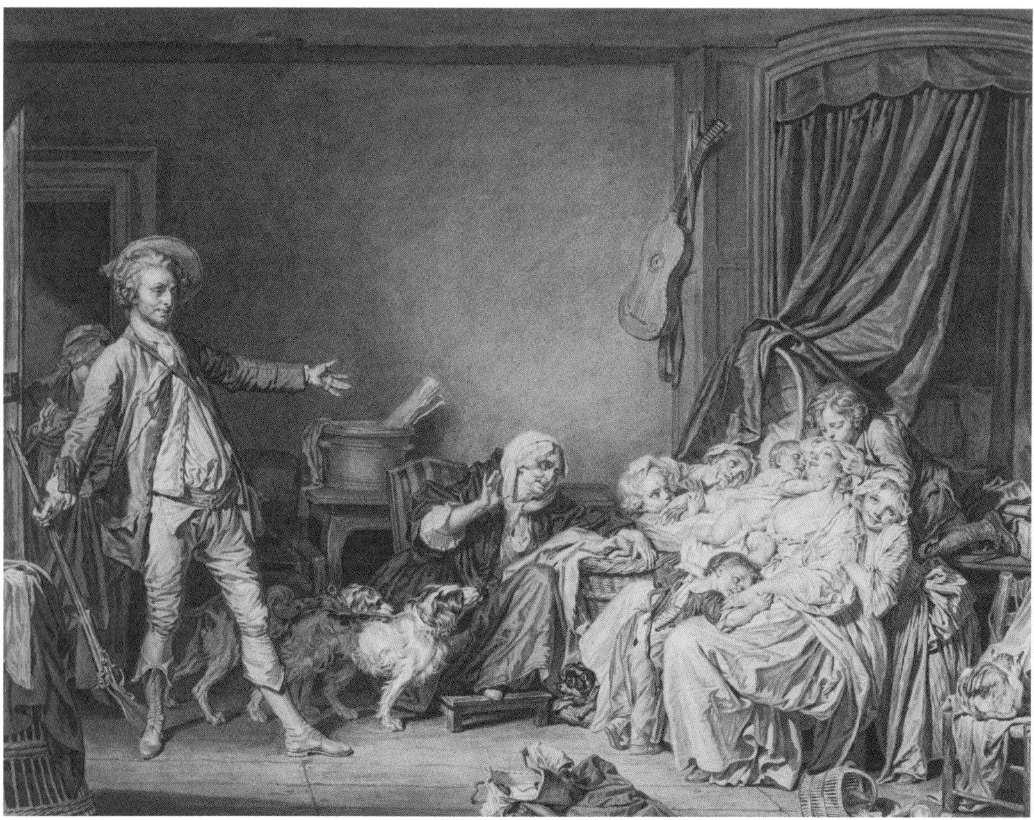

36

In this humble action, the mother's role in the formation of her children is presented through the combined application of religious instruction, the maintenance of order within the home and, by extension, of the persons within its walls.

the happy mother

In his account of the 1765 Paris Salon, the philosopher and art critic Denis Diderot describes a new painting by Jean-Baptiste Greuze in terms that suggest the artist has portrayed his wife in the throes of orgasm: 'This open mouth, these swimming eyes, this unstable posture, this swollen neck, this voluptuous fusion of pain and pleasure make all respectable women lower their eyes and blush in its vicinity.'[11] Diderot ponders the role context plays in rendering an expression that seems obscene in one work an invitation to moral contemplation in another. For, later in the exhibition, this selfsame expression of near-stifling pleasure reappears in an elaborate sketch that is much more to Diderot's taste.

Greuze's *La mére bienaimée* (*The Well-Loved Mother*, 1775) **36** is an orgy of maternal affection. Head flung back, the mother's lake of milky bosom wells out above a mountain of linens and silks upon which clamber six young children, each claiming a kiss or enfolding themselves around a limb, pinning her in position. Onto this scene bursts the father, hunting gun in hand, enraptured by the spectacle of unrestrained domestic bliss.

Diderot approvingly notes the bustling composition, the strained emotional response of the mother, and well-observed petulance of a daughter at her mother's lap. He also praises the work's moral content: 'It preaches population, and paints a sympathetic picture of the happiness and advantages deriving from domesticity; it announces to any man with soul and feelings: Maintain your family comfortably, make children with your wife, as many as you can, but only with her, and you can be sure of a happy home.'[12]

Greuze was not offering a candid vision of his own domestic bliss. Madame Greuze – born Gabrielle Babuti – was here performing in her capacity as artist's model only. (The couple had violent differences, aired by the artist in a public pronouncement against his wife, whose lovers had included Diderot.[13]) Rather, this was a dramatic tableau on a fashionable moral theme.

Three years earlier, philosopher Jean-Jacques Rousseau had published *Emile, or On Education* – a radical treatise charting the formation of a fictional child from infancy to adulthood. Book I of *Emile* took aim at high-society Parisian mothers who tended to place infants with a country wet nurse for their first three years of life. Besides insinuating that fashionable mothers preferred not to nurse their own children so that their bodies remained available for other adventures, Rousseau located this moment of rupture as a general source of social ills. Rather than being tended by a wet nurse who would confine him with tight swaddling bands, a baby's education was the natural duty of the mother (why else had God given her milk? asks Rousseau). Once he is of age to require a tutor, let that teacher be his own father. *Emile* recasts the family as the moral foundation of society, one in which a mother will find blissful satisfaction in the fulfilment of her natural role, and from which the contented father will never be tempted to stray. *The Well-Loved Mother* gives form to this ideal.

Like Greuze, and indeed Diderot, Rousseau's own domestic arrangements were far removed from this ideal – his five children conceived out of wedlock with Thérèse Levasseur died

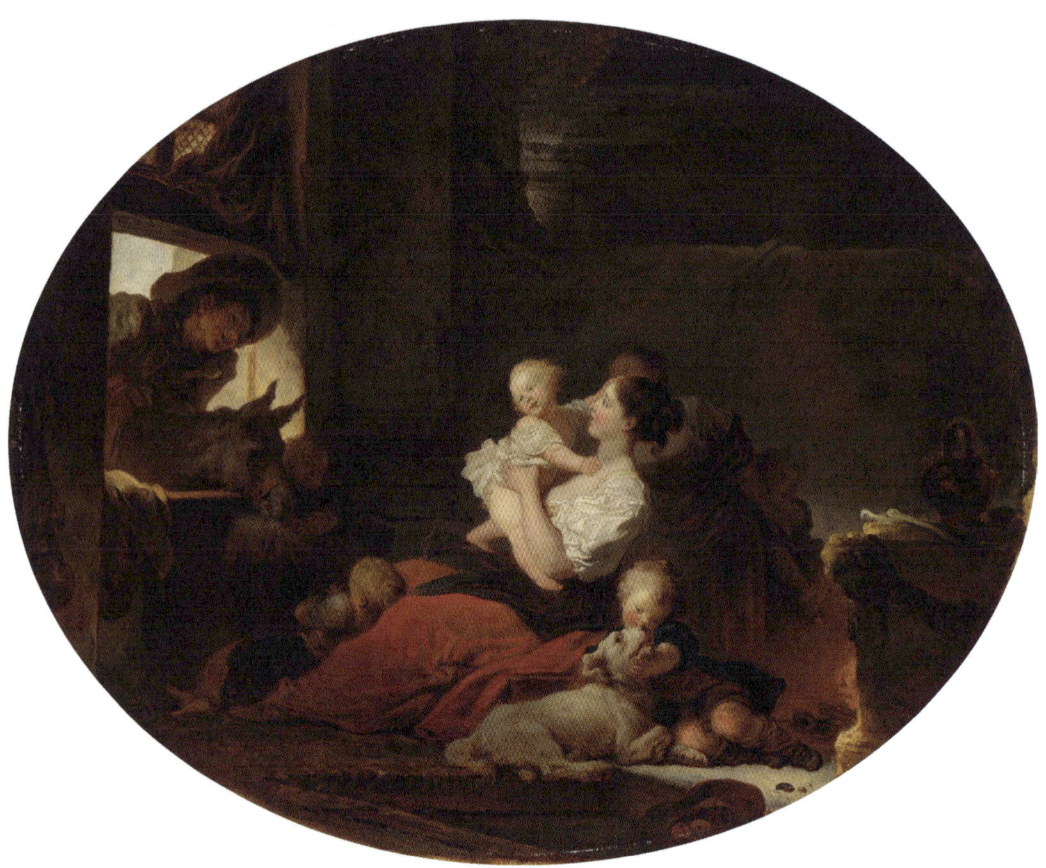

37

in the foundling hospital to which he persuaded her to consign them. Nevertheless, the self-sacrificing spousal constancy and maternal contentment detailed in his epistolary romance *Julie or the New Eloise* (1761) and the polemical views on wet-nursing and swaddling outlined in *Emile* hit home. Under the influence both of Rousseau's writings and Greuze's sentimental scenes of family life, the happy mother and nurturing home became popular subjects for French paintings of the period.

At the illuminated centre of Jean-Honoré Fragonard's *The Happy Family* (*c.* 1775) **37**, a winsome peasant sits with her blouse lowered holding a loosely robed baby aloft. Through an unglazed window, a man and his donkey gaze on fondly as four children play around her skirts. This happy family are camped in the ruins of an Italian villa with boxes for chairs and the promise of nothing but a couple of leeks and apples for dinner, yet the mood Fragonard evokes is of blissful contentment centred on maternal love. So successful was the composition that he produced three versions in oils and one in watercolour to be used as the basis for a print, revisiting the theme of familial happiness and motherly love in several other works of this period.

Enlightenment ideas on the family were perhaps less immediately practical than they were conceptual, informing social ideals in the period leading up to and following the French Revolution. Made visible in art, maternal breastfeeding progressively came to be accepted among women of the bourgeoisie and aristocracy. Seen as the duty of Republican mothers, nursing became emblematic of the Revolution.[14] In plaster busts, popular prints and even a public fountain, the French Republic herself was pictured with her breasts opened to all, a nationalist updating of the figure of Charity.[15]

This trend was reflected in the fashion for draped and uncorseted dresses *à la Grecque*, which emphasized the breast and permitted easier access.[16] Maternal breastfeeding climbed steadily in popularity over the 19th century, up to the introduction of bottle feeding in the 1880s. Nevertheless, from the 17th century right up to the beginning of the 20th, it remained common practice for French women of the middle and upper classes, as well as the urban proletariat, to entrust their children to wet nurses.[17] The practice remained so entrenched that the 'Roussel Law' was passed in 1874, to formalize the relationship between wet nurse and client.

Rousseau and his contemporaries transformed the way the institution of family was understood, issuing a call to affection taken up enthusiastically by parents who recalled the loveless formality of their own upbringing.[18] In place of a sprawling, dynastic network based on unions of convenience, an idea of the family emerged that was centred on the parents and their children – the nuclear family as we now recognize it – held together through bonds of love as well as duty. Rather than defective mini adults, children were viewed as humans in their uncorrupted, natural state on whose correct formation the future health of society rested. As the counterpart to the 'natural' child, motherhood was positioned as a woman's 'natural' role – in explicit contrast to the high society woman of ideas – and childrearing the source of her true happiness.

fallen angels

In Britain, the ideal of the family home as the moral core of society reached its ultimate expression in the Victorian era. The dutiful wife and mother became a cultural type, epitomized by the titular

37.
Jean-Honoré
Fragonard,
*The Happy
Family*, *c.* 1775

heroine of Coventry Patmore's narrative poem *The Angel in the House* (1854–62), published after the death, from tuberculosis, of his wife Emily – the domestic seraph of its inspiration. Born Emily Augusta Andrews, care was her life's duty from an early age. The eighth of twelve children, she lost her mother when aged seven, and she took over household duties for her minister father. Quick and studious, she tutored her younger siblings in classical and modern languages. Through her father she knew critic John Ruskin. Emily and her sister were later credited with introducing him to the Pre-Raphaelite Brotherhood – part of the girls' circle as bright young women in London. Aged twenty-seven, Emily Patmore was painted by one of their number **38**. John Everett Millais portrays her stiff and upright, hair neatly pinned, face clean of makeup, dress sombre save for the velvety flourish of a rose-pink bow flopping beneath her immaculate lace collar. A posy of flowers is pinned or perhaps held in front of her – pink carnation, lily of the valley, a pale jonquil – emblems of grace and purity. It is a quiet parlour study, in spirit a companion piece to Millais's suggestive narrative painting *The Violet's Message* (1854). A world away from the Pre-Raphaelite 'stunners' with their torrents of hair and jewel-bright costumes, Emily performs the archetype of modest motherhood, her face radiant against the shadowed background just as the pale posy shines against her dark dress. To me she looks a little tired – she was mother to two already, the youngest, Tennyson, then only a year old – and at first glance older than her years. I see her face prematurely sombre and resigned from years of care. Emily expired in 1862 at the age of thirty-eight, leaving Coventry Patmore with six young children.

It took almost seventy more years for the 'Angel in the House' to be declared dead. Virginia Woolf announced the murder by her own hands in 1931, in her speech to the National Society for Women's Service entitled 'Professions for Women'. Woolf described the shadow this paragon had cast over Queen Victoria's reign – and how the voice of the Angel had whispered in her own ear instructing her to be sweet, pleasing and flattering to men. Woolf frames the killing of the Angel in the House as an act of self-defence – made more taxing because, like Greuze's well-loved mother and Rousseau's Julie, she was a fantasy rather than a mortal woman. 'She died hard,' Woolf notes, after metaphorically flinging her ink pot at the Angel. 'Her fictitious nature was of great assistance to her. It is far harder to kill a phantom than a reality.'[19]

38.
John Everett Millais,
*Mrs Coventry
Patmore*, 1851

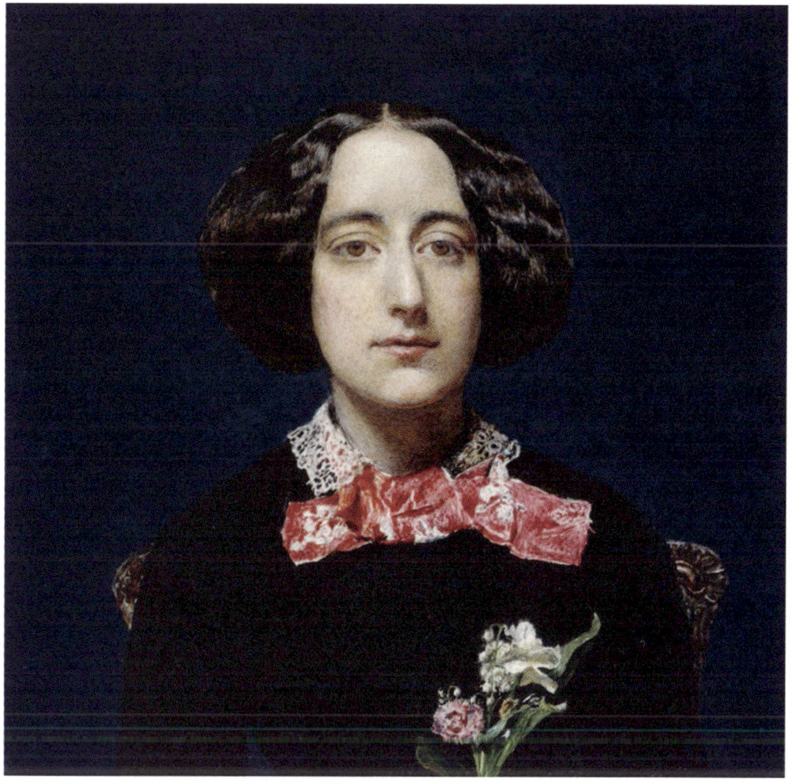

38

We should remember this gulf, this fantasy, when looking at Emily Patmore, for it will have directed Millais's hand as much as her husband's. Emily was not passive, but industrious. Around the birth and care of six children she fit the authorship of an instructional volume on behaviour for servants and two books of children's verse, all published under the pseudonym Mrs Motherly.

·

The Victorian Angel in the House had a dark sister – and she was likewise an object of considerable fantasy. She was the 'fallen woman', the angel plucked of her wings. The 'fall' was a moral one, from chaste respectability to social outcast. The fallen woman might have been carried away by passion, she may also have been raped, enslaved into prostitution, lied to or abandoned. If she conceived a child outside of marriage she was considered ruined. For aristocratic families and the haute bourgeoisie, power and capital were bound up in legitimacy: wealth and titles followed the bloodline. All women, rich and poor alike, who became pregnant out of wedlock risked social exclusion. This 'fall' is still

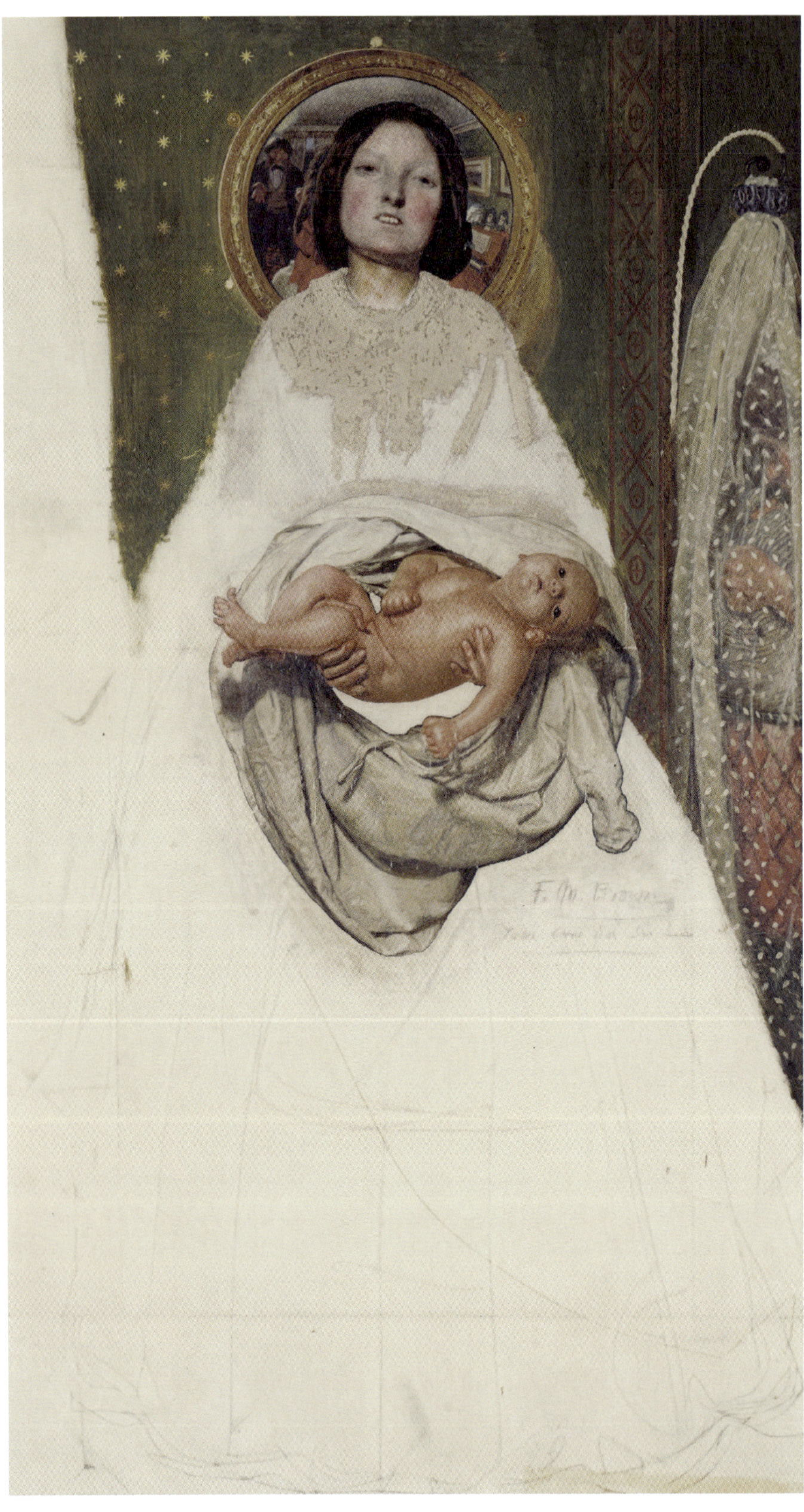

implied when we describe women as having 'fallen' pregnant – a term that implies sex outside marriage and the accompanying fall from grace.

As a subject for art, the fallen woman is ripe with potential – a beauty ruined by forbidden love. She's there in William Holman Hunt's *The Awakening Conscience* (1853), rising startled from her lover's lap as they sit at the piano, a discarded glove prefiguring her vulnerability to abandonment. Her downfall is charted in the three panels of Augustus Leopold Egg's *Past and Present* (1858): the weeping wife revealed as an adulteress in the first panel, who is seen shivering beneath a bridge with a baby in her arms by the third. The young woman George Fiddes Watt paints in *Found Drowned* (1848–50) has fallen both literally and metaphorically – a suicide, whose redemption is suggested by a single star shining above her as she lies cruciform on the bank of the River Thames.

While these works are animated by the frisson of scandal, we should no more assume that the artists were moralising in the conventional sense than the great novelists of the period. Charles Dickens himself became a public campaigner, petitioning on behalf of a woman who applied to place her newborn with the Foundling Hospital that 'society has used her ill and turned away from her, and she cannot be expected to take much heed of its rights or wrongs...she is degraded and fallen, but not lost.'[20] Dickens also persuaded the philanthropist Angela Burdett Coutts to establish Urania Cottage as a 'home for fallen women' in London's Shepherd's Bush.[21]

In Ford Madox Brown's *Take Your Son, Sir* (1851–92) **39** a beseeching mother proffers her infant to a horrified older man, seen reflected in the mirror. With the gold frame forming a star-girt halo, and her (unfinished) body cloaked like the sheltering robe of the Virgin of Mercy, this mother is presented as saint rather than sinner. Art historian Rosemary Betterton describes the vividly rendered child revealed amid the tormented folds of a shawl in terms of an anatomical drawing, with the grey drapery suggesting a uterus – a shocking hint both of sex and the mother's fragile mortality.[22] Using his wife Emma and young son Arthur Gabriel as models, Madox Brown makes visible the spectre of death hovering over the fallen woman. This choice turned out to be unbearably poignant for Madox Brown, who left the painting unfinished after Arthur died in 1857.

While Madox Brown's unwed mother carries a righteous power, the fallen woman was more often imagined sentimentally:

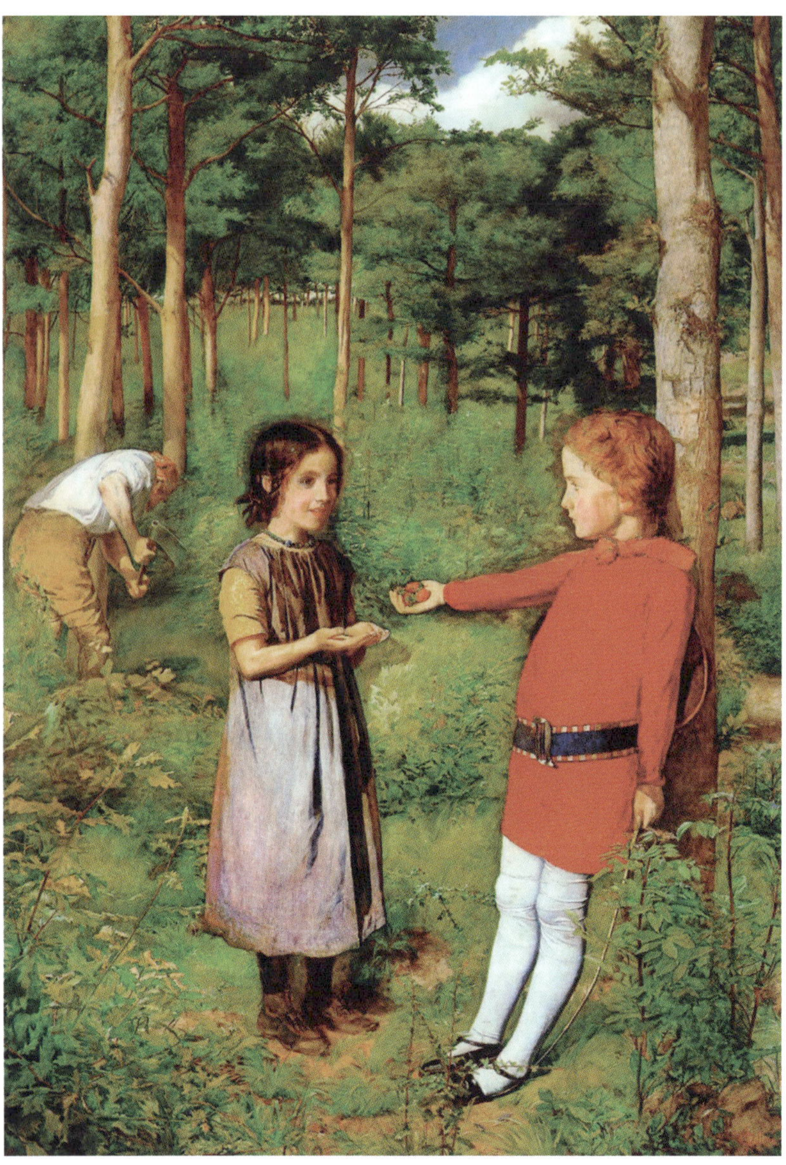

40

beautiful, friendless, in need of rescuing. Millais presents her in prelapsarian form in *The Woodsman's Daughter* (1851) **40**, which takes its title taken from a ballad by Coventry Patmore – he of *The Angel in the House*. 'Innocent Maud' accompanying her father into the woods is watched in fascination by 'the rich Squire's son', who offers her fruits which she received 'with an air/ So unreserved and free,/ That shame-faced distance soon became/ Familiarity.' In Patmore's poem, we first encounter Maud as a young woman mad with grief, no baby in sight, lying beside the deep mill pond as bubbles rise ominously from its rotting weeds. Millais pictures

40.
John Everett Millais,
*The Woodsman's
Daughter*, 1851

her instead as a young girl accepting berries from a boy in archaic costume as her father labours, oblivious, in the background. Patmore's poem was well-known, and literate viewers would have inferred the seduction, pregnancy and infanticide that was to follow. In portraying Maud as a trusting innocent rather than a ruined woman, Millais directs the blame for her downfall to her male seducer, echoing a distinction between the deserving and undeserving fallen made by institutions of the time.[23]

When it opened in 1741, London's Foundling Hospital took all abandoned babies irrespective of their parentage, turning mothers away only when the hospital was full. During the 19th century, the procedure changed: only the children of unmarried women would be accepted, contingent on the governors' investigation of the mother's circumstances.[24] What the mother was asked to prove, tacitly, was the possibility of redemption – that this was her first child, that she was otherwise 'pure of habits', that the relief of this child would open the path for respectable employment and perhaps even marriage. The euphemism of the admissions board distinguished between premarital relationships, abandonment, 'criminal conversation' – a consenting relationship in which one or both parties was married – and 'seductions' involving physical force, coercion or intoxication, many of which would now be classified as rape.[25] Women whose petitions were rejected by the board faced a future on the social margins: the workhouse or perhaps prostitution, a child brought up in poverty. As Watt's *Found Drowned* reminds us, many took their own lives.

While artists, writers and social campaigners showed sympathy for unwed mothers, in sentimentalizing them as fallen innocents they reinforced a feminine ideal of childlike purity. There is no space here for a woman's sexual appetite or agency. After studying the petitions made to the Foundling Hospital while preparing an exhibition on the fallen woman, art historian Lynda Nead noted how the applicants compliantly offered the required narrative. 'How could a woman ever have written that she loved and desired a man so much that she was willing to risk everything for sex? This is an archive of silences and of secrets that are spoken, in part, through an authorized philanthropic language of female sexual passivity.'[26]

mary, mary

Painter Mary Cassatt hovered between worlds. An American in Paris, she was a skilled professional who trained her eye on the domestic realm, and an unmarried woman whose most celebrated subject became the mother and child. Griselda Pollock, in her classic monograph on Cassatt, enumerates the restrictions she faced as a woman artist in late 19th-century Paris. Unlike her male contemporaries she was unable to study the nude, receive men in her studio, hang out in cafés or explore the seamier phenomena of urban life. There is 'a positive side to this particular coin,' notes Pollock, 'for Cassatt knew the world of women, the drawing room and childbearing as few men in that period could have done'.[27] As an artist associated with the group of independent painters and sculptors later known as the Impressionists, Cassatt had access to the private realm of bourgeois domesticity at a cultural moment in which the everyday of modern life was held a fresh and exciting subject for art and literature.

Cassatt often pictures women within restraining structures – opera boxes, balconies, framed mirrors – or the stifling abundance of home interiors full of clashing pattern and polished surfaces. In tightly laced costumes enrobing them to their fingertips even when taking tea, all that is left as an expressive zone is that little window of the face. Perhaps unsurprisingly, in her more formal studies of women, Cassatt's most pronounced

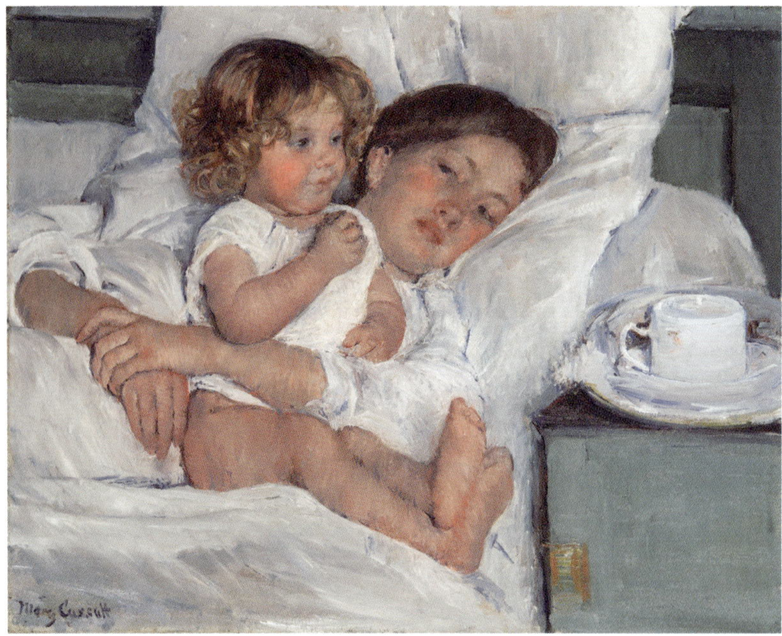

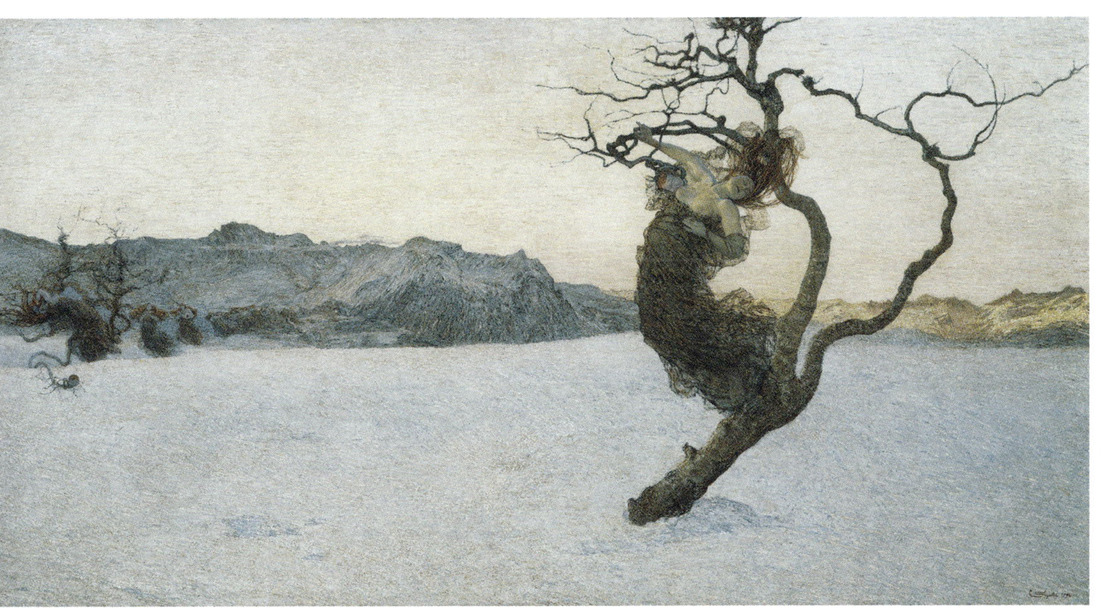

42

skill is in capturing a claustrophobic atmosphere of listlessness, apprehension and boredom.

Her mother and baby paintings stand apart from this close-corseted world, both for the dynamic relationship between the figures and for the orgy of baby flesh on display. It does Cassatt a disservice to read these works as straightforward portraits of maternal bliss. Notwithstanding their wealth and privilege, these lives were constrained, held apart from the public world of men and work. Cassatt was well-read, politically involved and bitterly aware of the fight women had to engage in to 'be *someone* rather than *something*.'[28] She would later become a supporter of the campaign for women's suffrage. Nevertheless, I find a luxuriance in Cassatt's mother and baby paintings **41**. In *Breakfast in Bed* (1897) the artist's sister-in-law Jennie is half sunk in a soft mound of pristine white pillows and sheets, with her chubby toddler Ellen Mary beside her. Both bodies are painted in the tones of a lavender dawn, melding one in with the other. Sitting upright and bare bottomed, Ellen Mary is alert, intent on breakfast, while her mother takes a few moments of calm repose, holding her daughter loosely in her arms while the child is distracted. Cassatt's paintings offer a view onto a world in which women had little freedom, and even contact with members of their own sex was bound by social rituals. Motherhood is that rare context in which physical contact and expressions of affection were not only permissible but celebrated.

41.
Mary Cassatt,
Breakfast in Bed,
1897

42.
Giovanni Segantini,
The Evil Mothers,
1894

the new woman and social anxiety

There is a suite of Symbolist paintings by the Swiss artist Giovanni Segantini that I have encountered scattered across various museums over the last thirty years. At first glance they are wildly romantic, all rugged landscape, twisted trees and tumbling hair, but look closer, and something sinister emerges. In *The Punishment of Lust* (1891) Segantini pictures women in a state of suspended animation, floating amid snowy mountain tops. This barren terrain is imagined as the place of torment for those who have sought abortions. In *The Evil Mothers* (1894) **42** women who have rejected maternity appear ensnared in the tangled trees of an Alpine landscape. Trapped, their bared breasts now nourish babies sprouting from the branches, bringing these women to a state of 'wholeness' as nurturing mothers.

Segantini's paintings stand in curious relation to the fetishization of the maternal body in art around the turn of the 20th century. Paul Gauguin, Gustav Klimt, Maurice Denis and others in this period glorified pregnant and maternal bodies. Women's generative powers were celebrated and the mother presented in an idealized 'natural' or 'primitive' form. Such paintings were in fact created against a backdrop of radical change and can be seen as a reaction to it. This was the era of feminism, the battle for women's suffrage and the emergence of the liberated 'new woman'.[29] We might view Segantini's *Evil Mothers*, and the voluptuous baby-eaters of Bram Stoker's novel *Dracula* (1897), as forms of mythic caution against women with 'unnatural' appetites, who enjoyed non-procreative sex, wished to work outside the home and fought for a political voice.

The political and social context for the turn to maternity in art in the early 20th century was complex. As a result, the work of an artist now seen as one of the most important to address the subject from a woman's perspective has suffered shifting readings. From 1898, Paula Modersohn-Becker was based in the rural artist's colony of Worpswede near Bremen, Germany. In her short life her great subjects became the mother and child, for which she often took models from the local farming families. Children she painted as autonomous, self-contained, hinting at the inner lives even of babies. Her later paintings of the mother body, made in 1906 and 1907, are radically and shockingly nude **43**. Rather than soft and sexually inviting, these women are monumental, blocky, rendered in jarring impasto: the last of them read as symbolic rather than sensual bodies.

43.
Paula Modersohn-Becker, *Kneeling Mother With Child at her Breast*, 1906

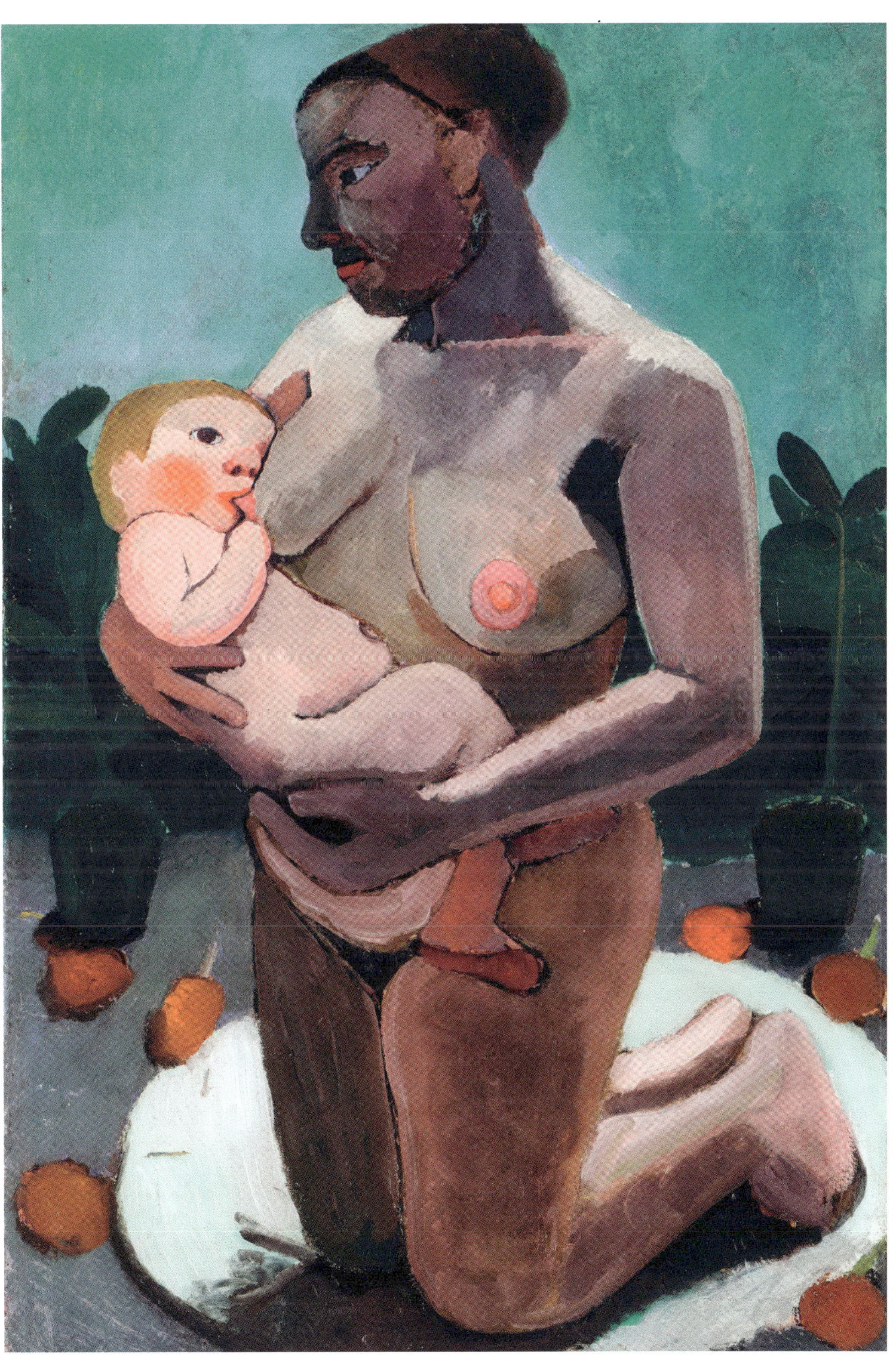

43

Some feminist art historians of the 1970s and 1980s condemned this treatment of the mother – and the rural, peasant mother in particular – as reactionary.[30] Little wonder: these were highly charged subjects. Modersohn-Becker's younger contemporary, the photographer Erna Lendvai-Dircksen, documented peasant women and children in rural Germany. They were presented as emblems of wholesome, traditional values that stood against the decadence of the modern city in her 1932 book *Das deutsche Volksgesicht* (*The Face of the German Race*), and Lendvai-Dircksen continued to work under the Third Reich, aligned with Nazi ideals. Her photographs remain contentious.

Such was not Modersohn-Becker's story. Far from rejecting urban life, she longed to escape Worpswede for the cultural ferment of Paris. Her happiest years were spent in the buzz of the French capital where she sketched from the nude at the academies, marvelled at Paul Cézanne's work and stayed in step with new ideas in painting. She was distinctly ambivalent about the prospect of her own motherhood and was involved in the socialist-aligned League for the Protection of Mothers and Sexual Reform, which campaigned for reproductive rights. Like Cassatt, her paintings of mothers and babies were made as an outsider, looking in. Her treatment of the subject shifted over the course of her brief career, from relatively sentimental depictions of the peasant mother as a heroic moral figure, to something closer to a universal archetype.

As a subject for German art in particular in this period, the mother carried multiple associations, often contradictory, from both extremes of the political spectrum. She bore the weight of anxiety over women's changing position in society, for in the eyes of the 'new woman', motherhood started to be understood as a choice rather than an inevitability. Germany was experiencing a declining birth rate, due to industrialization as well as the increased availability of birth control. Following the huge loss of life during the First World War there was talk of a 'population crisis'. In Germany, a woman who left her children to work outside the home, or who was, for other reasons, judged to have insufficiently devoted herself to childcare was labelled *Rabenmutter* – a 'raven mother'. Her obverse, the 'good' mother – the unpaid mother-caregiver-nurturer who devoted herself to childbearing, nursing and keeping home – was an ideal promoted by nationalist movements. She would provide the workers, and the cannon fodder, of tomorrow.

By contrast, the urban working mother was often depicted as the ultimate victim of poverty in a highly divided society. In his mother and child paintings of the 1920s, Otto Dix offers tired, emaciated, sickly and miserable figures, claustrophobically framed by the built fabric of the city. An image by Käthe Kollwitz from the Images of Misery series (1908–9) **44** shows pregnancy as a burden to a working class woman. Unlike the middle class 'new woman' she had no easy access to contraception and was more likely to be prosecuted for the crime of abortion.

With the formation of the Weimar Republic in 1918, German women gained the right to vote, and as a group, acquired political heft. Led by the League for the Protection of Mothers and Sexual Reform, abortion became a heated subject, prompting public demonstrations and protests. Attempting to woo female voters, the Communist Party embraced the cause, and lobbied for its legalization throughout the 1920s and into the 1930s, commissioning Kollwitz to design a poster to publicize their stance.

Paragraphs 218 and 219 of the penal code punished women who procured an abortion and those who assisted them with five years in prison.[31] In 1931 two doctors in Stuttgart – Friedrich Wolf and Else Kienle – were arrested for helping women seeking abortions, sparking mass protests by thousands of women.[32] At the invitation of the Communist women's magazine *Der Weg der Frau* (*The Woman's Way*) artists become a visible part of these protests, with Kollwitz, Dix, Hannah Höch, Edvard Munch, Alice Lex-Nerlinger, Emil Nolde and Otto Nagel contributing work to the exhibition 'Frauen in Not' ('Women in Need').

In this same period, Modersohn-Becker's representations of motherhood were appropriated by those on the political right. Several works – including *Reclining Mother and Child II* (1906) **45** – were purchased by the nationalist entrepreneur Ludwig Roselius. In 1927, twenty years after the artist's death, Roselius opened the Paula Becker-Modersohn Haus in Bremen as part of a propagandistic museum complex dedicated to German art and artefacts, holding Modersohn-Becker up as an example of a true Nordic artist, forging a new German tradition.[33]

There is nothing intrinsic to the paintings that merits such a reading. Indeed, in the following decade, Modersohn-Becker's mother and child paintings would be condemned by the Nazis for lacking a 'sensitive maternal-womanly quality' and came to be considered examples of 'degenerate' art.[34] By the early years of the 20th century, the mother body had become a free-floating

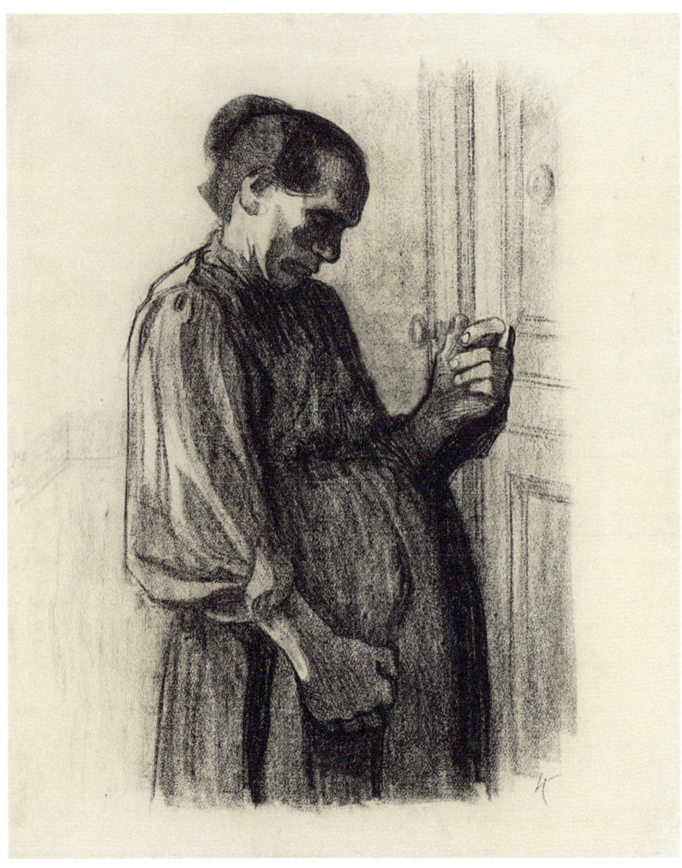

44

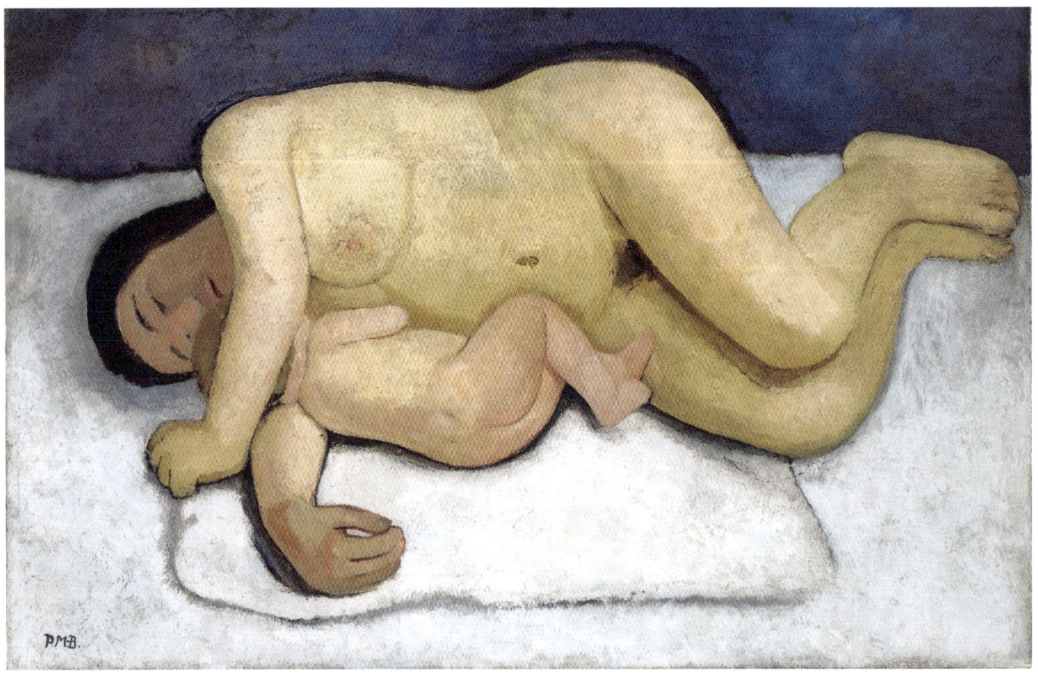

45

political symbol. It is one that still carries great potential for misinterpretation and co-option in our own time.

bordering on death-worlds

In the lithograph *Hope for the Future* (1945) by African-American artist Charles White **46**, a working mother cups a vigorous newborn in her blocky and powerful hands. White adopts a centuries-old pictorial convention, framing this Madonna-like figure with a window. Nailed from raw wooden boards, the lopsided structure appears less solid than the woman seated before it. Her face is wary, turning one way as though to look out of the window, but with her narrowed eyes cast in the other direction as though she cannot bear to do so. Just visible is a noose hanging from a jagged tree: an emblem viewers of the time would have associated with lynching – acts of public execution without due process, overwhelmingly carried out on Black bodies.[35]

White grew up on the South Side of Chicago during the Great Depression. Radicalized as a teenager by Alain Locke's *The New Negro* (1925), he openly questioned the absence of African-American history in his school's curriculum. A scholarship student at the Art Institute, White emerged with the desire to make art that was 'meaningful.' Encounters with political murals by Diego Rivera and David Siqueiros in Mexico City, as well as Käthe Kollwitz's emotionally charged prints persuaded him that powerful art could emerge from popular media.[36] *Hope for the Future* was made in 1945, a moment that for many in the victorious United States would indeed have seemed a time of hope, but the mother in White's lithograph is haunted by decades of violence that included the lynching of Black veterans.[37] Between 1882 and 1968, 4,743 lynchings were recorded in the US, with Black men targeted in particular.[38] Within that number were five members of White's own family in Mississippi.[39]

Seventy-five years later, Titus Kaphar's *Analogous Colors* (2020) **47** pictures another moment of haunting. A mother in a richly coloured rural kitchen clutches her infant close against her chest, eyes closed and brow furrowed, as though troubled by a presentiment of death. Her child is visible as nothing more than an empty silhouette giving onto the shadowy whiteness of the wall behind. Emerging from a deep red sweater, the mother's left hand is blue, which, against the shock expanse of white space, forms the colours of the US flag. Here, the white represents the erasure of another Black body. In June 2020, at the height of

44.
Käthe Kollwitz,
At the Doctor's,
1908–9

45.
Paula Modersohn-
Becker, *Reclining
Mother and
Child II,* 1906

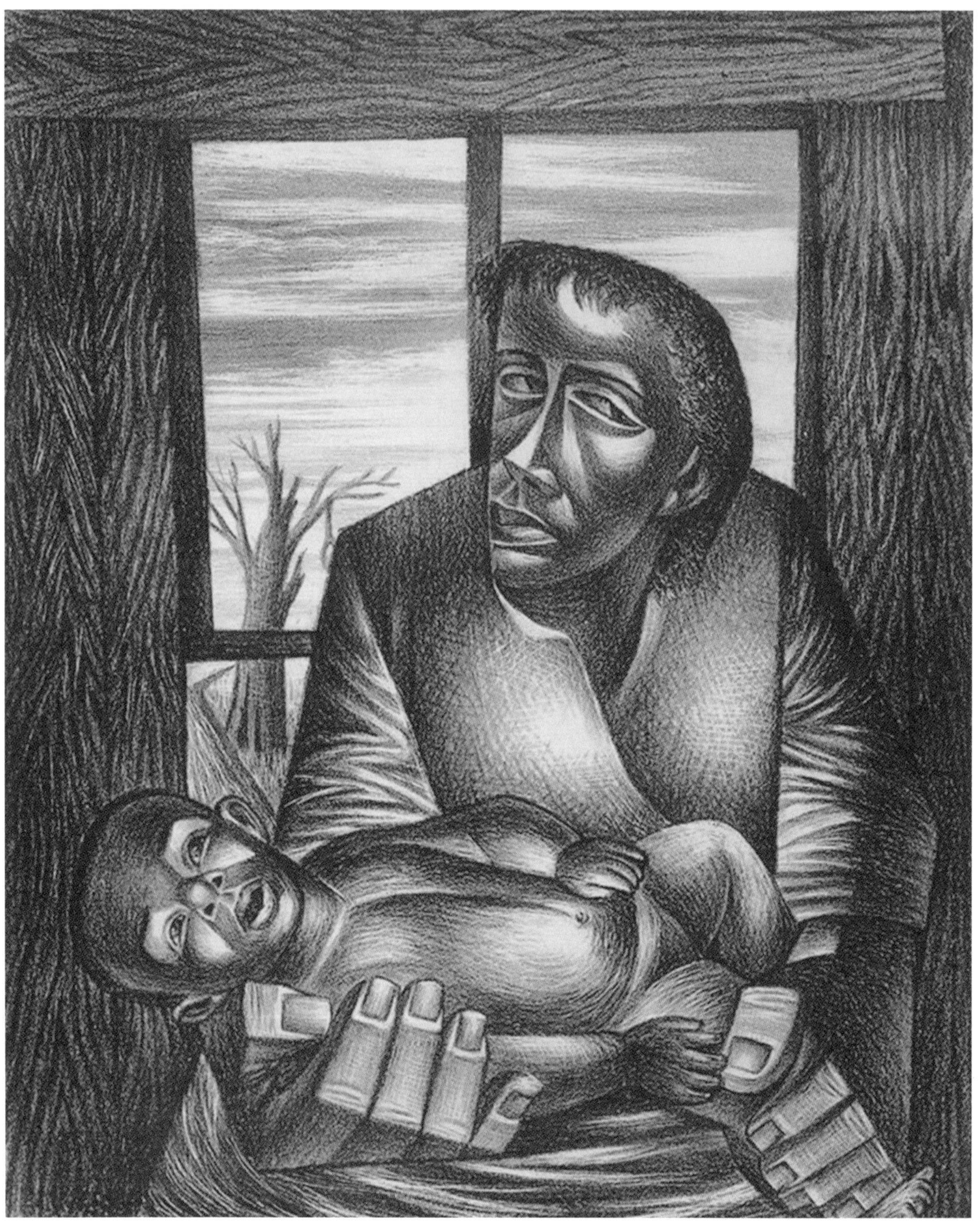

46

46.
Charles White,
Hope for the
Future, 1945

the #BlackLivesMatter protests, *Analogous Colors* ran on the cover of *Time* magazine bordered by the names of thirty-five men and women who had died as a result of racist violence, many at the hands of the police. 'In her expression, I see the Black mothers who are unseen, and rendered helpless in this fury against their babies,' Kaphar wrote, inside the magazine.[40]

In *Birthing Black Mothers* (2021) gender studies scholar Jennifer C. Nash notes the enduring archetype of the grieving Black mother. 'Black mothers in the United States have become spectacularly and dangerously visible through the frame of crisis, one that insists on their spatial and temporal location in a death-world'. In this death-world, the violent threat of structural racism appears as part of a continuum of violence stretching back to slavery. Nash proposes alternative paradigms in the new visual cultures emerging around breastfeeding and celebrity motherhood, but warns of the 'enduring and troubling tradition of rendering Black women generally, and Black mothers specifically, into symbols,' even if in the era of #BlackLivesMatter they are 'symbols of tragic heroism rather than deviance.'[41]

enter the MILF

In all US states apart from New York the cover model of the August 1991 issue of *Vanity Fair* was concealed by a sheet of paper hiding her body from the neck down. 'Many retail chains refused to carry the issue altogether,' recalls photography curator Susan Bright.[42] The cause of this outrage? The heavily pregnant body of movie star Demi Moore photographed naked (if demurely positioned) by Annie Leibovitz. Moore was not the first celebrity portrayed with her baby bump exposed, but she was the first to appear on the cover of a popular magazine. Leibovitz's portraits of Moore provoked a rapid cultural shift. Moore's *Vanity Fair* cover was also, as Bright notes 'the first [image] to objectify the pregnant form in mainstream culture.'[43] The pregnant and maternal body were laid open to scrutiny and admiration. Not only *could* they be sexy, but the implication was now that they *should* be. Expectant mothers could no longer hide beneath tent-like smocks. By the end of the decade, helped along by the Spice Girls, and fashions for crop tops and bumster jeans, baby bumps (mine among them) were worn publicly exposed. In the 1990s, the women's press acquired an obsession not only with celebrity pregnancy, but with the loss of 'baby weight'. The celebrity mother body was policed in the most invasive way, expected to conform at all stages to the prescribed degree of allure.

Within this continuing atmosphere of extreme scrutiny, the impeccably confected portraits issued by Beyoncé Knowles-Carter during and after her second pregnancy can be seen as a powerful gesture – one of the most famous women in the world taking control of the iconography around her maternity. The pregnancy 'reveal' portrait by Awol Erizku issued on Instagram in February 2017 showed the expectant mother in Agent Provocateur lingerie with her head gauzily veiled, kneeling before a bower of roses. A month after the birth of Sir and Rumi Carter, Beyoncé issued a portrait by Mason Poole in which she is positioned holding her twins before a flowering archway, with her legs, shoulders and a flash of midriff exposed amid a foam of mauve ruffles and a pale blue cloak. In fashioning both portraits, Beyoncé turns knowingly to Western art history, melding the tumbling hair and exposed flesh of Venus (or, more accurately, Charity) with the veil, blue robe and *hortus conclusus* (enclosed garden) of the Virgin Mary. Fashioning a vision of contemporary maternity, she puts in play a tension between the suggestion of sexual availability and the forbidden.

47.
Titus Kaphar,
Analogous Colors,
2020, featured on
the cover of *Time*,
15 June 2020

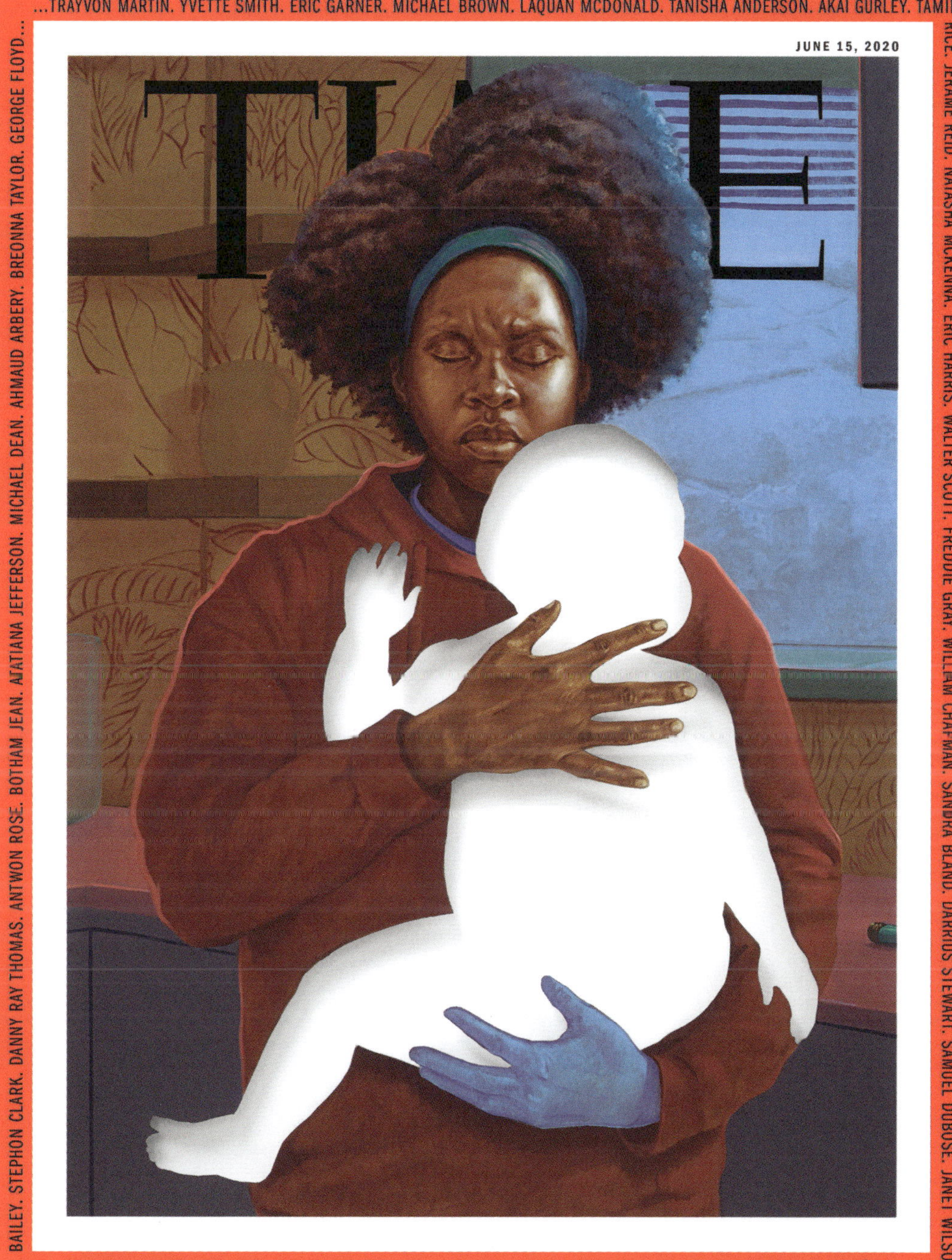
...TRAYVON MARTIN. YVETTE SMITH. ERIC GARNER. MICHAEL BROWN. LAQUAN MCDONALD. TANISHA ANDERSON. AKAI GURLEY. TAMIR
RICE. JERAME REID. NATASHA MCKENNA. ERIC HARRIS. WALTER SCOTT. FREDDIE GRAY. WILLIAM CHAPMAN. SANDRA BLAND. DARRIUS STEWART. SAMUEL DUBOSE. JANET WILSON.
CALIN ROQUEMORE. ALTON STERLING. PHILANDO CASTILE. JOSEPH MANN. TERENCE CRUTCHER. CHAD ROBERTSON. JORDAN EDWARDS. AARON
BAILEY. STEPHON CLARK. DANNY RAY THOMAS. ANTWON ROSE. BOTHAM JEAN. ATATIANA JEFFERSON. MICHAEL DEAN. AHMAUD ARBERY. BREONNA TAYLOR. GEORGE FLOYD...
JUNE 15, 2020
TIME

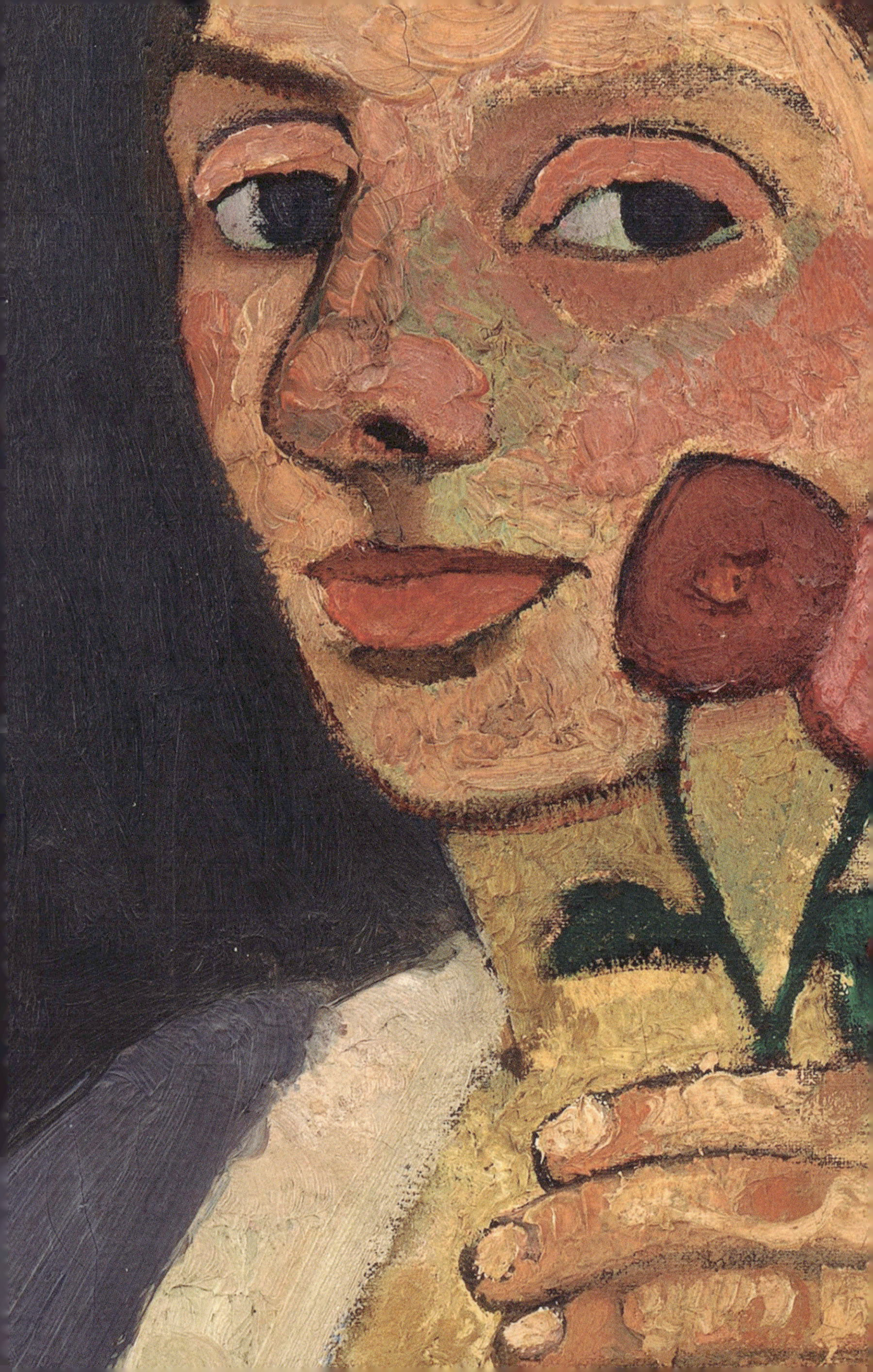

the artist as mother

the shifting 'i'

In *The Mirror and the Palette* (2021) writer Jennifer Higgie proposes the self-portrait as a form of special significance for women. Historically less able to access models (and nude models in particular), a woman's self, seen in reflection, became a readily available subject. Women's self-portraits perform as an assertion – of presence, of practice, of world view. They can be a way to work through love, loss, illness and ageing. Through self-portraiture, Higgie writes, a woman could navigate 'the confusion she's experienced between the reality of living in her body and the lies she's been told about it.'[1] For artists experiencing physical and psychological transformations associated with pregnancy and motherhood, self-portraiture offers a process of thinking through making, a way to get to grips with the shifting 'I'.

The British cover of Higgie's book carries a self-portrait of Paula Modersohn-Becker holding two stylized flowers to her face **48**. A narrow painting made in 1907, its format echoes Fayum mummy portraits, a debt to which can also be seen in the heavy-lidded and stylized rendering of her face. You wouldn't notice unless you knew to look for it, but the artist's right hand rests on her swollen belly. For this is a pregnancy self-portrait, the earliest known. Modersohn-Becker had been fascinated by what it meant – how it felt – to occupy a pregnant body. The previous year she painted herself stripped to the waist, distending her belly in masquerade as I did myself as a teenager, to see how she might look with child. While mothers and children were important subjects for her, she struggled against the constraints of her own marriage, and all cares that took her away from painting.

Her flowers recall the memento mori that garnish Lucas Cranach's paintings. Here, their presence reads like an omen.

This was to be Modersohn-Becker's final self-portrait. She died nineteen days after giving birth. In his tribute *Requiem for a Friend* (1908) Rainer Maria Rilke wrote of how she had:

> *...died as women used to die,*
> *at home, in your own warm bedroom, the old-fashioned*
> *death of women in labor, who try to close*
> *themselves again but can't, because that ancient*
> *darkness which they have also given birth to*
> *returns for them, thrusts its way in, and enters.*[2]

•

In the preceding chapters, I explored the mother as subject – the symbolism and values associated with and imposed on her. Here, I look instead at the artist as mother – how she has chosen to represent herself through self-portraiture, and why she might choose to do so. Reflecting real experiences of motherhood rather than confected ideals, these portraits also help us understand how artists have balanced creative lives with the demands of mothering, pregnancy or efforts to conceive.

Frida Kahlo painted herself for many reasons – to work through the pain of her injured body, a rupture in her marriage, a new love affair. Sometimes simply to remind people she was there. Her marriage to muralist Diego Rivera was tumultuous, and her feelings about pregnancy distinctly changeable. Motherhood would separate her from Rivera, she would no longer be able to share his peripatetic life and he would inevitably stray (as he did, and had, so many times). There were concerns about Kahlo's health. Her doctor in Mexico worried she was not robust enough to carry a child.

In 1932 while Rivera was working on frescoes for the Detroit Institute of Arts, Kahlo realized she was pregnant. She requested a termination from a doctor in Detroit. All he would prescribe was quinine and an emetic of castor oil, a revolting concoction that caused only light bleeding. Defying her doctor in Mexico, she decided to go ahead with the pregnancy. Typically, she also ignored medical advice to rest, instead taking her time in Motor City as an opportunity to learn to drive. During the fifth month of pregnancy Kahlo started bleeding heavily and suffered a painful and devastating miscarriage. As with other traumas, she worked through this in her art, requesting pencils, paper and medical textbooks during her thirteen days in hospital. In *The Henry*

49.
Betye Saar,
Anticipation,
1961

Ford Hospital (1932) **50** she portrays herself as a tiny weeping figure on a bloodstained bed in a barren wasteland, with the Ford Motor Company's River Rouge plant on the horizon. Tethered to the six red ribbons she clutches are symbolic objects – anatomical drawings of the female abdomen and pelvic bone, a foetus, a snail and crushed flower, and a piece of machinery – evoking a conceptual clash between the industrial mindset of Detroit and the soft unpredictability of the human body.

•

'How do you handle being a mother and being an artist?' an interviewer asks Betye Saar, in 1977. 'What's the difference?' she replies, laughing.[3] The richly textured screen print *Anticipation* **49** was made in 1961 when Saar was pregnant with her third daughter and shows the artist in a purple dress holding flowers in her lap – an emblem of the blossoming underway within her increasingly heavy body. Saar is best known for politically charged

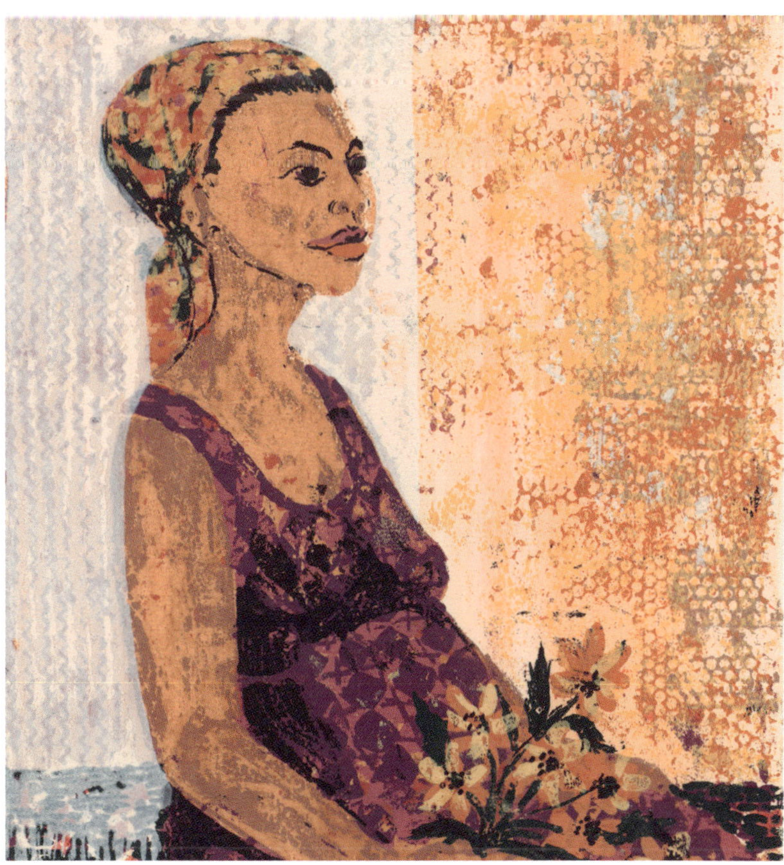

49

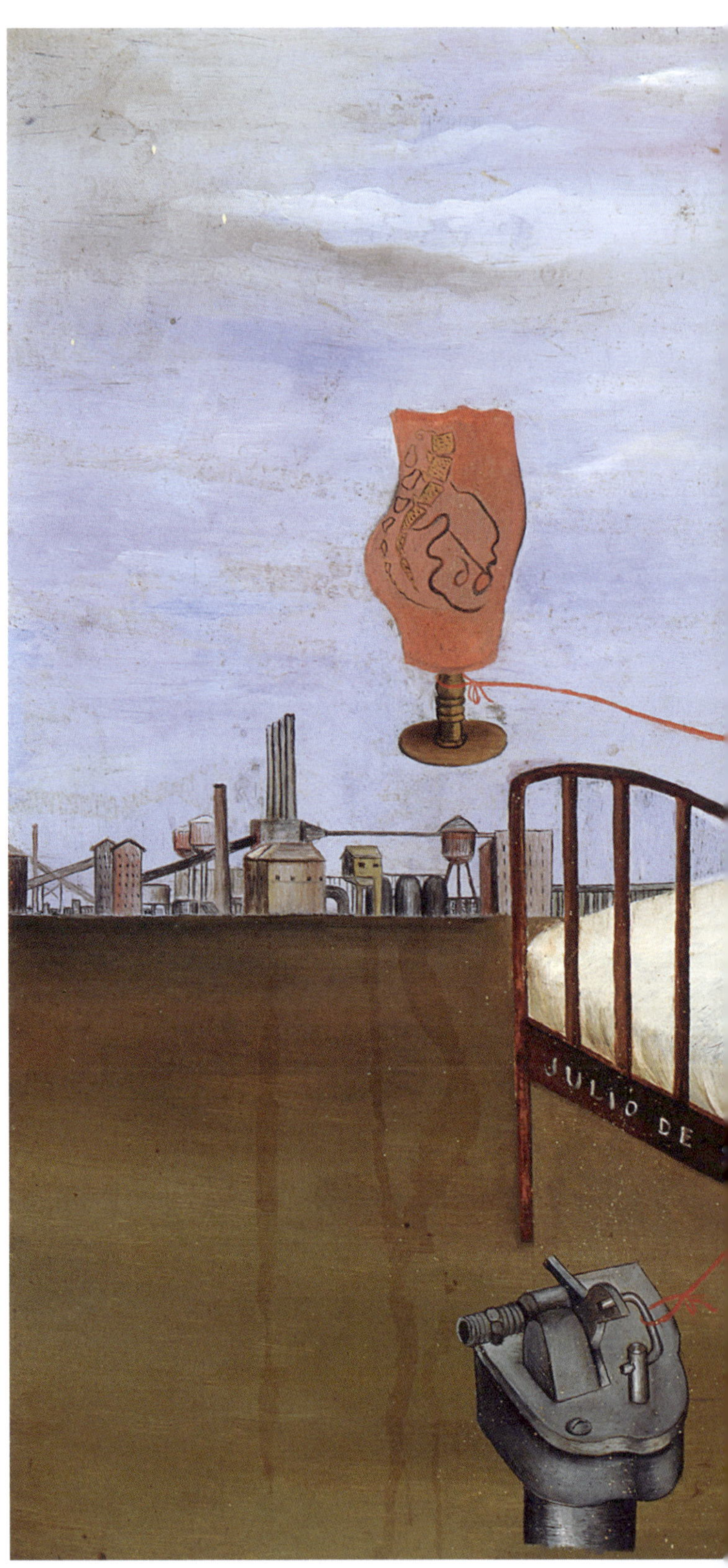

50.
Frida Kahlo,
*The Henry Ford
Hospital*, 1932

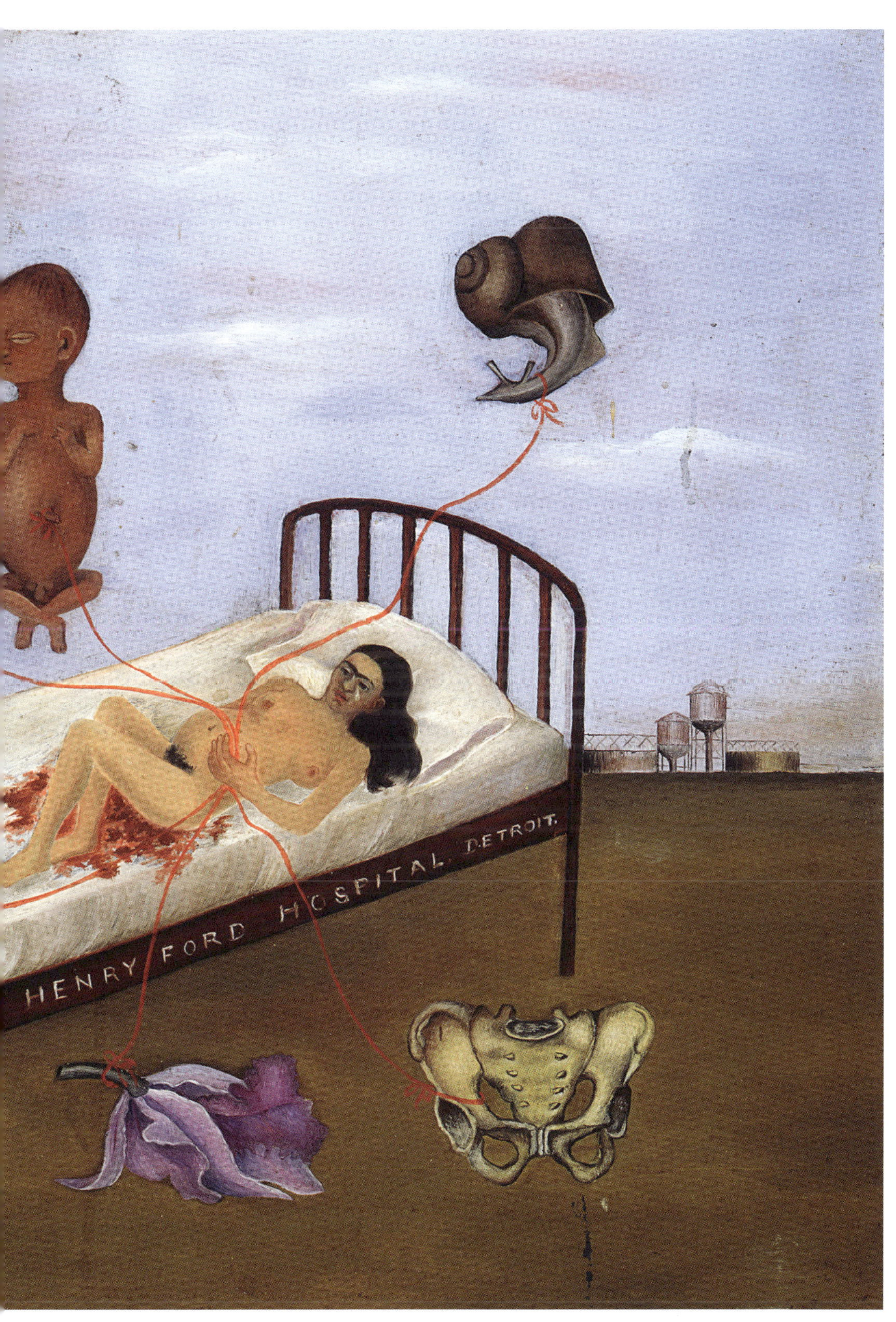HENRY FORD HOSPITAL. DETROIT.

assemblage works, but those, she explains, only became possible when her children were older. In early motherhood she focused on printmaking and graphics: *Anticipation* is one of the first works she made after deciding her path lay in art rather than design ('You know at that time blacks were not particularly encouraged in the arts' she patiently informed an interviewer in 1975.)[4]

Saar has spoken of events that sparked a radical shift in her art in the late 1960s – formally, an encounter with the mystic box sculptures of Joseph Cornell, politically, the assassination of Martin Luther King – with the implication that her prior work was more personal, less focused. Yet there is something quietly revolutionary about this gentle self-portrait. Before the advent of the Women's Movement, pregnancy was rarely depicted in art, still considered a private subject. In the early 1960s, when 'Jim Crow' laws in Saar's home state of California imposed segregated schools and forbade mixed marriages, a pregnant self-portrait by a woman of colour seems a strong assertion of visibility, of presence.

hide and seek: a detective story

The visibility given to artists' statuses as mothers has fluctuated according to wider societal trends. In certain periods it was considered highly desirable, in others, almost a source of embarrassment. In the 19th and for much of the 20th century, as the role of art shifted after the invention of photography, Western women artists struggled to be taken seriously. To add motherhood to the mix was beyond the pale, read as evidence of insufficient commitment to art's calling. As this period coincided with the foundation of major public museums in Europe and the US, little wonder that artist motherhood is not well-represented in their collections.

Back in the listless pandemic days when time seemed giddyingly expansive, I searched the entire online painting database of London's National Portrait Gallery for works in which artists identified themselves as mothers. I had Mary Beale's self-portrait of 1666 in mind as a starting point. Beale, a successful portraitist of the Restoration period, shows herself in a lavish silk robe with one hand resting on an unfinished picture of her two sons. On the wall hangs her palette, a tool identifying her as the author of the painting within the painting as well as the self-portrait itself. Surely if Mary Beale was portraying herself as a mother in the 17th century, plenty of other artists must have, over the years? I scrolled and clicked through the centuries and found nothing until Chantal Joffe's monumental and assertive *Self-Portrait with Esme* (2008) **51**. Joffe's 3-metre-high painting presents mother and child as real, naked bodies – vulnerable, but impossible to ignore. It offers the bond of care between mother and child as something grand and magisterial, fit to be celebrated. We encounter the towering mother as a child might, as a figure embodying the whole world. In this venerable and extensive portrait collection, Beale and Joffe were separated by 342 years of British painting during which the artist as mother was not visible.[5]

This issue is not confined to historic collections. The artist as mother has not been readily apparent in books or displays on the avant-gardes of the early 20th century, or even – with one or two specific exceptions – in surveys of feminist art. Yet women have continued to make both art and children. Part of my goal in researching art and motherhood was to inscribe the artist mother as a cultural type. So why couldn't I find her?

The answer is complex. For some artists, the studio is a refuge, separating the spheres of art and family. Artist mothers have pursued a great variety of subjects – we should not demand self-portraiture of them if it lies outside their usual domain. Those who do paint the figure also face an issue that corresponds to 'single parent photo syndrome'. As a lone parent (at least before the age of the smartphone) you were likely to have fewer pictures of yourself with your children because there was no partner on hand to hold the camera. Historically, mother and children were available as models for the artist father in a way they were not to the artist mother.

respectable, professional

Professional artists in Europe prior to the 19th century faced a crucial limitation: while they may have sketched all manner of personal subjects, this variety would not have been reflected in work offered for sale. A professional painter was expected to specialise in a genre and cultivate a signature style.[6] While there were 17th century Dutch artists, for example, who were also mothers – Rachel Ruysch being among the most celebrated – their art was made for the market, and as such, corresponded to those subjects for which they were recognized and valued. In Ruysch's case, these were floral arrangements in which rare blooms were animated by flitting insects and creeping lizards. There is a portrait of Ruysch with her husband and one of the couple's ten children, in which her status as an artist is clearly indicated. She leans

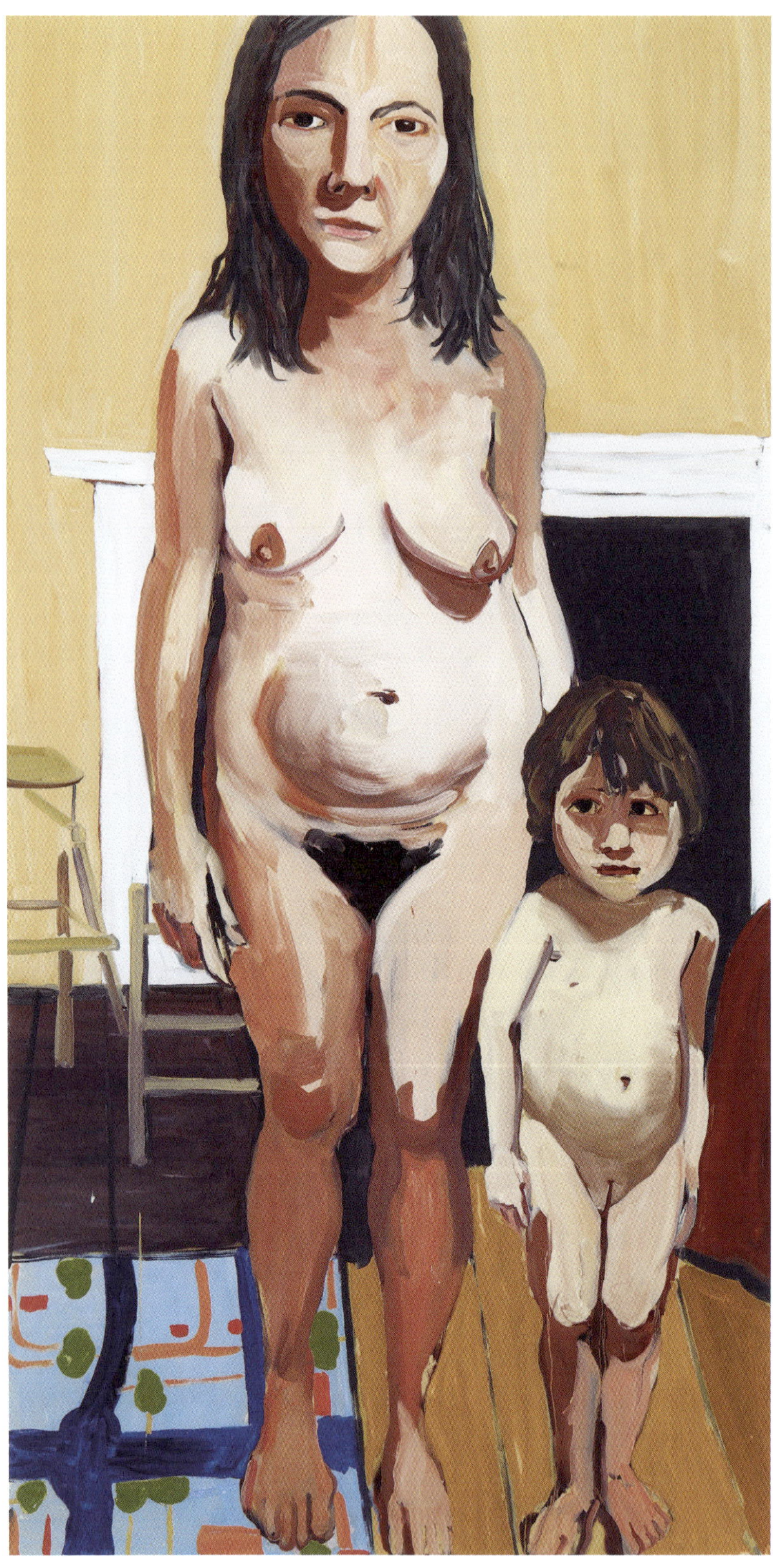

on a table beside voluptuous blooms while her husband Juriaen Pool gestures proudly to her easel. The picture was painted by Pool – a portraitist and printmaker – rather than Ruysch, the still life specialist.

Let us revisit Mary Beale, who flourished during the relative social liberation that followed the restoration of the monarchy in 1660. These were the years in which women first appeared on the British stage and the writer Aphra Behn found fame. Beale nevertheless worked within social constraints. Although recognized as an accomplished painter in the 1650s, the self-portrait of 1666 **52** was created before she professionalized her practice. During her first years as a mother, the family lived on her husband Charles's civil service salary, which he lost during the plague years when the Beales left London. On their return in 1670 Mary set up studio in Pall Mall, near to the Royal Palace and to her mentor, the court artist Peter Lely, to whose lavish formal portraits Beale represented a less costly alternative. Demand was such that her income supported the family, while Charles worked as her bookkeeper and studio manager, mixing colours and preparing canvases. As the Beales' sons grew up, they were coached by their mother and completed sections of her portraits. This success was built on well-laid groundwork. 'Beale prospered, in part, because in the 1650s and '60s she prepared society to accept her work by cementing a personal reputation as virtuous domestic gentlewoman, accomplished amateur writer, and artist,' writes art historian Helen Draper. 'For Mary to work at a public profession, with Charles as her assistant, each fostered a creditable persona with which to protect themselves from social disapproval.'[7] Mary Beale's self-portrait showed her not only to be skilled, but also respectable. Her status as a mother not only enhanced her role as an artist: it became part of the persona that allowed her to flourish professionally.

Painted 120 years later, Élisabeth Louise Vigée Le Brun's *Self Portrait with her Daughter Julie* (1786) **53** is a rare picture of a woman embracing her daughter – a counter-image to centuries of Holy Virgins and mothers brandishing heirs to the family line. As discussed in the previous chapter, late 18th-century France was embroiled in a moral panic in which that mythic creature the 'natural' mother and her role at the centre of a loving family emerged as a new ideal. Dressed in an unstructured gown *à la Grecque* the artist and her daughter perform these roles in anticipation of approval. A favourite of Marie Antoinette in a period of intense social insecurity, Vigée Le Brun – as with the

51.
Chantal Joffe,
*Self-Portrait
with Esme*, 2008

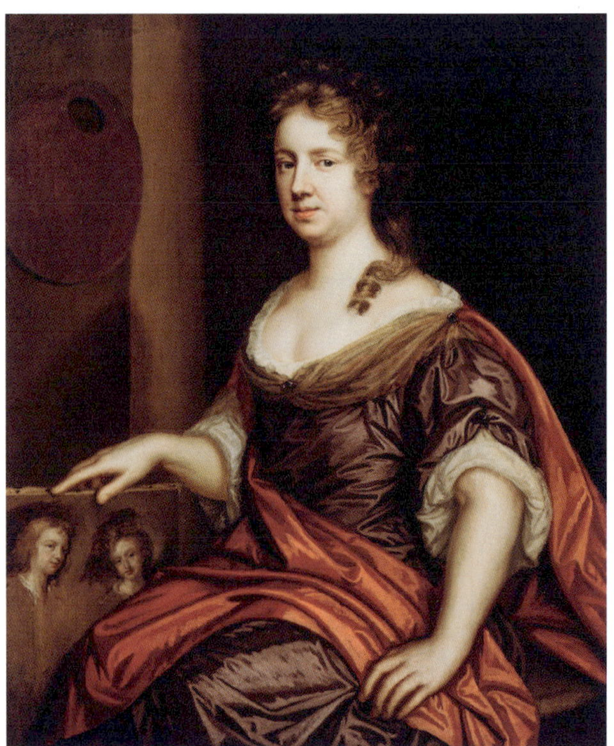

52

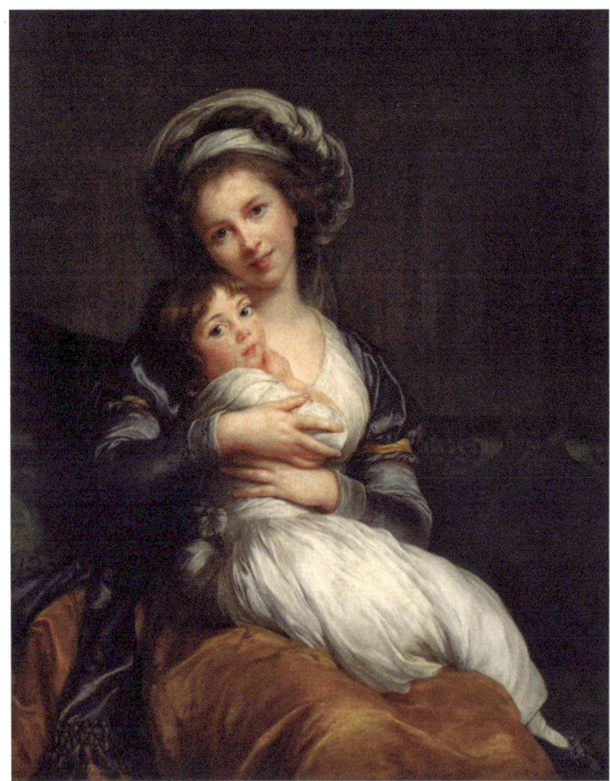

53

Queen herself – was the victim of salacious rumours. One critic suggested that she had 'intimate' knowledge of her sitters.[8] This self-portrait offered a wholesome riposte.

Vigée Le Brun was summoned to attempt similar maternal magic with Marie Antoinette, whose legendary extravagance and reputation for whimsical fancy contributed to her mounting unpopularity. The artist's *Self Portrait with her Daughter Julie* was presented at the 1787 Paris Salon, the same year as *Marie Antoinette and Her Children* – Vigée Le Brun's sentimental portrait commissioned as a propaganda gesture to align the monarch with the new maternal ideal. Clutching a baby boy, the Queen receives an embrace from her daughter, in a gesture reminiscent of Greuze's *The Well-Loved Mother*. The older son gestures toward an empty bassinet, indicating the recent loss of another child. No repositioning would be enough to warm the French public to their Queen. Within two years, a period of revolution commenced during which Vigée Le Brun and her daughter were forced into exile, and her patron lost her head.

Public revelations of mothering may have been good business strategy in Restoration England and late 18th-century France, but the disconnect between the home and the professional sphere became firmly entrenched in the 19th century. Professional women, artists or otherwise, have been expected to keep their motherhood out of sight. As recently as 2018, the then New Zealand premiere Jacinda Ardern made headlines around the world as the first world leader to attend a meeting of the United Nations General Assembly with her baby. In 1982 the US editor of *Cosmopolitan* magazine Helen Gurley Brown published her book *Having It All*, promoting a life plan encompassing motherhood, a career and a raging hot sex life. Today the notion of 'having it all' seems more trap than aspiration.

Billie Zangewa's shimmering silk appliqué *Every Woman* (2016) **54** presents us with a vision of this impossible ideal. Zangewa is apparently 'having it all'. Elegant and sexy in high heels and figure-hugging trousers, we seem to have caught her en route to a high-powered business meeting. Carving out a few minutes to tidy away toys, she stands a giant amid the miniaturized ephemera of a child's life. Yet Zangewa's choice of medium for this self-portrait tells a different story. Look closely and you will see the stitching, the edges of raw silk left rough, drawing attention to long associations with domestic work. The unhemmed lower edge of *Every Woman* reminds us that we're not

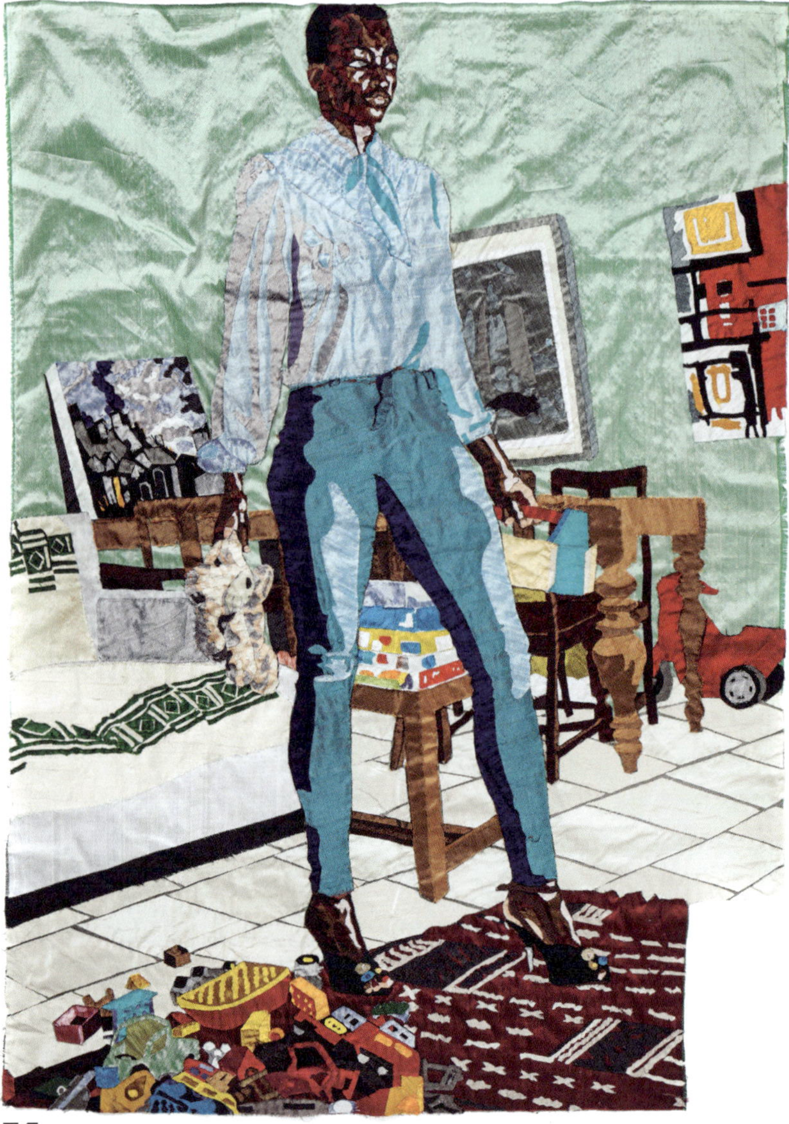

54

seeing the full picture: out of sight, another Zangewa sits sewing
at her kitchen table in Johannesburg.

that ancient darkness

When I lecture on artist mothers, I often start with a *Madonna
and Child* painted by Artemisia Gentileschi in 1613, the year she
gave birth to the first of her five children. The 'girlboss feminism'
version of Artemisia's life has her as a violated woman with a
taste for bloody revenge – it doesn't tend to consider Artemisia
as a mother. Considerable scholarship has been applied to the

early lives of historical women artists and the influence of artist fathers, but there has been substantially less investigation into the impacts of marriage and maternity. Artists are considered as daughters, in other words, but not so much as mothers.

Art historian Frima Fox Hofrichter's research into nursing and family planning in 17th-century Europe, suggests it is unlikely Artemisia painted the nursing Madonna based on lived experience of breastfeeding.[9] Married in 1612, at the age of nineteen, she had four children over six years. Although the pacing of these births would allow for her to have nursed, it is more likely as a Florentine woman of her social position that she would have placed them with a wet nurse. The well-observed intimacy of this *Madonna and Child* is instead thought to derive from the artist's studies of the family servant Tuzia and her son.[10] The likely impact of wet-nursing for Artemisia was two-fold. On the one hand, it released her from the labour of breastfeeding, leaving her free to paint. On the other, she was unwittingly putting her children at risk. In this period, infant mortality was higher among babies tended by a wet nurse. Three of the four children Artemisia bore in Florence died. The overwhelming weight of work, childbirth, debts run up by her husband and the deaths of her children may well have contributed to Artemisia leaving Florence for Rome in 1620, a move that marked the start of her mature career.

Hofrichter compares Artemisia's career after marriage with that of Judith Leyster. In 17th-century Holland, maternal nursing was promoted as an emblematic gesture of love and care. According to Dutch moralist Jacob Cats: 'One who bears her children is mother in part, but she who nurses her children is mother completely.'[11] It was believed sexual intercourse would taint breast milk, harming the supply and perhaps the baby. A pattern can be seen among Dutch women of the time, with births paced evenly every couple of years, suggesting twelve months or so of breastfeeding before the recommencement of sexual contact and a subsequent pregnancy.

Leyster was married in 1636 aged twenty-seven. She had five children, of whom only two survived her. All of Leyster's significant known works predate her marriage, which has led some scholars to assume she was not permitted by her artist husband to continue professional work under her own name as a married woman. Hofrichter instead proposes that the break in Leyster's artistic output represents the labour of childbirth and breastfeeding, as well as a period of grief for her lost children. Dated works by Leyster after marriage do exist, among them two drawings of tulips executed for a sales catalogue in 1643, made in the months after the baptism of her daughter Helena. Anyone who has worked from home with very young children will recognize that this switch – from oil paintings to small botanical studies – might reflect the challenges of life as a new parent. As well as considering the maternity of artists such as Artemisia Gentileschi and Judith Leyster, we should also consider their multiple bereavements. There can be a glib assumption that because infant mortality rates in Europe were so much higher in the past, parents took the death of a child in their stride. I would argue, however, that we should allow for the idea that these artists suffered terrible heartbreak.

This ancient darkness endures in our own time. Born in 1954 in Tanzania, Everlyn Nicodemus has explored expressions of cultural trauma in sub-Saharan Africa and its diaspora as both an artist and an academic. In the painting *My Mutilated Humanity* (1982) **55** she places her own pregnancy within a broader social and historic context. The drug thalidomide is synonymous with arguably the greatest medical scandal of the 20th century. First marketed in Europe in 1956, thalidomide was recommended for conditions including colds, flu and, crucially, morning sickness. It took five years for a connection to be made between the drug and its catastrophic impact on foetal development. Some 10,000 babies were affected worldwide, half of whom died mere weeks after birth. Thalidomide was officially withdrawn in 1961. Nevertheless, trials of the drug and its derivatives for conditions including leprosy continued through the 1970s in African countries including Tanzania and Ethiopia.[12] Nicodemus and her daughter were among those affected. The horrifying grief of *My Mutilated Humanity* is the mourning for an imagined future lost. The mutilation of the title marks not only the drug's physical impact on mother and child, but the psychological trauma caused by scientists and pharmaceutical companies who continued to submit populations in Sub-Saharan Africa to illegal and under-regulated clinical trials well into the 1990s. One of Nicodemus's earliest paintings, it was made as part of a larger project to work visually through damaging experience.[13] A few years later she would commence her *Woman in the World* (1984–86) project for which she gathered oral histories 'connected to domestic violence, to marriage as a prison, to women's bodies being used as experimental fields and to old women's stoic resignation.'[14] For Nicodemus, the informal combination of first-person testament and visual art was a riposte to the 'authoritarian interpretative

55.
Everlyn Nicodemus,
*Min Stympade
Mänsklighet*
(*My Mutilated
Humanity*), 1982

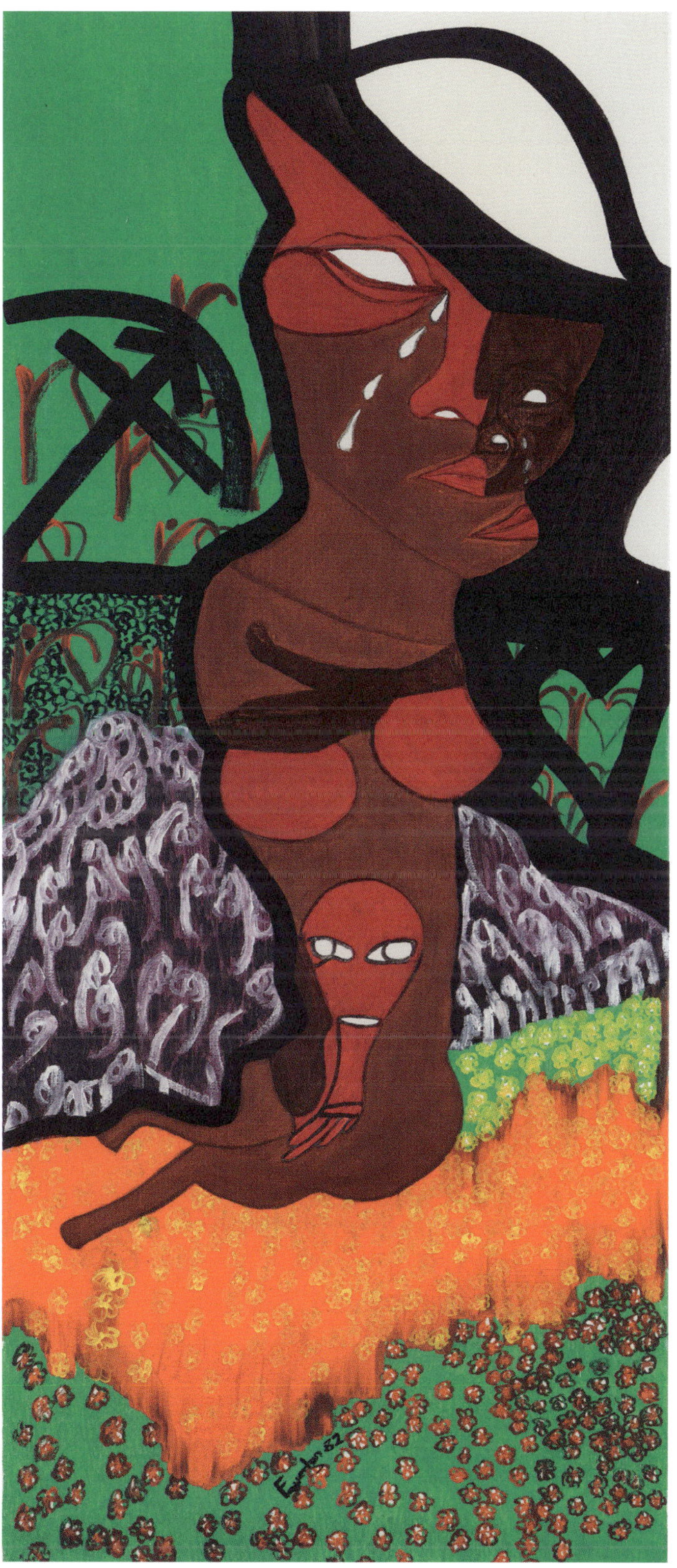

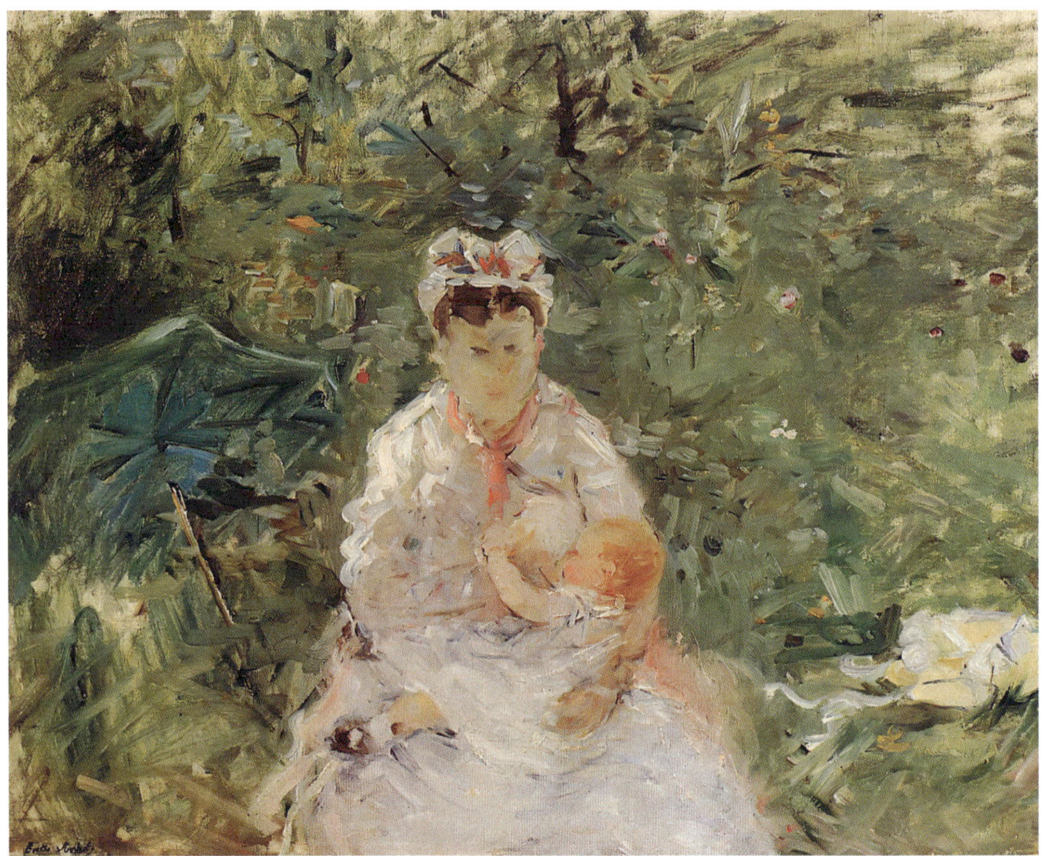

56

control of humans as objects of study' she had encountered as an
anthropology student.[15]

I would like to propose awareness of that ancient darkness
as something we carry with us when we consider the maternal
experience art historically. The absence of the artist mother may
in many cases form a shadow gap that we might also name grief.

artist, mother, teacher

In an essay from 1988, feminist art historian Linda Nochlin scru-
tinizes *The Wet Nurse Angele Feeding Julie Manet* (1880) **56** by
the French painter Berthe Morisot. It is a loosely rendered garden
scene dominated by intense greens with, at its centre, a breastfeeding woman in a white bonnet trimmed with pink ribbons. Nochlin
notes that this is not an Impressionist update on the Madonna and
Child but a work scene. The seated figure is the nurse Angèle hired
by Morisot for her daughter Julie. In 1874 France passed a law
professionalizing the relationship between wet nurse and client.

Wealthier households now hired live-in nurses and provided them with a healthy diet and uniform, including dresses that buttoned at the chest, a cloak and parasol for propriety and shade, and a pale bonnet decorated with two long ribbons.[16] Look out for that ribboned bonnet and you will spot the wet nurse all over French art of this period, a figure of considerable prurient interest. In Nochlin's reading of the painting, 'two working women confront each other...across the body of 'their' child and the boundaries of class, both with claims to motherhood and mothering.'[17] Morisot, in other words, is showing us the circumstances under which the creation of this painting has been made possible.

Thinking of how Morisot instead represents herself as a mother, I would like to turn to a later self-portrait – *Berthe Morisot Drawing with her Daughter* (1889) **57** – a dry-point etching of the artist working as her daughter looks on. Morisot is seated, intent on her reflection. Her daughter Julie, now ten or eleven, leans in, her head touching her mother's. The positioning of their bodies speaks to deep affection, but while Julie looks at the drawing, watching her likeness appear, Morisot gazes outward, breaking through the bubble of familial love. As with the painting of Angèle, this work explores the conditions of making art as a mother. Morisot is the focus of both the work and the child's attention. Rather than a compliant nurturing figure, she portrays herself as an educator demonstrating her drafting skills.

In their research-led project *The Birth of the Image* (2016–20) the British artists Hermione Wiltshire and Clare Bottomley revisit familiar subjects from Renaissance and Baroque art. Their staged photographs reimagine the portrayal of women in relation to birth, motherhood and midwifery. The project expands on the limited roles afforded to women art-historically, portraying them as custodians of knowledge to be passed down through practice and oral tradition. In *...and another thing...* (2020) **58** Wiltshire herself appears stretched on a bed, half covered by a thin cloth, in a pose familiar from Andrea Mantegna's 15th-century *Lamentation over the Dead Christ*. In Mantegna's painting, Christ's body is watched by three weeping figures: his mother, St John and Mary Magdalene. In the restaging Wiltshire is alive and holding forth in philosophical style. Her two daughters listen with a rapt attention flesh-and-blood mothers can only dream of. Wiltshire's performance in the role of sage alludes to her real-life status as a professor of photography at London's Royal College of Art, where her working partnership with Bottomley grew out of their relationship as teacher and student.

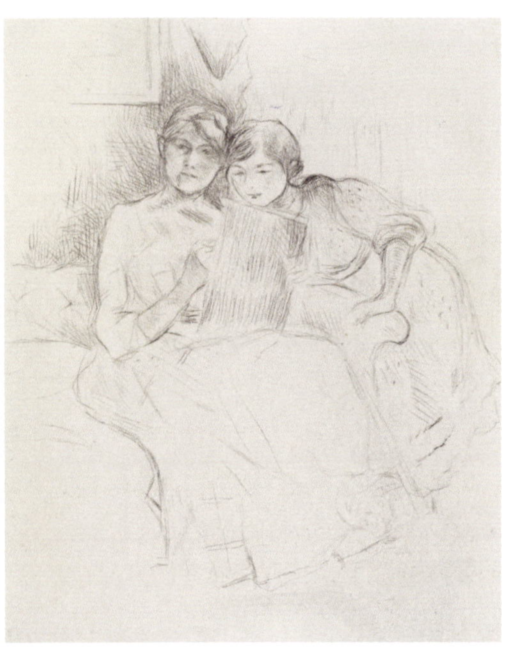

57.
Berthe Morisot,
*Berthe Morisot
Drawing with her
Daughter*, 1889

58.
Hermione Wiltshire
and Clare Bottomley,
*...and another
thing...*, from the
series *The Birth
of the Image*, 2020

59.
Suzanne Valadon,
Family Portrait,
1912

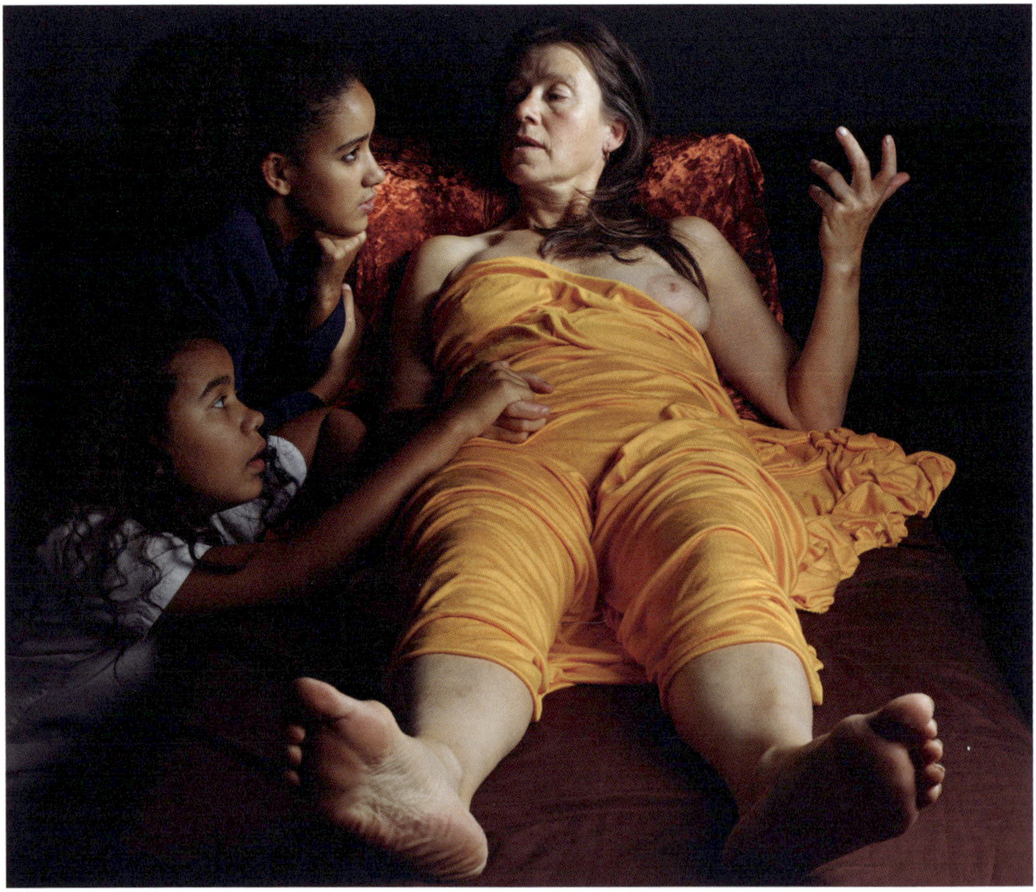

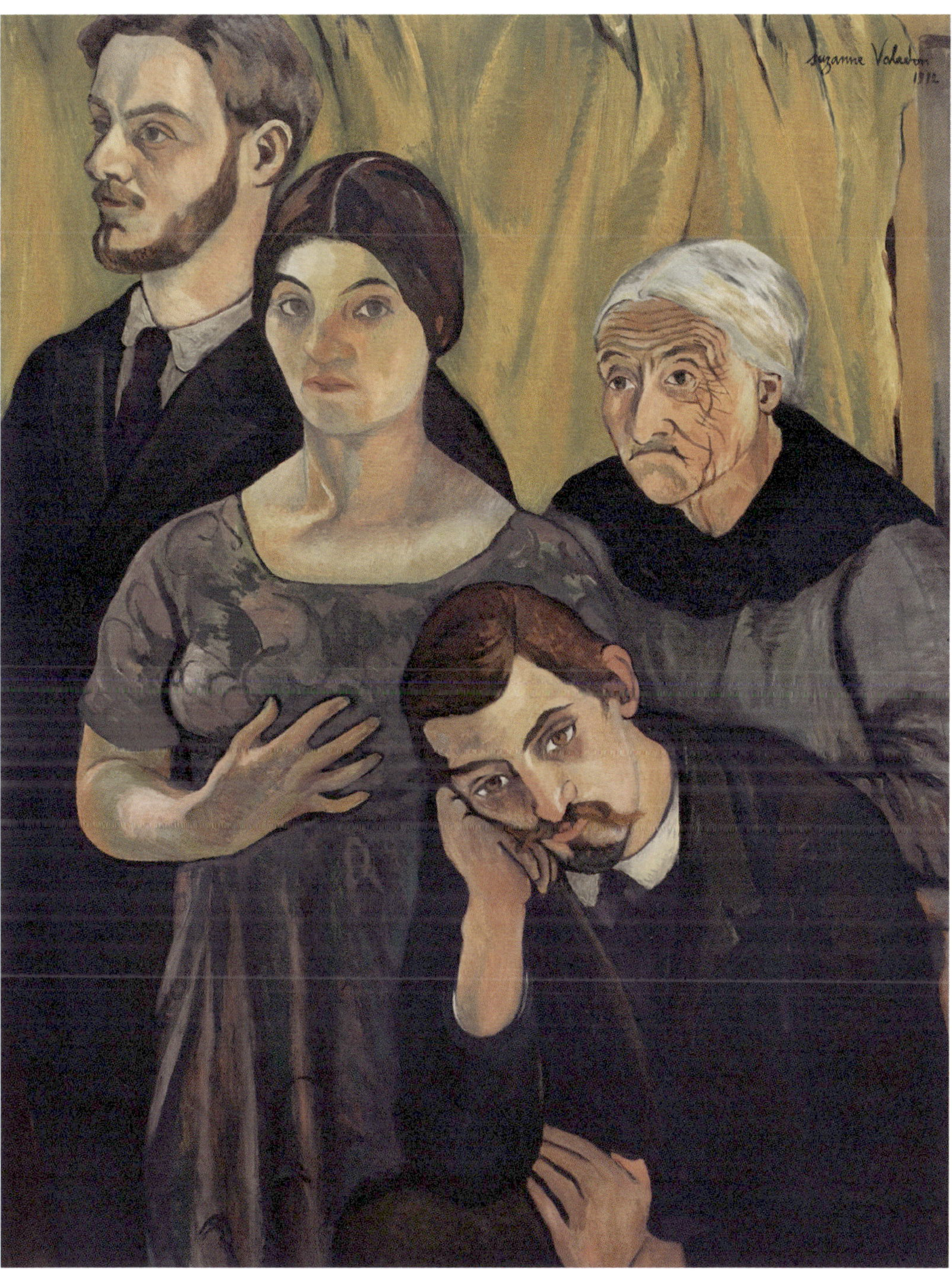

59

This role as the custodian of knowledge offers a significant paradigm for how the artist mother might represent herself. Mary Beale trained her sons as studio assistants. Artemisia Gentileschi taught her daughter Prudentia, who also became an artist. The French painter Suzanne Valadon's son Maurice Utrillo entered the artworld under her tutelage. When we think of the bodies of knowledge held by women and passed down mother to child, skills in drawing, painting, sculpture and printmaking, preparing colours and canvases, working with patrons and running a studio should also be part of that story.

a vision filled

Valadon's *Family Portrait* (1912) **59** depicts an unconventional ménage. Standing at its centre, the artist gazes at us steadily, one hand clasped to her chest as though claiming ownership. Around her, crammed into the field of the painting, are the three most important people in her life dressed in sombre tones, against which Valadon's pale dress stands out. Behind to her left stands her mother Madeleine, whose hollow face testifies to a lifetime of labour. Madeleine raised Valadon and her sister as a single parent, supporting them through domestic service. Valadon was sent to work aged ten and had found success as an artist's model when she became pregnant at eighteen (the two facts are not unconnected – candidates for paternity included her recent clients, Auguste Renoir and Pierre Puvis de Chavannes.) After the birth, Madeleine took care of Valadon's son Maurice so that she could work. It has been customary for art historians to describe Valadon as self-taught. In truth she learned by observing the painters for whom she modelled, and with the guidance of Edgar Degas and Henri de Toulouse-Lautrec. In caring for Maurice, Madeleine Valadon thus not only made it possible for her daughter to earn a living, but also to acquire skills in the profession that would engage her once she entered her forties.

In front of Valadon sits Maurice, now in his late twenties. From early childhood, he had been prone to 'congenital nervous excitement'. By his teens he was troubled and drinking heavily: it was under medical advice that Valadon taught him to paint. Maurice worked side by side with his mother in the studio until his early fifties. This then, is still a scene of active mothering, of ongoing care for an adult child. Maurice Utrillo's stepfather, the painter André Utter, described the son as 'a sort of disciple of his mother.'[18] The fourth figure in the scene, Utter, stands at the

60.
Ishbel Myerscough,
All, 2016

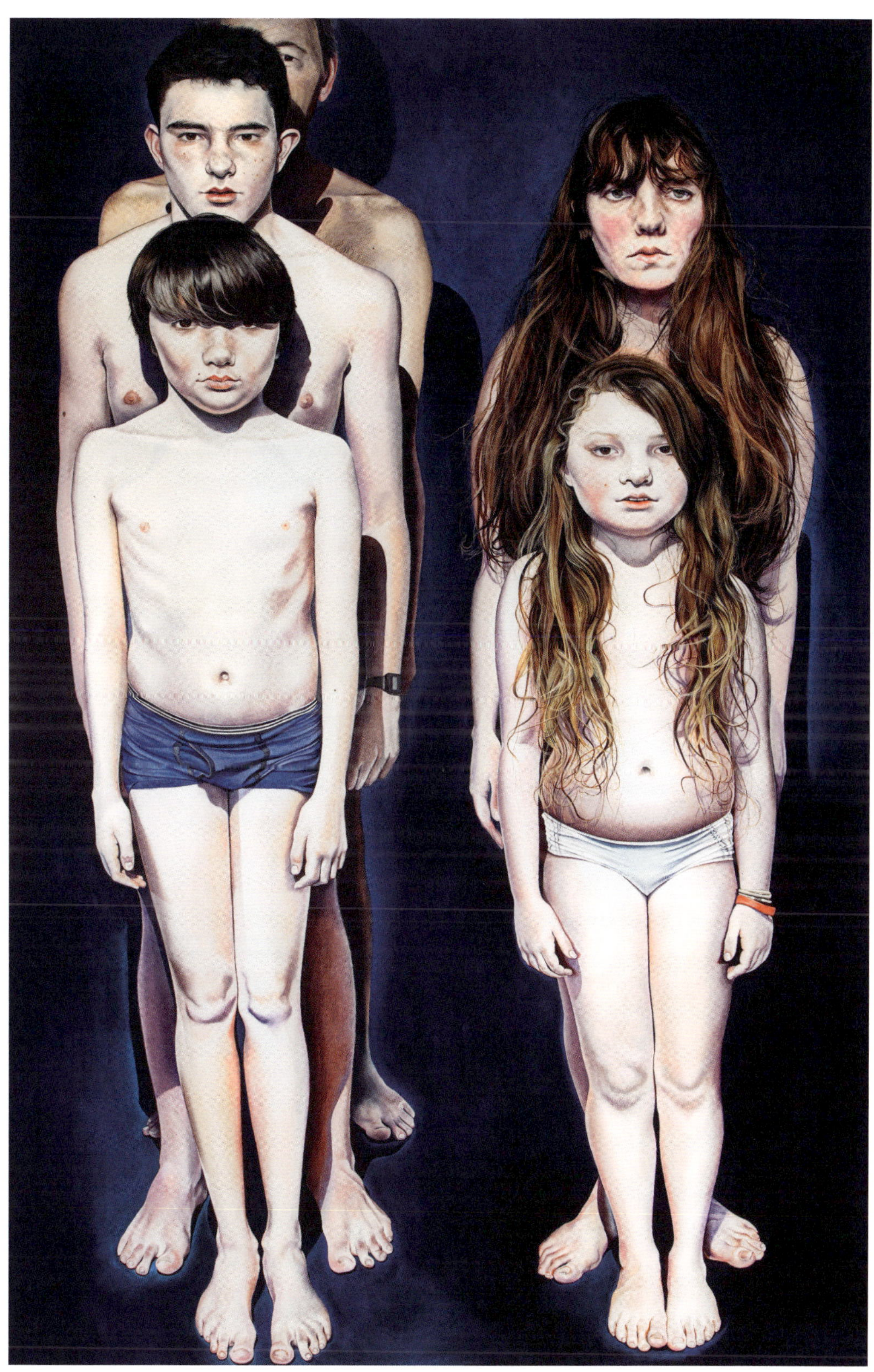

back left. A friend of Maurice and three years his junior, Utter's romantic relationship with Valadon commenced when he was twenty-three and she a married woman of forty-four, unable to paint because of domestic responsibilities. In 1913, Valadon abandoned her suburban marriage, applied for a divorce and set up home with Utter and Maurice in a studio in Montmartre. Steady and practical, Utter offered Valadon not only romance, but the freedom to paint professionally, while he negotiated with dealers and arranged exhibitions for both mother and son. Valadon's *Family Portrait* is a painting that acknowledges the circumstances of its production. Valadon presents herself as a mother, supported by the network of care that made this painting possible: Madeleine Valadon who cared for Maurice as a child, and Utter who supported her transition into the professional artworld.

In Ishbel Myerscough's *All* (2016) **60** the artist and her family are crammed into pictorial space so tightly that the father's head is cropped. Stripped to their underpants, we are presented with their naked reality – their all, all at once, all together. As with Valadon's *Family Portrait*, the fullness of the composition suggests an entire world caught within its boundaries: these are the people that fill this London-based artist's thoughts, the minutiae of whose lives keep her preoccupied, and beyond whose cares and needs it can be hard to see. In dividing the family along gender lines, Myerscough has described *All* as a kind of ladder or progression, in which the life experiences of the parents will gradually transfer to their children, whose lives might fill with their own children in turn, progressively pushing the older generation further back and obscuring them from view. The 'all' of the title extends beyond the figures that we see on the canvas to the act of painting them – for this full world view of Myerscough's encompasses both her role as a mother, and her life as an artist.

hail the many marys!

The Virgin Mary's crimson and ultramarine robes cast a long shadow over the iconography of motherhood, in life and in art. She is flawless, serene, self-sacrificing and ripe for subversion. Leni Dothan's short, looped video *Sleeping Madonna* (2011) **61** shows the Israeli-born artist and her son nodding off mid feed. With a light touch, the film alludes both to the exhaustion experienced by new mothers, and to the labour of nursing, like being trapped in a repeating cycle. Dothan has described the representation of women in Renaissance art as tantamount to a series of 'visual contracts' which continue to influence social, political and religious expectations of motherhood. *Sleeping Madonna* became the first in a series of performances to camera which concluded in 2022 when Dothan's son turned thirteen – considered a Jewish boy's coming of age. In *Playing Dead/Pieta*, Dothan robes herself in mourning black, and invites her son to lie across her lap playing dead, which he does with vaudeville flair.

Catherine Opie's *Self-Portrait/Nursing* (2004) **62** concludes a trilogy that commenced with *Self-Portrait/Cutting* in 1993. The 'cutting' is a line drawing incised into Opie's back, photographed as she stands against blue rococo wallpaper. Into the artist's pale skin is carved a queer child's dream of quotidian comfort: two skirted figures holding hands outside a dinky house. Opie could not foretell the progress of her own life, but as it happens this trilogy charts a progression from the lesbian S&M scene in her thirties to domesticity on her own terms in her forties. While it is posed in echo of the *Madonna Lactans*, Opie's tender portrait with her son has become iconic in its own right: a powerful revisioning of the act of mothering. Long before her own parenthood, Opie was fascinated by the domestic. She documented families colouring outside the lines, composing themselves along expanded structures of love, support and kinship. Her own pregnancy, in 2001, was 'confusing for people...the fusion of me being butch and sporting a moustache,' she recalls. 'I always wanted to have a baby, but the stereotype of a mother was ingrained in people's psyche, and it was not a butch woman. That's why making *Self-Portrait/ Nursing* was so important to me. It was about showing my body [as a mother], illustrating that this is what I desired, and I was going to give it to myself.'[19]

The self-portraits of Renee Cox's *Yo Mama* series show the artist first as a younger woman (1980), then, in photographs made between 1992 and 1996, pregnant, nursing, posing as a pan-African Madonna, holding one child, then two. This was a period during which Black mothers in the US were being vilified in parts of the media as irresponsible 'welfare queens' and 'crack addicts', disproportionately arrested for so called 'prenatal crimes' by the police and pressured to have Norplant contraceptive implants by Medicaid. In 1997 sociologist Dorothy Roberts's devastating investigation *Killing the Black Body* positioned the country's 'dehumanizing attempts to control black women's reproductive lives' in the 1990s within a legacy that stretched back to 'slave masters' economic stake in bonded women's fertility', 'the racist strains of early birth control policy', and 'sterilization abuse of Black women

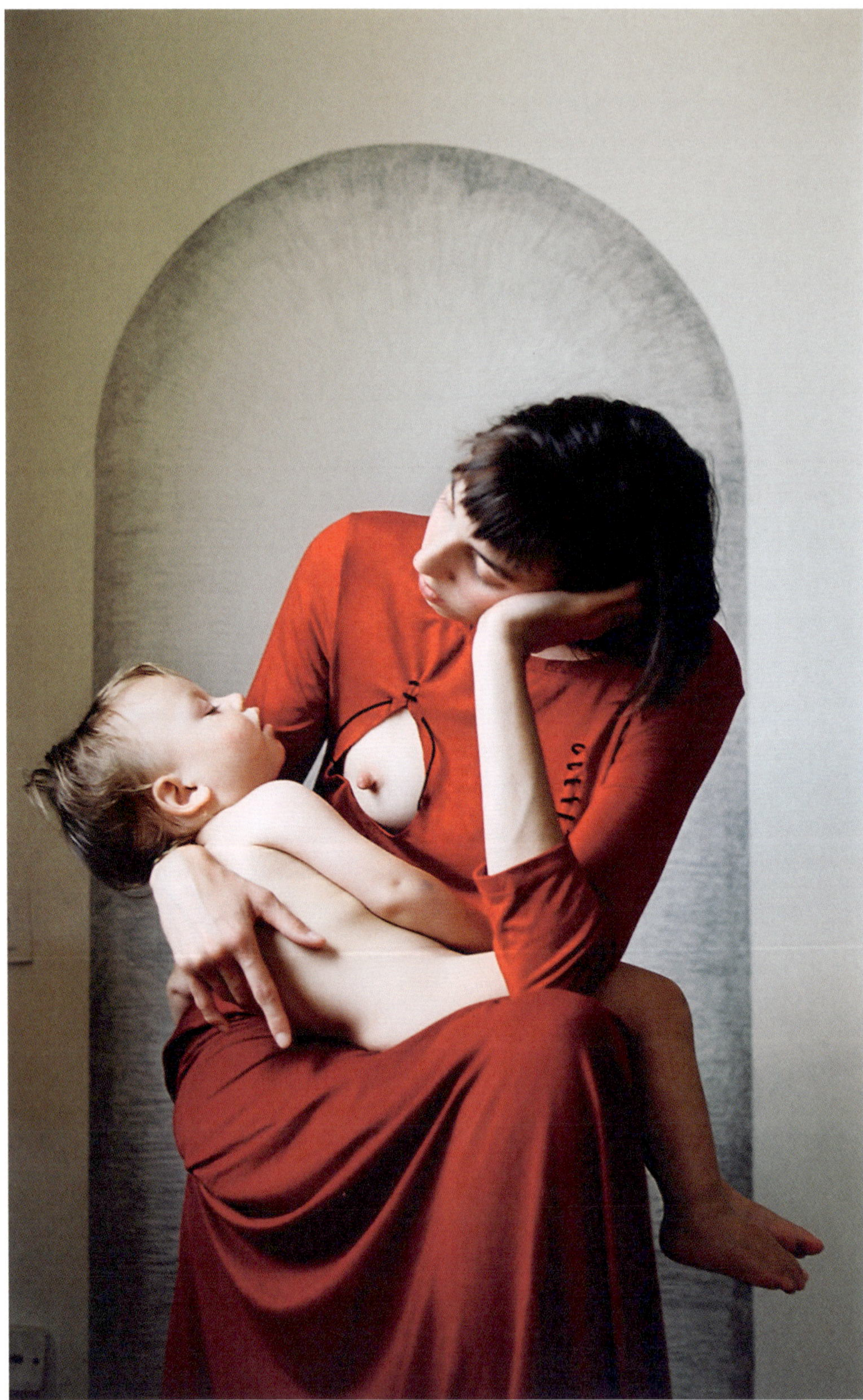

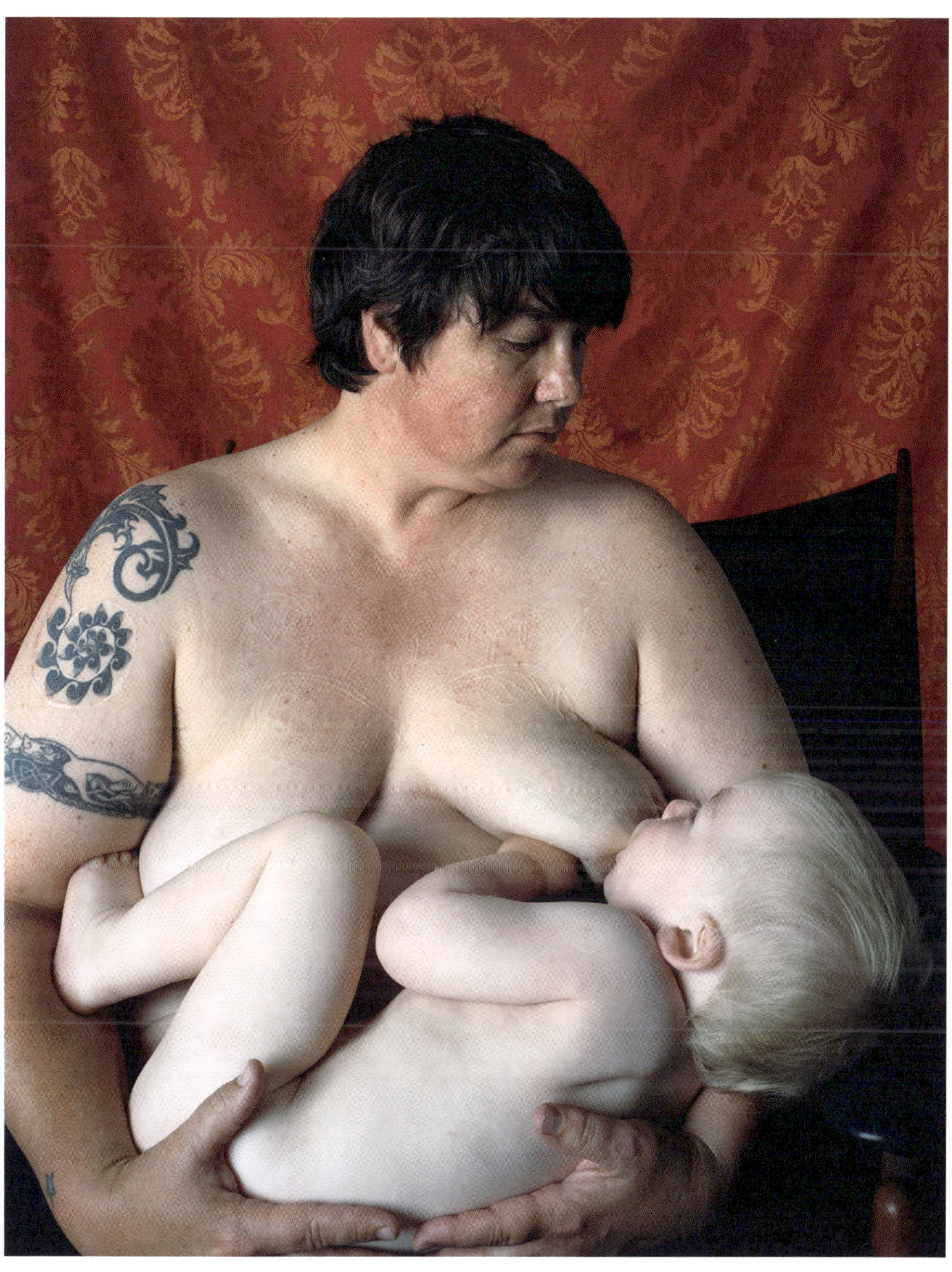

62

61.
Leni Dothan,
Sleeping Madonna,
2011

62.
Catherine Opie,
*Self Portrait /
Nursing*, 2004

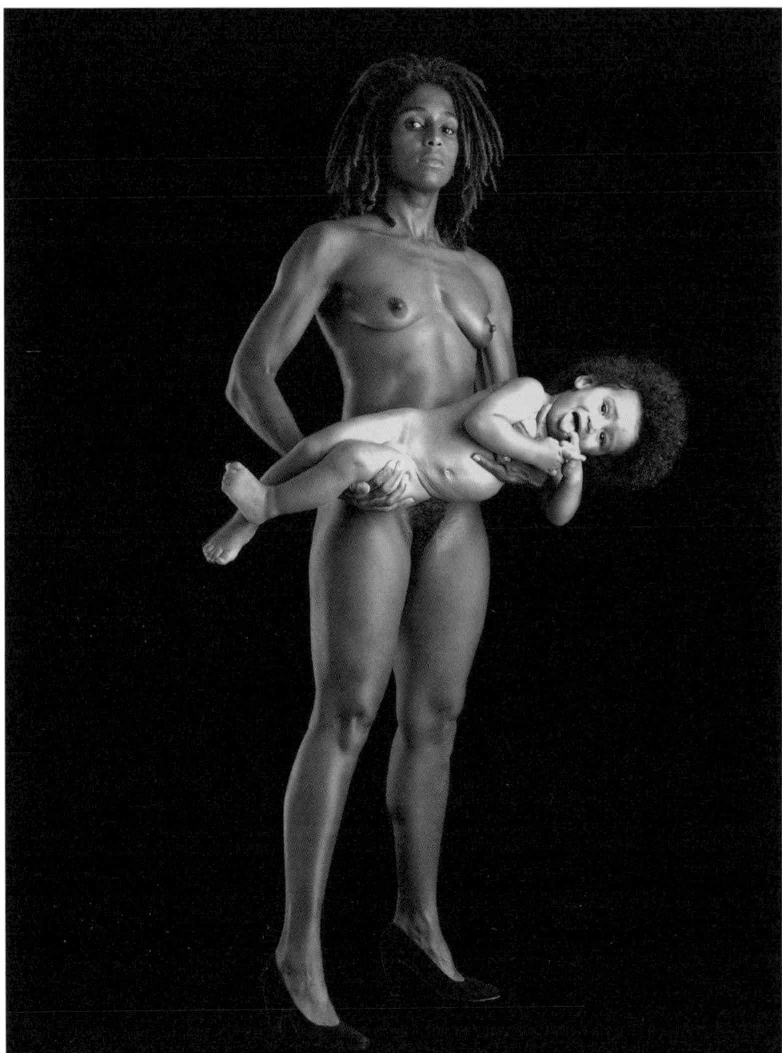

63

during the 1960s and '70s'.[20] Against this cultural backdrop Cox crafted a vision of Black motherhood that busts through the tabloid stereotypes but also rejects the demure ideals represented by the Virgin Mary. In *THE YO MAMA* (1993) **63** she poses naked but for high-heeled shoes, her body toned and glossy, a strapping infant carried lightly in her muscular arms. It suggests motherhood as a source of formidable power. While this mother is a potent object of desire, she is not here to please.

Nurture threads through Janine Antoni's work. In one of her earliest performance works, *Loving Care* (1993) – titled after the box dye used by her mother – the artist painted a gallery floor using her long hair, methodically mopping the audience out of the space. Other performances have explored the gendered power relations of washing and eating. During a rural residency in Sweden in 2000, the New York-based artist spotted an old bath installed in a cattle barn: an object designed for the human body repurposed as a drinking trough. It started a chain of ideas about the relationship between different bodies as sources of nourishment. The photograph takes its title – *2038* – from the numbered tag carried by the cow leaning over to drink as though suckling from her breast, transforming this from a creche scene into an interspecies re-staging of the nursing Madonna **64**. It is a moment of intimacy within a relationship hitherto conducted at one remove: Antoni was weaned off her mother onto cows' milk, a substance that appeared in a carton from the grocery store. Cow 2038 stands in for the unseen, unknown wet nurse. Antoni performs a symbolic act of reciprocity with an animal who will spend most of her life lactating to feed the offspring of another species.

The still composure of the Holy Mother comes under scrutiny in Jenny Saville's *Reproduction Drawings (after the Leonardo Cartoon)* (2009–10) **65**. Scaled as though for a cathedral, in these drawings Saville shows herself heavily pregnant with one child while wrangling another. The outlines echo and recur as Saville adjusts her position to accommodate the wriggling baby. The works' scale performs a spirited defence of both the 'minor' medium and 'minor' subject. They are larger by some degree than Leonardo da Vinci's 'Burlington House Cartoon' (*c.* 1499). The shifting bodies of Saville and her son fulfil all four roles in Leonardo's drawing, in which Mary is (oddly) seated on the lap of her mother Anne with the infants Jesus and John. Saville's visual doubling arises from the action of drawing itself – or more specifically, the interrupted nature of drawing while mothering. These drawings are reproductions in spirit of Leonardo, showing Saville engaged in the work of human reproduction. Their form is determined by the repetitive process of working alongside young children – art made in short bursts interspersed with the same gestures reproduced again and again.

beyond the 'i'

In Carolee Schneemann's 1994 text *Anti-Demeter*, the artist recalls her reaction to pregnancy as a young woman. 'You are not invited into my body. I did not invite an alien being, a 'child,' into my future. I had a mountainside to climb' she writes. 'I was taken over. I was no longer an 'I'.' Schneemann travelled from

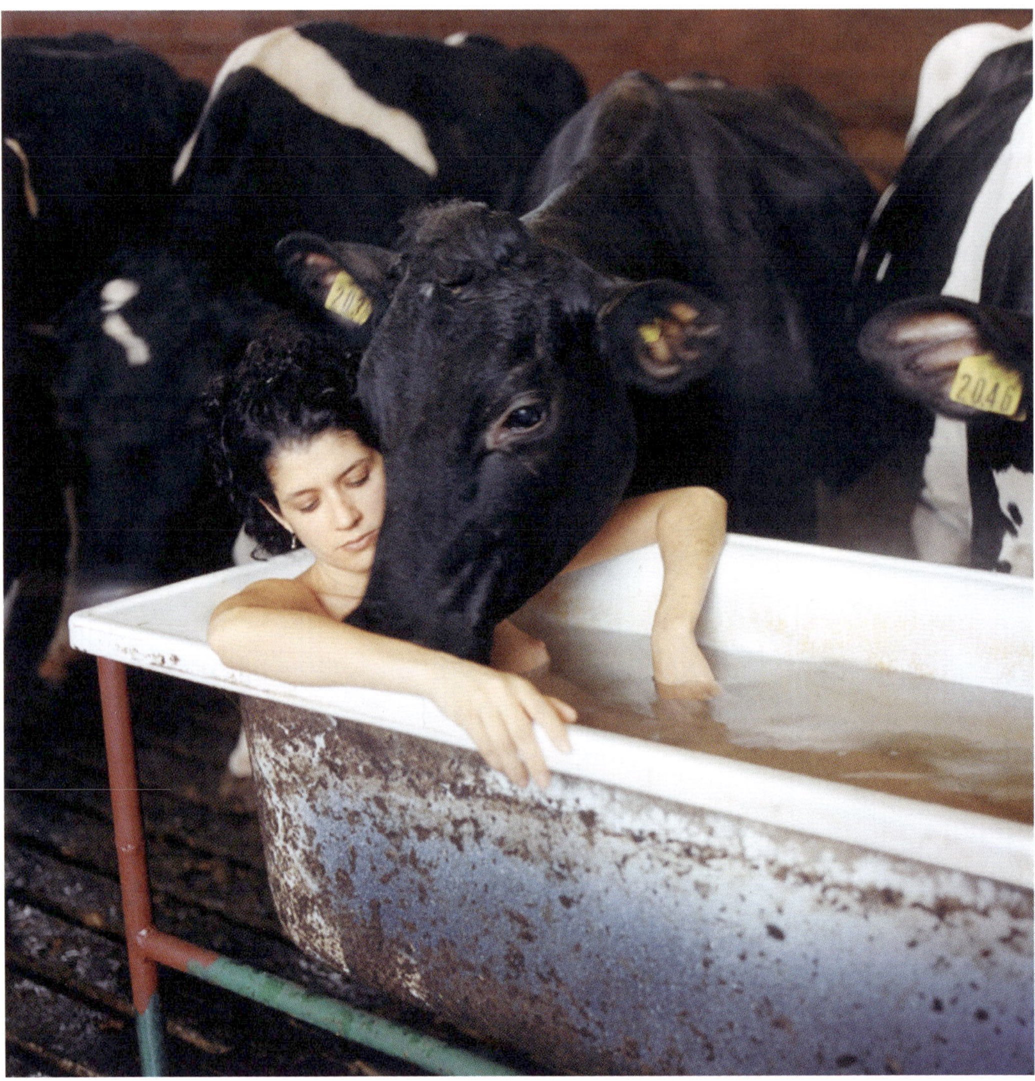

64

64.
Janine Antoni,
2038, 2000

65.
Jenny Saville,
*Reproduction
Drawing II
(after the Leonardo
Cartoon)*, 2009–10

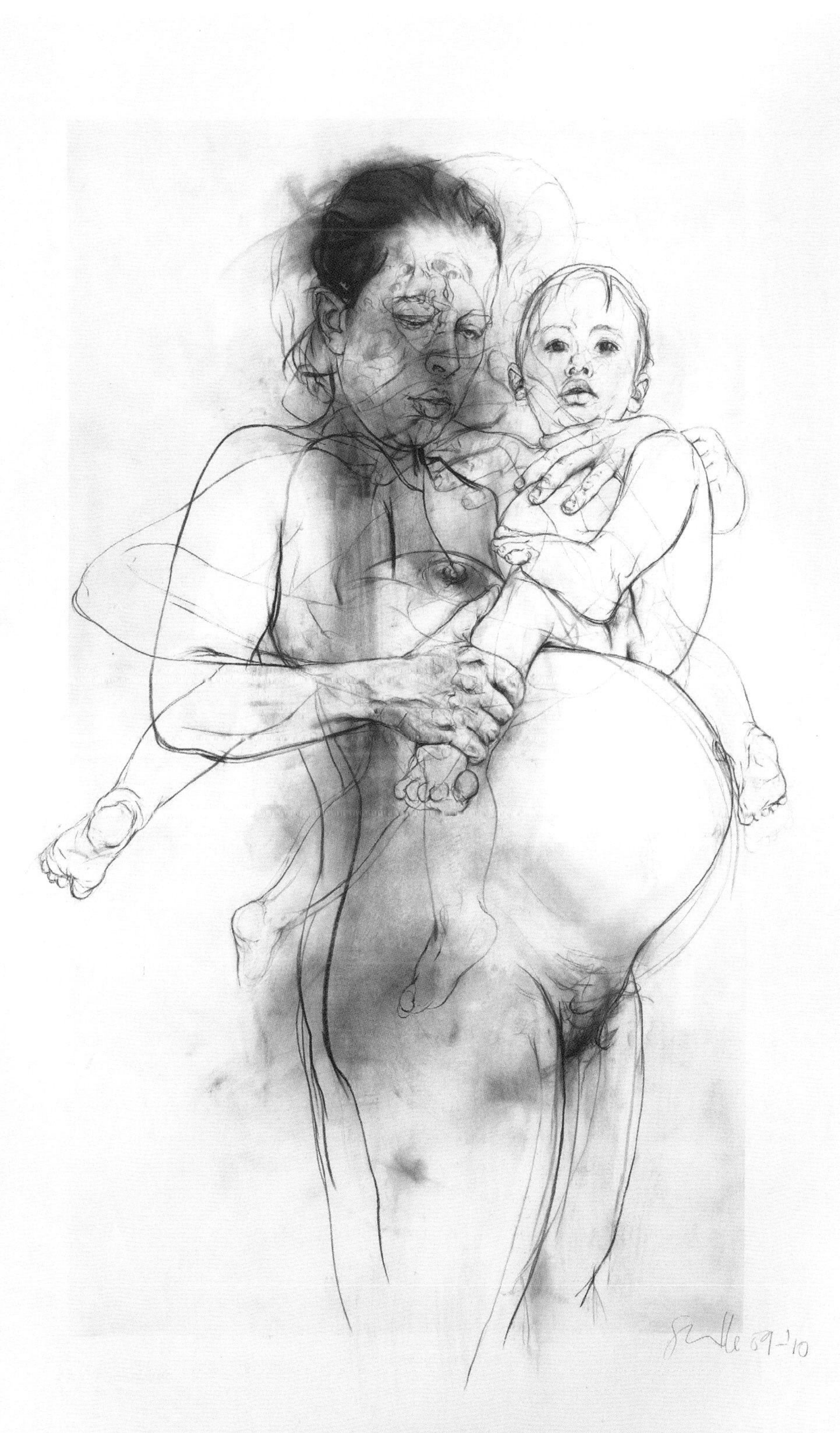

upstate New York to Cuba for an abortion, administered without anesthetic. Decades later, what she recalled was less the pain of the procedure than the terror it removed: that she would not make it through the hostile, patriarchal terrain of the artworld if she had another body to carry. That her self was under threat of erosion. That she was no longer an 'I'.

Anti-Demeter portrays Schneemann's mother as a furious and frustrated drudge whose creative outlet was her sewing machine, whose maternal breasts were consumed by cancer, and whose touch she rejected as though domestic imprisonment might transmit like infection. Her siblings direct their love instead towards the handsome father whose repeated acts of insemination have pinned their mother into the home as surely as a lepidopterist pins a butterfly to card. Many artists of Schneemann's generation associated motherhood with frustrated creativity, the loss of self, isolation and ill temper. Some considered motherhood antithetical to the feminist project – a trap that would return women to the domestic sphere. Artists reflecting on the maternal experience during the 1960s, 1970s and 1980s felt doubly sidelined – by the boys' club who wrote them off as part-timers, and by the Women's Movement that dismissed them as reactionary and conformist.

When British painter and printmaker Eileen Cooper became pregnant in the mid-1980s, she was aware that earlier women artists had maintained a career with the support of servants but could see no role models that reflected her personal background. Motherhood was not part of her life plan – and certainly not a subject she had intended to explore. So, on giving birth she was surprised to find herself 'absolutely consumed by motherhood.'[21] Cooper recalls the stinging backlash when her first works exploring motherhood were exhibited in 1985. Art critic Sarah Kent, writing in *Time Out*, described her 'as '2.4 children' – a phrase used in the 1980s to designate an average family, deployed scathingly to suggest Cooper had departed the serious artworld to join the normies. *Putting Down Roots* (1985) **66** is like a fairy tale altarpiece with the child and mother's face appearing on either side of trunk-like legs. The mother self is divided: her torso lying on the ground with the roots springing out of or perhaps through her, and legs above, pinning her to the ground. Cooper had been studying Frida Kahlo's use of doubling to express contradictory instincts: this painting is celebratory, nevertheless we see the weight of the old self pressing down on the new maternal identity. 'I never intended to make pictures about having a family, but I suddenly realized what that was: putting down roots,' she recalls.

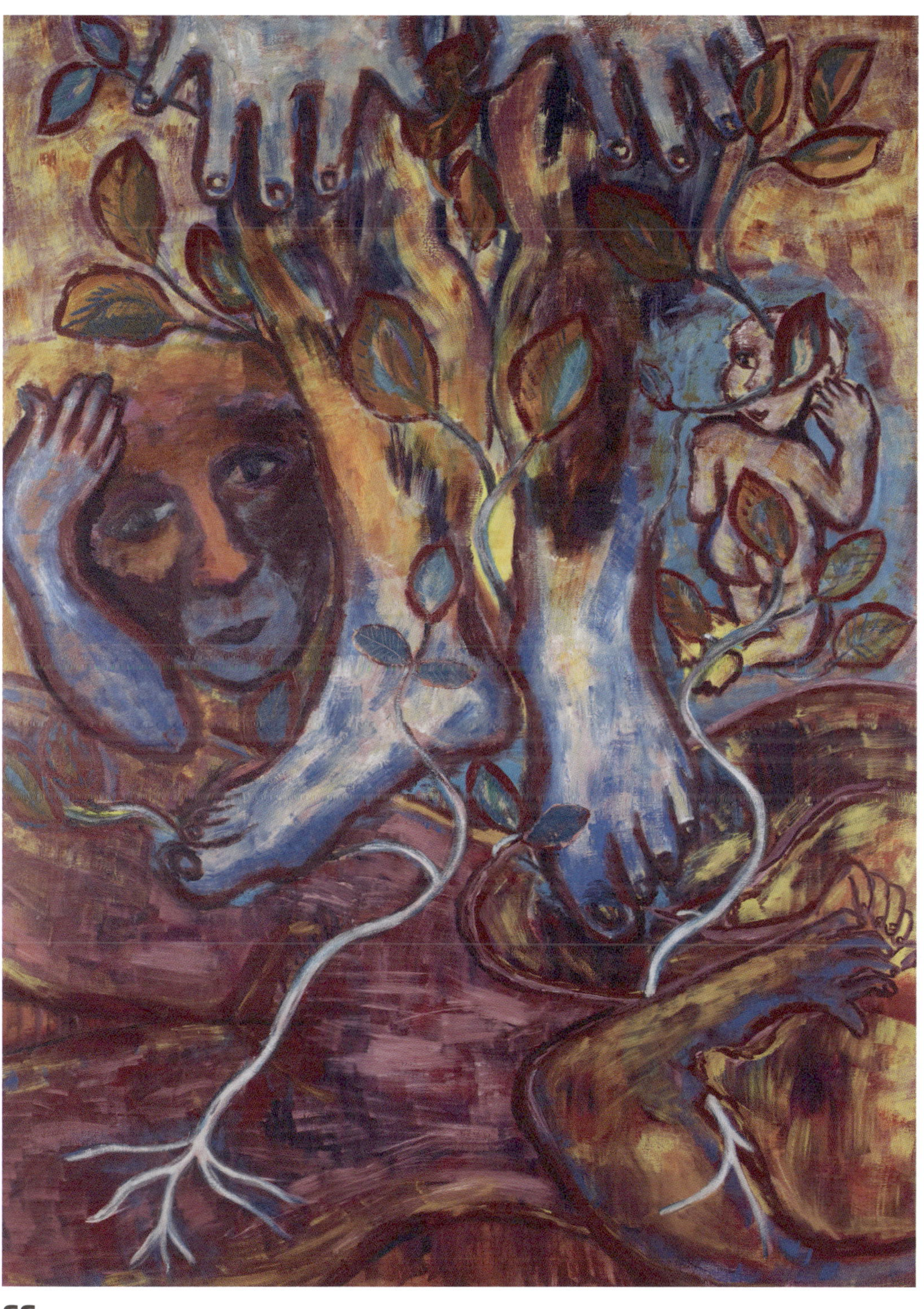

66.
Eileen Cooper,
*Putting Down
Roots*, 1985

'The title came after the image.' This was a painting that went beyond the fractured 'I' to suggest something more expansive: plural selves and the connections beyond them.

While writing her memoir *Self-Portrait* (2019), British painter Celia Paul read back over notebooks from the days after giving birth to her son Frank in December 1984. They reveal overpowering emotion – a desire to 'give up everything for him', to lose herself 'in this powerful tide of maternal love' but also a contrary instinct. 'I must save myself too', she writes.[22] Paul was then twenty-five, and her lover – Frank's father – sixty-two. As a single mother she risked losing all she had worked for as a young artist, so her mother offered to look after Frank at her home in Cambridge so that Paul could continue painting in London. There are no self-portraits of Paul with Frank as a young child – 'I felt I was too powerful,' she told me. 'I would be looming over him in a way that didn't seem fair.'[23] Instead she drew him alone or cuddling his grandmother until he became a teenager and refused to sit anymore. The two double portraits titled *Frank and Me* were painted during that period of softening that often occurs between a parent and child after their student years: the calm after the storm of necessary separation. The shape of the family was also shifting: 'Around the time his father was dying he said he would sit for me again. He had time to give and gave it willingly.' In the painting of 2011 **67**, Frank lies back on the maternal curves of a pillow and watches his mother's reflection in the mirror with a comfortable smile which she returns. In their mingled gaze, mediated by spectacle lenses and mirrored glass, Paul sees 'an intense connection, a profound intimacy' enjoyed during this particular episode of closeness between mother and adult son.

67.
Celia Paul, *Frank and Me*, 2011

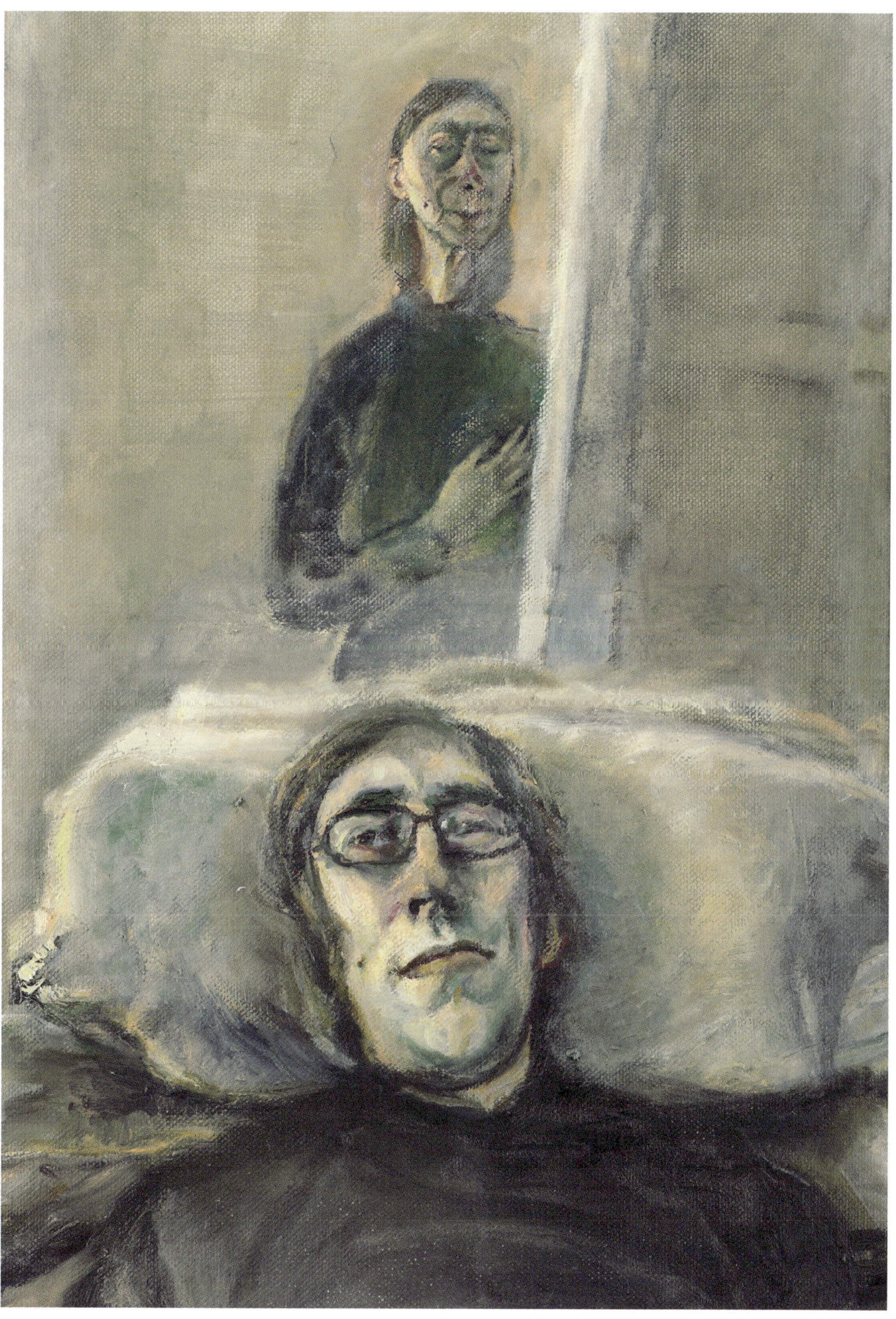

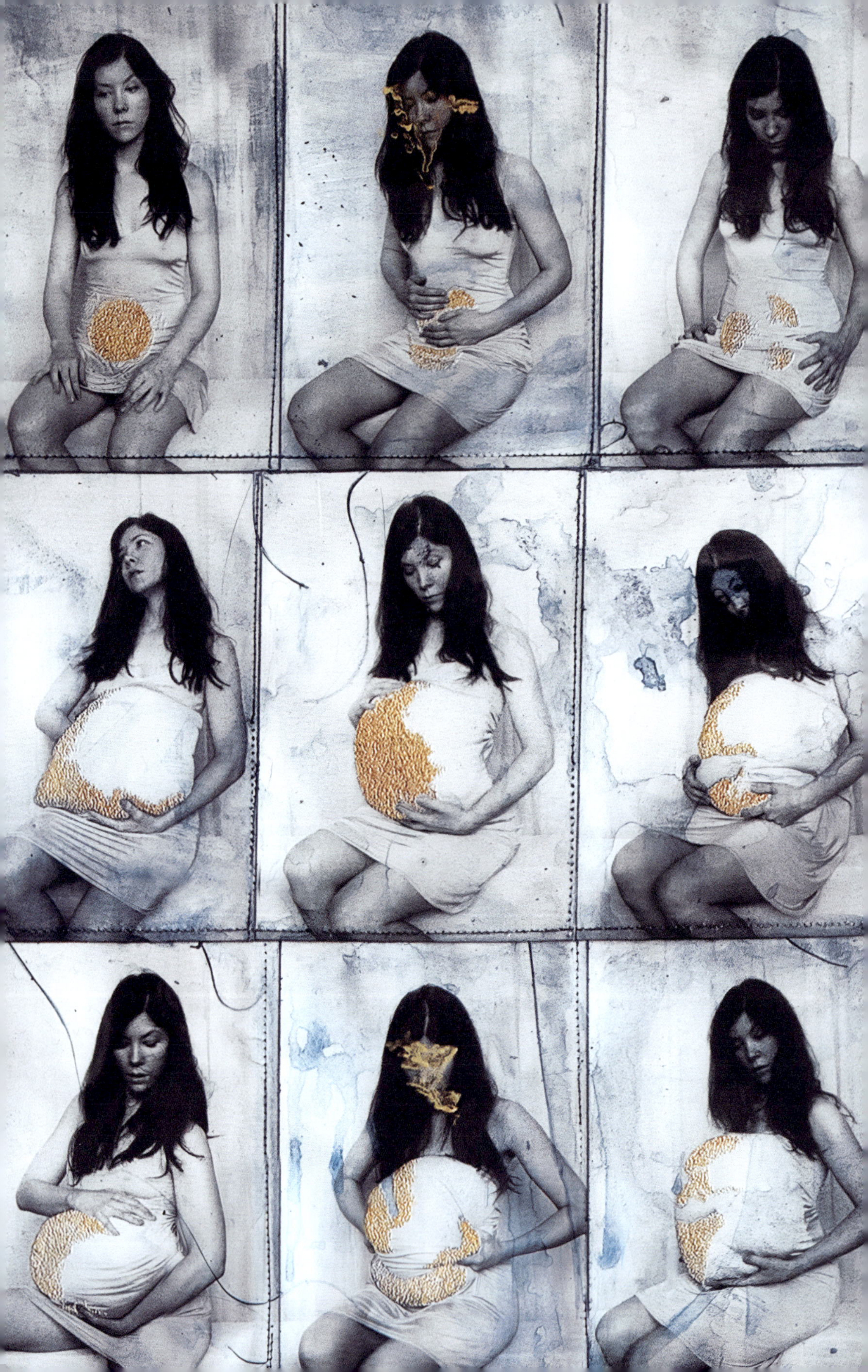

creation

It is commonplace to describe the creative act in terms of child-bearing: the seeding of an idea, its long gestation, and the tortuous labour of its realization. This analogy resonated in particular with sculptors in the early 20th century – the artist imagined drawing smooth flesh out of brute stone.[1] In *Matter* (1908), a lost sculpture by Jacob Epstein, the godlike creator is a muscled and moustachioed male sculptor holding aloft a baby partially emerged from its matrix – its mother rock. The irony here will not be lost on the artist mother, since it is this process – of conception, pregnancy and labour – that progressively drives her from the studio. After birth, full-body parenting forcefully precludes much other activity: it is the hot centre of things at which the creation of art must cede for a while to that of life. For much of art's history, this literal process of baby-making and nurture invalidated a woman's status as an artist. The creation of new life was glorified as analogy only.

conceptions and misconceptions

Christian art abounds in paintings of conception, though sadly seldom as racy as that description suggests. In the Annunciation, Mary is visited by the Angel Gabriel who bears tidings of a miraculous conception taking place within her. As early as the 4th century, the knotty issue of how Mary conceived while remaining a virgin was resolved by the idea that the Holy Spirit entered her body through that respectable orifice, the ear. In a heavily gilded 14th-century altarpiece by Sienese painters Simone Martini and Lippo Memmi the Holy Spirit appears above the Annunciation as a dove encircled by eight angels. The dove opens its beak sending golden rays toward Mary's head which meet Gabriel's words *Ave gratia plena dominvs tecvm* – Hail, full of grace, the Lord is with thee! – inscribed in the surface of the painting. The angel's proclamation and the Holy Spirit enter her ear as one, the miracle of conception coinciding with its pronounce-ment. On the floor between Gabriel and Mary is a deep-bellied vase carrying flowers, alerting us to the blossoming vessel of her womb. In both the Christian and Islamic traditions, Mary herself was the miraculous offspring of an older childless woman, Anne, as was John the Baptist (son of Elizabeth). The writers of these ancient texts understood fertility as a fraught arena.

•

In a sculpture by New York-based artist Lea Cetera, the pink sands of time pour between twinned blown-glass models of the uterus, ovaries and fallopian tubes. As the title of this hourglass reminds us – *You Can't Have it All* (2022) **68**. Parenthood hangs in the balance between two timescales. The first is counted in hours – how competing demands of work and self-fulfilment might be balanced against demands of care. The second time-scale counts the years of fertility – the dreaded 'biological clock' which must be held in consideration against economic variables, romantic status and career progression.

68.
Lea Cetera,
*You Can't Have
It All*, 2022

69.
Wangechi Mutu,
Fertility Heal IX,
2018

Cetera explores the relationship between body and machine under capitalism. This manifests both in metaphor (the biological clock, the fertility window) and in an emerging area of commer-cial medicine that promotes the idea that fertility can be 'hacked'. A growing number of women this century have pre-emptively frozen their eggs, having been encouraged to do so before the age of thirty-five.[2] 'Banking' viable eggs offers security to those concerned about their fertility declining, theoretically extend-ing the age they might start a family. Concerns have been raised about the irresponsible marketing of this expensive and invasive procedure. Targeted ads promote egg freezing as a lifestyle choice, as though it were a juice cleanse or spin class.[3] Stoked by scare stories and direct marketing from fertility clinics, people in their early thirties now report anxiety about fertility long before they consider starting a family.[4]

Lumpy and human scale, Wangechi Mutu's *Fertility Heal* works (2018–19) **69** look non-specifically obstetric: between a uterus and a pelvis, hard and earthen. Each is constructed around a pair of high-heeled shoes – a power motif in Mutu's work – caked with a paste of red Kenyan mud. All are encrusted with potent materials: quartz shards, seashells, *Rhus Natalensis* wood and

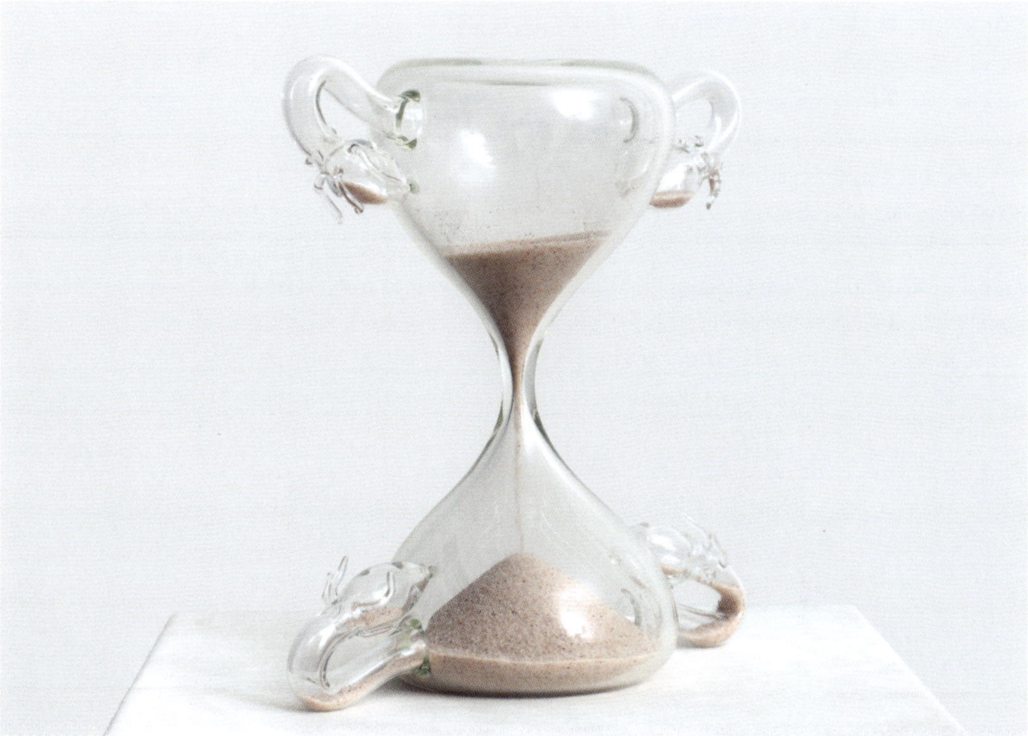

68

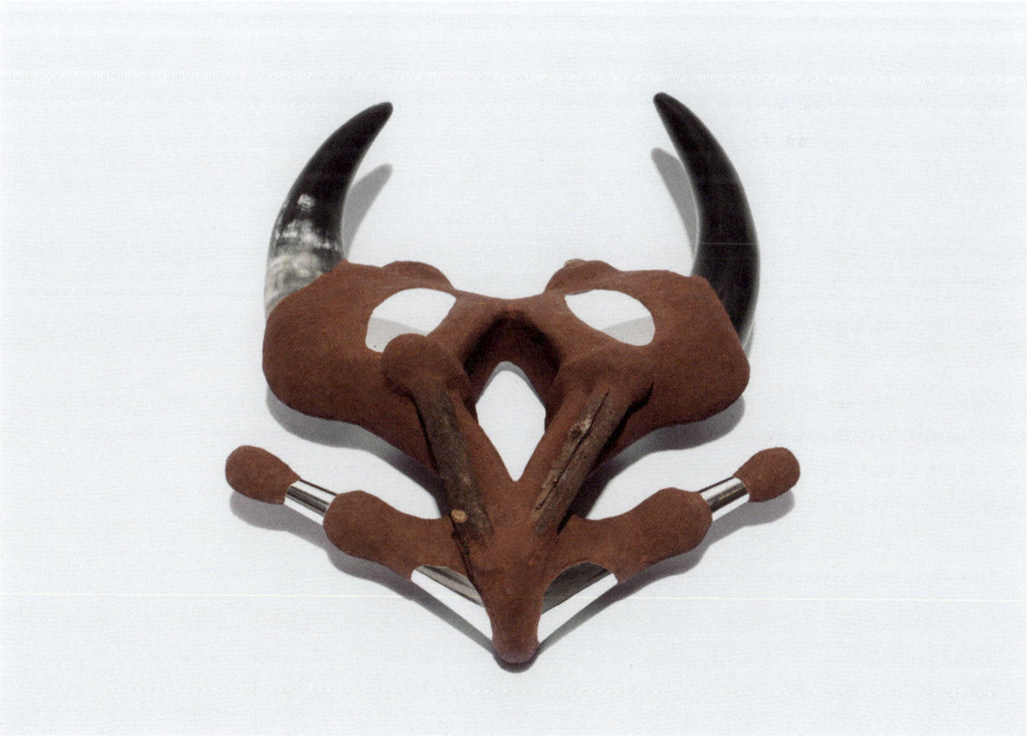

69

cow horns. This is the stuff of magic: equipment for incantations, protective spells or summoning into being. In many creation myths the first humans were modelled from clay. With their blend of performative feminine sexuality, wellness-era mysticism and the primal material of the human story, the *Fertility Heal* works have a talismanic quality.

Those struggling to conceive can turn to an expanding menu of alternative practices. Of course, we'll try anything when we're desperate, but the search for alternatives is also driven by experience of diagnostic bias in the healthcare system. Women and non-binary people are more often misdiagnosed than men, in part because for many decades the 'standard' body used for diagnosis and drug testing has been male. Women of colour are particularly susceptible to misdiagnosis – a systemic failure that contributes to disproportionately high maternal mortality rates among Black women in the UK and US.[5]

•

Lindsey Mendick's characteristically brave and confessional work *Hairy on the Inside* (2021) **70** uses the trope of the werewolf to explore the artist's experience of polycystic ovarian syndrome (PCOS). Originally installed at the London gallery Cooke Latham, the extravagant mise-en-scène included a waiting room lined with anxious wolves in hospital gowns, their sculpted ceramic extremities stuck with acupuncture needles, and hairy claws protruding from Crocs clogs. In a video shot by her partner Guy Oliver, Mendick recites a checklist of symptoms – PCOS is a leading cause of infertility, characterized by elevated male hormones that typically cause excess hair growth, acne and weight gain. She concludes, grimly, that 'in the eyes of society, I'm officially unfuckable, aren't I?' Mendick shares memories over footage of werewolf transformations lifted from 1980s horror movies. Friends commiserate about her lost fertility. It seems the done thing. But actually, what bothers her is the facial hair – something that in this era of body positivity she feels pressure to accept but doesn't wish to. 'The truth is, I don't want a baby,' she admits. But she's not sure which came first: the diagnosis or the decision.

Those whose fertility is a journey rather than a given acquire a new vocabulary – sonography, ovulation induction, intrauterine insemination, egg harvesting, IVF. This emotionally charged and physically demanding process may last for years, but for the woman who ends up childless not by choice, only a few intimates

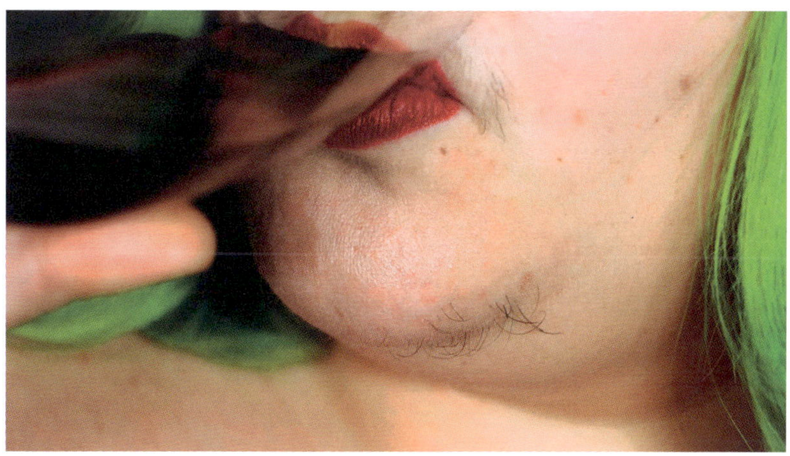

70

may ever know. Unlike the pregnant woman who carries a baby to term, she has nothing to show at the end of it.

In Jessa Fairbrother's *Role Play (Woman with Cushion)* (2017) **71**, the artist performs cycles of attempted conception as though she were the waxing and waning moon, with a cushion standing in for a swelling and shrinking belly. Rivulets of gold like the vibrations of the Holy Spirit in the Annunciation enter and shift around her body suggesting the child she imagines forming within her, only to leach out again, leaving her preparing to start the process again. It is a work that makes visible some of the gruelling process the British artist went through before accepting, eventually, that she would not become a mother. The fifty-six panels of *Role Play* are stitched into a quilt – historically a piece of handiwork passed down by the mother. Fairbrother is the last in her maternal line – there is no daughter to pass this quilt on to.

great with child

It seems apt that the touring *Acts of Creation* exhibition began at Bristol's Arnolfini. Founded in the 1960s by artists Jeremy and Annabel Rees, this British gallery was named after a work by Jan van Eyck known as *The Arnolfini Portrait* (1434) which hangs in the National Gallery in London. With her belly swelling beneath a magnificent swagged green robe and her delicate hand resting on its bump, to the modern eye Giovanni Arnolfini's wife appears to be pregnant. When the painting was purchased for the nation in 1843, the Victorian public read a scandalous suggestion of premarital sex (a woman on her wedding day, already big with child!)[6] Yet in the Ghent altarpiece, created by Jan van Eyck and

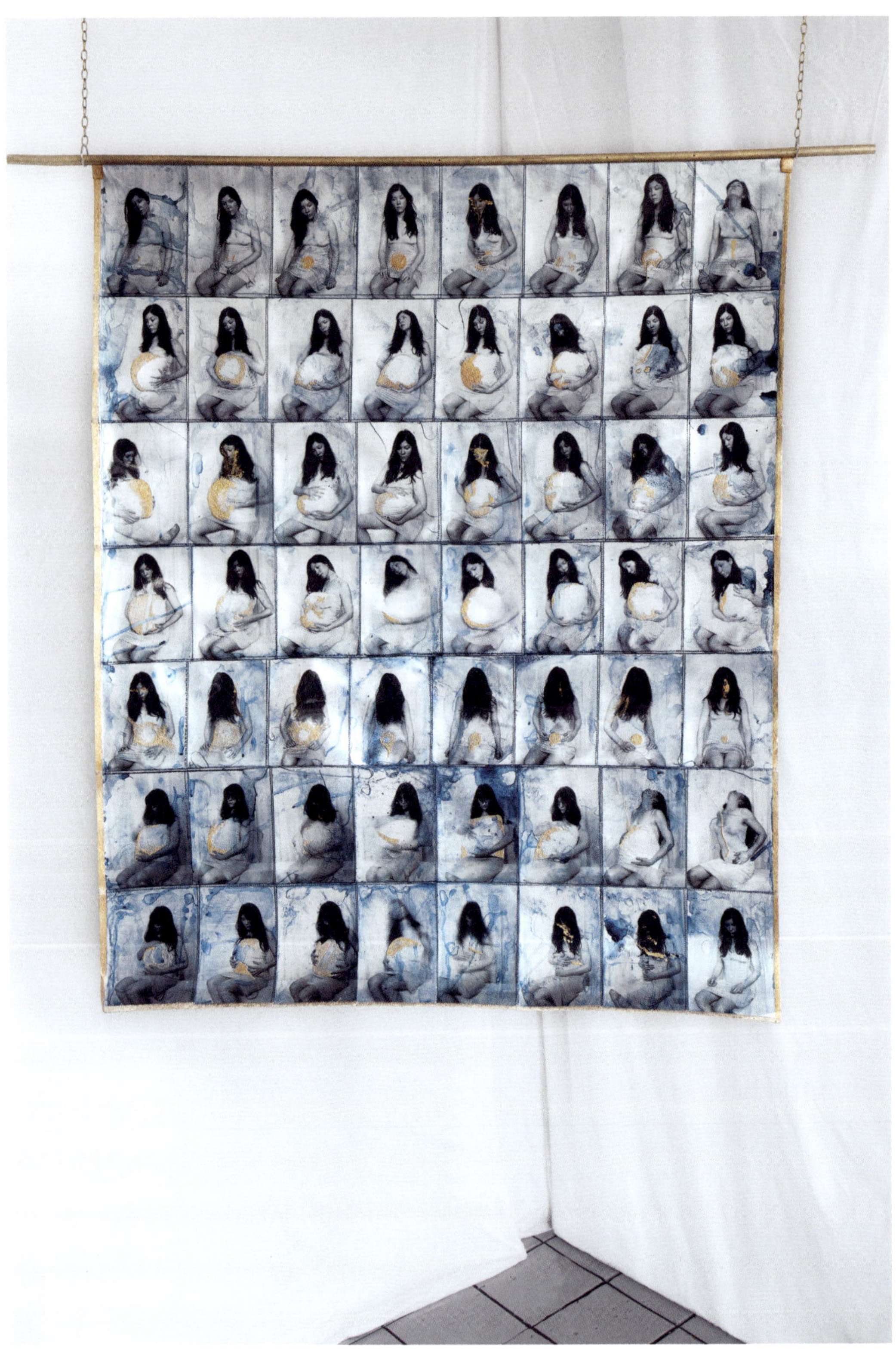

**71

his brother Hubert, the naked belly of Eve is likewise domed, as is that of the Virgin Mary at the Annunciation. Jan van Eyck was a pioneer in the naturalistic rendering of the human body and painted women with narrow chests and big tummies. He lived in an era when women expected to bear eight children or more and spent much of their adult lives either pregnant or nursing. We might well ask what impact that had on Van Eyck's understanding of what a 'normal' shape was for a woman's body. For long periods of European history, depictions of actual pregnancy were the subject of superstition. In 17th-century Holland and 18th-century Britain, the condition was considered indecorous.[7] While a woman's status might be indicated by a hand gesture, or the symbolic placement of plants, it was unusual to appear 'big bellied' in a formal portrait. Art historian Karen Hearn identifies one period that was an exception: the reign of Queen Elizabeth I. Examining a handful of magnificent Tudor pregnancy portraits in which noblewomen drip with pearls and gold embroidery, Hearn speculates that they broadcast dynastic succession during a period of public anxiety about Elizabeth's lack of heir. Ironically, the 'Virgin Queen' inspired a brief vogue in visible pregnancy.

If the pregnant body was taboo, the naked pregnant body was infinitely more so. By convention the female nude in art represents not only an ideal but an invitation: to look, to fantasize, to possess. As Alice Neel pithily put it: 'A pregnant woman has a claim staked out; she's not for sale.'[8] By the 1930s Alice Neel was living an unconventional life in New York's Spanish Harlem (see also pages 201–3), where she would later bear two sons to different fathers (neither of whom she married) and paint at night while her children slept. 'Women were always the sacrificers,' she explained, of her hard-won balance between art and motherhood. 'I used to feel guilty about being an artist, because I used to think the way the normal world thinks: there's a certain function for women, that they have to do the ordinary things. I couldn't, so I was the world's best conniver.'[9]

Neel's female nudes of this decade show women as individuals revealed, whether self-conscious, languorous or assured. Some thirty years later, with her children grown up, Neel's creative and professional blossoming produced a radical series of nude pregnancy portraits, in which the subjects' varied responses to their condition – aching, anxious, delighted, transformed – are manifest. In one of the earliest, *Pregnant Maria* (1964) **72**, a heavily pregnant woman is arranged on rumpled bedsheets. She looks luscious and comfortable, and gazes towards Neel with shadows of exhaustion beneath her eyes. Neel's pregnancy portraits are remarkable both as feminist rewritings of the nude, and for the contribution they make to representing the range of women's experience in visual culture. These are not just studies of 'the pregnant body' as form – they engage with individual experiences.

Pondering pregnancy, I would like to dip into three bodies of work from the late 1970s. All were controversial in their specific context. Discussion and representation of pregnancy was still rare – the body itself considered almost obscene. The Women's Movement had encouraged exploration of the female body and its sexuality, but the pregnant experience was, in certain quarters, considered too domestic and, by implication, too heteronormative as a subject: as yet it had been little explored or expressed by women in their own terms.

A dancer since childhood, Senga Nengudi was sensitive to the physicality of pregnancy – the expansion and contraction, the shifting weight.[10] Searching for a material that would express that experience sculpturally, she turned to used tights, which she stretched and pinned and filled with sand to echo the yielding weight of flesh. During the 1960s, Nengudi lived in LA, and interned at the Watts Towers Art Center while at college in

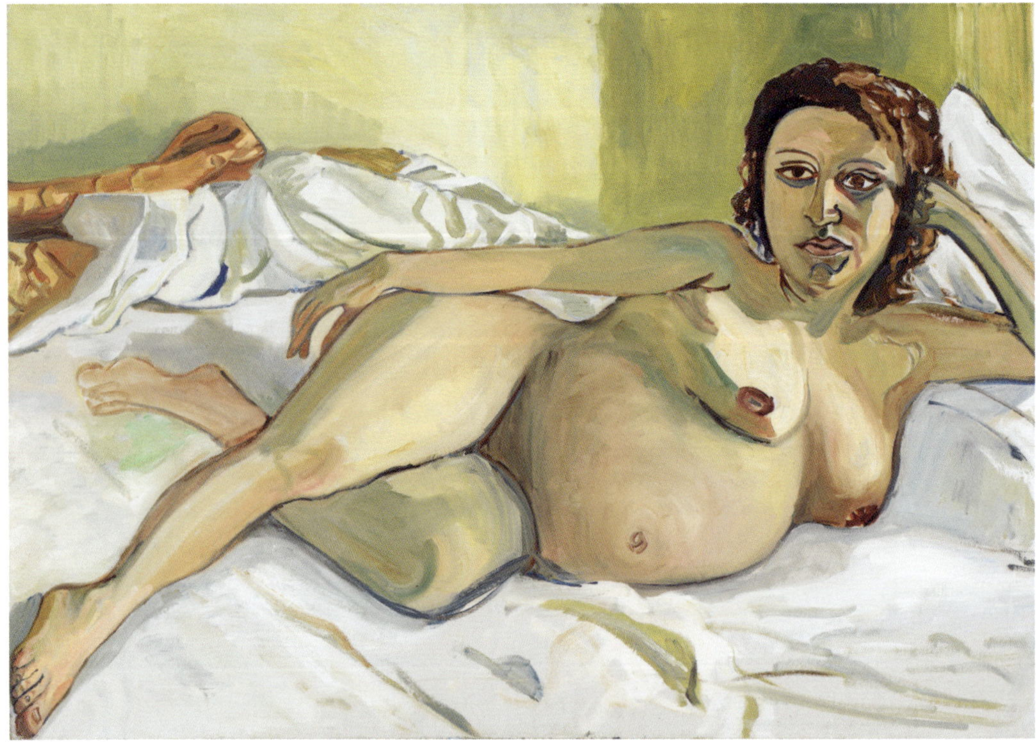

1965. Working with everyday objects chimed with her interest in the Japanese Gutai art group, studied during a student residency in Tokyo in 1967. Her commitment to found objects also reflected a shift in mood that followed the Watts Riots of 1965. It was a politicization that 'changed the way Black artists dealt with materials and subject matters...from very classical drawings...to really reflecting on the culture and trying new materials.'

The first version of Nengudi's *R.S.V.P.* was an installation of ten stretched and knotted pairs of tights, their gussets filled with sand, at the Just Above Midtown gallery in New York in 1977 **73**. Described by the artist as 'abstracted reflections of used bodies', the series that followed went through dozens of variations.[11] The installations were often animated by performances by Nengudi and fellow artist Maren Hassinger. Just as Nengudi's own body might be seen as an artefact displaying the impact of pregnancy, so *R.S.V.P.* took its exhibited form from the movement of human bodies within the material.[12] At the time, *R.S.V.P.* was an awkward fit within Black arts scenes more focused on sociologically rooted and figurative work.[13] In 2013 an interviewer asked Nengudi whether she considered herself a political artist: 'I was stating – and I guess still state, really – what it feels like to be

72.
Alice Neel,
Pregnant Maria,
1964

73.
Senga Nengudi,
R.S.V.P, 1977/2003

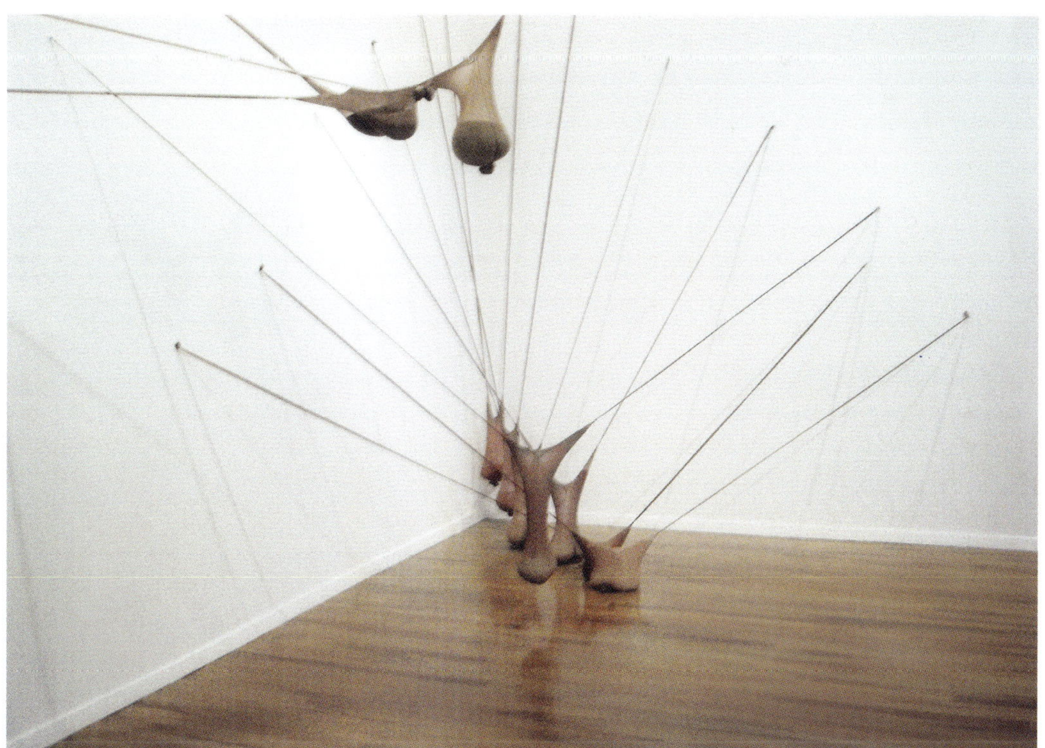

an artist who is Black, who is American, who is a mother, who is a daughter, who is a wife….In my classes I would often say, "Being born Black is a revolutionary act in this country."'[14] The soft sculptures came as part of the artist's personal rebirth – created in the same era she exchanged the birth name Sue Ellen Irons for a chosen name. *R.S.V.P.* suggests the female body weighed down and overstretched, but also elastic, sensual and miraculous.

Annegret Soltau's embroidered photocollages instead express the sense of being trapped in one's own body, of losing control. Made in 1978 while she was pregnant with her second child, the German artist's expanding form becomes increasingly prominent as the series evolves. *Schwanger* (*Pregnant*) shows Soltau's body pierced with needle marks, cut up and held together with black stitches – her flesh made strange. In *Ausgeliefert* (*Vulnerable*) **74** she is tethered to the table, bound like a fly caught in a spider's web. In *Auf dem Geburtstisch I* (*On the Birth Table I*) the viewer looks along Soltau's legs toward her vast domed belly, splintered with tears that radiate from her pubis – the moment of birth imagined as a violent explosion. Black thread connects craft practice and surgery. During performances in the mid-1970s, Soltau wrapped her face in tight threads, to the point where she could no longer see or speak, before releasing herself with a pair of scissors.

These stitched and torn works were Soltau's riposte to the wholesome vision of maternity promoted in adverts and the women's press. Exhibiting at a radical feminist gallery in Berlin[15] she fell foul of both progressive and conservative elements within the city's art scene. Her nakedness as a pregnant woman was considered offensive: 'For men it was not a suitable subject of art-making,' she recalls. 'And for women my art was problematic because they were divided and rejected motherhood in order not to fall back into old gender roles.'[16]

As in Berlin, so London. Describing the critical reception of her photographic installation *Ten Months* (1979) **75** Susan Hiller noted that 'The piece was deeply disturbing…to other people who find it hard to accept the right of a woman to be both the artist and the sexed subject of a work.'[17] Stretching along one long wall are ten neat grids, each accompanied by a fragment of text. Each grid carries twenty-eight grainy black-and-white photographs of Hiller's growing bump. The number reflects the days in a lunar month – and indeed Hiller's belly looks increasingly like the moon.

74.
Annegret Soltau,
Ausgeliefert
(*Vulnerable*), 1978

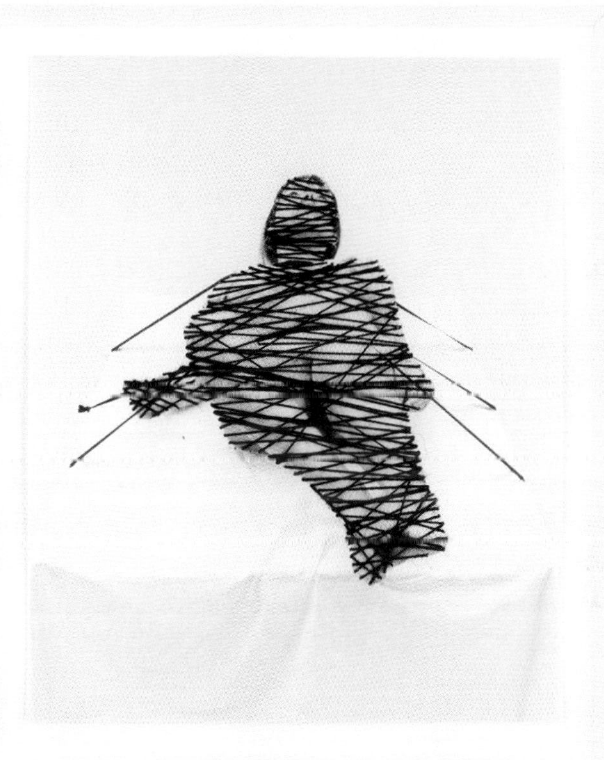

During her pregnancy three years earlier, Hiller photo-graphed her changing body and kept a journal to record 'the internal and external changes of that period.'[18] The average pregnancy lasts 280 days – ten lunar months – which provided an organizing principle for the work. Hiller cropped each photo-graph to show only 'the section of the body you couldn't talk about, the pregnant part.'[19] Just as she'd 'excerpted' the body, she took excerpts from her journals, which are typed and presented below and above the grids. These fragments are polar to the whimsical and infantilized portrayal of pregnant women in popular culture, in which they are treated as though intellectually diminished. Hiller instead offers meditations on language, gender, power, the body and the creative act, reflecting an intense process of reading and theorizing during pregnancy. The text for month six reads: 'She speaks (as a woman) about everything although they wish her to speak only about women's things. They like her to speak about everything only if she does not speak "as a woman", only if she will agree in advance to play the artist's role as neutral (neuter) observer. She does not speak (as a woman) about any-thing, although they want her to. There is nothing she can speak of "as a woman". As a woman, she can not speak.'

labours

Within Louise Bourgeois's enormous body of work, informed by many years in psychoanalysis, the trope of mother/child attach-ment recurs obsessively, examined from both perspectives. The pink cloth sculpture *DO NOT ABANDON ME* (1999) **76** shows a mother umbilically attached to a newborn, the cord stretching navel to navel. It presents a moment of becoming – the birth of the mother concurrent with the birth of the child. Bourgeois's soft sculptures are pieced from old clothes, upholstery fabrics, table linens, blankets and other domestic textiles. Made when the artist was eighty-eight, this is a mother and child pulled from deep memory, constructed in materials that accompanied her passage through life. Bourgeois reflects on the complexity of birth as an experience – the body rupturing, breaking its borders, splitting into two individuals. It is a trauma which inscribes itself on both body and mind. As the baby emerges from the birth canal like a spaceman floating from the mother ship we hear the words of the title *DO NOT ABANDON ME* as spoken by the parent rather than the child – she is the figure left behind. By the time the infant has language enough to understand and

75.
Susan Hiller,
Ten Months,
1977. Following
spread: Susan Hiller
in front of *Ten
Months* at the
Hayward Gallery,
London, 1980

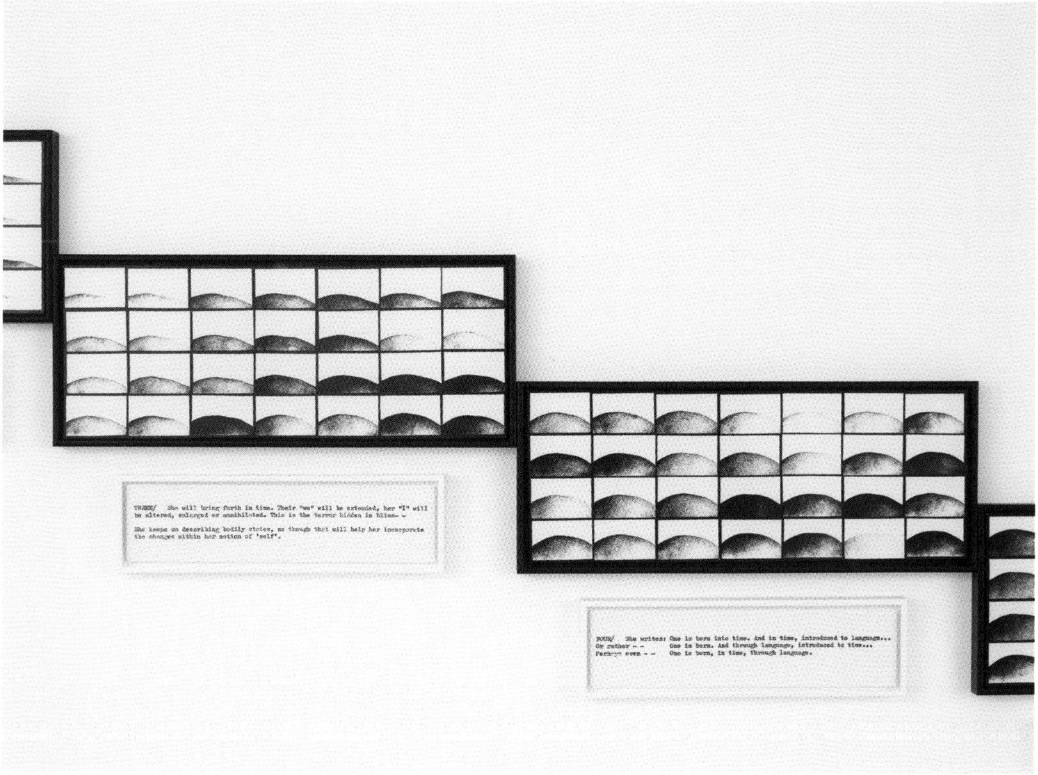

THREE/   She will bring forth in time. Their "we" will be extended, her "I" will
be altered, enlarged or annihilated. This is the terror hidden in bliss--

She keeps on describing bodily states, as though that will help her incorporate
the changes within her notion of 'self'.

FOUR/   She writes: One is born into time. And in time, introduced to language...
Or rather --   One is born. And through language, introduced to time...
Perhaps even --   One is born, in time, through language.

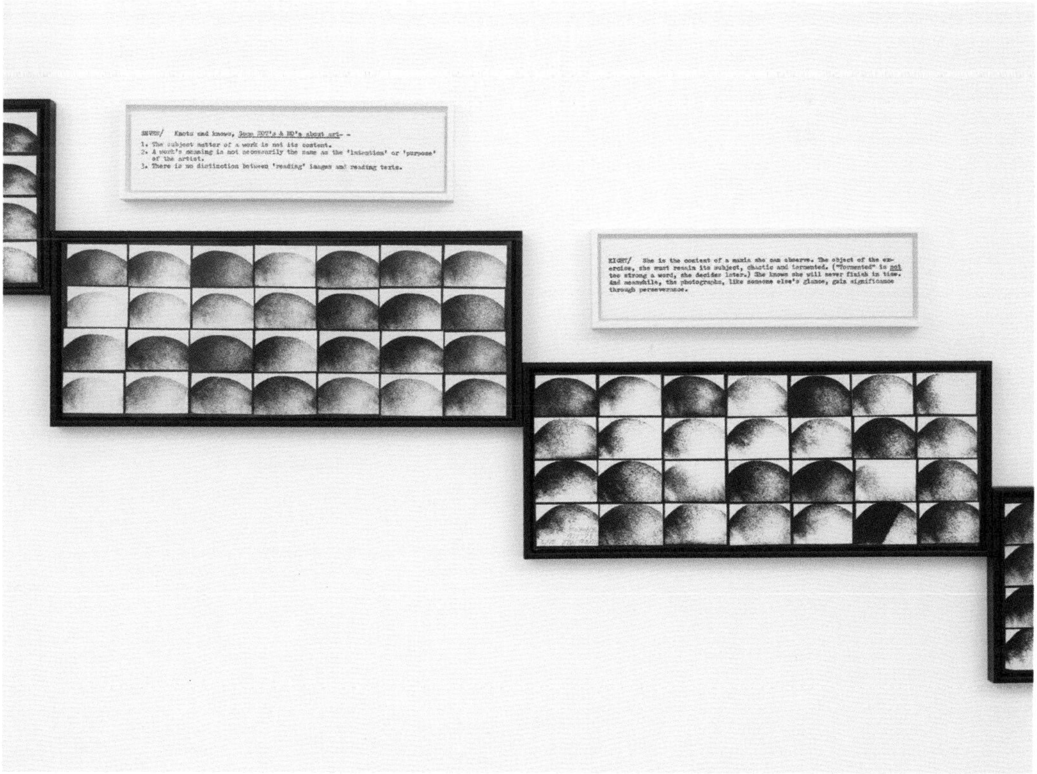

SEVEN/   Knots and knows, Some DOT's & DO's about art- -
1. The subject matter of a work is not its content.
2. A work's meaning is not necessarily the same as the 'intention' or 'purpose'
   of the artist.
3. There is no distinction between 'reading' images and reading texts.

EIGHT/   She is the content of a mania she can observe. The object of the exercise, she must remain its subject, chaotic and tormented. ("Tormented" is not
too strong a word, she decides later.) She knows she will never finish in time.
And meanwhile, the photographs, like someone else's glance, gain significance
through perseverance.

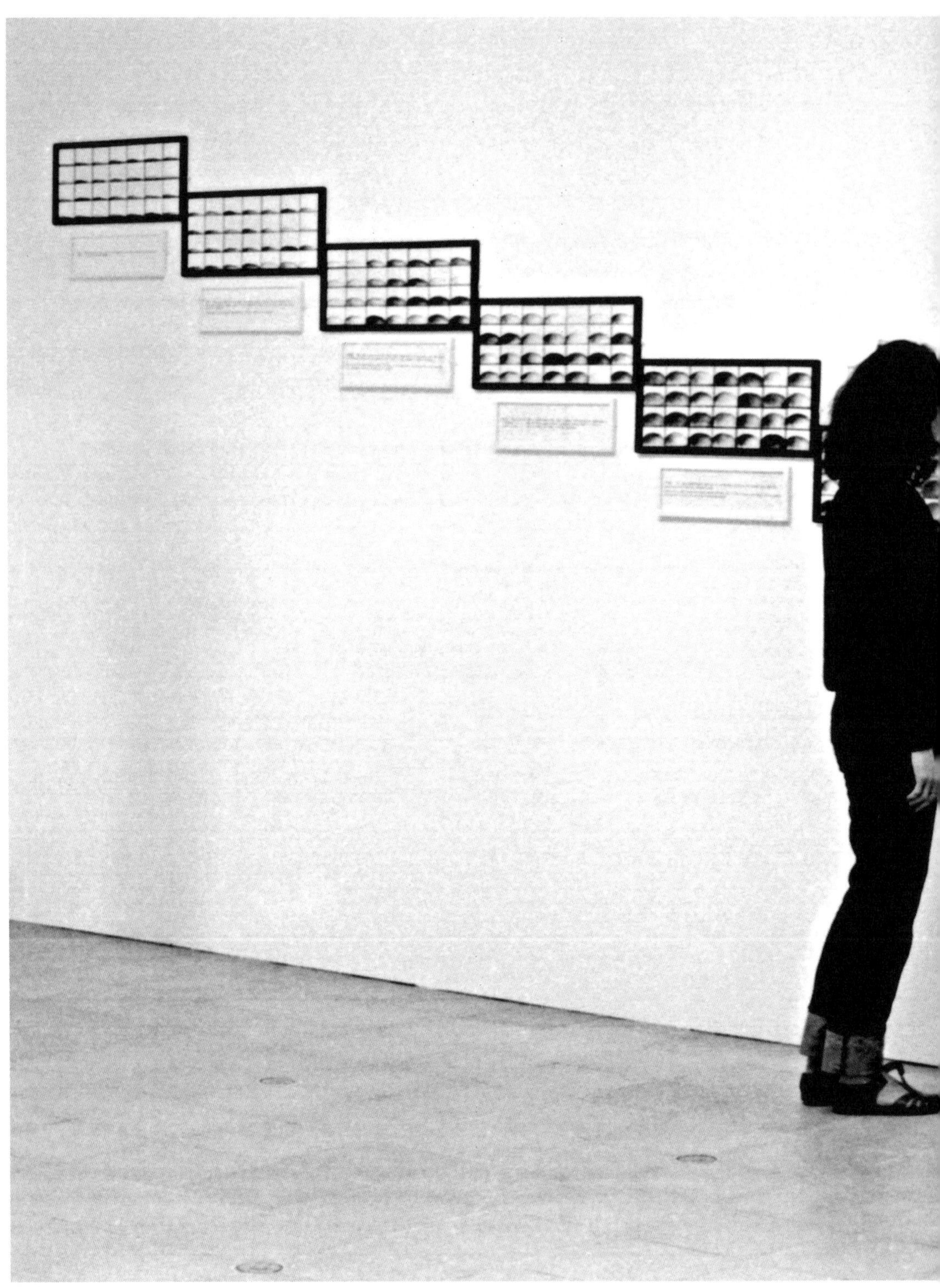

75

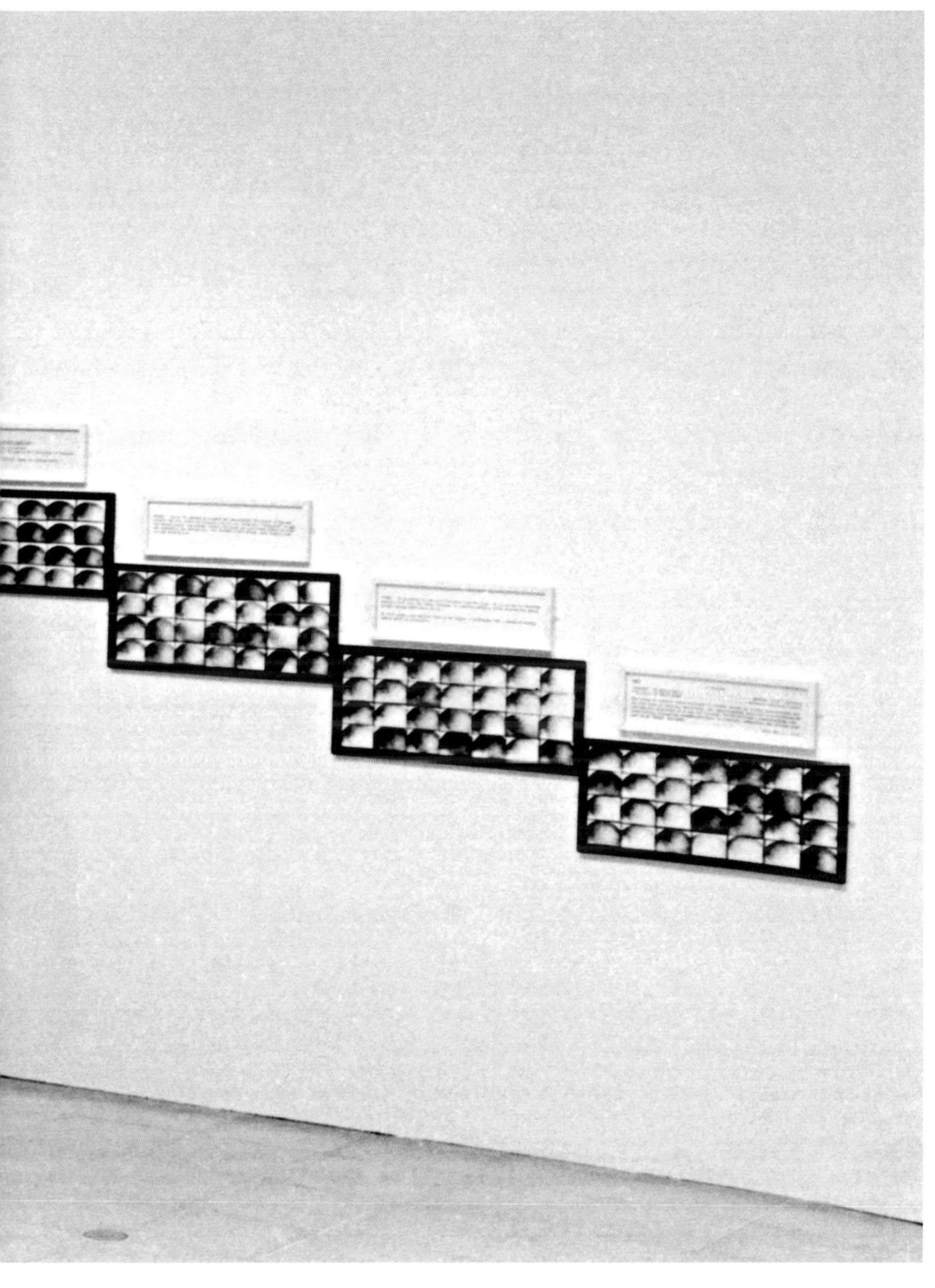

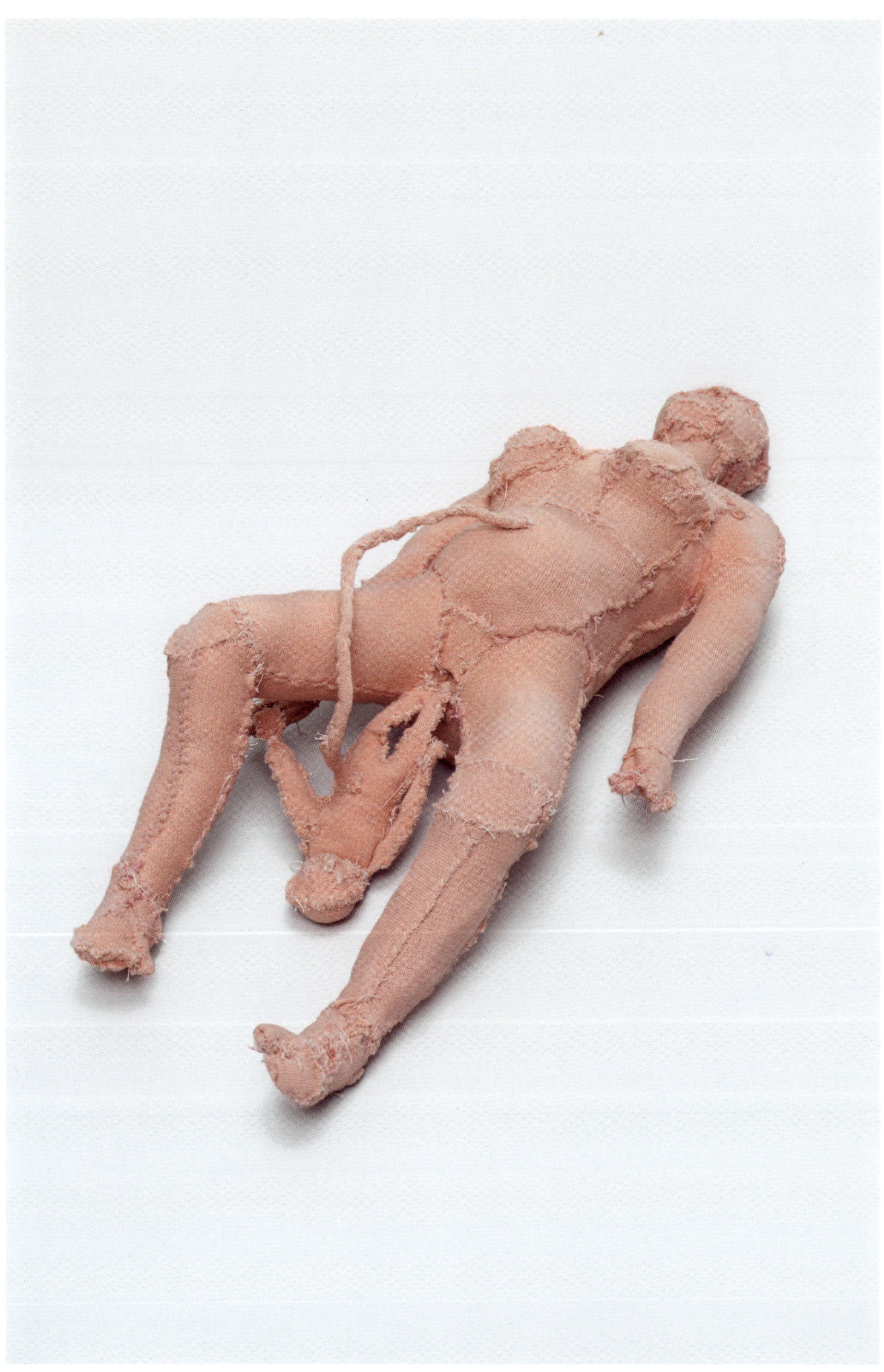

answer, the distance between them as two individuals will be definitive.

Pregnant, it is hard to see beyond the moment of birth and imagine the new parenthood beyond. Visions of coming pain and hormonal tumult consume the imagination. The rational mind wrestles with the prospect of submitting to the body. Cinematic convention portrays birth according to the drama inherent in the form – the waters that break at an inopportune moment, the frantic race to the hospital, a delivery that is all screaming climax. The vision we are fed is of control lost, of a woman made monstrous by labour. In real life, control is more often ceded – passed from the individual to the medical team. Decisions about induction, epidural and surgical intervention are couched in the language of consent but experienced less as a series of open choices than life or death decisions made while in a state of sweating agony. The birth plan I was invited to make while pregnant amounted to little more than fantasy fiction. I suspect I am not alone. Giving women knowledge and agency in childbirth is a long-running project within the feminist model for women's healthcare. There arc many (often competing) schools of practice, but the guiding principles are to inform expectant parents of what happens within the mother body during childbirth, and to teach strategies by which they can experience some degree of control. Positive and transformative as these movements are overall, the term 'natural' is often deployed in ways that lead those whose birth did not go as expected (and they are many) to feel they have in some way failed. It should not be necessary to state, and yet somehow I very often do, that childbirth is not a competition.

Hermione Wiltshire, who performed the role of sage in the last chapter, has worked to challenge conventional representations of birth – shifting away from the medical gaze, foregrounding women's histories and knowledge, and defying the tendency to portray the female body in terms of abjection. In the series *Preparing For Birth* (2008) **77** – commissioned by the Birth Rites Collection – we encounter enormously pregnant women whose bodies appear to protrude from the wall, floating as though weightless. The women are fully engaged in preparatory birthing exercises involving visualization and breath work led by doula and yoga teacher Kathleen Beegan. *Nicola Preparing for Birth* holds out her hands in a diamond, picturing her baby's passage through the birth canal. She opens her mouth to gulp in breath, her full body filling further. Wiltshire compares this scene to her experience of National Childbirth Trust (NCT) antenatal classes,

76.
Louise Bourgeois,
*DO NOT ABANDON
ME*, 1999

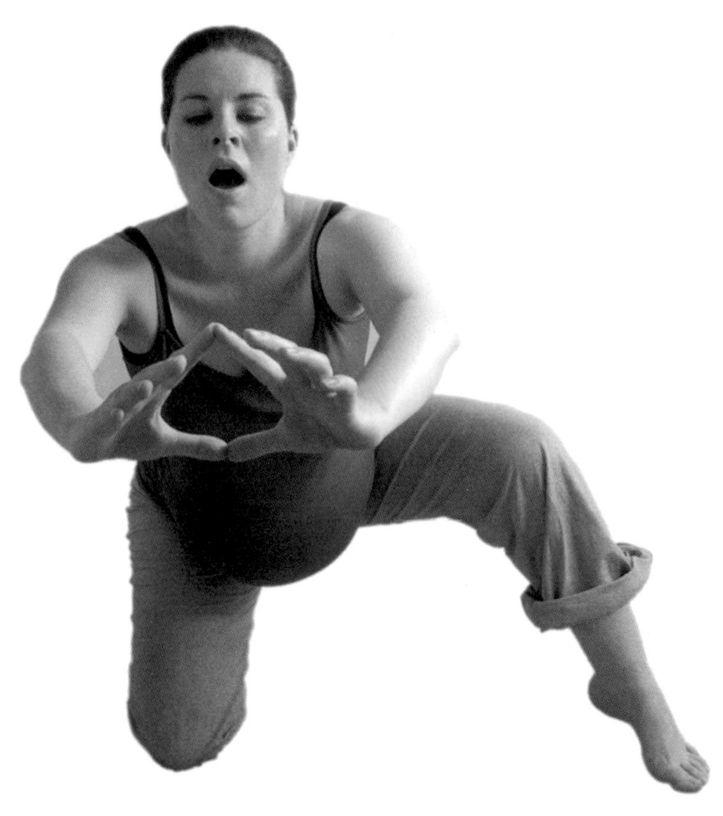

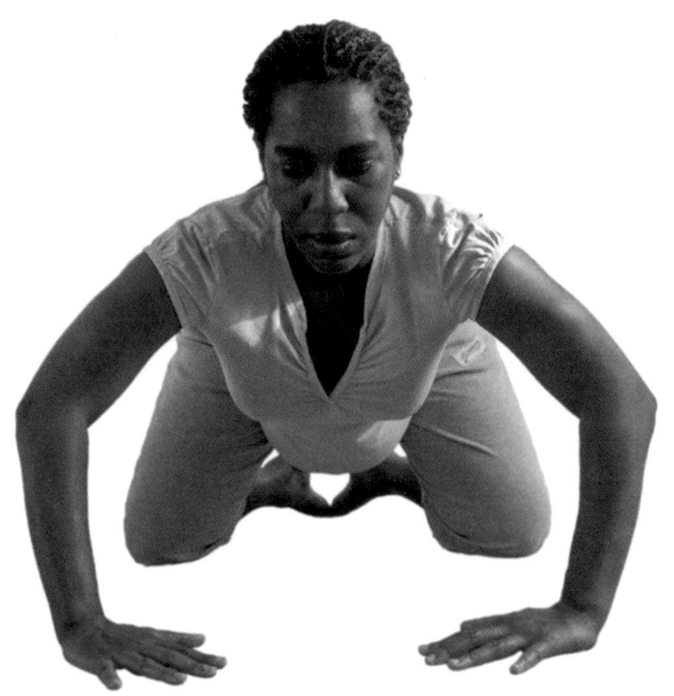

77

which she felt evaded references to the vagina and to the moment of crowning. Acutely focused on the interior of the body, these women are trying to think their way into the unimaginable space of birth, performing their preparatory drills as though readying for battle.[20]

•

When the Canadian-born poet and artist Heather Spears died in 2021, she left behind an extraordinary and under-explored body of work. I had seen a few digitized examples of Spears's drawings of women in labour but was quite unprepared for the work itself, her capacity for empathy and sense of mission. The Spears box in London's Wellcome Collection archive contains several thick folders, each bearing a woman's name, location and date. Each folder holds dozens, if not hundreds of individual drawings **78**. As I turned the pages of the first folder it became apparent that I was witnessing the entire process of one woman's labour: the onset of contractions, the periods of respite, time spent standing up and walking, shifting positions on the bed or floor, her interactions with partners and children. Sometimes the process lasted days – Spears kept drawing throughout, dashing off sketches by the dozen. She documented the cervix being measured, the administration of epidurals, the baby crowning, or an emergency C-section. In some folders the final few pages carried blood stains – Spears had been right there, in the action. Every sequence ended with a photocopied drawing of a newborn. Perhaps she passed the original to the parents? The drawings themselves express the speed things progressed at different stages of labour – some are detailed and leisurely, others just a few expressive marks. There is no sense of mounting urgency until the end – instead there are islands of activity, and great periods of waiting. I cannot imagine a most honest and evocative account of a woman's labour.

Spears lived most of her adult life in Denmark, and her route into the labour ward started with a desire to understand the anatomy of babies. For over three decades she drew in various Neonatal Intensive Care Units (NICU) around the world. At the Rigshospitalet in Copenhagen, she was given access between the hours of 11 p.m. and 3 a.m., drawing standing up and racing to capture the particular motion of premature babies' limbs: 'so loose and graceful,' as she described them, 'different from any human movement that had been around to be observed and drawn before.'[21] Spears had discovered her ideal subject at a perfect moment in

77.
Hermione Wiltshire,
Preparing for Birth,
2008

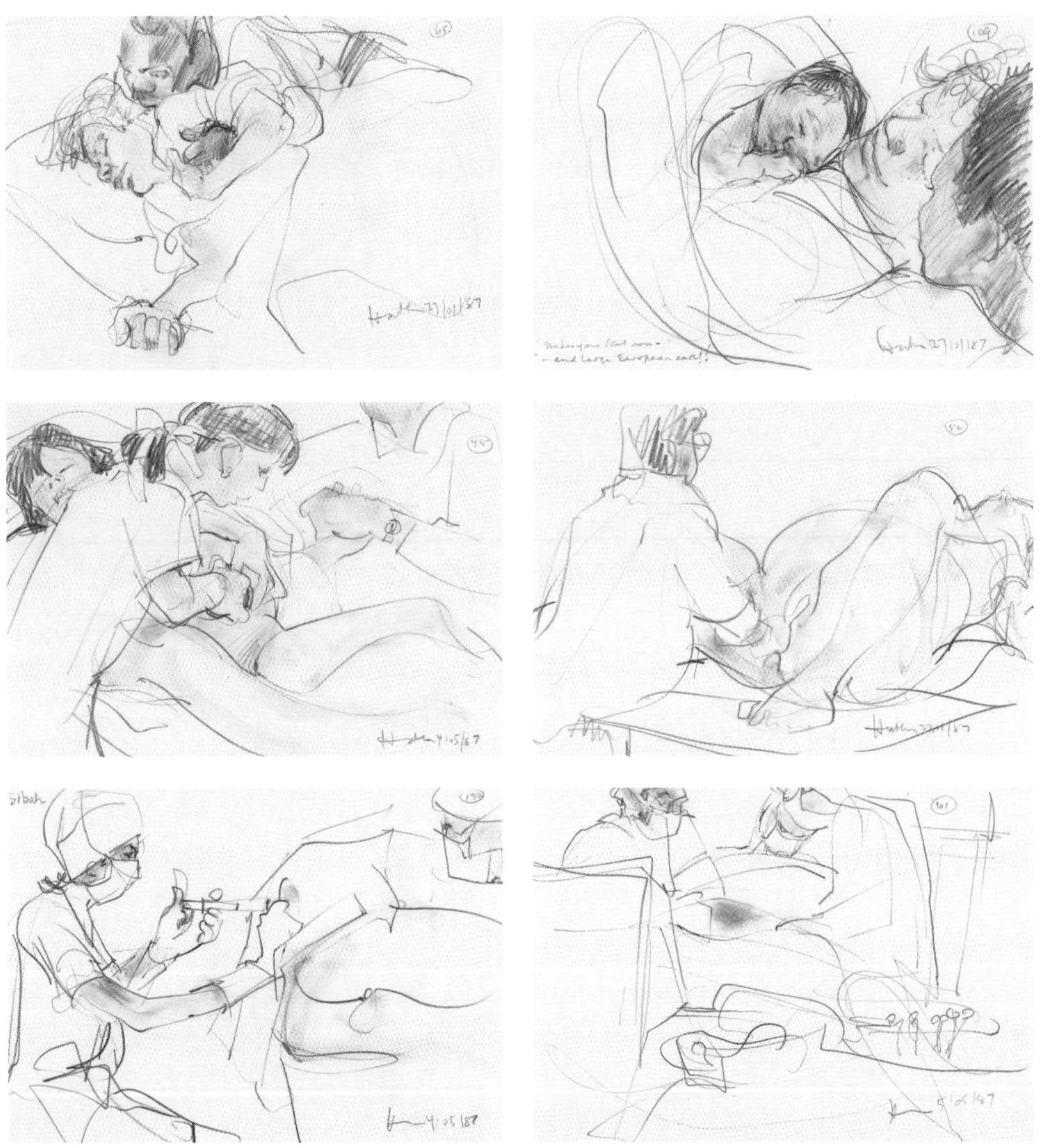

78

78.
Heather Spears,
*Studies/Drawings of
Labour/Childbirth,
Rigshospitalet 26–27
January 1987*, 1987

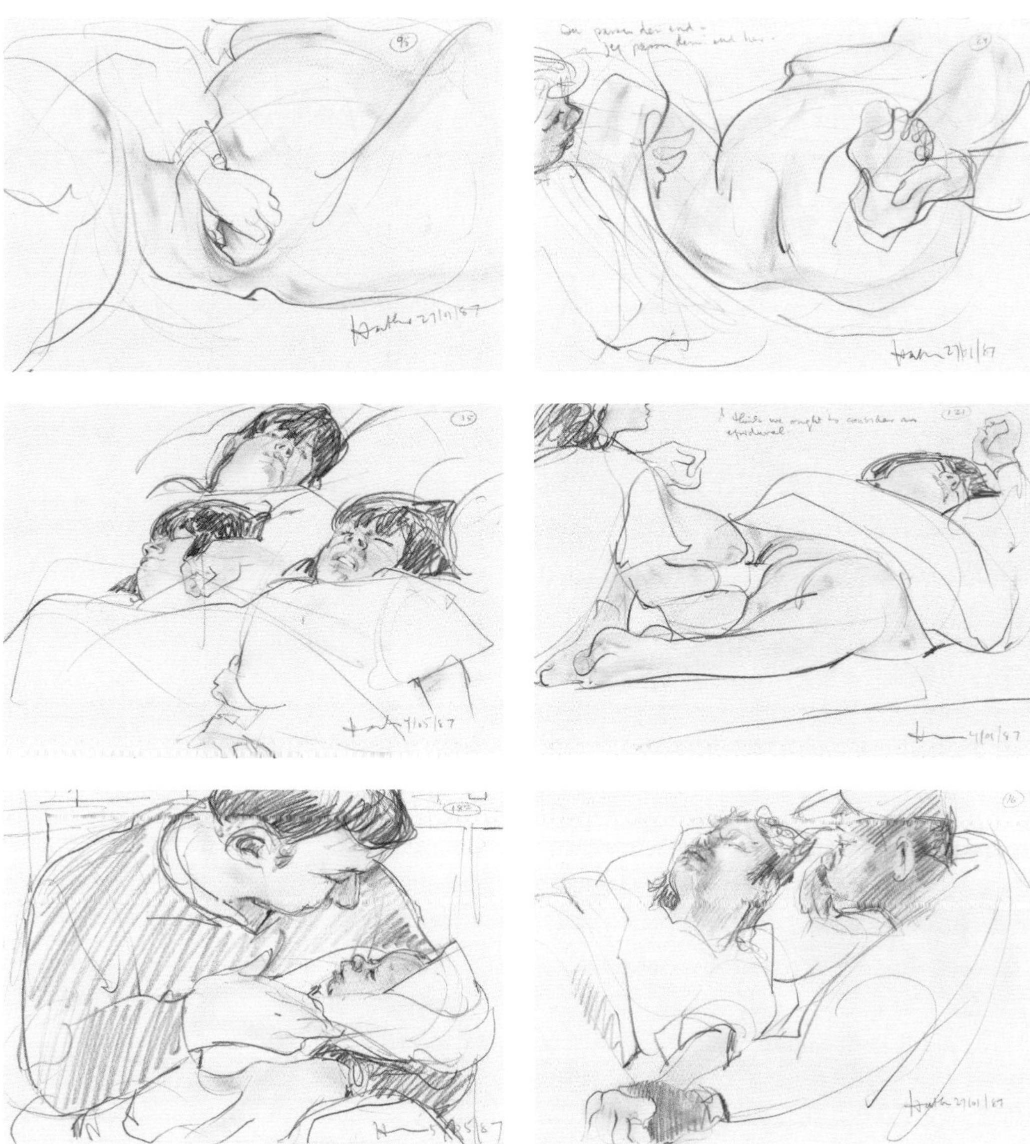

history: in a blog written as her sight failed and such work became impossible, she described the history of the incubator from the 1860s, when it was presented as a curious attraction to the paying public. By the early 1980s when Spears first approached a hospital in Canada, NICUs were well established, and ever younger babies were being saved. Through her involvement with neonatal units, Spears started drawing women in labour. On occasion she was also invited to draw portraits of stillborn babies for grieving parents. 'I love to draw anyone who is in a state of perfect presence, as kids are all the time,' she told an interviewer in 2015. 'People of all ages become beautiful doing something difficult and completely absorbing, from musicians, athletes, women in childbirth, kids just being alive, great joy, great grief. The uncertainty about how long I've got focuses me – as with drawing people in motion, or a stillborn baby.'[22]

rejoice!

Rejoice! A baby has been born! **79** If this chapter is tinged with melancholy and anxiety, it is in part because we often turn to art to think through difficulties and trauma. Our tribulations can seem weightier than our joys. It is perhaps also because we harbour suspicions about art that is too celebratory. The received wisdom has been that motherhood is a minor subject, and art about babies sentimental, indicating a maternal softening – perhaps of the brain, as well as the body. Yet what could be more captivating a subject than this fresh being with its mercurial, emergent self, its fleeting hints of mood, so unselfconscious in response and movement? I think there are few artists to have had a baby who have not felt compelled to draw or paint it. Out there in bottom drawers and dusty portfolios there is a hidden museum of unseen baby art.

after birth

A trip to the Neonatal Intensive Care Unit is not on anyone's birth plan. In the UK, one in seven babies will spend time there, but the NICU is seldom mentioned on the hospital tour offered during your third trimester. Much like the medieval women we encountered in Chapter 1, whose visual environments were believed to influence the formation of their child, expectant mothers of today are often shielded from things imagined distressing, whether images of crowning or the procedures followed if an infant is unwell. These

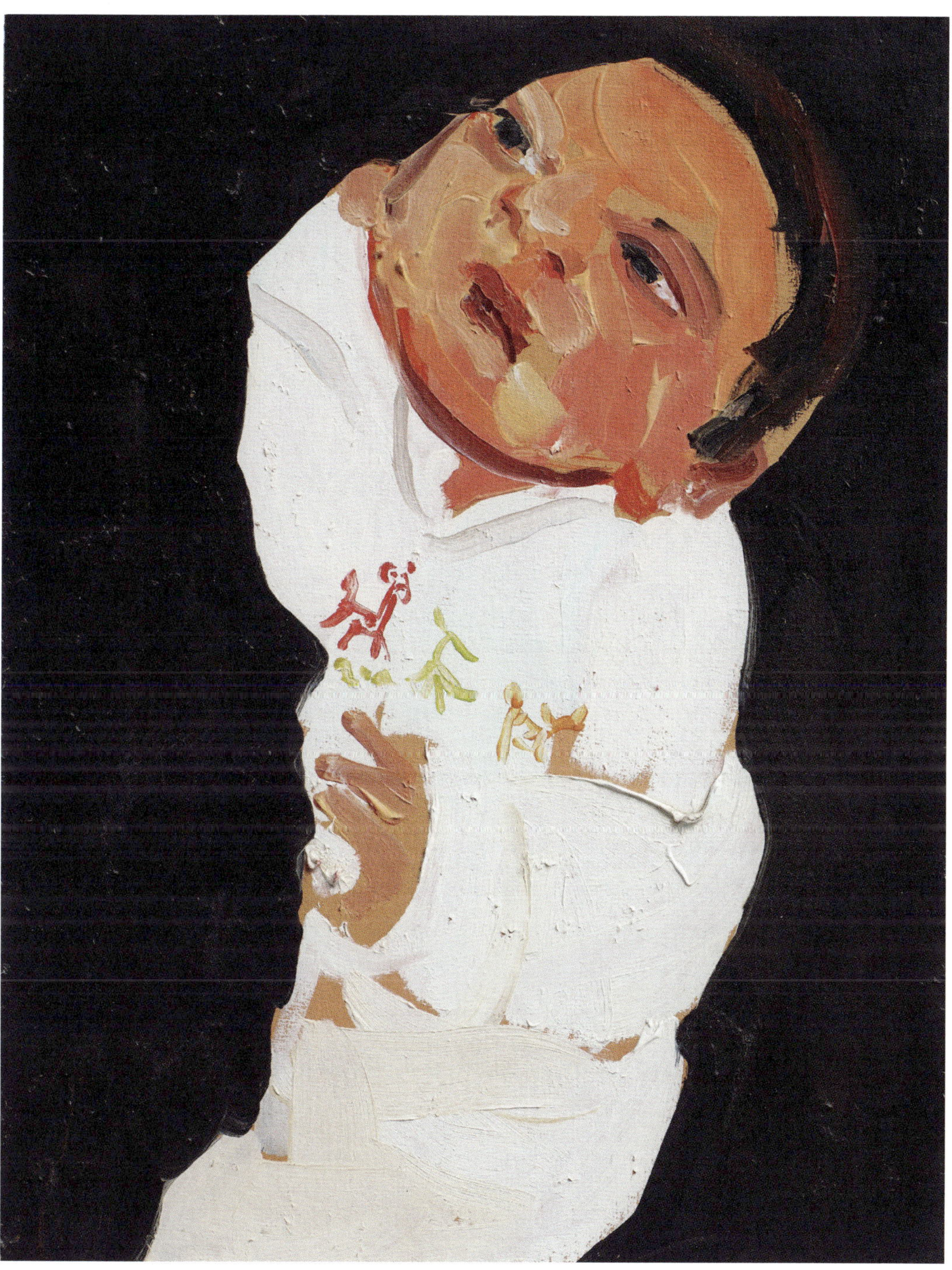

79

79.
Chantal Joffe,
*Esme (First
Painting)*, 2004

include the reality of being physically separated from your baby for the first weeks of its life, of placing a newborn in the hands of a surgical team, of watching your own child hooked up to machines inside an incubator, of trying to express milk for a baby with which you are not permitted skin contact.

Fani Parali's *Incubator/Flight* (2022) **80** was made following a traumatic birth. In a pencil drawing we see her tiny son as she did during the earliest weeks of his life – a featherlight creature, a life so delicate, suspended within the welded steel frame of an incubator. This bandaged body is nevertheless filled with a fighting strength that will carry him through surgery and intensive care. In the accompanying sound work a woman's voice is engaged in non-verbal communication. *Incubator/Flight* is part of the Greek-born artist's wider series *Early Universe*, which imagines how a parent can be present in a space their body cannot enter: through voice, through smell, through observation. *Early Universe* evokes the world shrinking around those in crisis – parents whose whole universe is suddenly contained in the metal frame of an incubator. Trust, the voice and the use of metal frames to extend and constrict the body had all been features of Parali's work before parenthood. Here, the trust is not a bond to be nurtured between performers but extended to others responsible for a child's care.

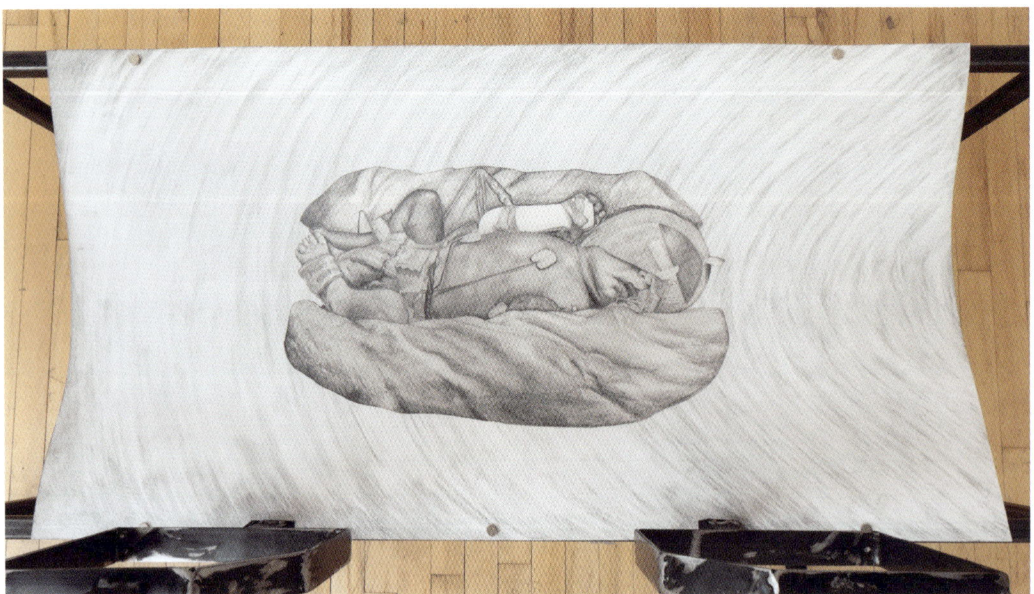

•

The Dutch photographer Rineke Dijkstra looks to people in a wavering state, whose identities are loose, transitional, transforming: intoxicated clubbers, adolescents in the park, a recruit making his way through the French Foreign Legion. Her portraits of three mothers immediately after giving birth were made in 1994, the same year she photographed young Portuguese matadors as they stepped out of the bullfighting ring. These are portraits of the face and body newly emerged from trauma – blood-spattered, shocked, conquering. Julie stands in her corridor in The Hague, wide-eyed, looking at and somewhat through Dijkstra **81**. Her body tilts awkwardly, bending to the weight of the tiny pink baby held tight against her chest. Beneath the paper mesh surgical pants, we see a thick pad, and her belly still taut and domed, as it remains for so long after birth. A fish tattoo hints at an identity that pre-existed the one of 'mother'. This is a portrait of a woman feeling alien in her own skin, and a little daunted by the new dependent life in her arms.

And yet we become accustomed. There is a transformed life on the other side. In Claudette Johnson's languid, smoky, self-portrait *Afterbirth* (1990) **82** the British artist contemplates her changed body – the marks on the skin, the folds on the belly, the battle scars of pregnancy and labour. The wrinkles and stretch marks are rendered in a wandering line that make their existence as a writing on the body feel congruent with Johnson's style. She is seeing herself as a mature woman, monumental and relaxed, one arm cast behind her head as though she'd caught sight of herself at rest on a hot day. I love the softness of this work, the steady, almost drowsy gaze, and the way the artist's body fills the frame. It feels like an assertion of the self after birth – of a new identity, one complete in itself, not defined by a child's presence.

eating and being eaten

'Milk is an Ur-substance, an originary substance, a primal liquid. It is the first substance to enter the mouth, to touch the tongue, to fill the belly. Milk flows from one to another. It is the first fluid to be incorporated into the body ex utero. Milk is associated with beginnings – the beginnings of life, the beginnings of civilizations, the beginnings of the world in origin and creation myths.'[23]

Thus opens *Deeper in the Pyramid* (2018) a book published as part of Melanie Jackson and Esther Leslie's multiplatform submersion into the rich and profitable world of milk. Following

80.
Fani Parali,
Incubator/Flight,
2022

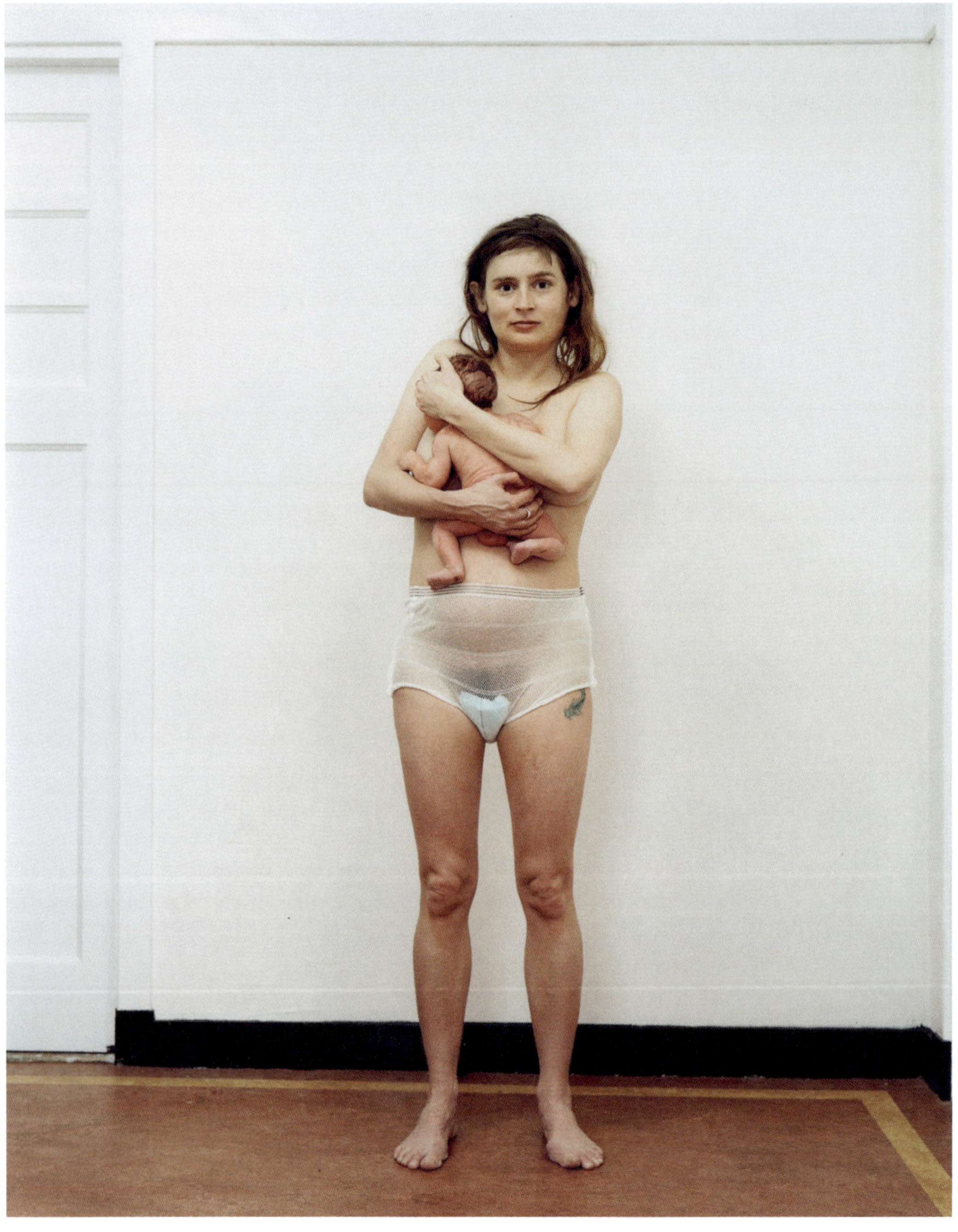

81

81.
Rineke Dijkstra,
*Julie, Den Haag,
Netherlands, February
29 1994*, 1994

82.
Claudette Johnson,
Afterbirth, 1990

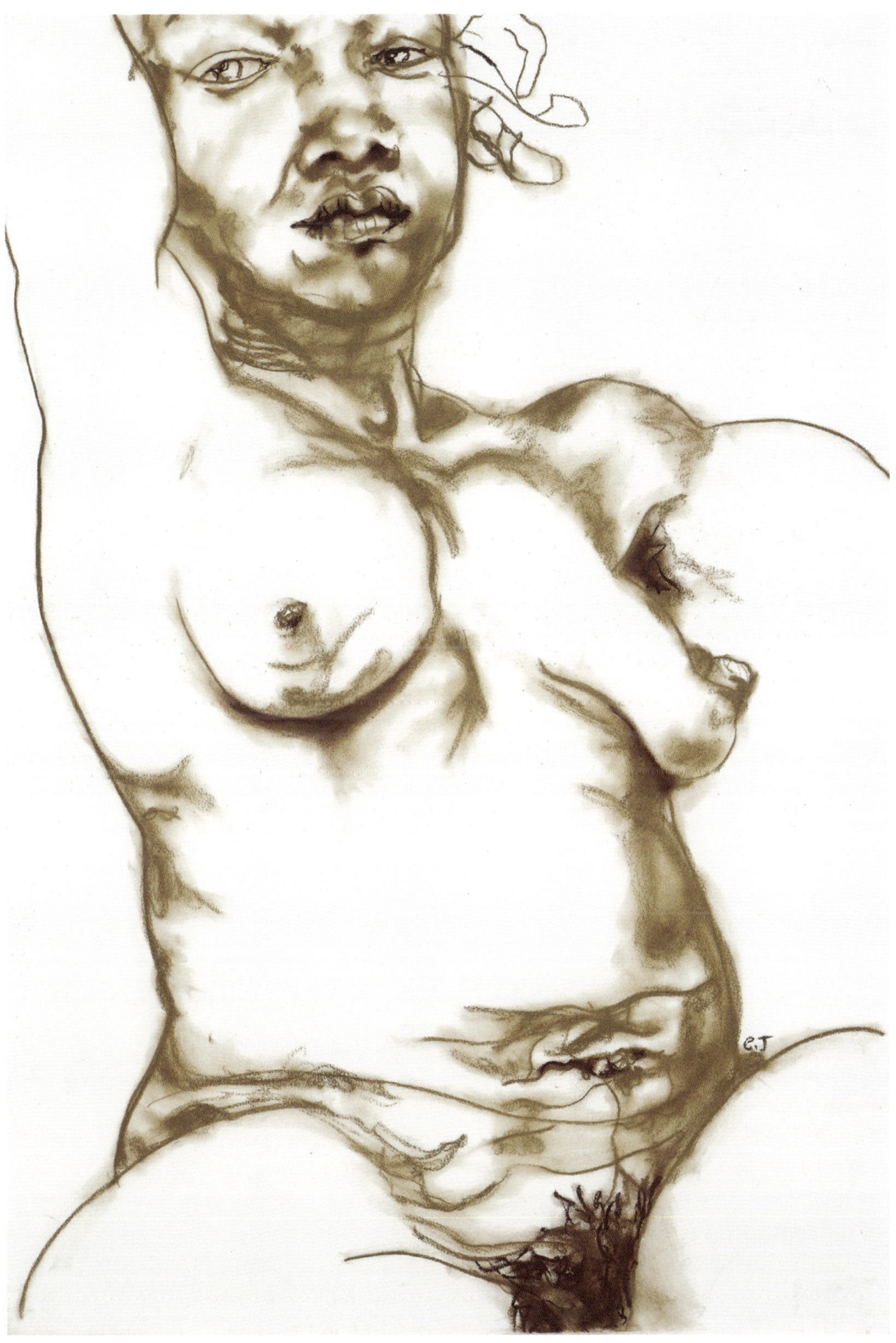

the currents of the international milk market, they explore its promotional tactics, its impact on local economies and the global environment. Swimming deeper into the milk economy the artist/writer duo notes how this substance is processed into stable components to be traded at leisure. They examine milk's iconography, its rebranding as a homogenous white liquid, its associations of cleanliness and purity, and co-option as an emblem by the far right. Between mechanized milking parlours and 16th-century Tintoretto paintings, Jackson and Leslie also look at nursing through an economic lens. The first formula milk was developed in Germany by Justus von Liebig in 1867: within two decades twenty-seven brands had reached the market. In this shift toward 'scientific motherhood' a case was made for formula feeding through the implied connection between the precise weights and measurements applied to the powder, and the documentation of infant flourishing according to growth charts. At different times, in different ways and in different territories, formula feeding has been promoted as superior to breast to mothers who can ill afford it. Exploring the economics of breastfeeding, *Deeper in the Pyramid* reproduces an advert for a hands-free breast pump that promotes the vision of a (young, slim, conventionally attractive, white) mother simultaneously engaged in waged work at her computer and doing the unpaid labour of feeding her child by mechanically expressing breast milk while at her desk. Behold 'the newly-freed bodies of a female workforce that need not leave its desks to do the work of reproduction'. they write, with, I imagine, a curl in their lip and one eyebrow raised.[24]

·

One breast protrudes from the darkness. Accompanied by the cooing hum of a suckling infant a tiny hand flaps and slaps and punches at the breast. Droplets flow from the nipple, wettening the hand, which spreads milk as it moves. Cut to: an adult female mouth sucking sensually at what, as the camera pulls back, is revealed to be a thumb, above which the mother strokes her nose as babies do for comfort. Cut to: the bite of clashing teeth. Cut to: the bite of clashing teeth threatening to consume the baby ('I'm going to EAT YOU UP!' we say, nibbling provocatively). This is Catherine Elwes's *There is a Myth* **83**, made in 1984 – a time when, in her hometown of Oxford, the only public place a woman could bare her breast to feed her child was the café at the Museum of Modern Art, but bare breasts were 'on display across

83.
Catherine Elwes,
There is a Myth,
1984

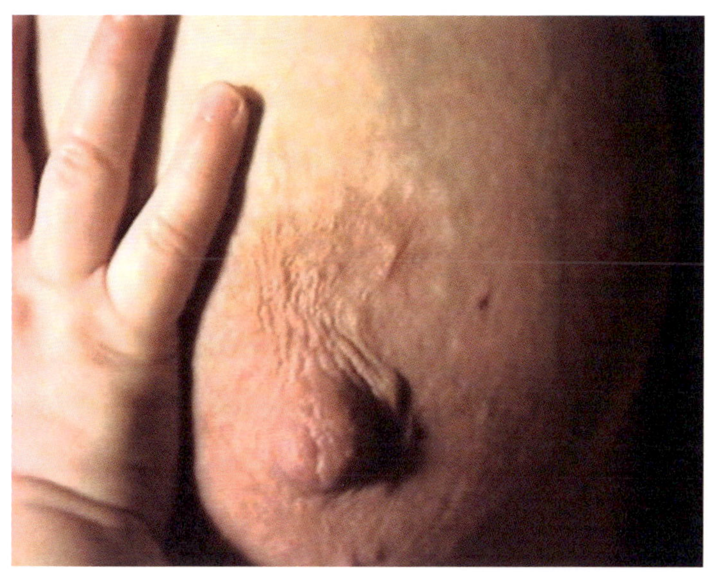

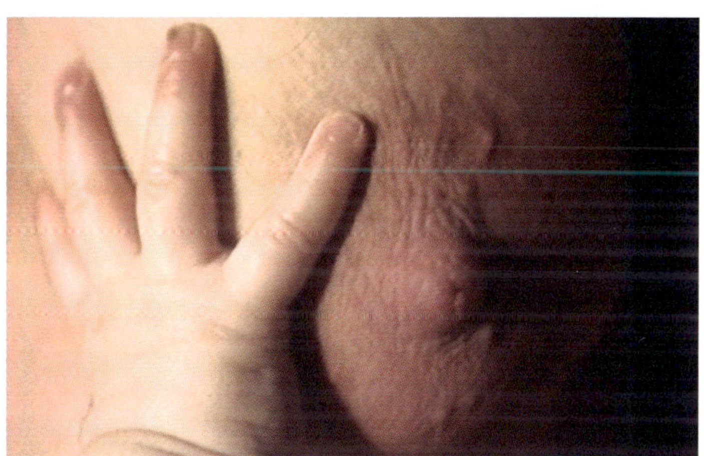

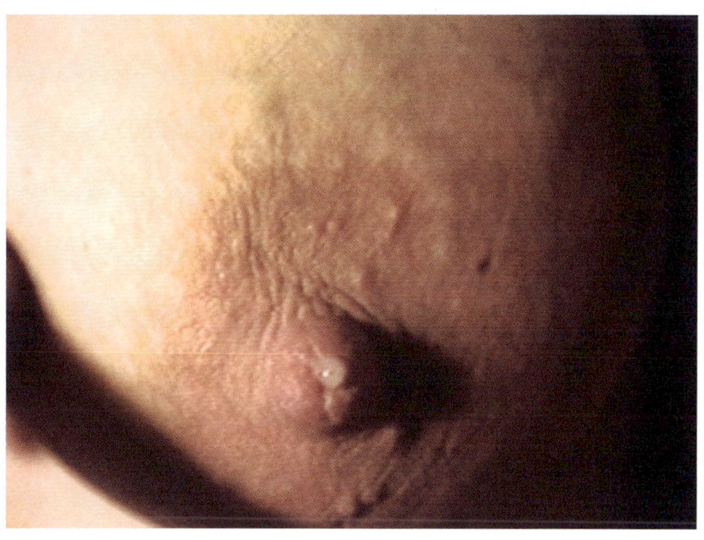

top rack magazines at every newsagent in the city.'[25] Elwes's back-ground was in performance. While an undergraduate at the Slade School of Art, London, in 1979 she spent three days behind glass in a white room, dressed in white and visibly menstruating, responding to questions on the window in felt tip pen. The following year, Elwes co-curated the landmark exhibitions – 'Women's Images of Men' and 'About Time' – at the ICA. She was centrally positioned within debates about both the representation of the female body, and motherhood as a subject for women's art. Observing the way her contemporaries (notably Mary Kelly, see pages 171–3) veiled the lived experience of motherhood in theoretical discourse, and others focused on the grit of domestic labour, Elwes felt there was more complexity to be teased out. There was 'the potential to disrupt adult heterosexual formations and release a deeper and more transgressive sensuality. I wanted to preserve the perverse eroticism of the mother/child bond without exposing my son' she wrote.[26] In *There is a Myth*, Elwes proposes the mother as creative power, and both giver and taker of life. She is the monster: exposing her breast but placing it off-limits for sexual pleasure; the prick tease simulating fellatio; the witch, eater of babies. She is also engaging with the intimacy and ambivalence of nursing; suckling the baby on the other breast, out of sight, while receiving its tiny involuntary blows on her exposed nipple; she comforts herself; she bares her teeth; she toys with consuming the flesh that was so recently part of her own body.

•

In 2022, Caroline Walker painted her sister-in-law Lisa in the days up to and immediately after the birth of her first child. The mother and her environment are tracked with a knowledgeable eye. Walker seeks out and finds the blurry vigil of night feeds, and the attendant water bottles and glasses crowding in around a nursing mother trying to keep her milk flowing, consuming so that she can be consumed. On the opening night of Walker's exhibition at the Stephen Friedman Gallery in London I watched women pause in unexpected shock before one specific work: a still life of plastic feeding and pumping bottles, uncoupled and drying in a white tray **84**. Something about that plastic – tough enough to boil on a stove top, smooth and curved in echo of the maternal breast, cuffed in garish yellow as though the selecting mother was herself infantile. I had not fed a newborn for almost twenty years, but the textures and tones of this paraphernalia, at once medical and emotional, freighted with such anxiety, touched something long buried. The maternal fear of lacking amplitude, of never being enough.

The watercolour paintings of Camille Henrot's series *Wet Job* (2018–23) **85** are slick with the suggestion of fluids – blood, milk, drool, bathwater. Within this wash are bodies that trouble the boundaries between self and other. Her mothers kiss, nibble and threaten to consume their delicious infants. The babies suckle, ingest, and deplete the parent. Henrot the nursing mother is, as one title tells us, both Saturn and Saturn's children, the consumed and the consumer. In French, the words for 'tongue' and 'language' are the same – *langue*. Taken into the infant mouth, the mother body is a vessel of language – we speak in our 'mother tongue'. Into this slippery relationship, Henrot inserts that cyborg accoutrement of the modern working mother, the breast pump. It is an apparatus that allows her to spend time apart from her child in her other identity as artist. Plugged into this machine, the figures in the paintings morph and become gelatinous as though something more than milk were being sucked from them.

self-expression

The essay that binds the artist publication *Milk Report* (2019) by Conway and Young opens with a quotation from Marxist-feminist theorist Silvia Federici: 'They say it is love. We say it is unwaged work.'[27] Open the pale blue pages, and you find a ledger of accounts: time codes in a six-digit formula. 00:17:00, 00:23:00, 00:08:00 and on and on. These are the periods Young spent breastfeeding in the first six month of her baby's life – a total of 720 hours and 7 minutes. As a physical object *Milk Report* repositions the labour of nursing within the economic system. 720 copies of the report were printed, each retailing at £8.21 – the UK hourly living wage in 2019. If all the copies sell, Conway will 'earn' a wage of £5,916.95 for breastfeeding her child. The economics of breastfeeding are not as simple as this apparent quid pro quo suggests. The liberty to engage in this labour rests on 'a cushion of circumstance and privilege' which might include maternity leave, financial stability and a supportive partner. Even as she feels consumed by the relentless cycle of nursing, Young is aware of a larger economy of care around her. As the mechanism by which the labour force is reproduced, the unpaid mother body has a particular status

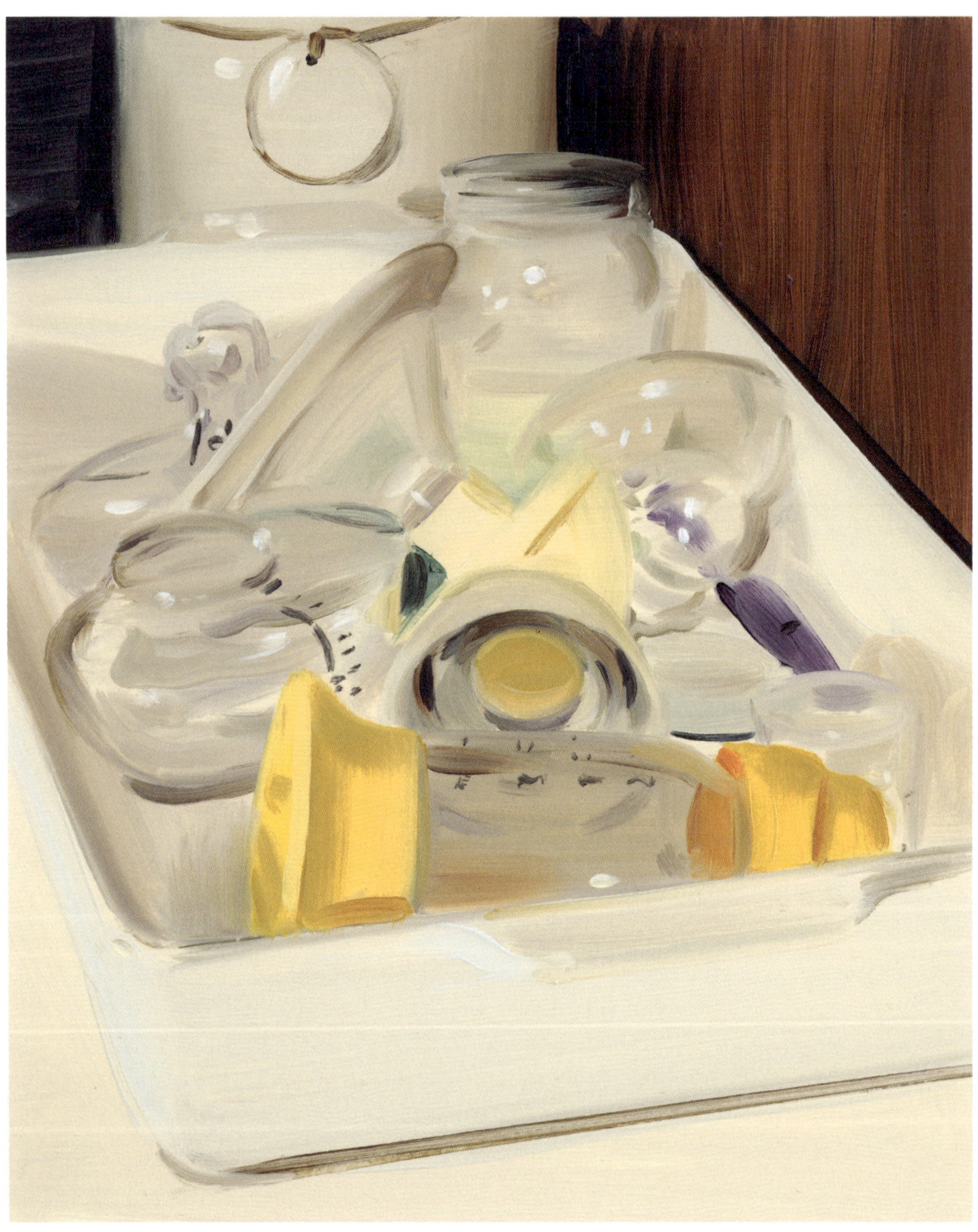

84

84.
Caroline Walker,
Bottles and Pumps,
2022

85.
Camille Henrot,
from the series
Wet Job, 2019

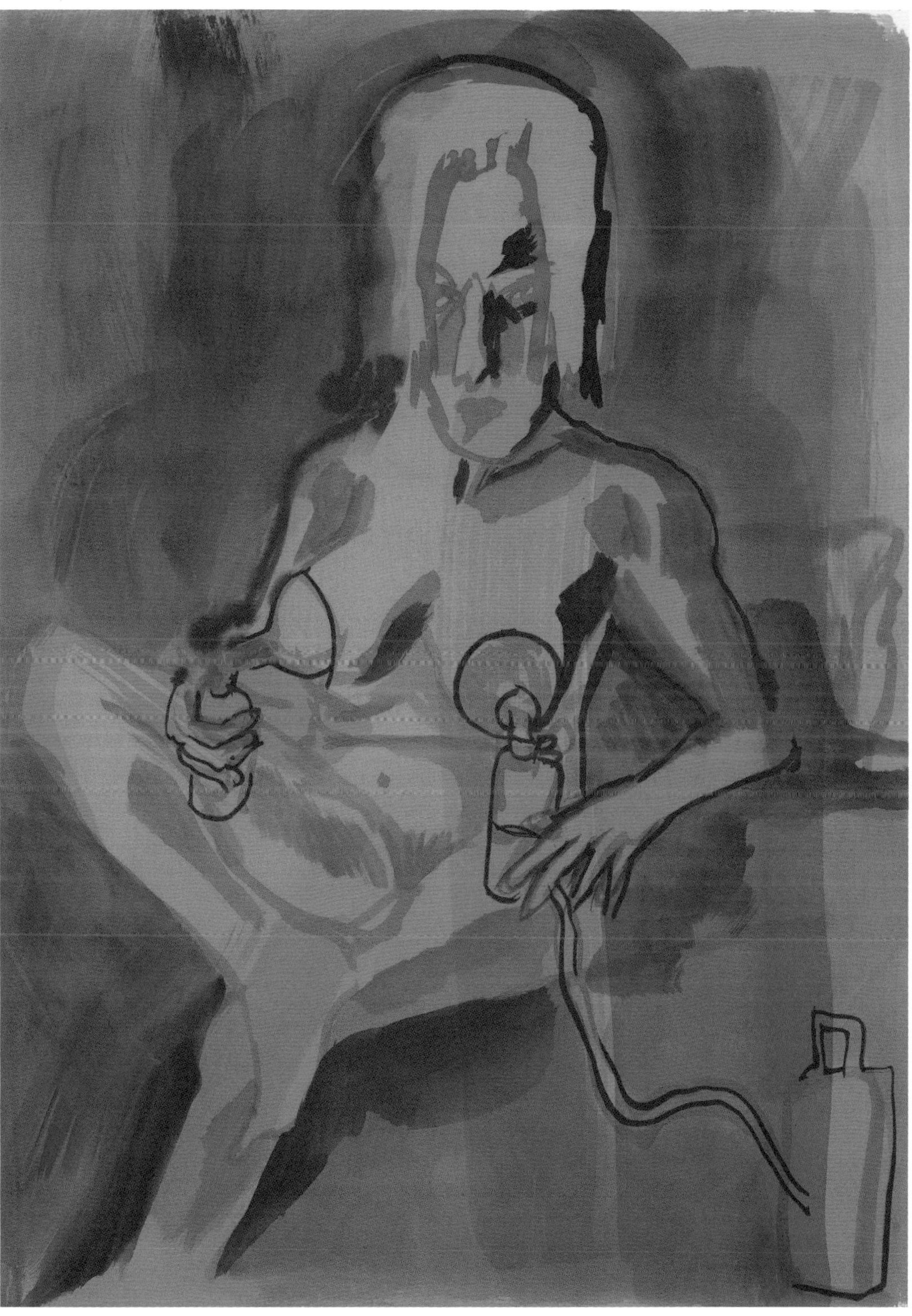

85

under capitalism: 'This milk is future producing,' Conway and Young write. 'This is concrete labour.'

When milk is ejected from the body, it is described as being 'expressed'. The mother body expresses nourishment and protective bacteria rather than – perhaps at the expense of – a poem or dance. In *White Ink* (2018) **86** Carmen Winant collages black-and-white images of nursing mothers over text written in white on fifteen sheets of black paper in an even, looping hand. The text is from Hélène Cixous's fabulous roar of an essay 'The Laugh of the Medusa' (1975/6) in which the philosopher calls for new forms of writing (*écriture feminine*) in which women will write themselves. Cixous enumerates the radical changes to society this might bring about: the positive assertion of women's sexuality, new ways to love, and a 'thrilling era of the body' in which women can, without judgment, opt to birth and raise a child free of old maternal and paternal codes.[28] Winant made *White Ink* in the same year she installed 2,000 found images of women in labour, *My Birth*, at the Museum of Modern Art in New York – a riposte to the near invisibility of real childbirth in contemporary art. In response to Cixous's call for a new form of writing, Winant the new mother apparently dips her pen in breast milk and makes a reproduction, copying out a fragment of 'The Laugh of the Medusa', which is not completed but rather repeated within the work. Across the surface of the text hover images of women mid expression, the white ink of their milk flowing from breast to mouth.

•

Tabitha Soren's *Motherload* is a chronicle of a year of broken sleep. The title of one photograph from the series is particularly irresistible: 'My Great American Novel' (2007/21) **87**. This North American's 'novel' is a suite of 400 multiple exposures shot from above her bed documenting a body in motion as she rouses to nurse her baby night after night. The work suggests the work not done while doing the work of parenting. Instead of writing a magisterial work of fiction – an act for which she might receive public praise – Soren has nourished and nurtured a child for a year in hundreds of small private actions. Like a novel, *Motherload* is divided into chapters delineating periods of significance: 'The Night the Panic Attacks Started', 'The Month the Baby Slept Through the Night', 'The Month I Could Walk Without Peeing on Myself'.

Between Winant's faithfully copied fragment of text, and Soren's sequence of broken nights, we might propose a form of

86.
Carmen Winant,
White Ink, 2018

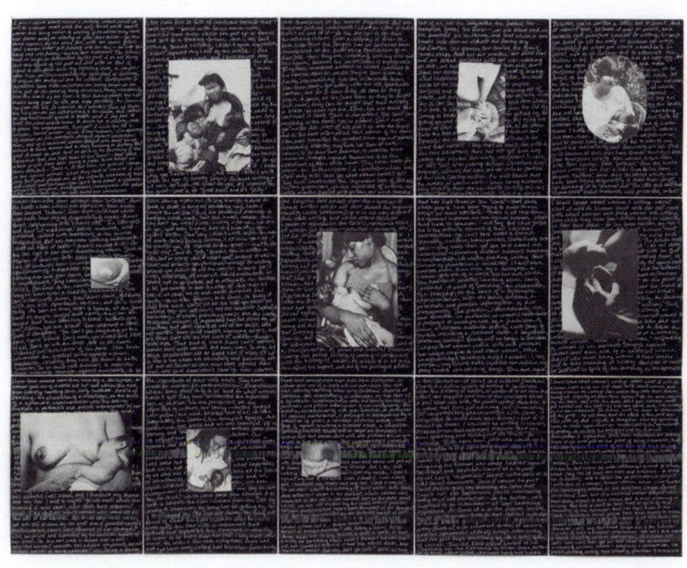

have been amazed more than once by a description a
woman gave me of a world all her own which she had
been secretly haunting since early childhood. A world of
searching, the elaboration of a knowledge, on the basis
of a systematic experimentation with the bodily
functions, a passionate and precise interrogation of her
erot...

was ashamed. I was afraid, and I swallowed my shame
and my fear. I said to myself: You are mad! What's the
meaning of these waves, these floods, these outbursts?
Where is the ebullient, infinite woman who, immersed as
she was in her naïveté, kept in the dark about herself,
led into self-disdain by the great arm of parental-conjugal
phallocentrism, hasn't been ashamed of her strength?
Who, surprised and horrified by the fantastic tumult of
her drives (for she was made to believe that a well-
adjusted normal woman has a divine composure), hasn't
accused herself of being a monster? Who, feeling a funny

'expression' in response to Cixous – one that emerges from the structures and strictures around the artist-mother body after birth. It is an art of fragments and scraps, work made in the times in between, in a state of hallucinatory sleeplessness and perpetual interruption. An art that can bear a long period of delay (fourteen years in Soren's case) between the moment a work is imagined and when it is executed and shown.

the monkey and the cow

It's hard to imagine the legendary Amazon queens Marpesia and Lampedo breastfeeding, yet it seems they did, for after her death in battle Marpesia was succeeded by her daughters Orithyia and Antiope. The image of these warrior woman – who dubbed themselves 'daughters of Mars' the god of war – sits uncomfortably with the soft patience we associate with nursing. Amazons were said to have removed their right breasts to improve agility with sword or arrow, but as Giovanni Boccaccio reminds us in *De Mulieribus Claris* (*Famous Women*, 1374) the left breast was left intact so that it might suckle a child.

For the sculpture *Amazon* (1992) **88** Irish artist Dorothy Cross dressed a tailor's mannequin in cowhide and a single udder. It's an ungainly object that recalls the sensation of feeling all breast – a body dominated by the provision of milk. Like Sylvia Plath, many mothers will remember feeling cow-heavy[29]. To call ourselves bovine suggests braindead compliance. Cross instead offers us a model body that is both milk cow and warrior queen, ferocity and nurture coexisting.

During the 1950s, the American psychologist Harry Harlow conducted an infamous series of experiments testing the bond between mother and child. Was a baby's connection to its mother based on the provision of food or was there something more important at play? Harlow's methodology was controversial, even at the time. Working with baby rhesus monkeys he provided them with two surrogates – a mother made of wire, and a mother covered in soft cloth. Some monkeys were suckled by the wire mother, and others by the cloth mother, but all returned to the soft body and spent as much as seventeen hours a day clinging to it. Harlow observed that comfort and security were more important than the provision of food to the bond between child and mother. After further distressing tests, he concluded that the presence of this maternal body emboldened the infant to explore the world and overcome its fears.

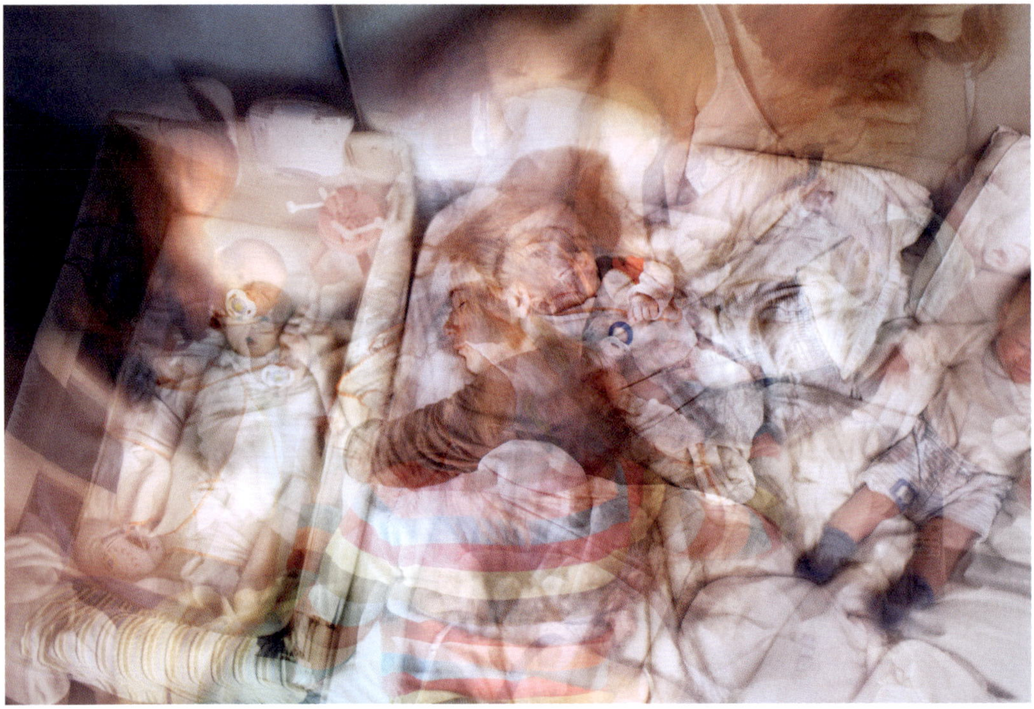

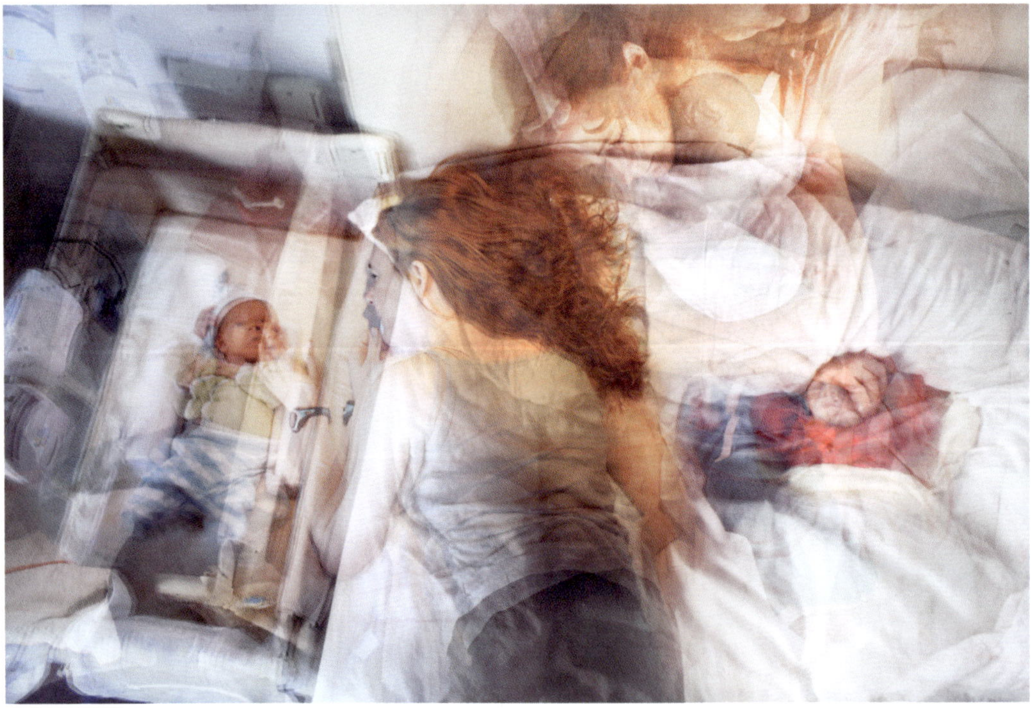

87

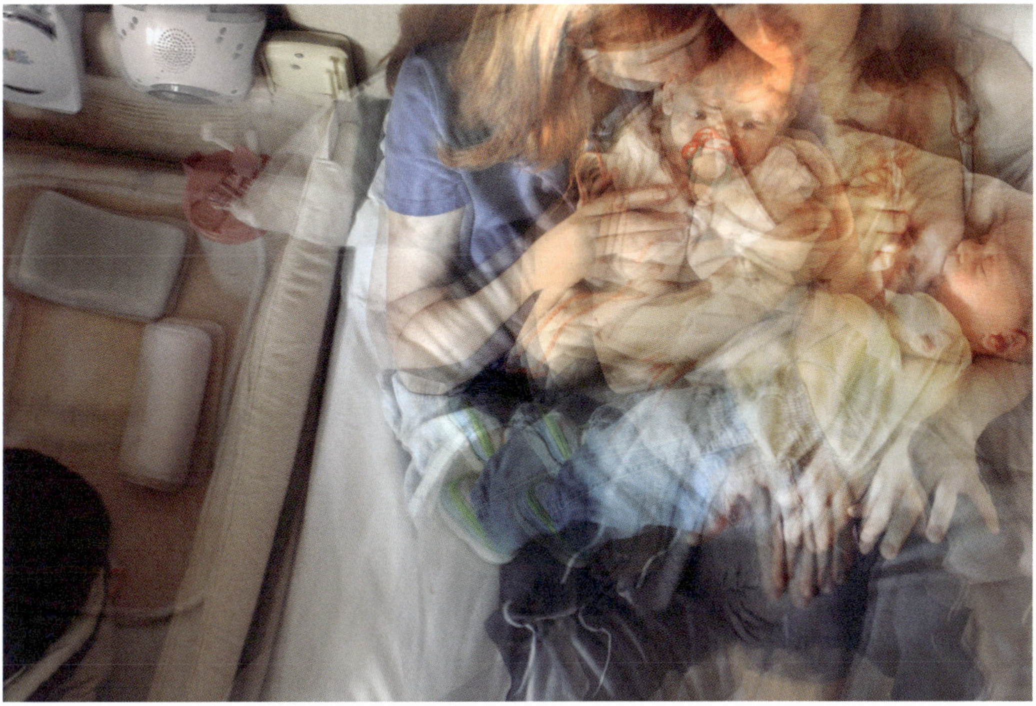

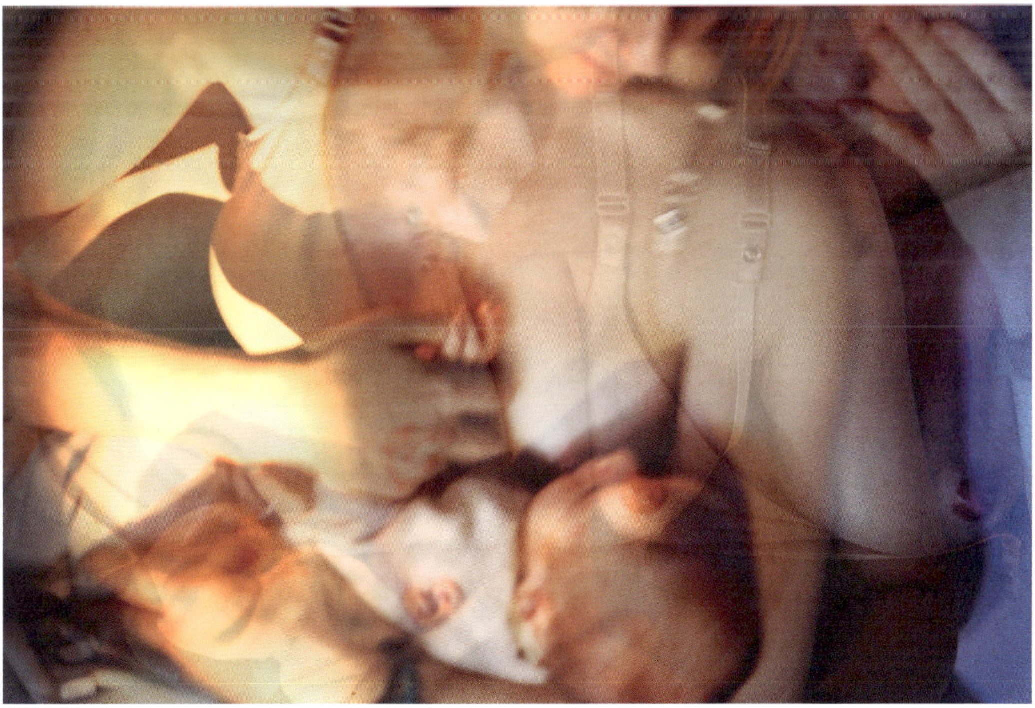

87.
Tabitha Soren, *Motherload* (clockwise from top left): *My Great American Novel, All 400 Photographs*, 2006–7/2021, *The Month the Baby Slept Through the Night*, 2007/2022, *The Night the Panic Attacks Started*, 2006/2022, *The Month I Could Walk Without Peeing on Myself*, 2007/2022

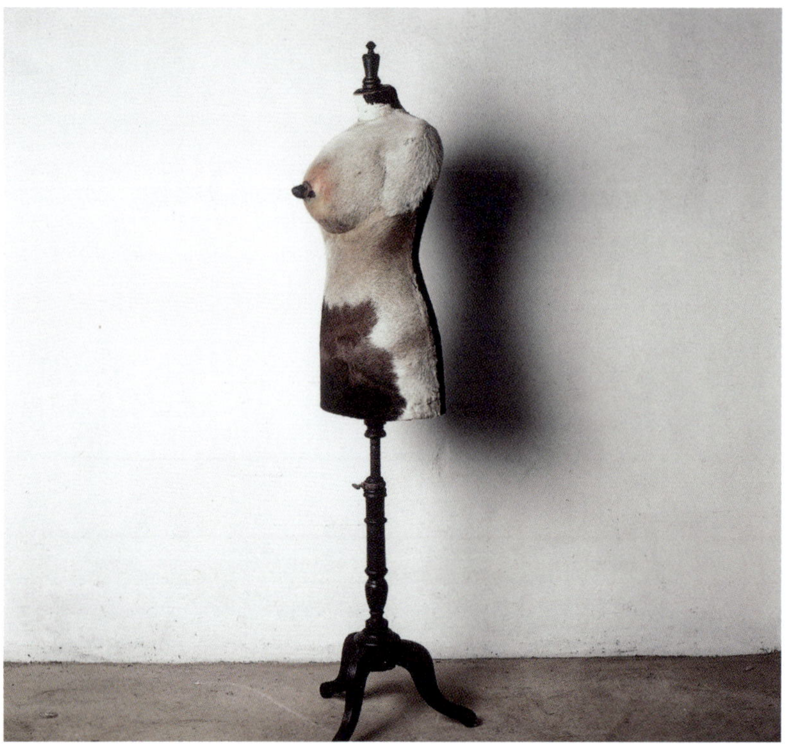

88

British sculptor Cathie Pilkington encountered a photograph of Harlow's experiments in an exhibition in 2004 and faithfully translated the figures into the sculpture *Surrogate* **89**.[30] Then a new mother, Pilkington describes making the work as a way to take ownership of the complexity carried in the image: the rough approximation of a mother figure onto which the baby monkey clings, the clinical dissection of the infant/mother bond, the horror of being witness to cruelty and the curious reassurance that infant attachment is not rooted in biological motherhood. In those all-at-sea days nursing, Pilkington saw her own fears reflected in the baby monkey and suggests the work as a self-portrait in the satirical tradition of *singerie*. As well as a meditation on motherly love and nurture, she invites us to read *Surrogate* as a portrait of the artist as a young monkey, desperately clinging to the debased medium of sculpture.

88.
Dorothy Cross,
Amazon, 1992

89.
Cathie Pilkington,
Surrogate, 2007

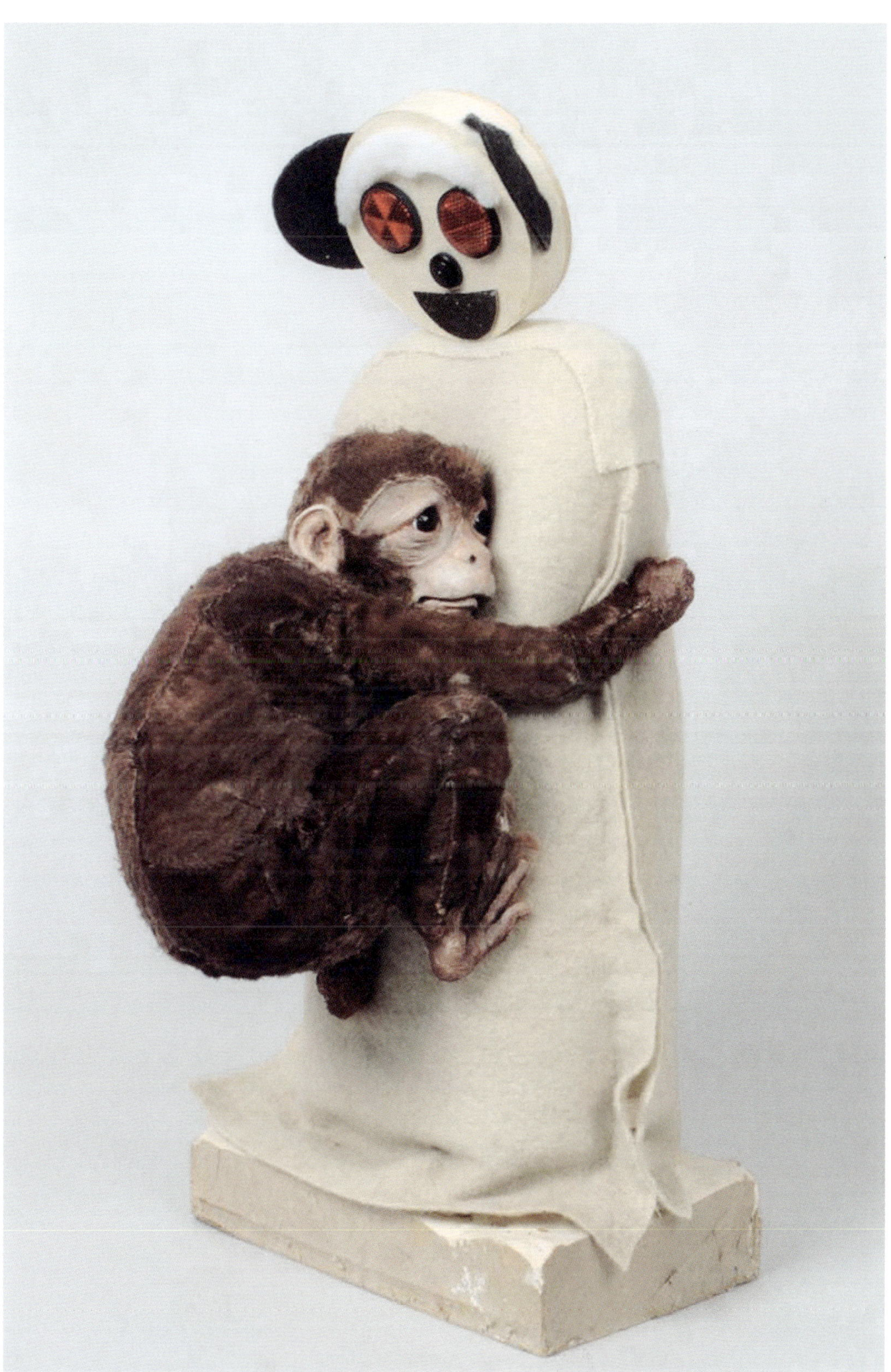

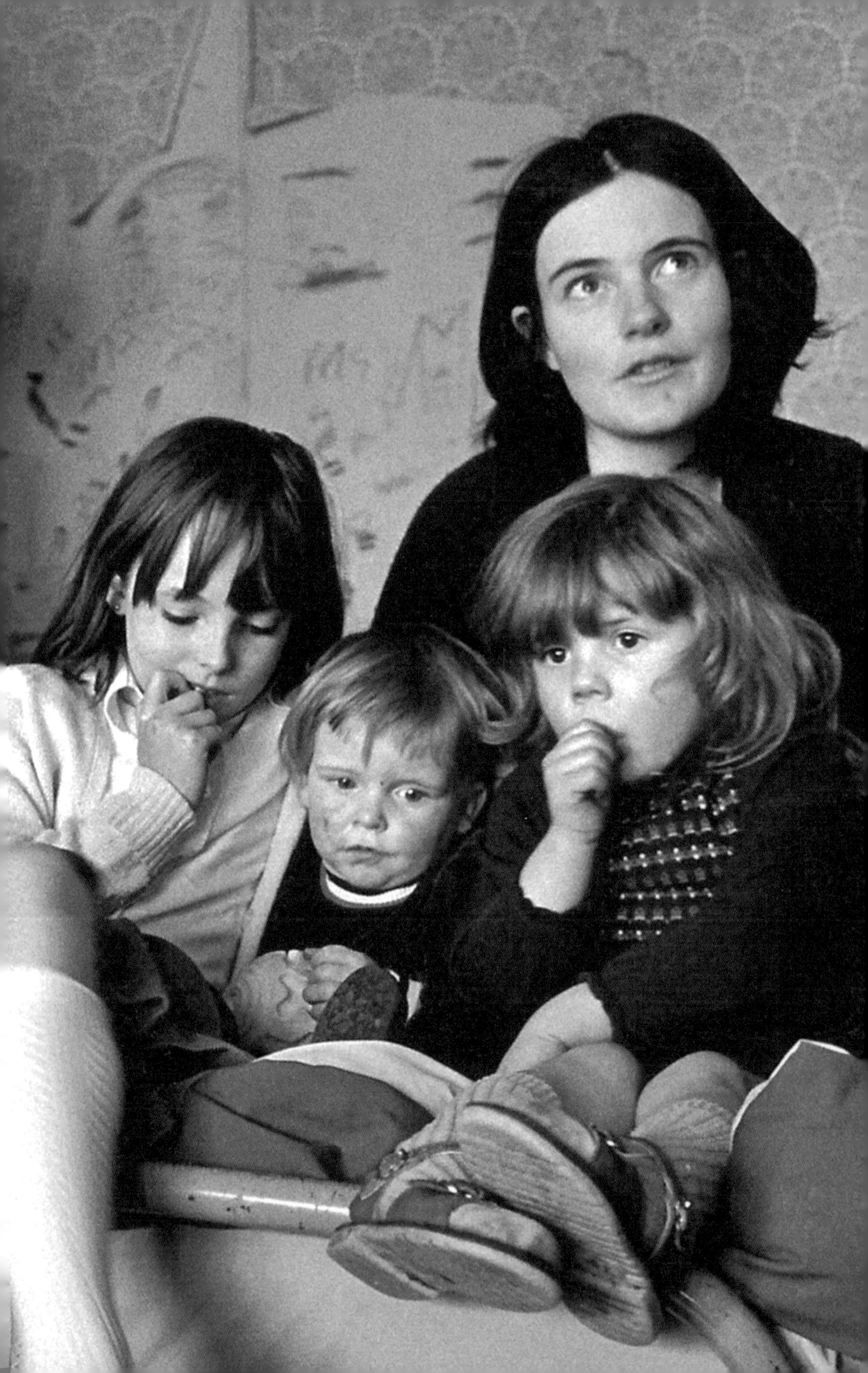

maintenance

We are seen as nagging bitches,
not as workers in struggle.
Silvia Federici, 'Wages Against Housework'[1]

Mothering continues. There is the excavation of mashed carrot from between kitchen tiles. The expression of pride over bowels appropriately moved. There are receipts, accounts and detergent. There is buttering, slicing and sandwich bagging. There are the snotty days (phlegmy weeks, aching months...) off school. Decades spent tessellating swimming lessons, birthday parties, maths coaching, school plays, dental check-ups, sporting fixtures, playdates, dance classes, eye tests, inoculations, exams, and other 'who-needs-what-where-when?' logistics. In the years to follow, debt, drugs, heartbreak and the struggles and upsets of young life will drive spawn back to the mother pond. You can express care through a myriad of actions, but you cannot fix everything. Mothering gets you down. Mothering is hilarious. Mothering is love.

In the abstract 'motherhood' evokes the fresh-faced years of pregnancy, birth and nursing. Perhaps they are easier to sentimentalize because we don't remember passing through these stages as a child so are free to make them in our own image. This chapter looks beyond, at artists responding to the ongoing experience of mothering in the everyday. Much of the territory corresponds to the world of housewifery and unpaid domestic labour that has been such an important focus of feminist writing over the past century. We encounter artists and collectives who reimagine the kitchen table as a site of radical action, and home as a place of resistance. We also find acts of love tempered by exhaustion, and exhaustion tempered by love. Artists who propose quotidian motherhood as a fit subject for advanced art and the mother as a figure who is sexually active and (God forbid) cool.

I began the last chapter noting how conception, gestation and birth are used as analogies for the creative act. This chapter is titled in honour of artist Mierle Laderman Ukeles and her *Manifesto for Maintenance Art* (1969). After having a child, Ukeles realized 'the creating, the originating, that's the easy part.' Her studies had offered no cultural language that gave value to the repetitive ongoing labour of caring for a child. 'Nothing educated me for how to bring a wholeness to taking care, not only creating life, but maintaining life.'[2] The modernist glorification of the artist as a 'free being' failed to acknowledge the complex supporting structures that made that freedom possible. Ukeles's manifesto opens with a distinction between two systems of enterprise, one rooted in the Death Instinct, the other in the Life Instinct. On one side is 'Development', which encompasses acts of 'pure individual creation; the new; change; progress' and other gestures we associate with art and the avant-garde. On the other is 'Maintenance', which keeps the pure individual creation free of dust, preserves the new and sustains change. Development depends on Maintenance. 'After the revolution,' she asks, 'who's going to pick up the garbage on Monday morning?' The *Manifesto* accompanied a proposal for a three-part exhibition titled 'CARE'. In the first, Ukeles would move into the gallery with husband and child and perform her domestic activities as art: 'My working will be the work.' For the second, she would interview people – including visitors – about the care that kept them alive. For the third part, containers of polluted earth, air and water as well as the contents of a sanitation truck would be deposited at the gallery daily to be processed, purified and rehabilitated. The project provided a template for Ukeles's life's work. In 1973 she documented repetitive everyday actions – changing nappies, doing laundry, dressing and undressing her children to leave the house – and named them *Maintenance Art Tasks* **90**. Moving into the public sphere, Ukeles performed acts of maintenance, including mopping the steps and dusting a vitrine, at the Wadsworth Atheneum in Connecticut. In 1976 she invited 300 workers in main-tenance roles at a Manhattan skyscraper to designate an hour of their time each as art production. In 1977 she took up an open-ended self-appointed role as artist-in-residence at the New York Sanitation Department. In her first work, *Touch Sanitation*, she tracked down and shook hands with 8,500 sanitation workers and thanked them 'for keeping New York City alive.'

90.
Mierle Laderman Ukeles, *Maintenance Art Tasks*, 1973

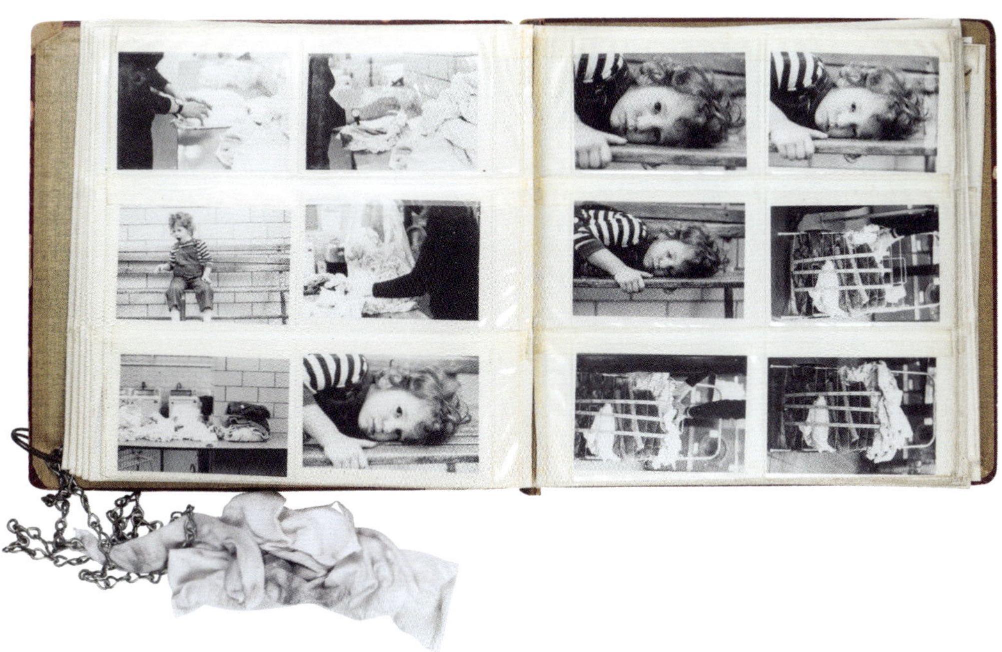

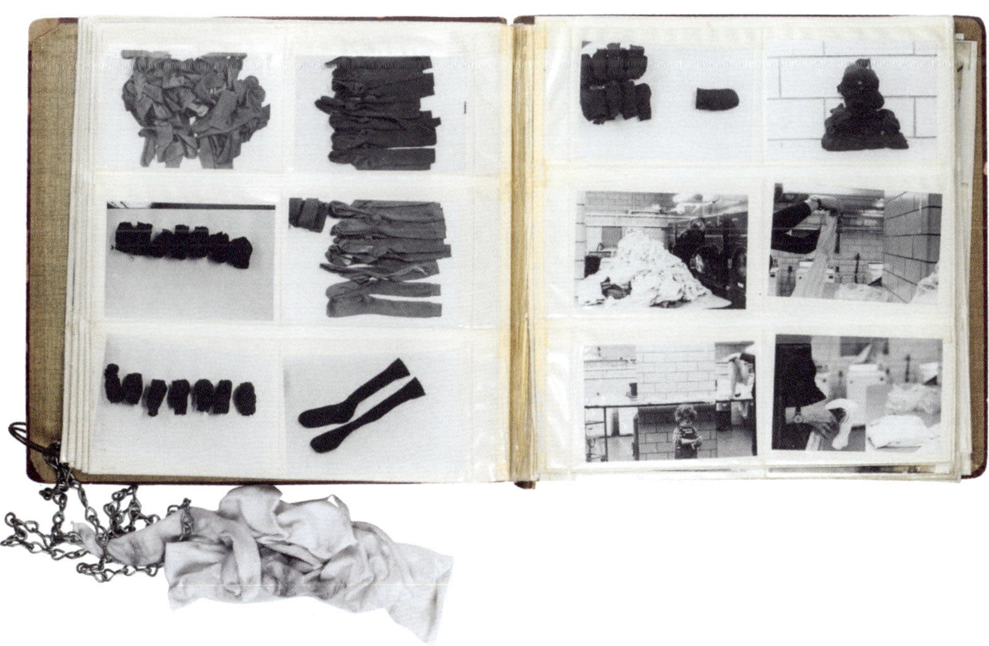

90

Across all these gestures, Ukeles raised questions about whose expertise is valued in a society, what kinds of labour are hidden or denigrated, and which are publicly celebrated.

the happy housewife heroine

Released in 1966, Gunvor Nelson and Dorothy Wiley's short *Schmeerguntz* **91** was described by the film critic Ernest Callenbach as 'one long raucous belch in the face of the American Home.'[3] The film is a jangly cut'n'paste of the feminine ideal promoted in the mass media, slammed up against the gunky, gross and ungainly reality of housewifery. Nelson filmed Wiley, heavily pregnant, as she changed fouled nappies, cleaned the toilet, pulled food from the plughole, suffered morning sickness, and struggled to dress

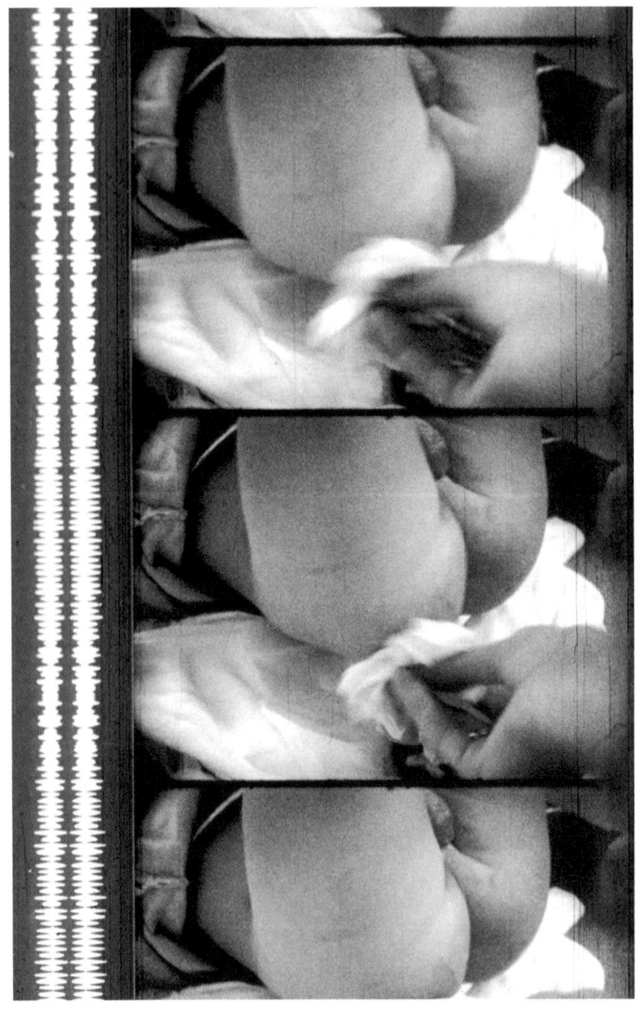

91.
Gunvor Nelson
and Dorothy Wiley,
Schmeerguntz, 1966

91

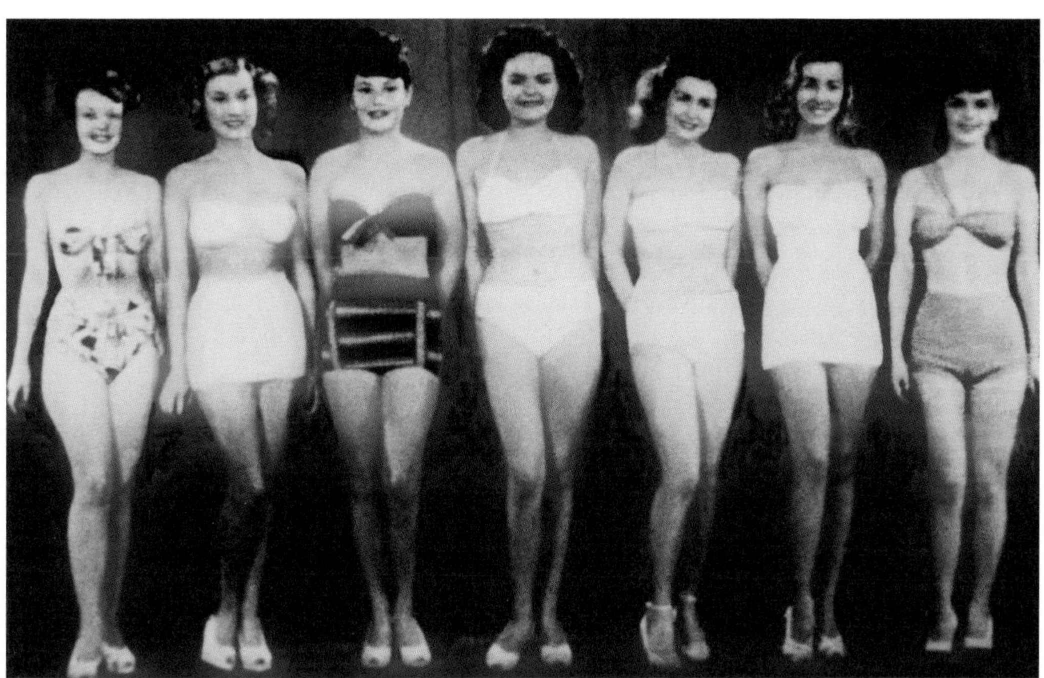

91

herself. Snippets of this candid home footage flash up in razor-fast edits between beauty contests and fashion plates. Over it all plays snippets from fairy tales, Bach's portentous organ chords and that jazzy 1960s pop that signals carefree youth.

Like Ukeles, Nelson and Wiley located their interest in repressed aspects of the everyday within a broader social purpose: peeling back the gloss that was being lacquered over Western society in the mid-20th century. Wiley recalled 'looking at all the gunk in the sink and [thinking] of the contrast between what we do, and what we see that we 'should' be – in ads and things – and that was the idea right there, from the sink.' 'For me, that was America,' said Nelson, the matter-of-fact Swede. [4] *Schmeerguntz* reflected growing awareness of the role assigned to women in the US in the post-war period: that of the great consumer. Betty Friedan's incendiary work *The Feminine Mystique* was published in 1963. A punchy chapter dives into reports commissioned for US ad agencies between 1945 and 1960. Seventy-five per cent of the consumer advertising budget in the US was directed at women – for which Friedan reads 'housewives'. A new class of convenience foods, cleaning products and appliances were created to target the purchasing power of middle-class homemakers. The advertisers identified the woman most likely to buy their goods – houseproud but hungry for creative fulfilment – and set out to manufacture her through the suggestive power of marketing. A researcher interviewed by Friedan explains how the new products and appliances are promoted with the suggestion that domestic labour could become a fulfilling and highly skilled activity for the housewife: 'We have helped her rediscover the home as the expression of her creativeness,' he explains. 'We help her think of the modern home as the artist's studio, the scientist's laboratory.'[5]

VALIE EXPORT's photo collage *The Birth Madonna* (1976) **92** reimagines the Virgin as housewife. Perched on a new washing machine, her head is bowed, and her arms outstretched, as though cradling the dead Christ. Here, there is no body, only a bloodied towel spewing from the washer door. The perfections of this Madonna are burnished by a new attribute: that of the ideal consumer. EXPORT produced a series of Marys adoring home appliances: one venerates a vacuum cleaner; another cradles a knitting machine before a reproduction of Michelangelo's *Pietà*.

Born Waltraud Lehner in 1940, EXPORT rebelled all through convent education, and plunged into marriage and motherhood aged eighteen. These trappings of adulthood did not bring her longed-for freedom, so she applied for divorce – eyebrow raising in Catholic Austria – and left Linz to study in Vienna, leaving her daughter in her sister's care. She rebranded herself after Export cigarettes. In a 1968 self-portrait she poses cockily, hand on hip, brandishing a soft pack bearing her face and logo, irresistibly punk. EXPORT described the targets of her work as: 'Marriage, the Christian Church, religious themes and the traditional side of Vienna at the time – this fossilized Nazi realm.'[6] In restaging the Madonna and Child she draws a connecting line between sources of patriarchal control both historic and contemporary. On the one hand the Catholic Church, on the other, the constructed consumer cult of happy housewifery. A few years earlier, in *Women's Art: A Manifesto* (1973), EXPORT outlined art's importance within the women's liberation movement: 'We must destroy all these notions of love, faith, family, motherhood, companionship which were not created by us and replace them with new ones in accordance with our sensibility, with our wishes.'[7]

•

Among the post-war consumer goods marketed to women was a new class of branded medication touted as a relief to 'baby blues',

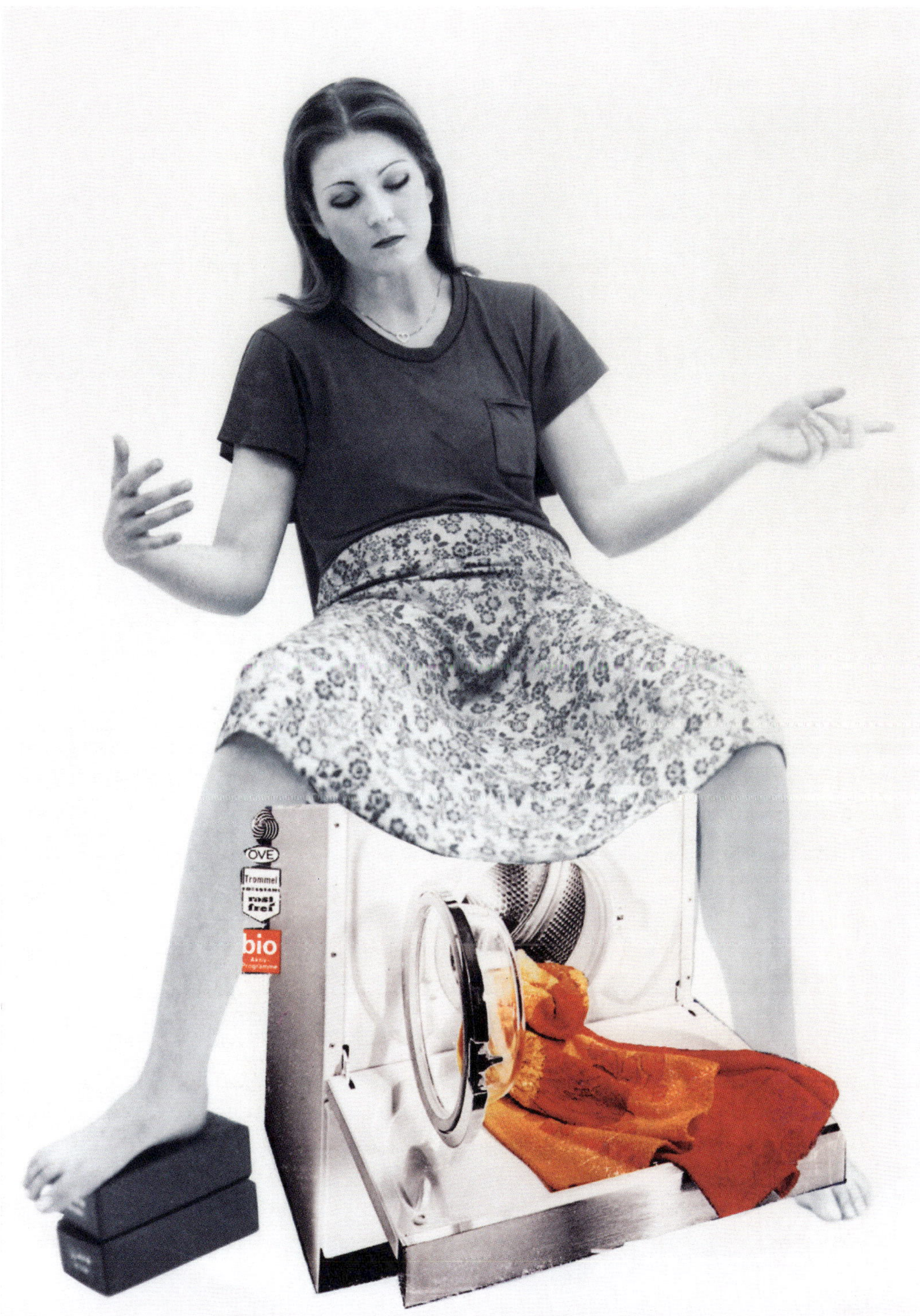

92

Don't take drugs, take action

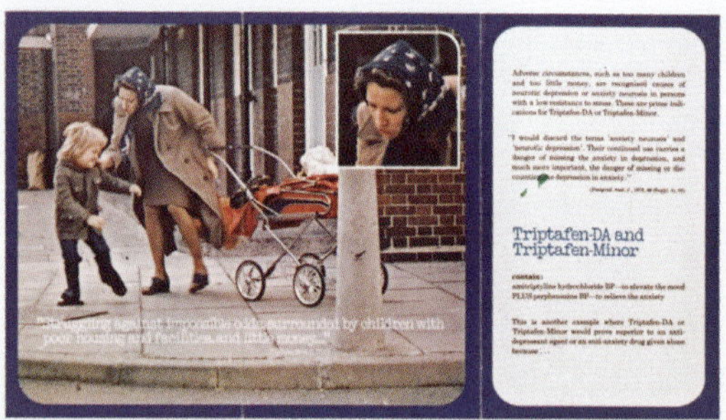

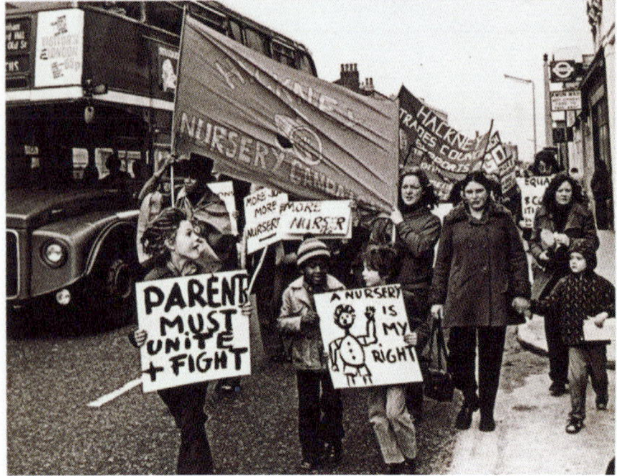

93

93.
The Hackney
Flashers, from the
series *Who's Holding
the Baby?*, 1978

depression, fatigue, distraction, anxiety and insomnia. For the
liberal prescription of tranquillizers including Miltown, Librium
and Valium, doctors were rewarded with 'bonus points' and gifts
from the pharmaceutical companies.[8] Tranquillizers were also
marketed directly to consumers, promoted as the cure to the ills
of modern motherhood. A 1968 ad for Miltown uses language
familiar to readers of *The Feminine Mystique*, outlining the social
pressures which led to women feeling overwhelmed, proposing pills
(rather than radical societal change) as the balm.[9] Consumption
rocketed, as did drug companies' profits. In the mid-1970s,
campaigns to combat prescription drug addiction located it as
the affliction of white middle-class suburbanites – housewives
hooked on 'mother's little helpers'. This was not the whole story.
In Britain, working class mothers, many struggling with poverty
and isolation were offered medication for stress and depression,
but little structural support.

Formed in 1974, the socialist-feminist photography collective
The Hackney Flashers took up the cause of working women and

mothers in a London borough still bearing bomb damage three decades after the Blitz. Hackney was, and remains, one of London's most diverse boroughs. In the early 1970s its working class and migrant communities suffered high unemployment, elevated levels of poverty and a housing crisis. The Flashers' first project *Women and Work* (1975) documented labour conditions including factory shifts and women's unpaid work in the home. This informed their next project *Who's Holding The Baby?* (1978) **93**, which charted the economic and social impact of the borough's parlous childcare provision and proposed a sustainable model for community nurseries and shared care. Documentary photographs, appropriated images, illustrations and texts were mounted on twenty-nine cardboard panels, laminated for display at community centres and libraries. Crucially, The Hackney Flashers outlined the impact class and wealth had on experiences of motherhood – their focus was a world apart from the affluent college-educated women studied by Friedan. *Who's Holding The Baby?* demonstrated how the lack of childcare prevented women in greatest need from returning to work, trapping them in poverty, isolated and depressed. It was a call to arms. One panel shows an ad for tranquillizers in which a woman pushing a pram near a housing estate snaps at her unruly toddler, beneath it are protestors carrying placards down the high street with their kids. Their provocative suggestion? 'Don't take drugs: take action'.

Collage is a classic tool of feminist subversion – it can be shocking and mordantly funny. Wit was an important weapon for The Hackney Flashers. Even the group's name nodded to sex pests of the era: gross men who lingered in public places waiting to expose themselves to passing females. Laughter is powerful. In 1990, the literary critic Susan Suleiman wrote of her admiration for Tracey Ullman (a comedian who, by delicious coincidence, would thirty years later play the role of Betty Friedan in the TV drama *Mrs. America*). Suleiman is struck by Ullman's descriptions of her mother's use of humour – albeit humour of the darkest and most powerful kind. After Ullman's father died when she was six years old, 'My Mom used to get out this pistol Dad had, and we'd have competitions in her bedroom to see who could die the best.' Laughing at her mother playing, says Ullman, 'was the greatest defense we had against the misery.'[10] Suleiman suggests that play and laughter allows the mother to be seen as an active, independent subject, rather than the still centre around which her children move: 'I believe that women – women artists in particular – must be strong enough to allow themselves this kind of play; and that one way to achieve such strength is for girls to imagine – or better still, see – their mothers playing.'[11]

I would like to imagine – although admit it is unlikely – that Suleiman wrote this after watching Bobby Baker's *Drawing on a Mother's Experience* **94** when it was first performed in 1988. Created eight years into Baker's life as a mother, it deploys humour rather as a skilful home cook might a meat tenderizer, softening before applying heat. Humour says Baker is 'a subversive act. It's the way women in my family deal with injustice.'[12] Even before motherhood, her work probed the feminine realms of feeding and familial relations. In performances she adopts the unthreatening white cotton uniform of the caregiver. In *Drawing on a Mother's Experience* she arrives with bulging department store carrier bags and announces that she's going to make a drawing about her experience as a mother. In a pastiche of the genius cool of the Abstract Expressionists, Baker 'draws' on a white double sheet in a variety of refrigerated media including slices of roast beef, milk, fish pies, stout, yoghurt and chutney. Each brings with it a story. Of preparation for her babies' births. Of her ravening hunger while nursing. Of her need always to do more – care for the children, go out to work, entertain. As a young mother she had felt tremendous pressure – financially, creatively, domestically – which drove her into both physical and mental illness. The work asks: 'How do you care for yourself? Who cares for you? Who runs the everyday?'[13] It is also outrageous. Baker is funny and playful. This mother makes a mess. As she pours stout and sifts flour, she flexes her art education, using the language of connoisseurship. Talking about chutney as though she were Clement Greenberg, Baker raises questions about the kinds of expertise valued in society: this 'mother's experience' that she draws on is the unwaged business of the domestic realm.

shit

You deal with a lot of shit as a mother. Metaphorical yes, but mostly actual physical shit. Born in Tehran, Tala Madani's life as a mother has been spent largely in Los Angeles – a city that social media informs me is populated by athleisure-clad momfluencers. Long interested in the grotesque, and the gooey possibilities of paint, Madani's sticky response to her own experience of parenthood has been *Shit Moms* (2018–) **95**, a series in which the mother has been reduced to a hopeless lump of matter. In some paintings, the 'shit mom' is hapless and passive, with bumptious toddlers

94.
Bobby Baker,
*Drawing on
a Mother's
Experience*, 1988

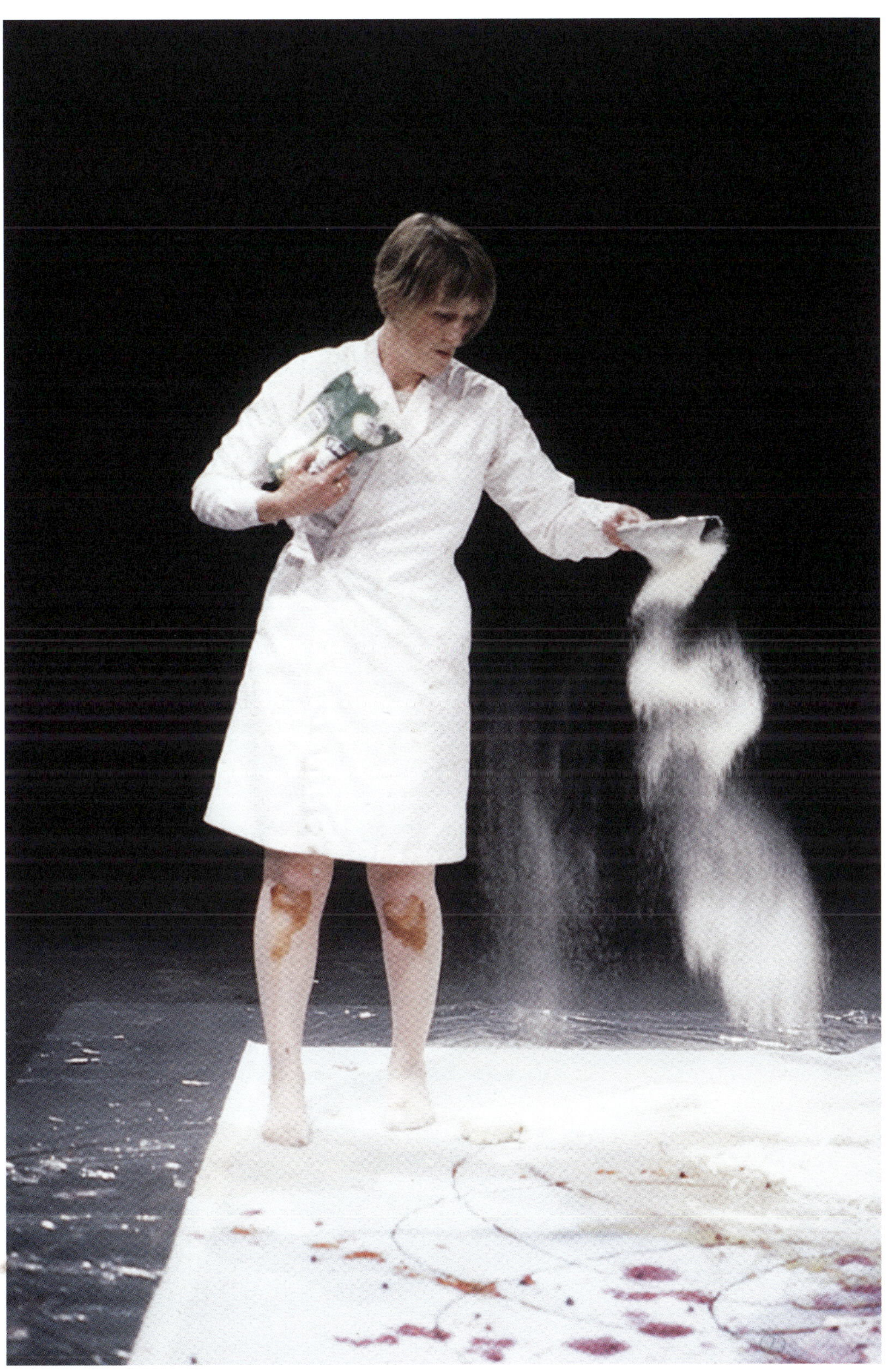

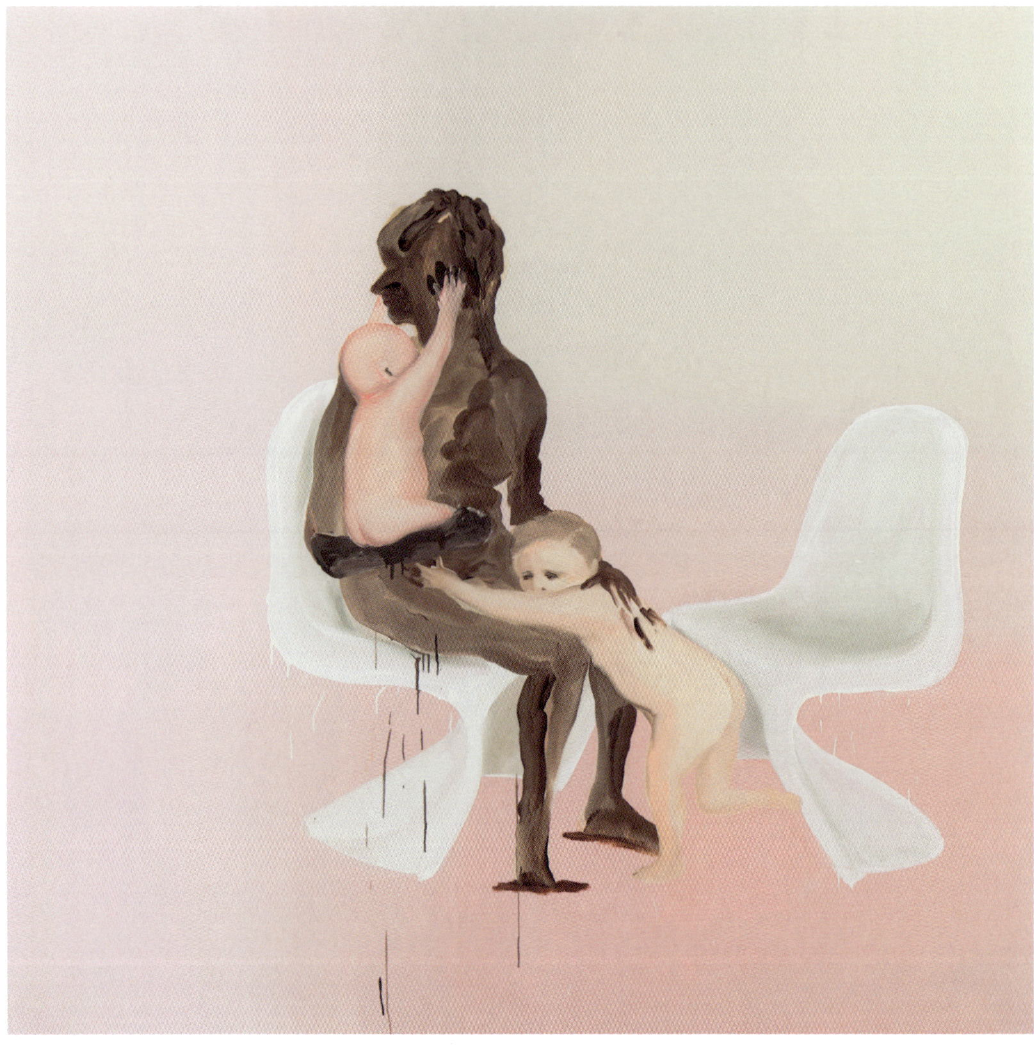

95

95.
Tala Madani,
Shit Mom (Remodel),
2019 from the series
Shit Moms (2019−)

using her as a trampoline, riding her like a pony, shovelling bits of her soft body into their mouths or smearing it down the walls. In an accompanying animation, the 'shit mom' wanders through immaculate sunlit interiors leaving streaks on the Persian carpets. As she throws her arms wide in excitement, she showers the room in sharticles. Cleaning up after herself, her gestures leave skid marks, compounding the mess. Madani's shit moms are grotesquely relatable for all who feel themselves judged and found lacking as a parent. As with Bobby Baker's subversive mess-making, Madani's mothers reclaim the territory of gunkiness from the child. In the face of maternal perfection, a world free of full nappies and unspecified goo, these mothers are allowed to be disgusting, to smear themselves, to fall apart. For all the suggestion of lost control and adulting fails, they have a liberating potency.

•

Dare I mention shit near Mary Kelly's *Post-Partum Document* (1973–79)? **96** When first shown, at London's ICA in 1976, Britain's outrage-hungry press generated much scandalized copy about Kelly's inclusion of used nappy liners. In truth *Post-Partum Document* is a rather sober installation, anything but sensational-ist. Six orderly sequences of documents and diagrams each chart an arena of infant development, from feeding and bowel move-ments, through early utterances to mark making – accompanied by observation, interpretation and the mother's diary. Denying us the pleasure of seeing or relating to either the child or mother body, the work is obsessive and intellectually rigorous, trans-lating the repetitive labour of child-rearing into the seriality of minimalist art. As it charts the gradual separation of child and mother, its language is psychoanalytic rather than sentimental. Having analyzed their relationship over six years, Kelly ends the work as her son writes his name and becomes an independent speaking and writing subject.

When we ask where motherhood is in surveys of feminist art, *Post-Partum Document* is the great what-about?-er-ist's weapon. Too often, it is the motherhood-related artwork included to the exclusion of all others. So much has been written that I don't feel a great need to add to the literature, save for a few observations. Kelly's work is sly – it wears the uniform of the conceptual and process art of its time, and speaks in psychoanalytic theory, while making a case for mother's work as an appropriate subject for advanced art. Crucially, amid the welter of psychoanalytic

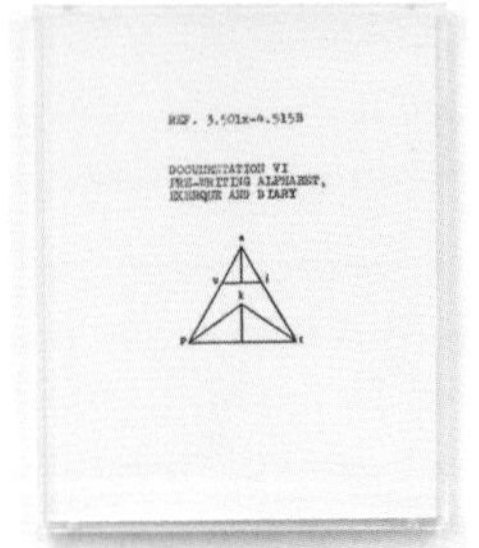
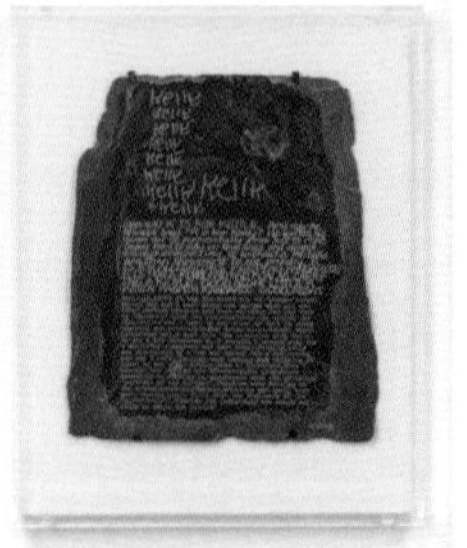
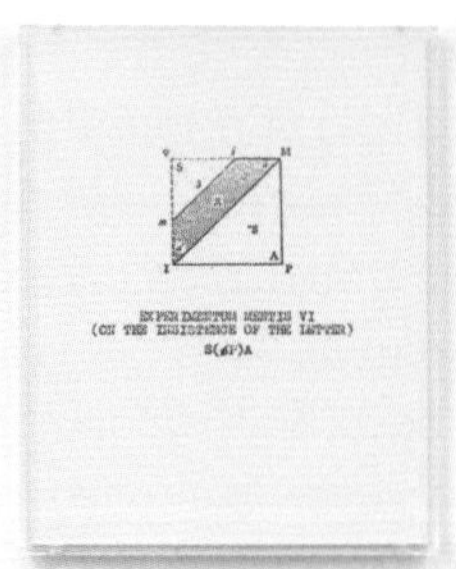
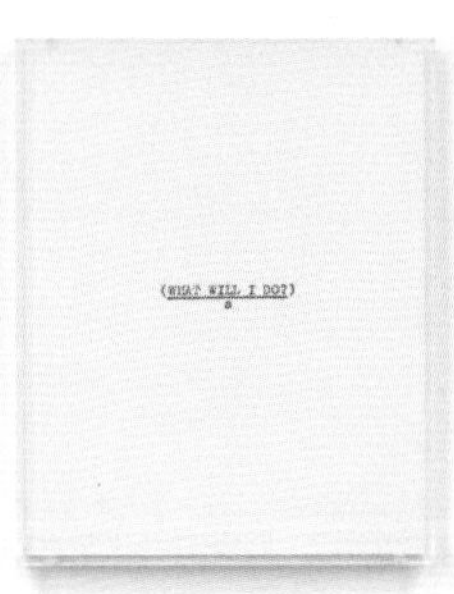

96

96.
Mary Kelly, *Post-Partum Document, Documentation VI: Pre-Writing Alphabet, Exerque and Diary/Experimentum Mentis VI: (On the Insistence of the Letter)*, 1978–79

writing that speaks of 'the mother', Kelly writes *as* a mother. She frees the mother to become the speaking eye, the seeing I. She makes what is for all mothers a difficult leap: rather than positioning herself as the child in relation to the mother, she positions herself as a mother in relation to a child.

cool and sodomitical mothers

In *Cool Men and the Second Sex* (2003) academic Susan Fraiman explores the Beat Generation's fetishization of outcast characters played by James Dean and Marlon Brando in the early 1950s.[14] Rejection of domestic norms is bundled into the untethered, roving, adolescent sensibility that informs cool. 'And it goes without saying that within this paradigm, the place occupied by the mother is by definition uncool', writes Fraiman.[15] Where would the rebel be without a mother to define himself against?

Looking at Hannah Starkey's mother figure carrying shopping across a Hackney park, I see Martin Sheen in *Badlands*, isolated against the great Colorado sky **97**. Starkey shoots at cinematic scale. Often, her women are alienated by the grandeur of their surroundings. Not here. Seen from a child's eye view, she is a towering figure lost in unknowable thoughts. Here is the mother positioned as hero: wary, thoughtful, strong, alert. Decades on from the cool of the Beat Generation, this mother is asserted as much more than a domestic convention to be rebelled against. In place of Sheen's shotgun, a white broom handle is slung across her shoulders. The plastic bags suspended from it testify to slender means: their blue the livery of budget shops and market stalls. Through thin plastic radiates the acid yellow of liquid floor cleaner, and the blaring graphics on a bumper pack of toilet paper. She's bearing tools of care. Who is caring for her, I wonder? Starkey notes that this woman is a single mother and writes of her admiration for those who raise their children alone.

The commonplace of portraying single mothers as super-women carries its own problems. There's a fine line between celebrating a woman's strength, and normalizing unreason-able burden. In describing a single mother's lot, the word often reached for is 'martyr', with its associations of selfless endurance and uncomplaining service. Evoking the crucifixion, Starkey looks not to iconography of the Madonna, but of her son. It is a startling image, in which competing associations – hero, rebel, superwoman, martyr – complicate conventions of the maternal.

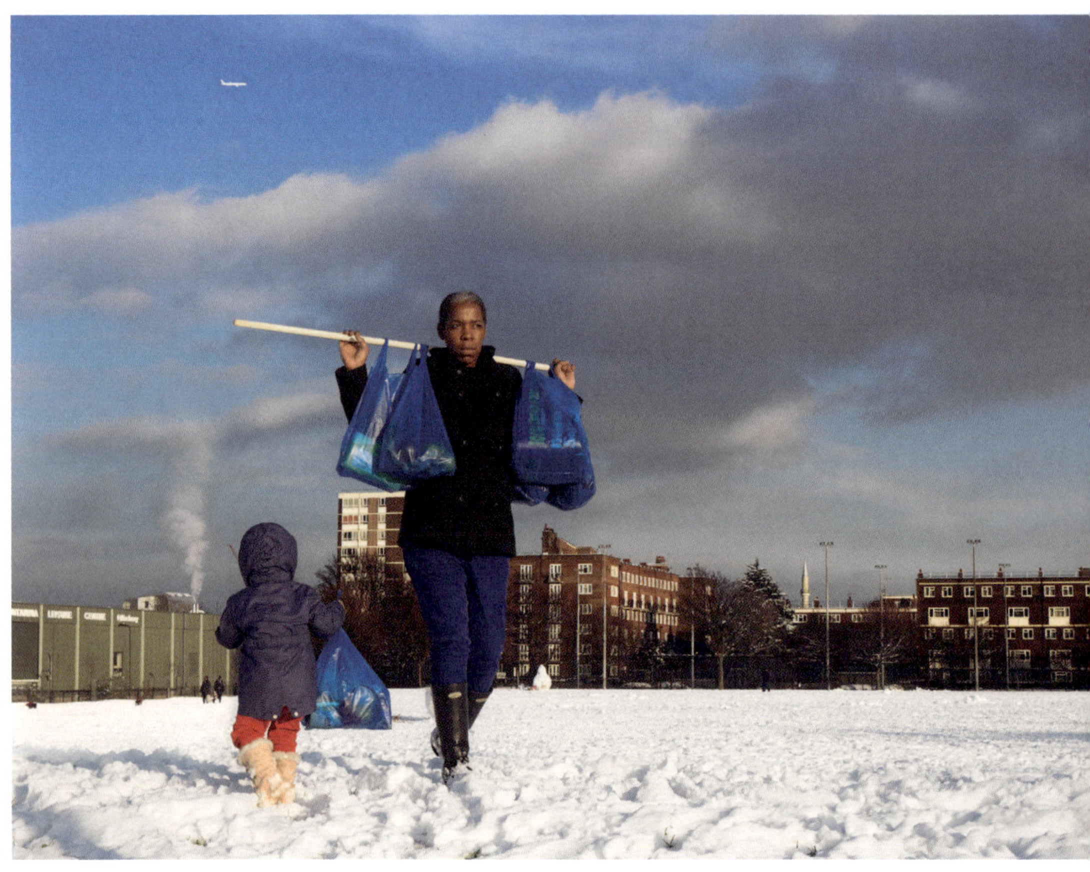

97

Shaking loose centuries of cultural debris, the mother stands, here, as saviour and life-force.

In *Cool Men and the Second Sex* Fraiman coins the term 'sodomitical maternity' to indicate a mother with a sexuality that is 'in excess' of her procreative capacity – a mother, in other words, who has sex for pleasure. It irons out the troublesome polarity Fraiman identifies between the counterculture rebel figure and the mother. Sodomitical maternity undermines assumptions about reproduction and the notion that selfless caregiving is intrinsic to a woman's nature.

We know how babies are made, yet there is squeamishness about maternal sexuality. Seeing Deana Lawson's *Baby Sleep* (2009), the viewer locks eyes with a luscious naked woman straddling a seated man, and then, with a shock, notices a slumbering infant in a swing chair. A narrative suggests itself, but there's something weird and stagey about the composition. Even in passionate thrall, her body curving toward her husband as she pulls him in to the scent of her neck, this mother is aware of being watched, and gazes toward us distractedly. The viewer has been invited to witness the reclamation of her body, her sexuality, and it feels uncomfortably voyeuristic. In 'Uses of the Erotic', activist and writer Audre Lorde describes intense, intentional erotic power as 'an assertion of the lifeforce of women'.[16] Lawson notes how Lorde frames the erotic as a source of creativity, foundational to an empowered feminist worldview in which there is space for spirituality, family and community. *Baby Sleep* acknowledges the coexistence of motherhood and desire, evoking the full force of a woman's sexuality. 'One of my other subjects saw the picture and said, "She looks like a succubus, like a woman who would eff the shit out of men and then leave them,"' Lawson says. 'I was actually thinking about a praying mantis, about a woman who was a bit forceful in a way that maybe complicates ideas of womanhood, sexuality, and motherhood.'[17]

97.
Hannah Starkey,
*Untitled, February
2013*, 2013

the subversive value of homeplace

In her 1990 essay 'Homeplace (a site of resistance)' bell hooks describes the domestic realm as a space from which Black women have pushed back against white supremacism. No matter this was a role assigned them by a sexist society. It is 'more important that they took this conventional role and expanded it to include caring for one another, for children, for black men, in ways that elevated our spirits, that kept us from despair, that taught some of us to be revolutionaries able to struggle for freedom.'[18] Hooks asserts a counter-position to the image of home as a place of oppression propounded by the predominantly white Women's Movement. She presents the home as a protective bubble constructed by Black women within a world of violent hostility, as 'a crucial site for organizing, for forming political solidarity.'[19]

These ideas feel intrinsic to Carrie Mae Weems's *Kitchen Table Series* **98**, made that same year. In her performance to camera, Weems's kitchen encompasses a world – of romance and family, education and collaboration, resilience and nurture – and one that centres Black women's subjectivity. In the opening image, Weems as the protagonist sits at a vanity mirror as a man embraces her from behind. She gazes at us, knowing and commanding. The series plays out over the blossoming and failure of a romance, the consolations of female company, motherhood, study and finally mature independence. At the end, Weems stares back again, this time standing with the cuffs of her black T-shirt rolled, hands laid flat on the table, occupying her power. In a 1995 conversation with Weems, bell hooks noted that critics are so 'fixated on the blackness of the images that they ignore the question of gender – of desire and power.'[20] Weems reminds hooks that the series is also about class, its images and text informed by working class experience and the milieu of blues music: 'A visual world that this music is played in, that's generated by the culture that the music creates.'[21]

around the kitchen table

At grassroots level, the 1970s Women's Movement spread through 'consciousness raising' groups – local gatherings at which issues of health, work, sexuality and the family could be openly discussed. Inequities in both public and private spheres were exposed, marital frustrations aired and women were encouraged to become acquainted with their own anatomies. Collective action, in art as elsewhere, became a way to amplify what had been too easily overlooked.

Let us return to The Women's Building in Los Angeles, first visited in Chapter 1. Founded in 1973, it was home to the Feminist Studio Workshop – an independent school for women artists. Dogs were welcome in the studios, but not children. In the founding incarnation of this explicitly feminist space, the principle that one could not be an artist and a mother lived on. Pissed off, a group of artists with children banded together, and, in 1974 formed the loose collective Mother Art. Their first act was to construct a place for children in the grounds – the *Rainbow Playground* – pieced together from wooden cable reels. 'It was a way of asserting that the ideal of feminism needed to include childcare and a place for children,' explains Laura Silagi, one of the four founding members, 'because children are a part of society and women's lives and you can't really divorce that fact from being a woman, being a feminist and being an artist.'[22] Mother Art were united by the constrained circumstances under which they made art, and their intimate acquaintance with the routines of housewifery. One of their most radical, joyous – and bizarrely controversial – projects, *Laundry Works* (1977) **99** was a performance series in five laundromats. Each was timed to the length of a single wash-dry cycle – the artists entered the laundromat, strung up a clothesline onto which they pegged artworks and poems printed on pillowcases, and handed out Xeroxed brochures. The laundromat was a gendered space that crossed class lines – one of the few sites at which poor mothers otherwise confined to the home could socialize. Supported by a

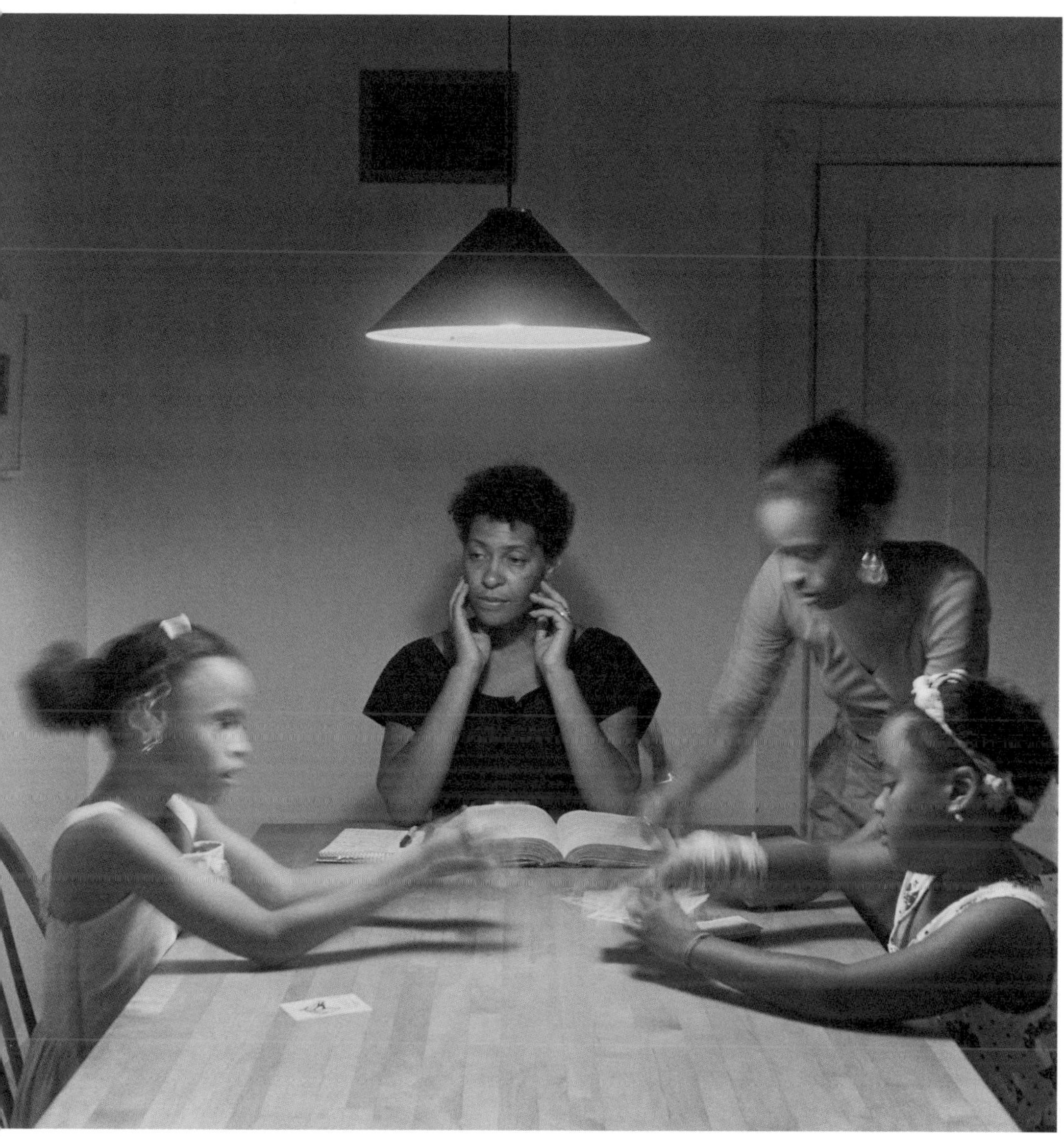

98

98.
Carrie Mae Weems,
Untitled, from *The
Kitchen Table Series*,
1990

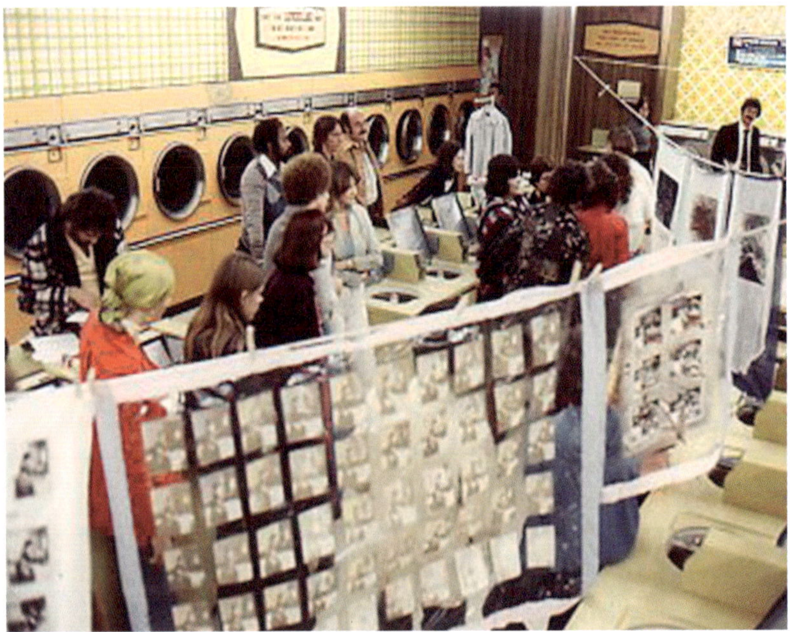

99

$700 grant from the California Arts Council, *Laundry Works* was cited as an example of waste in government spending by the then-governor of California, Ronald Reagan. The *Los Angeles Times* reported the Arts Council's hope of 'providing a little culture for housewives' under the headline 'Legislators Seek Ways to Cut Fat, Don't Have Far to Look', implying the very notion of programming art for those involved in reproductive labour was laughable.[23] The collective's response was *Mother Art Cleans Up*, in which they scrubbed the steps of City Hall and various local banks, directing attention to the real sites of waste.

•

At the Women's Art History Conference in London in 1975, artist Kate Walker stood up and asked who there made art on their kitchen table, between feeding the baby and doing the washing up? Su Richardson and Monica Ross answered her call.[24] The previous year, Walker had been a driving force behind *A Woman's Place* in South London – a collective dissection of the domestic realm within a squatted terraced house – as a creative response to the lack of space afforded art by women, as well as feminist art's pervasive problem with censorship. The exhibition laid into the heteronorms of family life. In Walker's contribution – *Death of a Housewife* – a female figure lay prone on the floor, surrounded by

99.
The Mother Art
Collective, *Laundry
Works*, 1977

100.
Feministo,
*Feministo:
Postal Art Event,
'A Portrait of
the Artist as a
Housewife'*, 1977

plastic baby dolls reaching their arms beseechingly: 'the mother lay, perhaps suffocated by the material excess of the home, but absolutely worn-out by housework.'[25] *A Woman's Place* addressed the domestic as *subject*. In looking to art made at the kitchen table, Walker turned to the domestic as *context*. Her encounter with Richardson and Ross, who had travelled to the conference from Birmingham, helped spark the *Postal Art Event* (1975–77) later known as *Feministo* **100**. A long-distance extension of consciousness-raising groups, the network connected over twenty artists who made works in snippets of available time and circulated

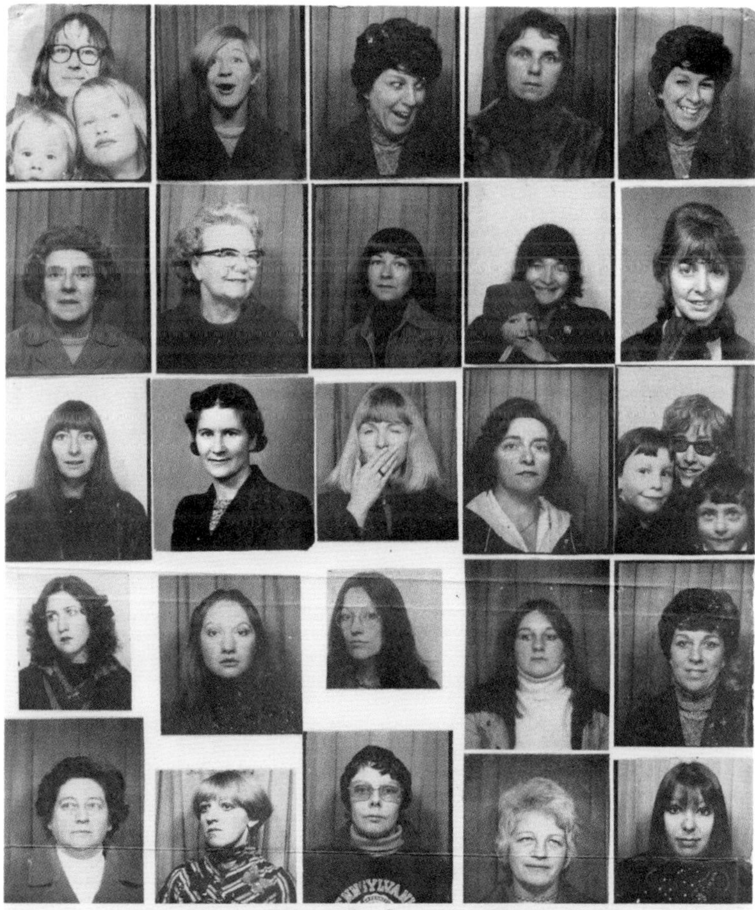

100

them by mail. They were diminutive – postcards, photo collages, knitting and crochet – and addressed intimate subjects including debt, exhaustion, food and sexuality. 'Most of the postal artwork was about relationships,' recalls Richardson. 'About the fact that once you were a mother you became a mother and nothing else. You're not seen as a person with a name.'[26]

Although made, shared, circulated and consumed in a domestic context, the postal artworks of *Feministo* were also exhibited. 'A Portrait of the Artist as a Housewife' (1977) commenced at London's ICA in an installation designed like a family home, with Richardson's irresistible crocheted *Burnt Breakfast* in the 'kitchen'. The show was reported in the feminist press and beyond, but as art historian Kathy Battista laments: 'What is particularly striking about *Feministo* is that much of the work has been lost. None of the work has gone into public collections that could preserve and archive such art…when art practice moves into the domestic space it is not valued, and clearly deemed unsuitable for a gallery or museum.'[27] As with Mother Art, members of *Feministo* became involved in wider political causes – including women's reproductive rights, the Campaign for Nuclear Disarmament, and the Greenham Common Women's Peace Camp. The kitchen table went from being a site of private making, to the production of political art and protest materials.

•

In 1987, the popular Mexican anchorman Guillermo Ochoa presented a segment of his prime time show *Nuestro Mundo* wearing a padded apron that made him appear heavily pregnant. Ochoa had been named *Mother for a Day* by the performance art duo Polvo de Gallina Negra **101**. On air they fed him pills to induce morning sickness and crowned him queen of the home. 'The audience immediately responded: the men were deeply offended, but the women enjoyed it.'[28] Formed in 1983 by Maris Bustamente and Mónica Mayer – recently returned from studies at The Women's Building – this was the first feminist art group in Mexico. Fierce, funny and ambitious, they adopted a name that offered potent protection. *Polvo de Gallina Negra* – Black Hen Powder – was a remedy to ward off the evil eye. Ochoa's baby bump was part of the long-running project *¡MADRES!* 'which literally means "mothers," but is also an expression that can be loosely translated as "Holy shit!"'[29] Launched when both artists were pregnant, *¡MADRES!* started as a postal art project, with seven monthly

101.
Polvo de Gallina Negra (Mónica Mayer and Maris Bustamante), *Madre por un día* (*Mother for a day*), 1987

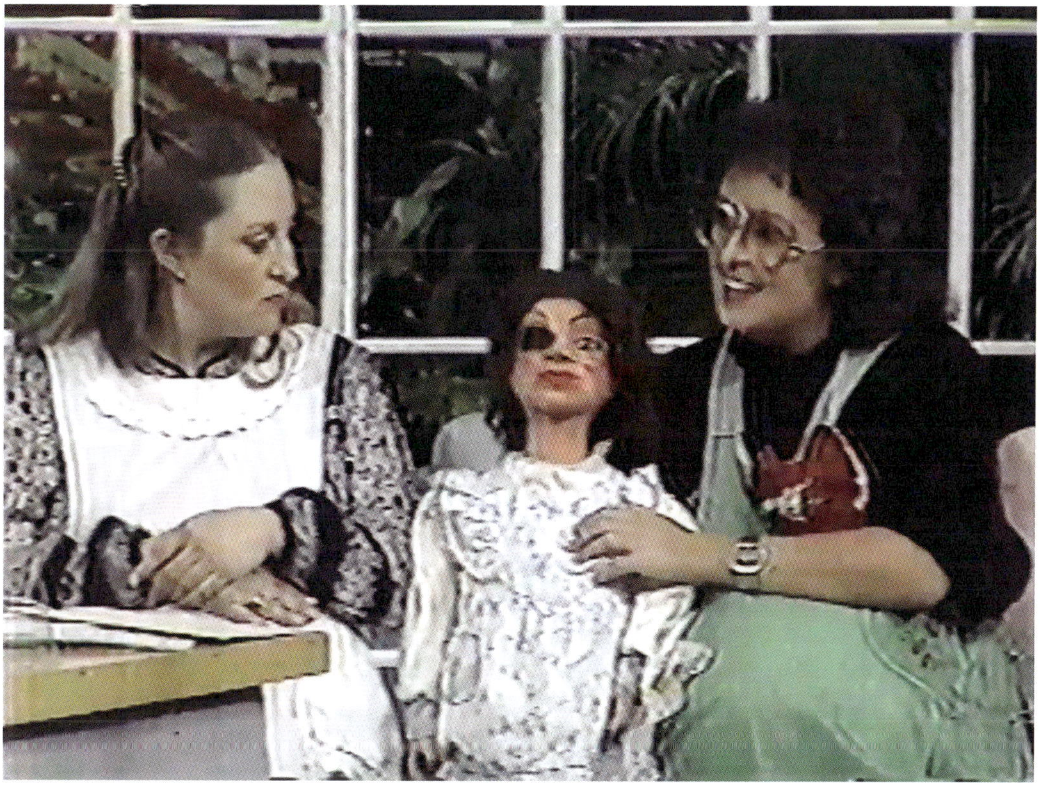

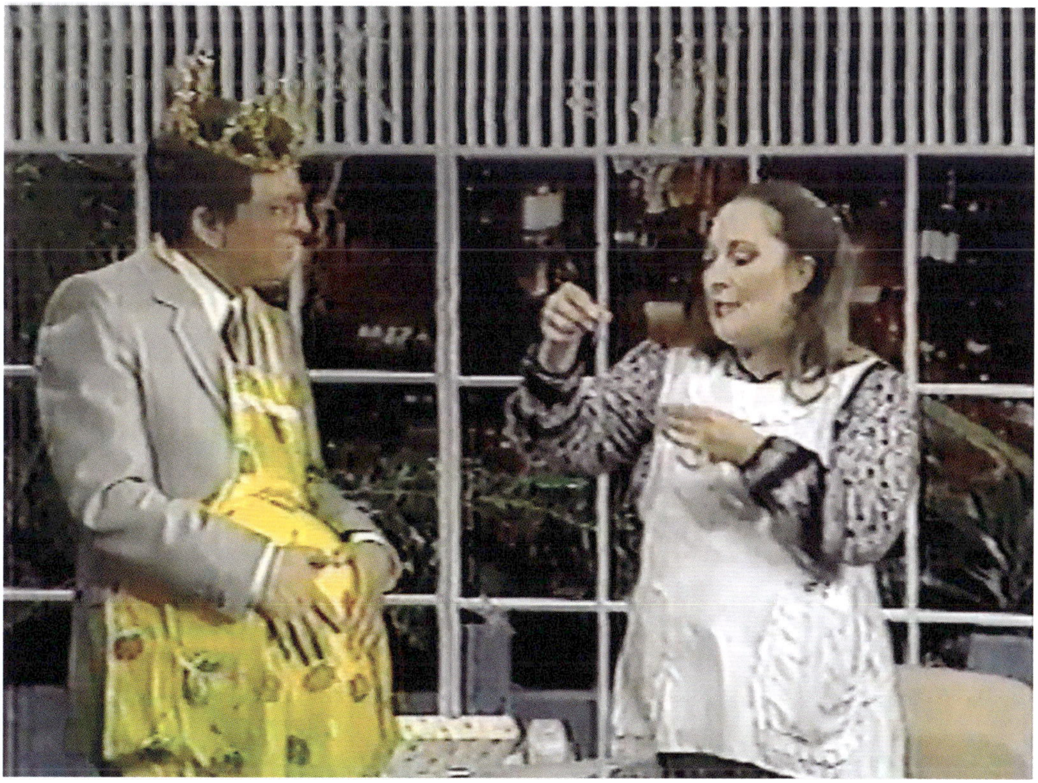

101

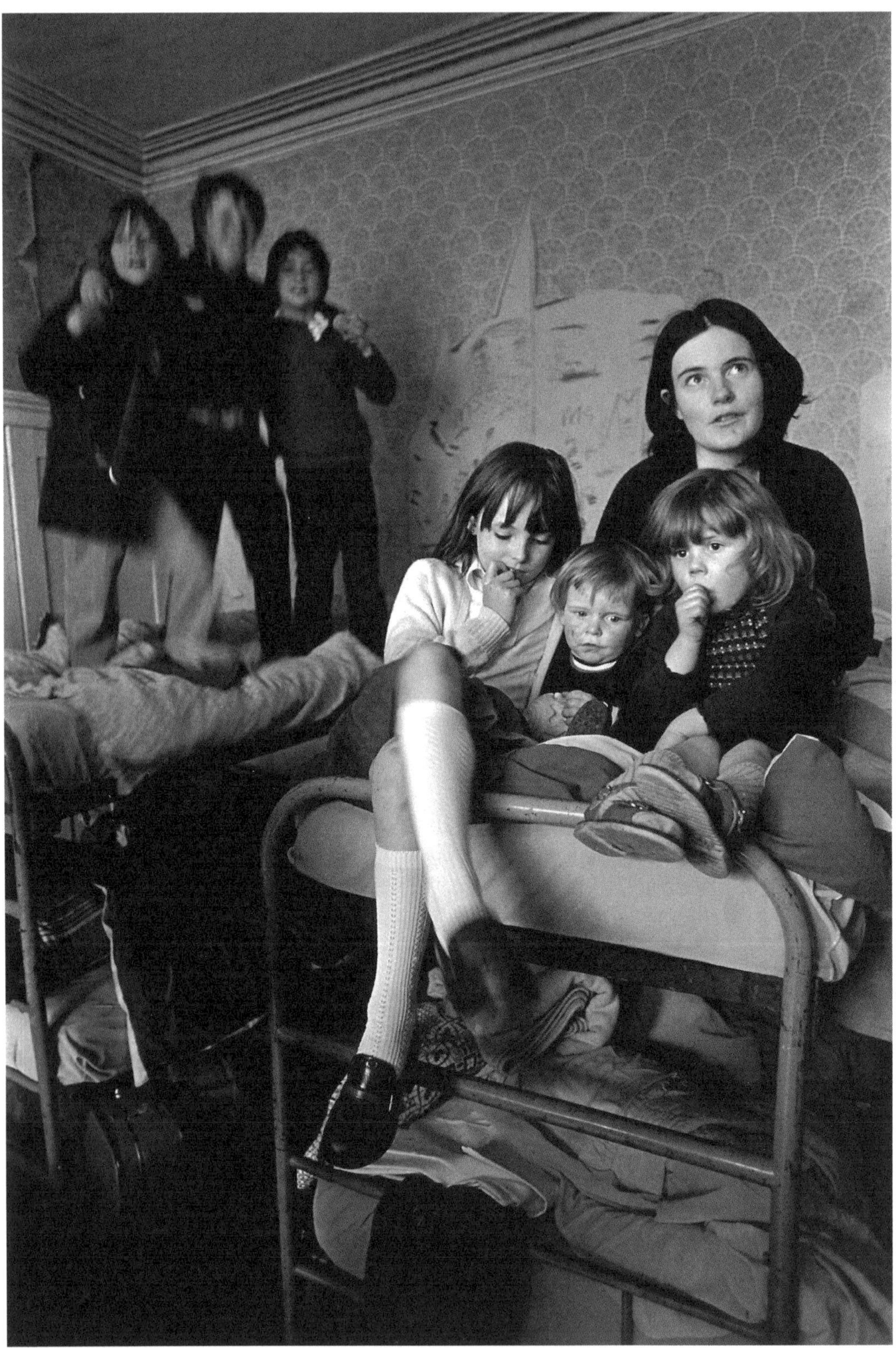

letters on issues including ambivalence, maternal mortality, clandestine abortions, depression and suicide sent. A competition invited people to submit a letter to their own mother expressing everything they wanted to tell her but were too afraid to. *Mother for a Day* aimed to 'show men the true and only road to authentic fatherhood by granting them the possibility of becoming Mother for a Day' – an honour they bestowed on six men, chosen 'for their intelligence, charisma, leadership and good looks'. During the final performance of *¡MADRES!* – for which Bustamente was pregnant again for real, she and Mayer announced that Polvo de Gallina Negra would become endogamous, with only their direct descendants entitled to join. As a political gesture, they constituted the collective a feminist art matriarchy.

the limits of protection

In this new world of consciousness-raising groups and collective action, subjects hitherto unmentionable were brought into public conversation. Black eyes, bruises and other evidence of domestic violence were conventionally ignored – abuse in the home was considered a private matter, not to be interfered with by police, the GP or church. In 1971, a woman came to a social centre set up by Erin Pizzey, lifted her jumper to show a body covered in boot-mark-shaped bruises and explained that no one would help her. Pizzey had grown up in an abusive family and understood the danger of her situation. She set up what became Britain's first refuge for battered women in Chiswick, placing discreet adverts in the papers inviting women to call if they needed help. Demand was overwhelming – within weeks eighteen women and forty-six children had moved into the small, terraced house, many arriving with appalling injuries, and only a few possessions crammed into black bin bags. So high was demand that Pizzey was forced to keep expanding, squatting properties when necessary, and eventually founding the nationwide charity Refuge.[30]

Christine Voge's photographs of the Chiswick Women's Refuge show great hardship **102**, but are overwhelmingly pictures of hope rather than misery. Occupants are crammed together, sleeping on bunkbeds and mattresses on the floor. 'There were women and children everywhere,' recalls Jenny Smith, who entered the refuge in 1973 with the youngest of her two children still a babe in arms. 'There were lengths of brown hessian hanging at the windows as curtains; mattresses snaked out of the bedrooms and up the hallways in any space that we could get them. It was a bit like a refugee camp, but it was wonderful...I cannot get away from the fact that Chiswick saved my life. You felt safe, you knew your children were safe; there was safety in numbers.'[31]

•

In the 21st century, surveillance is part of the parenting experience. CCTV has migrated into the home in the form of nanny cams and ever-smarter baby monitors. Night vision cameras have introduced a curious new aesthetic, in which the baby is observed as though the subject of a nature documentary or military operation. Whether this technology makes us more or less anxious as parents is a moot point. This apparently benign close circuit monitoring has been used to sinister effect in recent installations by artists including Ghislaine Leung. For her 2022 exhibition 'Balances' at the Maxwell Graham Gallery in New York,[32] Leung affixed baby gates to all thresholds and permitted access to works only during the two short days each week she could get to her studio. Monitors installed in the gallery broadcast images of the back rooms and offices: a reminder that as a modern parent your attention is inevitably split. Even on days allotted as studio time, the umbilical connection of surveillance binds you to your child, both ever present and not present.

•

There are limits to the protection parents can offer as children move into the world. In the US in particular, the territory of possible threat now extends to the school. A study of school shootings over the last five years shows rising incidents of gun violence on campus, to the extent that such incidents are, as the authors chillingly note, now 'relatively commonplace.'[33] In 2022, an eighteen-year-old entered the Robb Elementary School in Uvalde, Texas, killing two teachers and nineteen students. As a parent, the fear that your child will be caught up in a school shooting becomes part of your everyday – a threat against which you feel helpless. The Texas-based fibre artist Cassie Arnold was pregnant and teaching Middle School in 2012 at the time of the Sandy Hook school shooting. The massacre at Uvalde came on the last week of term for her two primary school-aged daughters. Arnold's *School Uniform (Bulletproof Dress)* (2022) **103** was knitted from Kevlar cord at the size of her daughter's tunics, as a way for Arnold to process the violent world her children inhabited. Intended as a satirical gesture, it soon felt uncomfortably close to real proposals in the wake of Uvalde, which included 'police shields. Bulletproof objects and backpacks for children. Vests for elementary kids in the classroom. Military personnel and single entrances for all schools.'[34] Although not, crucially, tighter legislation on gun ownership.

•

In the UK, you are more than five times more likely to be issued a stop and search warrant by police if you are Black than if you are white.[35] The highest rate is for males aged fifteen to nineteen.[36] In other words, if you are a Black teenage boy, you are very likely to be subjected to a 'stop and search' by the police. Barbara Walker's series *Louder Than Words* (2006–9) **104** uses

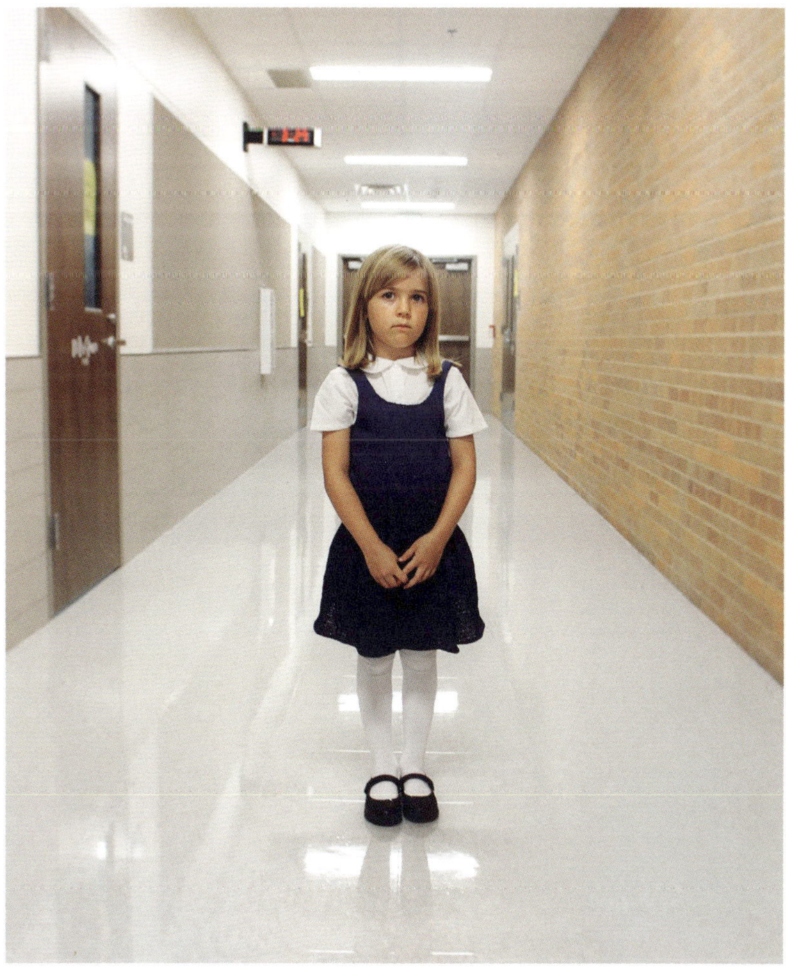

* Delete as Appropriate   WEST MIDLANDS POLICE
Search Record of Person/Vehicle/Stop Form   Ref
✓ AS APPROPRIATE
PACE   Ss.1-3 PACE 1984
DRUGS   S.23 Misuse of Drugs Act 1971
FIREARMS   S.47 Firearms Act 1968
POT   S. 13A   Prevention of Terrorism (Temporary Provisions) Act 1989
         S. 13A
CJA
CONSENT
STOP ONLY
Name (First
Address
Sex   M/F
Search/St
Search/St
Object
Grounds
Driver/Passe
VRM
Is Registered
Damage Caused
Details/Other
Arrested? Y/N*   Offence
Identity Group
Accompanied: Y/N*
1. Search/Stop* (Officers' Rank/No./Name/Station. In terrorist cases use Personal No. only)
.......(if required, cont. overleaf)
Signature
Supplied on (date)
Supplied by   Post/Personally*

scans of the police dockets issued to her son Solomon following many such incidents. On some dockets are painted sepia views of Birmingham, the areas in which Solomon had unwittingly become the subject of police scrutiny. On others Walker has drawn her son's face, studying this young man, trying to see what the police saw that she can't. As Eddie Chambers has written: 'What does one who is seen as a danger to society look like?... what are the consequences and implications of living in a world in which an individual such as Solomon is often judged by others (particularly those with power and in power) by the way they look, rather than by what or who they actually are.'[37] Thinking about Walker's experience as the mother of a Black teenage boy, I recall a distinction Jennifer Nash draws. 'The mainstream (white) maternal memoir is fundamentally about ambivalence – about the unwanted or partially wanted child, or about the changes... of self that a child can generate for a mother,' writes Nash. 'But the space for Black maternal ambivalence culturally is about the anticipated death of the Black child, particularly the Black son'.[38]

family romance

Emma Talbot has earwormed me, and I may never forgive her. A great double-sided painting on silk that hangs from a rod as though riding a trapeze, *The Mountain, Time after Time* (2016) **105** shows episodes from a mother's life with her son. From a raised hospital bed, she reaches toward a new-born in his plastic cot. A pool of light surrounds them as she breastfeeds in bed. They walk up the steps to their home, hand in tiny hand. In the centre of the front panel, we see him ascending swiftly, a blur of arms, up a climbing wall, as if he were scaling the silk itself like a cat up a curtain. As in many of this London-based artist's works, the faces are blank. We don't see our own face in our memories, and this is a work rooted in hers. It also invites us to project onto the figures as totems of the single mother/son experience. Lozenges of text carry Talbot's personal reflections and lyrics from Cyndi Lauper's love song *Time After Time* (1983). While the pictures illustrate a deep bond, the text expresses the limits of that connection – the things beyond a mother's influence, the point at which she must step back and watch her child make his own way. Lauper's ballad of growing up and moving on here becomes an expression of love from a mother to a child as he climbs out of her arms and into the world. *Time After Time* was a slow dance stalwart during Talbot's own teenage years. Here, it soundtracks

104.
Barbara Walker,
Untitled from the
Louder than Words
series, 2006–9

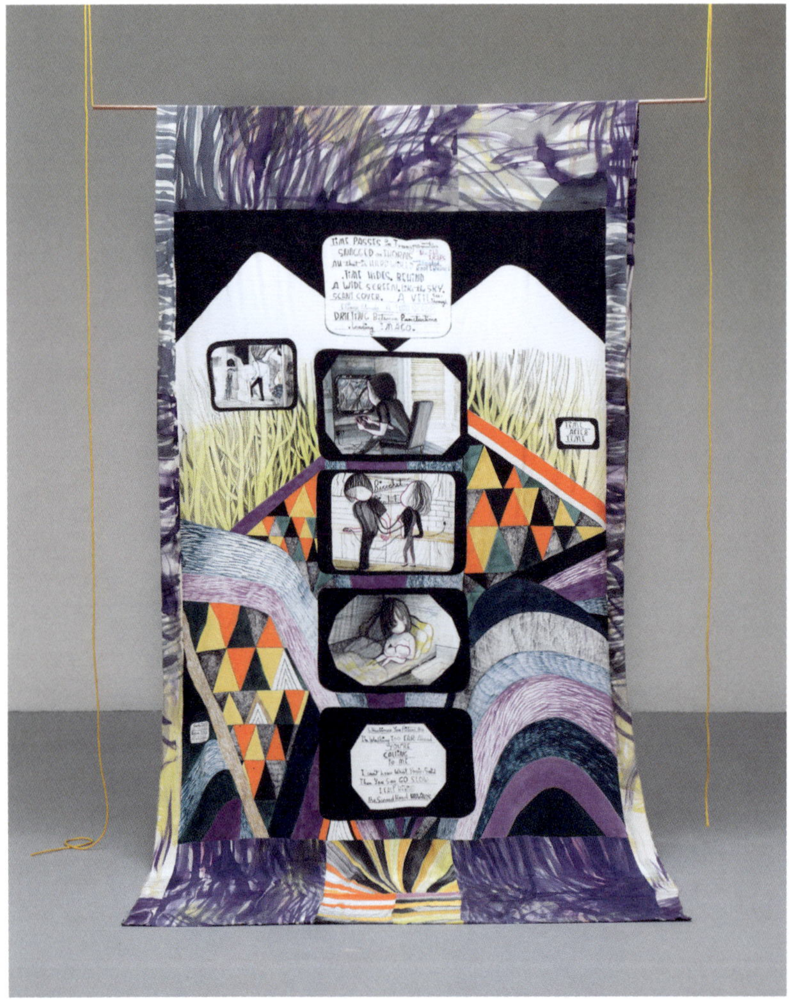

105.
Emma Talbot,
*The Mountain,
Time After
Time*, 2016

105

the deep and transforming relationship between parent and child
while acknowledging its limits and imperfections. Parenting is a
romance, one that carries its share of heartache.

•

I have written elsewhere on the ethics of parents featuring children
in their art, and in particular the work of Sally Mann.[39] I will not
revisit this territory, save to note my feeling that for a parent to
forbid themself from making or showing work featuring the children
who dominate their life and thoughts feels a perverse sort of cruelty
and a contemporary form of the competitive purity and calls to
self-sacrifice that have dogged the maternal experience since we
were first invited to compares ourselves to the Virgin Mary. Instead,

I would like to look at Mann's *Family Pictures* (1984–92) through this lens of maternal romance. Mann first started making work featuring her children in 1984, with a portrait of her daughter Jessie's face swollen with insect bites. The title of that work – *Damaged Child* – for me acknowledges the terrifying perfection and grace of young children, and our fear, as parents, of their suffering damage. 'I realized the image inoculated me to a possible reality that I might not henceforth have to suffer,' Mann has written in retrospect of the image.[40] To those who adore their children, these small creatures seem impossibly perfect. Mann documented her children at play and in moments of vulnerability on the family farm in Lexington, Virginia. There is an uncanny glamour to the photos. They pull us into the child's world of imagination that is in turn reminiscent of the hazy dreamland created by Julia Margaret Cameron over a century before. In *Emmett's Bloody Nose* **106**, Mann's young son has the calm heroism of a warrior after battle – you can sense her interest in the pattern of blood lacing his milk-clear skin. That Mann's work has been so wilfully misread is some indication of how tricky this territory is. I would like to invite an understanding of the maternal – or parental gaze – as one that can be idealizing, adoring and romanticizing of the child.

between art and life

Mann's family photographs are edited, arranged with a point of view. Yet, as the British feminist photographer Jo Spence argued, all family photo albums are selective. Spence's photographic memoir *Beyond The Family Album* (1978–79) addressed things left undocumented, and acknowledged the internal editing we learn even as young children, presenting ourselves to the camera in a conventionally appealing manner. Can there be such a thing as a truthful family album? Perhaps the answer is to participate more consciously: to understand the construction of the image as it is being made.

The ongoing *Regard* series (2015–) **107** by Anna Grevenitis has been created with her daughter Luigia: a portrait of the evolving relationship between a mother and daughter as she moves from childhood through her teenage years. They photographs are often humorous, with the French-born artist feigning an exploitative relationship with her daughter, who is seen giving a pedicure, or ironing while Grevenitis lounges eating macarons. Like many young girls, Luigia is fascinated by the beauty rituals that betoken adulthood – we see the pair applying mascara in

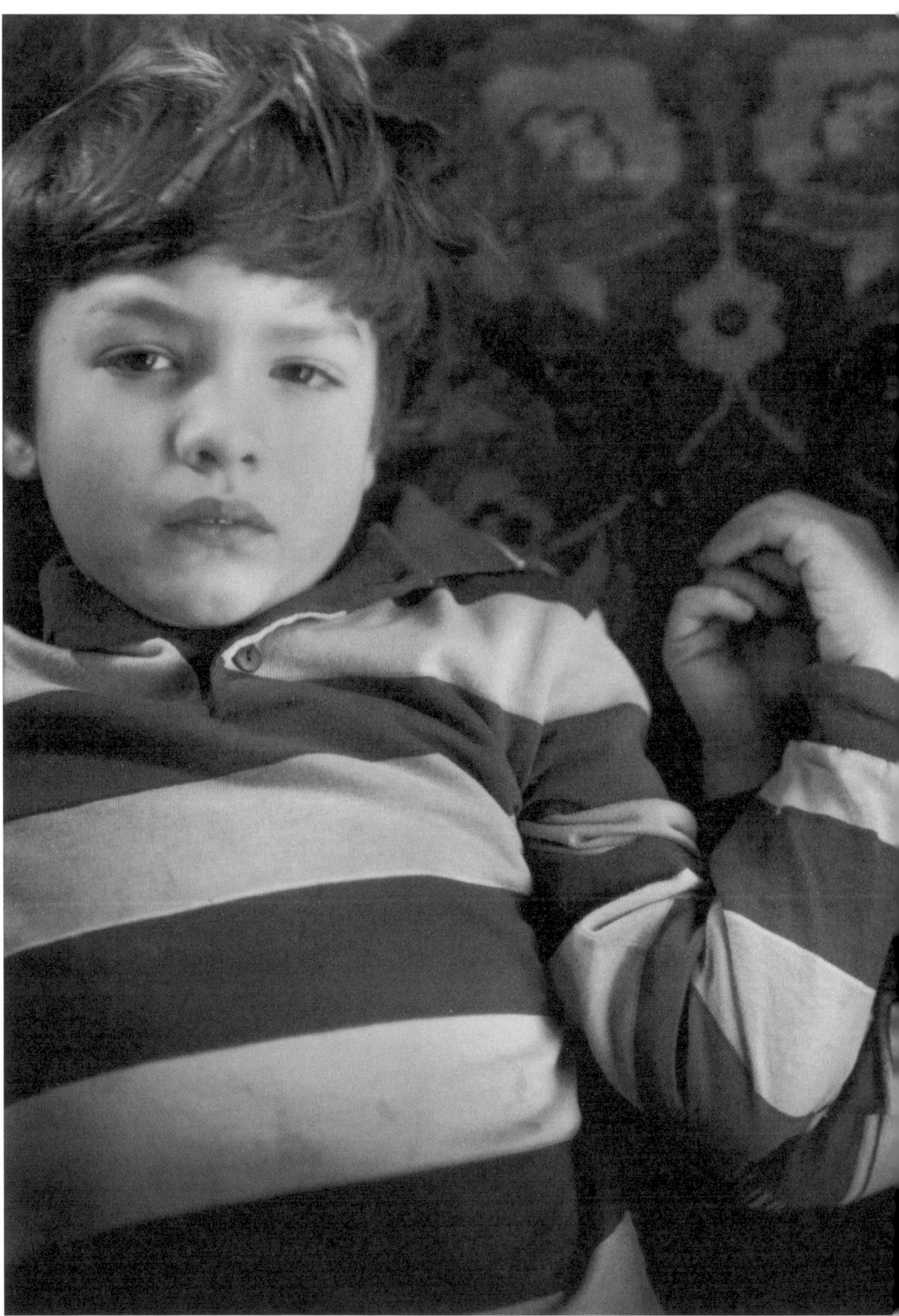

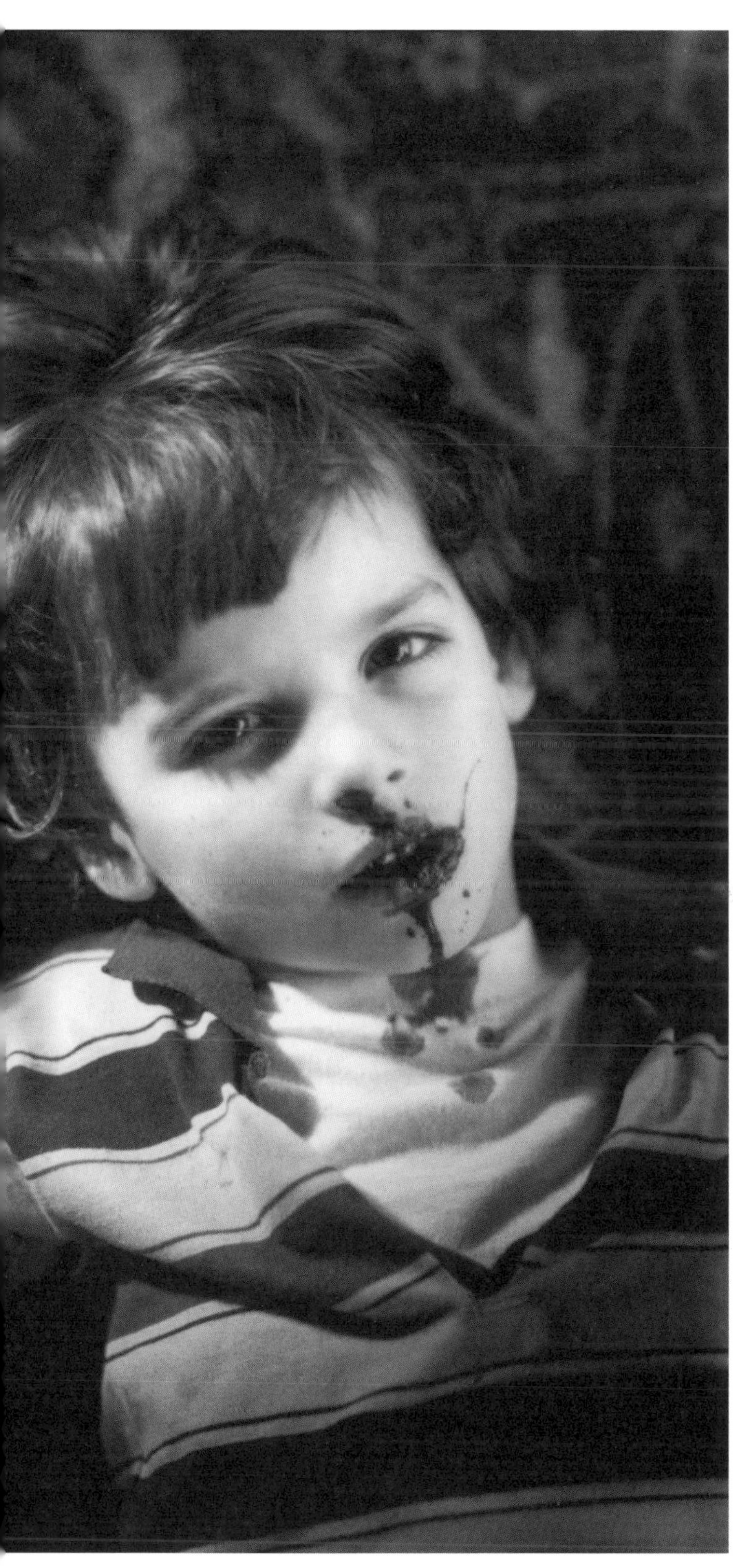

106.
Sally Mann,
*Emmett's Bloody
Nose*, 1985

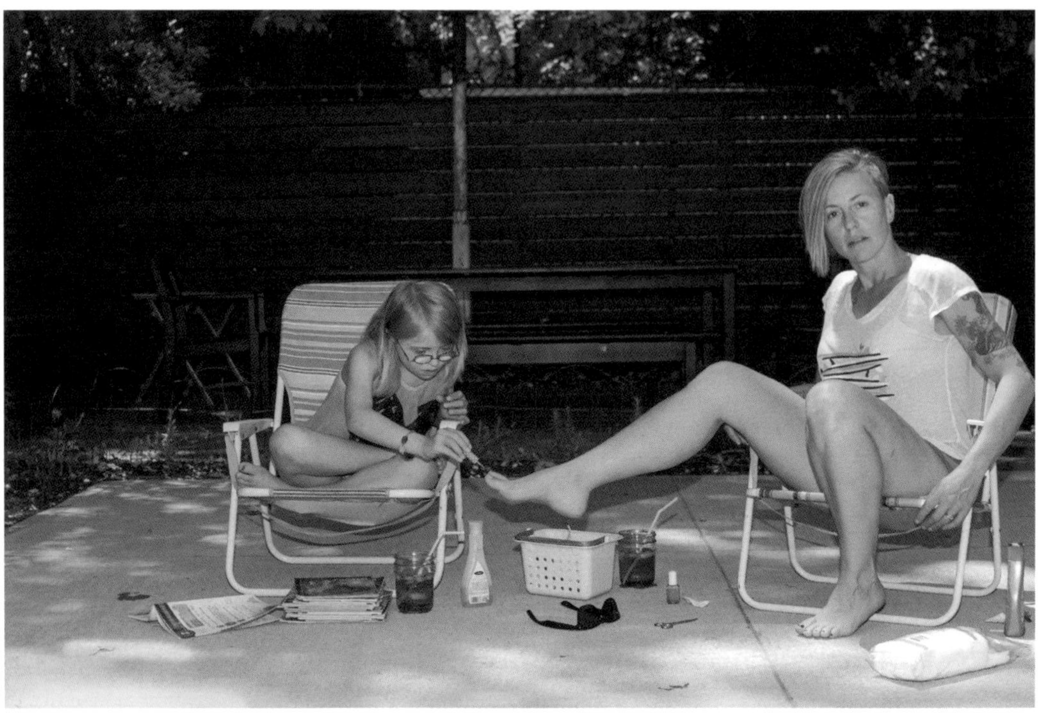

107

adjacent mirrors, and Grevenitis working dye into her daughter's long hair. Some photos feel more candid than others: we see Luigia upset, enfolded in a maternal embrace, or laughing as she tries on her mother's shoes. They have the vibe of family snapshots yet they are not, for in each, Grevenitis gazes at the viewer, deliberately and quizzically. This is the 'regard' of the work's title. Luigia has Down syndrome, and Grevenitis describes how their ordinary routine is punctuated by 'people staring, gawking, or side-glancing at her, at us. Even though their gaze feels invasive, I perceive it as more questioning than judging, at least most of the time.'[41] Grevenitis's stare is pre-emptive, but also protective. The 'honesty' of these photographs lies not in their carefully staged scenarios, but in the humour, vulnerability and ferocity that binds them.

To collaborate on works of self-portraiture gives a child a degree of agency. It also forcibly introduces personal life into the impersonal sanctuary of the gallery: not only is this artist a parent, but the act of making art cannot be cleanly separated from the boundless work of childcare. It is a rather different gesture for an artist to collaborate with their young child on the production of a painting or sculpture. Small children are not represented by commercial galleries. Their art is, by and large, not contemporaneously collected by major museums. The art of young children is not intentional, professional or trained, and while it may be envied for its untutored spontaneity by artists who are, it is a thing apart. For a celebrated artist to collaborate on a series of paintings with a child introduces interesting ambiguities into the art gallery.

Underground (1995) **108** is a grid of twenty-eight large inky painted heads by Marlene Dumas, each 'decorated, improved and worked on' by her daughter Helena, then aged six. Derived from photographic source material, the paintings before their adaptation relate to those in Dumas's *Models* (1994). The artist admits that she allowed Helena to play with them so that she 'could do other work'. *Underground* started, then, as a distraction offered by a busy mother buying herself studio time. Helena found the ink drawings 'a bit too boring' and introduced vivid colour and a set of fantastical narratives. 'She "re-casted" my models into her own stories. One was kidnapped, she said, and walked into a horse,' Dumas wrote of the series, when it was shown at the Tate gallery in London in 1996. 'Helena said: "It's easier to draw sick people. You give them a wound, you make them cry, and then you give them a Band-Aid".'[42]

Helena makes the portraits monstrous, comic and grotesque. In some she deploys the language of the primary school art room, drawing around her left hand then colouring it in. In others she embellishes faces as we might a photograph in a newspaper, adding earrings, hairpins, lipstick, tears and demonic eyeballs. One face indeed carries a Band-Aid on its forehead from which dribbles green droplets of blood – snot also oozes from its nose. Helena claims authorship of the works, writing her name on two of the pictures in red paint as though it were being spoken. While equally monumental, *Underground* has a very different presence to the neat black-and-white grids of *Models*: it is jittery, broken-up and garish. A little disturbing. The work has not entered the commercial artworld – it remains in Dumas's possession – but was exhibited in her glorious one-woman show at the Palazzo Grassi, Venice in 2022. The year before *Underground*, Dumas painted the work that opens this book – *The Painter* (1994). That work explicitly links the activities of mother and daughter – it could even be seen as a self-portrait – suggesting child's artmaking as a serious enterprise. Like her mother, Helena was learning about the behaviour of materials, making sense of the world, responding to colour. In *Underground*, Dumas is the supporting layer that allows her daughter to express herself, not separate, but part of a continuum.

107.
Anne Grevenitis,
May 25 2015, from
the *Regard* series,
2015–2020

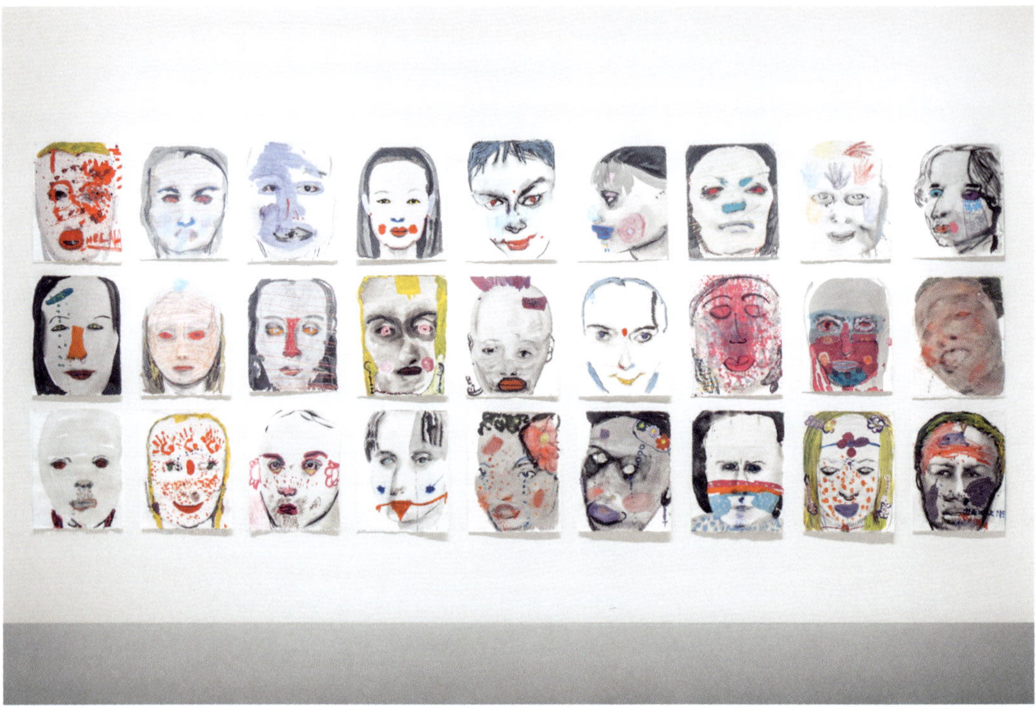

108

108.
Marlene Dumas
(in collaboration
with her
daughter Helena),
Underground,
1994–95

109.
Zineb Sedira,
Mother Tongue,
2002

110.
Daphne Wright,
*I Know What It's
Like*, 2021

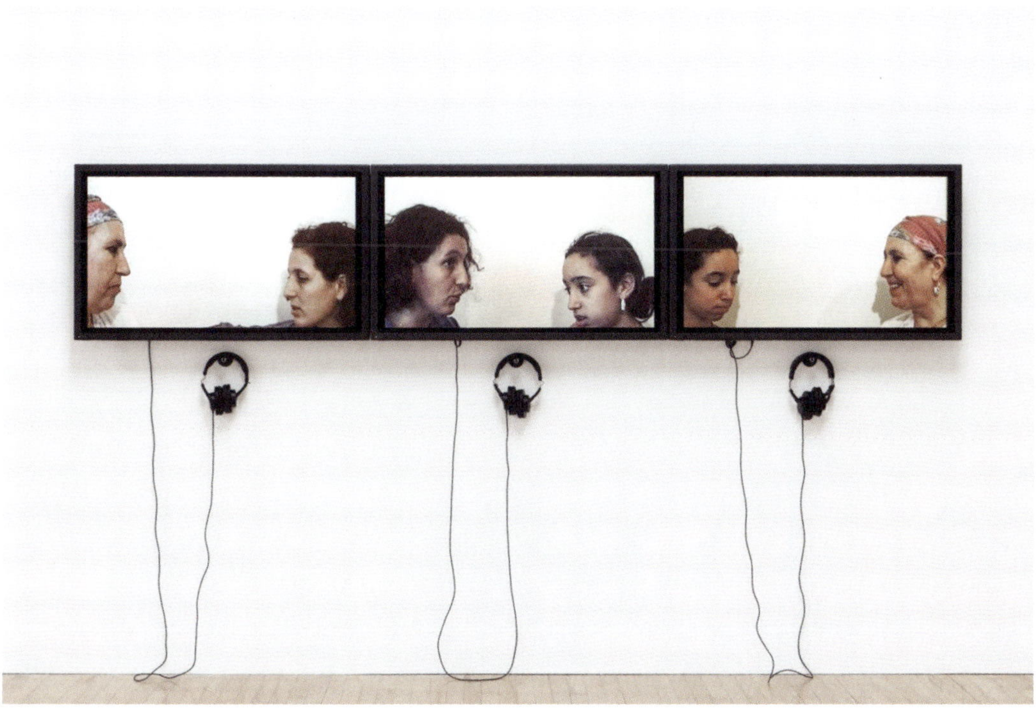

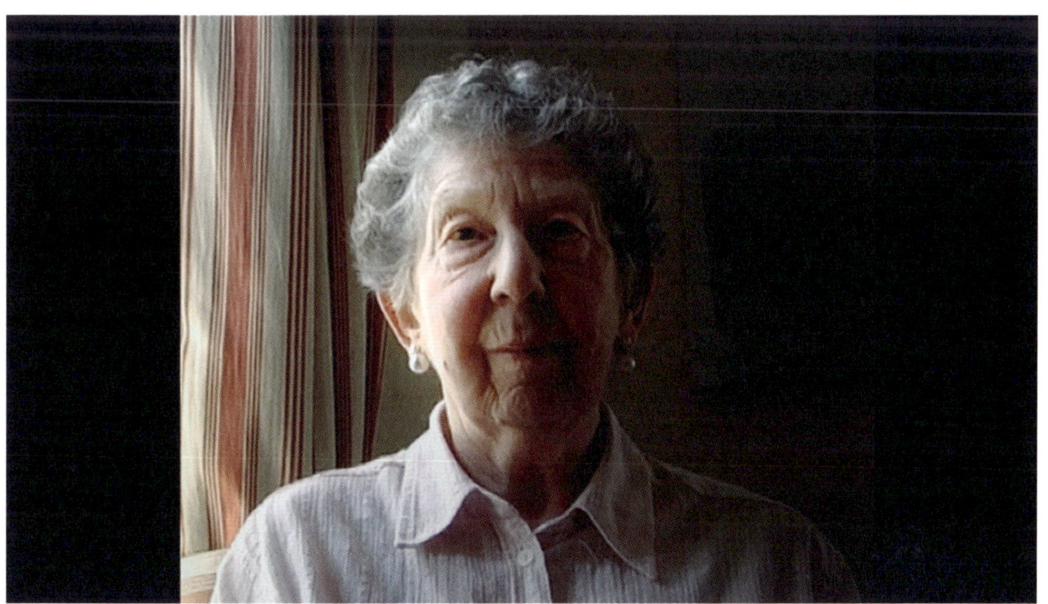

109

110

mother tongues

In her essay *Notes on Mother Tongues* (2020) Mirene Arsanios addresses the question of how to speak as a mother without a mother tongue. 'Some might say my language is French, but I would dispute that,' she writes. 'My language doesn't have a dominant language. Having many languages is like having many selves. My language often feels dispersed. She hesitates before she speaks. In what language will she tell her son his story?'[43] Arsanios spoke Spanish to her Venezuelan grandmother, and Arabic on the streets of Lebanon, was educated in French at the lycée in Beirut, acquired Italian from an Eritrean boyfriend and picked up English like an airborne virus. The choice of language is not neutral. She doesn't want to speak English with her son, because she wants him to know 'that English isn't the only language.' In her Francophone education she tastes the imperial aspirations of the global lycée system, and its drive to 'civilize' the tongue. She quotes theorist Frantz Fanon: 'A man who has a language consequently possesses the world expressed and implied by that language.'[44] For Fanon, the language of a colonized people carried the internalized inferiority complex imposed by the 'civilizing' nation. Our languages connect to our histories, they carry cultural memory. Which ties, then, do you opt to carry into the future as a polyglot speaking to your child?

In Zineb Sedira's *Mother Tongue* (2002) **109**, the artist, her mother and daughter appear in conversation across three screens. We hear them simultaneously: breaks in the discourse are not evident until we focus on individual screens. In the first, Sedira and her mother recall the routine of schooldays with the former speaking French (the language of her Paris childhood) and the latter Arabic (the language of her mother country, Algeria). In the middle screen, Sedira has a similar conversation with her daughter, who has been raised in London, and answers her mother's French with English. In the third screen, grandmother faces granddaughter, but the questions – Arabic from one side, English on the other – go unanswered. A cultural tie has been severed. Sedira – the linking point between the three generations with their three languages – is behind the camera, and remains silent, despite an appeal from her mother. 'I always believed that politics can be better engaged with through the personal – through voice and human experience,' Sedira has said. *Mother Tongue* was made at the end of the Algerian Civil War, after her parents' return to their mother country. It marked a turning point in the artist's relationship with her Algerian roots, stimulating her interest in the 'obliteration of minorities and stories of the past' and the political implications of language.[45] *Mother Tongue* presents the artist sandwiched between generations – mother to a growing child, daughter to an ageing mother. It is a position that can represent a doubling of care and concern. The easing of parental duties often coincides with the diminishing health of the older generation, and a shift in focus from providing care as a mother to providing care as a daughter.

Daphne Wright's *I Know What It's Like* (2012) **110** marks this circularity through language. As a sculptor, Wright is interested in everyday objects that carry the suggestion of personal history and emotion. Her knack for the uncanny carries into video works, often developed over long periods with professional actors. In *I Know What It's Like* an older woman (the actress Pameli Benham) is lit in a domestic chiaroscuro, with grey daylight filtering past a jolly striped curtain. The camera is still, as is Benham's gaze. She speaks in broken phrases – memories of breastfeeding a baby that give way to fragments suggesting a capacity for violence in lines lifted from Lady Macbeth ('…while it was smiling in my face, Have plucked my nipple from his boneless gums…'). Between these phrases, Benham makes strange sounds, articulated with the precision of an actor's vocal exercise: 'qua' 'mau' 'va'. As the film proceeds, she becomes less able to complete the lines of text, allowing them to fall into silence. Wright brings together two fragmented forms of expression, one linked to her role as a mother, the other to her role as a daughter. The strange, isolated sounds voiced by Benham are phonic blocks used by Wright's children as they learned to read. The incomplete phrasing was derived from the lossy pronouncements of Alzheimer's patients, signalling the ebbing of her own mother's capacity to communicate. The work is bound by the assertion of memory – 'I know how it feels' – as a woman towards the end of her life remembers the early weeks of motherhood, the arrival of new life and her experience of ambivalence. All these decades later, she is still a mother.

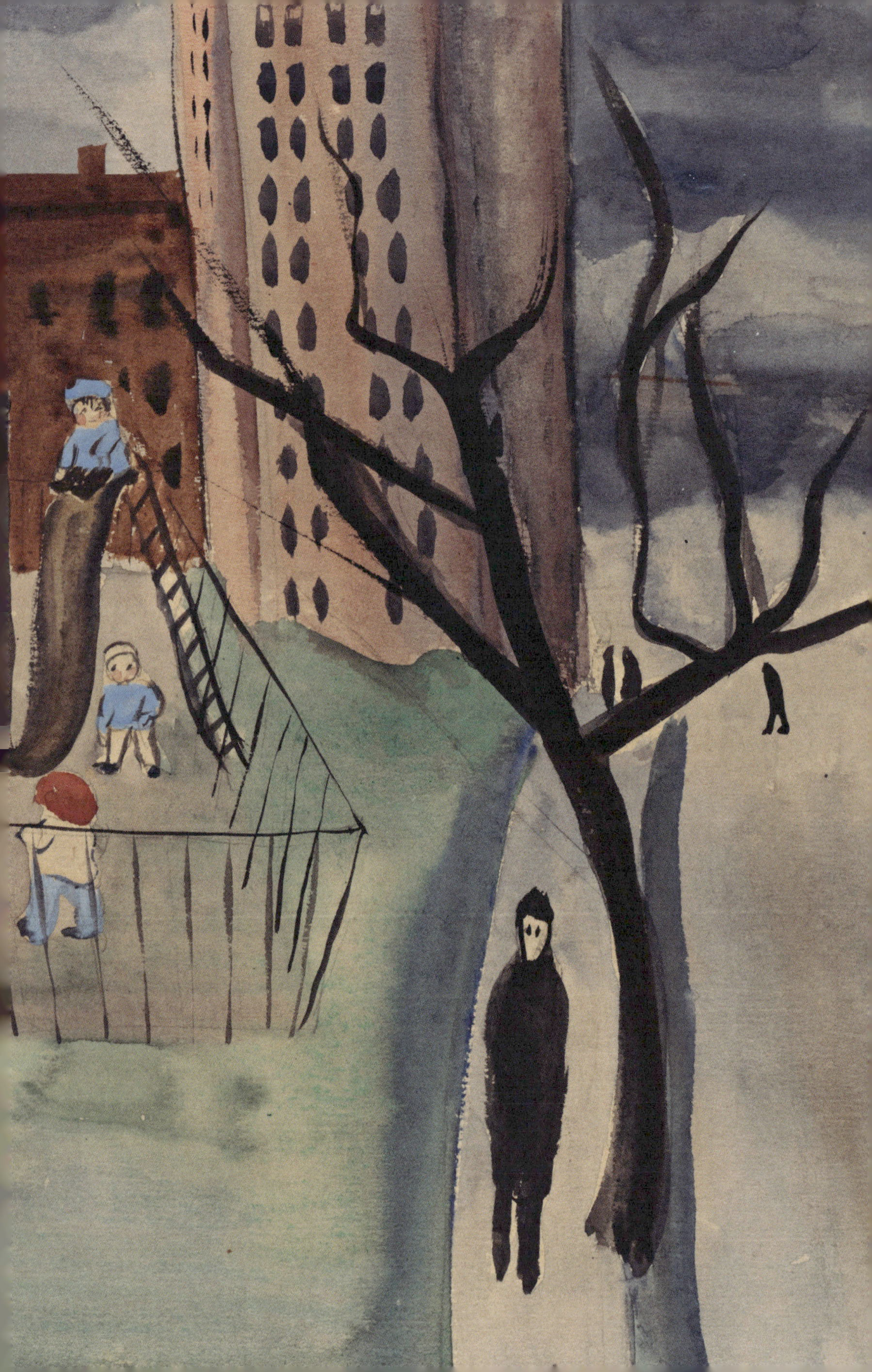

loss

Living in Istanbul with a toddler my nights were punctuated by visions of him sliding into a brief wave-sucked yawn opened between the sea wall of the Bosporus and a tethered barge, and watching him plunge into the wet blackness as the current slammed the boat back against the quayside. The death of a child is the actual stuff of nightmares. This is the chapter you don't want to read. It addresses the unspeakable in the realm of motherhood. This is the chapter I didn't want to write, so I have gathered a polyphony of voices to help speak about the unspeakable.

No one will be untouched by maternal loss, whether personally or at one remove. One in eight known pregnancies end in miscarriage. One in every two hundred pregnancies in stillbirth. In the US, the average infant mortality rate is 5.4 deaths per 1000 live births – 10.6 per 1000 for the babies of African-American women.[1]

Loss is an experience that can feel outside art's territory, too raw and relentless to impose considerations of style or form onto. *Blue Nights* (2011) – Joan Didion's memoir mourning her daughter Quintana Roo, who died aged thirty-nine – is fretted with Didion's awareness of her own frailty and limitations. There is a hollowness to the book that represented not only the absence of Quintana Roo, but this cool stylist's sense of futility. This was an exercise she had set herself – for what else is a memoirist to do in the wake of insupportable tragedy? Yet there is also a curious sense of inevitability to this mother's experience of grief, anticipated across a lifetime: 'Once she was born I was never not afraid.'[2]

I address loss here in an expanded sense, acknowledging the grief that accompanies miscarriage, stillbirth, failed IVF, absolute infertility, adoption, and obstetric violence. The losses encompassed by this chapter also include the loss of reproductive

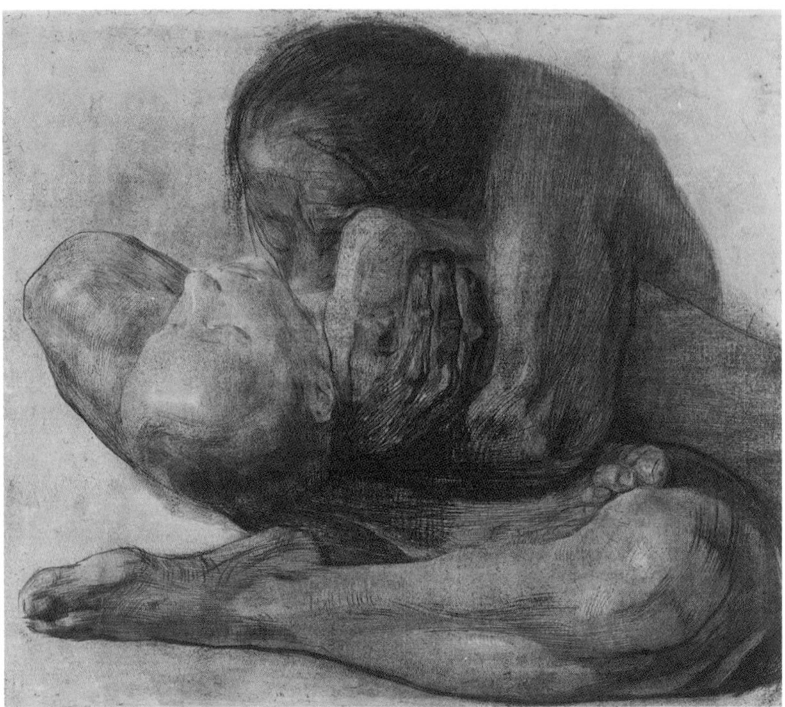

111

rights. It concludes with a bittersweet celebration: of art made to protest repressive abortion legislation and in defence of women's right to choose.

•

an altered condition of life

One of the most powerful and affecting evocations of maternal grief – Käthe Kollwitz's *Woman with Dead Child* (1903) **111** – is a work of empathy rather than autobiography. The composition was planned for her *Peasants' War* cycle – images of 16th-century labourers pushed to the brink as they work the land and fight for liberty. Instead, Kollwitz translated the composition into a stand-alone work, using herself as the model for the mother – naked and animal in her grief – posed in the mirror with her seven-year-old son Peter. The mother's body is folded deeply around the child, as though she is consuming it. She pulls the flesh that was once her flesh so close that the boundaries between the two bodies blur as the mother buries her contorted face into the chest of her dead son. While Kollwitz was not drawing on first-hand experience of maternal bereavement, the deaths of children weighed heavily on her. She was haunted by her baby brother Benjamin's death to meningitis and the culpability she felt about erecting a little temple to Venus with her nursery bricks. Was Benjamin's death divine punishment for her rejection of God? Kollwitz's husband Karl was a physician in a working class neighbourhood of Berlin. She observed infant and maternal mortality, violent abuse and desperate want at close quarters, and felt a duty to bear witness in her work. Death – of the child and of the mother – was a persistent theme for Kollwitz. Frequently, death appears personified, skin clinging to his writhing bones. We see him wrestle a mother to the ground or insert a long skeletal finger around a slumbering baby to rip it from the maternal breast. In these works, art historian Dorothy Price identifies a 'uniquely liminal space, peculiar to Kollwitz, between symbolism and social commentary'.[3] There was a grotesque prescience to *Woman with Dead Child*. Eleven years later, at the start of the First World War, Peter died in Flanders, aged only nineteen. 'I asked mother where she got the image of the mother with her dead child from – years before the war – which featured in almost all her pictures from that period,' her older son Hans wrote, many years later. 'She thought she foresaw Peter's death even then. She said she had been crying while working on these images.'[4]

•

In *Time Lived, Without its Flow* (2012), the poet Denise Riley describes the sensation of living in 'suddenly arrested time' following the death of her son. 'Hard to put into words, yet absolutely lucid as you inhabit it daily, this sensation of having been lifted clean out of habitual time only becomes a trial if you attempt to make it intelligible to others who've not experienced it,'[5] she writes, describing the prospect of giving written form to her experience as 'repugnant' over two-and-a-half years after her son's death. Compounding this insufficiency of words was a failure of vocabulary: in English, you can be a widow or orphan, but there is no word for the parent who outlives their child.

Similar isolation – suspended outside time and held separate from the world of the living – marks Alice Neel's *After the Death of the Child* (1927–28) **112**. In Chapter 4 we encountered Neel in the 1930s in Spanish Harlem. This small painting touches on the tragedy that preceded that phase of her life. Neel's first daughter Santillana died of diphtheria in December 1927, a month before her first birthday. Neel paints herself as a thin dark-clad figure, blank faced and huddled on a winter streetscape. A skeletal

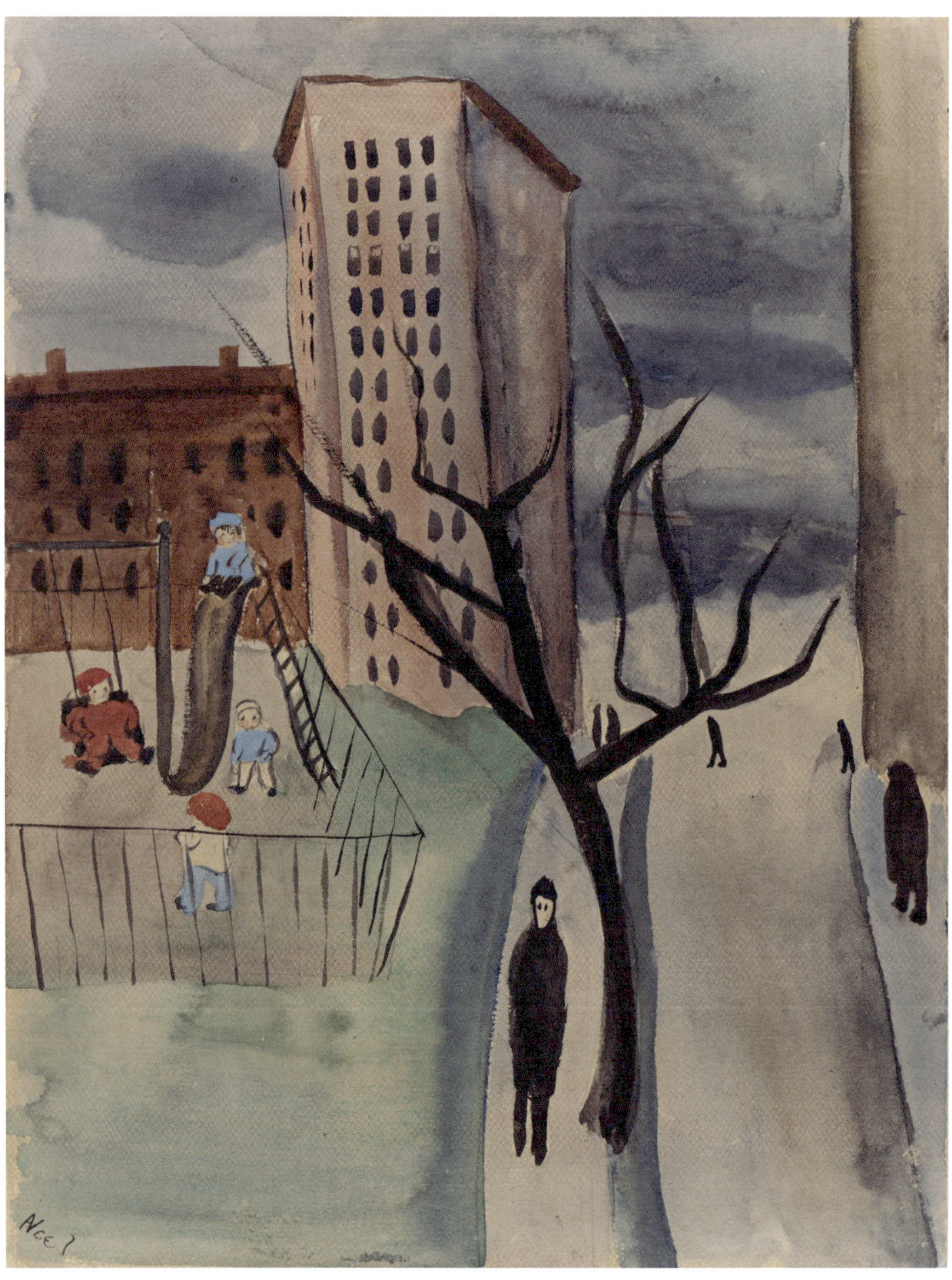

112

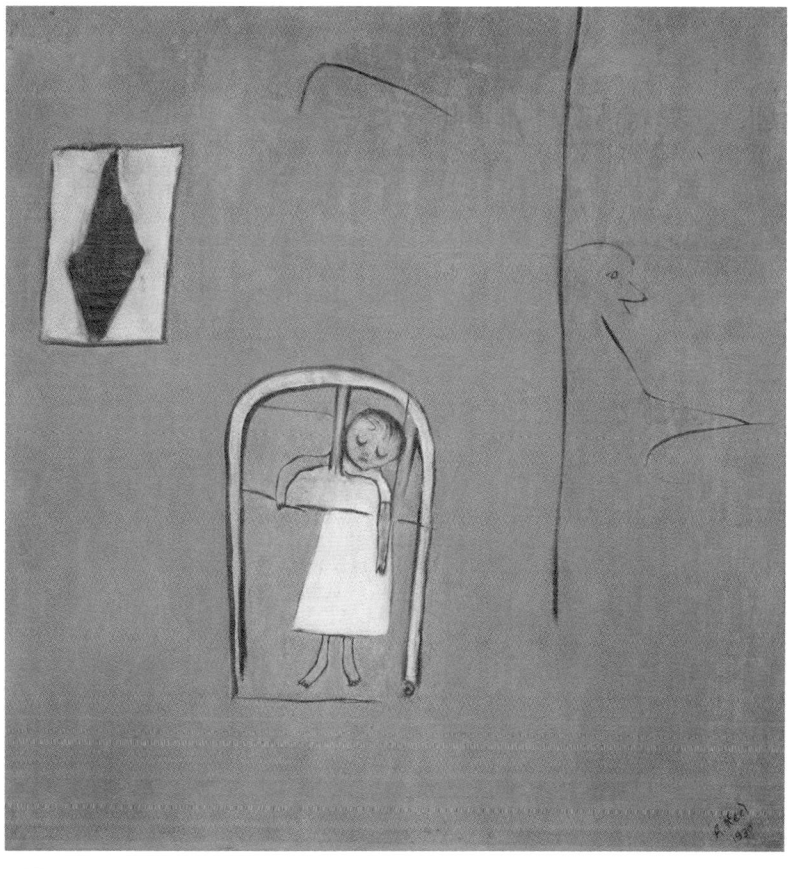

113

black tree looms over her, containing her body in a pointed arc, keeping her apart from the New York street life around her. To her right, in a separate world of bright colours and rounded figures, is a fenced playground in which small children swing and slide. Her head tilts towards it just slightly, but she has already walked beyond – the playground now occupies that other life that she may no longer enter.

In May 1930, Neel's husband Carlos Enríquez abandoned her and took the couple's second daughter Isabetta back with him to Cuba. Neel had a breakdown. There followed a year of on-off hospitalization, including time on the grim 'suicidal ward' of Philadelphia General Hospital. The ward was populated by women discarded by society – ill, old, mourning, desperate – under the autocratic rule of male doctors and their compliant nursing teams. Neel drew the ward and its inmates from memory after returning home in September 1931. It was in this broken year that Neel painted the withdrawn and desperate *Futility of Effort* (1930) **113**, inspired (if one can use such a word) by a story of a child that choked in their crib while their mother was ironing in the kitchen. It is a stark grey canvas, near empty but for a curtained window onto darkness, and a white cot from which a grey-faced infant is suspended, their head trapped between its bars. Neel created a public image of a hidden tragedy, giving form to private grief that felt unspeakable. Neel joined the Communist Party in 1935, and as she became more politicized she explicitly linked the death of Santillana (and other children born into poverty) to the dangerous precarity of their situation. In an undated note, she wrote: 'You see if I'd had the money...the baby maybe wouldn't have caught it like she did – and then if I could have paid the doctor I wouldn't have been so slow to call one.'[6] *Futility of Effort* was reproduced in the journal *Art Front* in 1936 under the alternate title *Poverty*, marking Neel's awareness of the socio-economic context that framed infant mortality.

•

The loop continues until the equipment gives in.
Melanie Stidolph, *Endless Reproduction*[7]

Elina Brotherus's *Annunciation* (2009–13) **114** tracks cycles: seasonal renewal expressed in tulips and cherry blossom; the photographer's working trips from Helsinki to Brussels, New York and Avallon; the annotated diary pages marking each passing year. Nestled within these other cycles are rounds of IVF treatment undertaken over the five years of the work's duration: life lived according to a strict calendar. In the staged self-portraits that punctuate the series, Brotherus waits at the end of a long table, framed by an archway like Mary in Fra Angelico's *Annunciation* fresco (1438–45). No angel comes. We are permitted access to the process Brotherus is going through, otherwise out of sight of the world. She injects herself in the belly, allows herself to be carried in hopeful daydreams (*She would go to Anne-Sophie's school* runs a self-portrait on a wisteria-covered balcony.) Again and again, we watch her sitting beside a pregnancy test, waiting for the result, then crumpling into tears. A toilet pan is tinged red with blood. In many self-portraits she can't bear to show her face. The series closes after she undergoes treatment in New York, and pictures herself gazing over the Manhattan skyline (*Last one in my line*) and then across the snowy wastes of a Finnish winter (*The End*). Brotherus presents *Annunciation* as a critical counterbalance to

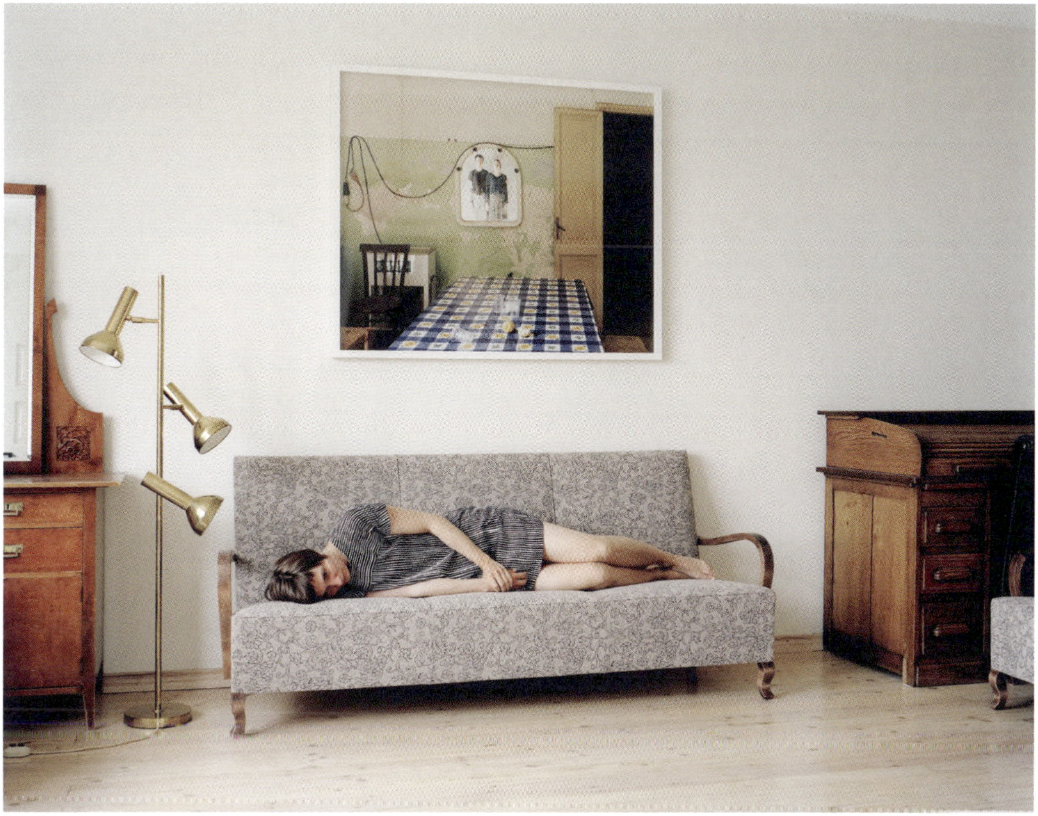

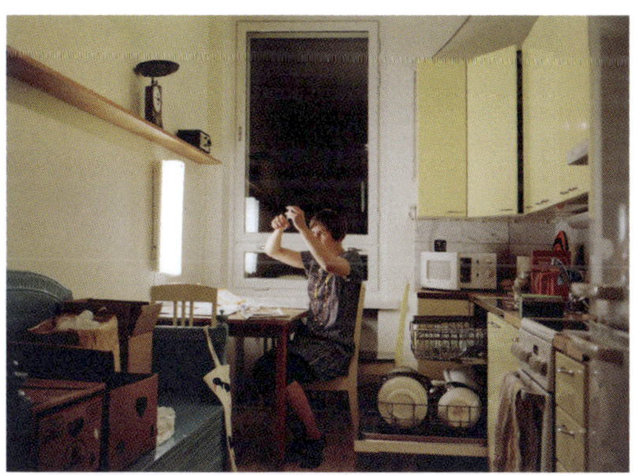

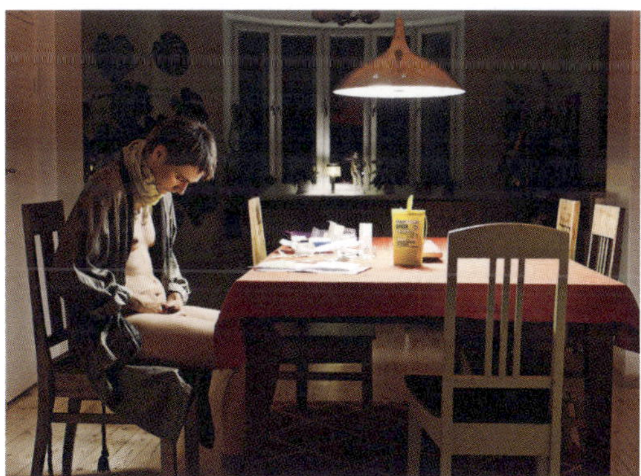

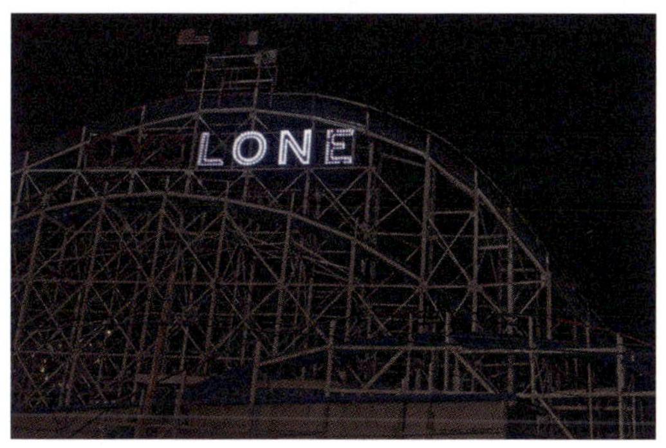
LONE

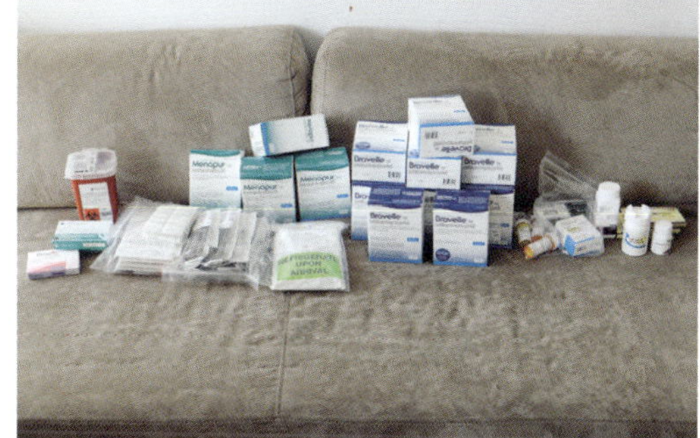

the portrayal of fertility treatments in the media in which a happy ending is presented almost as an inevitability. 'For the rest of us, this biased broadcasting is upsetting. It's as though the general public should not see the inconsolable reality but instead a cathartic "per aspera ad astra" Hollywood story,' she writes. Caught up in the hopefulness of each round of treatment, the resulting failure 'feels like mourning someone who died. The loss is very concrete. Not only does one lose a child, one also loses a whole future life as a family.'[8]

The End turned out not to be the end. Brotherus's next series *Carpe Fucking Diem* (2011–15) steps into a different future, one that holds humour, horror, love and pathos as well as physical discomfort. Her household grows to include the charming dachshund Marcello. She offers herself as the not so grown-up grown up, clutching Marcello with one hand as she flips us the bird with the other, titling the photo, with appropriate fuck-you defiance: *My dog is cuter than your ugly baby* (2013).

•

'Miscarriage', the US American novelist Louisa Hall writes, 'is another one of those things, like eating disorders and rape, that happen to most women.'[9] In *Reproduction* (2023), her novel of miscarriage, motherhood and experimental science, Hall takes as her narrator a college professor battling to carry a baby to term while studying the work of Mary Shelley. She reads Shelley's *Frankenstein* (1818) weighed down by intimate knowledge of the author's experience of stillbirth and maternal loss. In one journal entry after the death of her daughter Clara, born premature, Shelley recounts a dream: 'That my little baby came to life again – that it had only been cold and that we rubbed it by the fire and it lived – I awake and find no baby – I think about the little thing all day.'[10] It is irresistible for Hall's scholarly narrator to trace a line from this woman who dreams of animating the body through fire, and her creation Dr Frankenstein who harnesses lightning to spark life in dead flesh.

Horror also infuses the art of Renate Bertlmann. Since her work in 1970s Vienna, she's submitted the soft to the spiky, and shaken up gender codes. Playing with and inflating latex teats and condoms, it's not always clear which is which: both are used as extensions or proxies for the body, stuck on fingertips, or inflated like breasts or sexual organs. Maternity manifests in monstrous ways: fat phalluses are swaddled in place of babies or dressed in

115.
Renate Bertlmann, *Die Missgebildeten Menschen von Morgen* (*The Malformed Humans of Tomorrow*), 1975

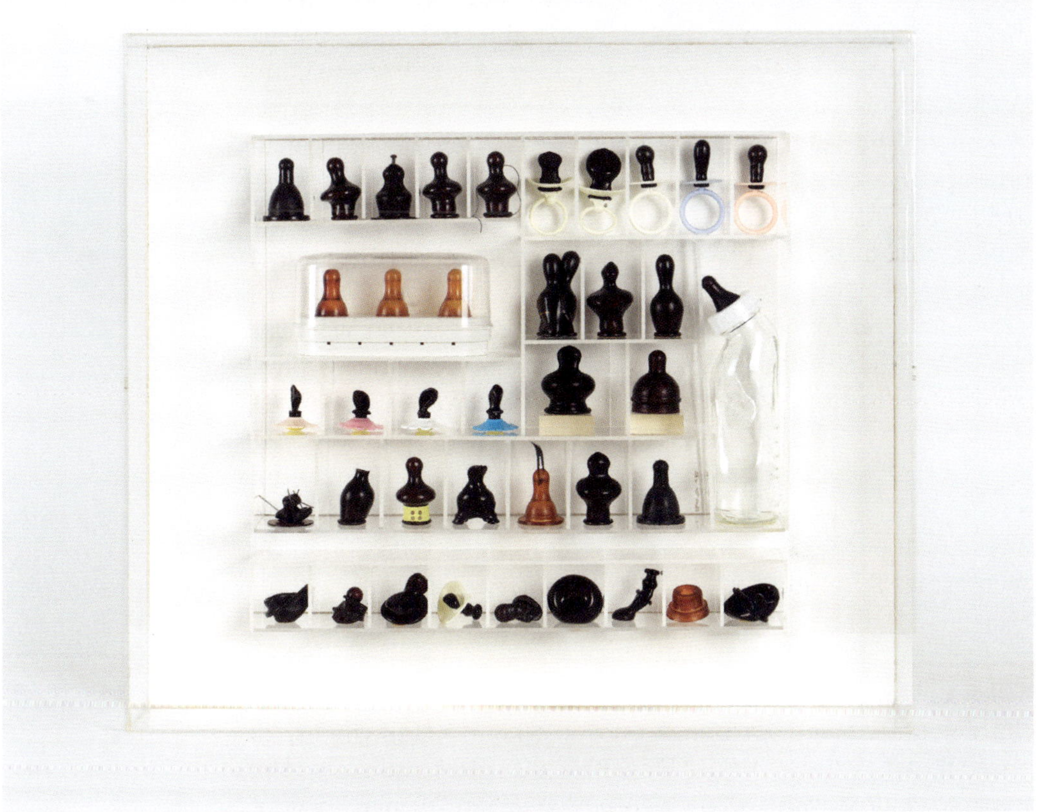

115

little girls' stiff-skirted frocks. Scalpels sprout from teats in a violent expression of maternal ambivalence. In the performance *Pregnant Bride in a Wheelchair* (1978) Bertlmann is wheeled into view in a crown and mask covered in latex pacifiers with a sign reading 'please push!' on her back. If she's pushed, lullabies play from a transistor hidden in her stomach. When the pushing stops the sound switches to a crying baby. Eventually the bride gives birth, delivering the bundled transistor from which loud wailing now emanates onto the gallery floor, then walks away – the mother as great abandoner – still in her wedding garb. *The Malformed Humans of Tomorrow* (1975) **115** gives these tropes a sharper twist. Latex nipples, pacifiers and a baby bottle are arranged on little shelves within a Perspex box like a trophy cabinet or series of portrait busts. Some are stuck with pins, nails or blades – dangerous objects that repel the body. Others are twisted, stuck, forced in on themselves or shrivelled. This is a line-up of babies that never happened – a brutal monument to Bertlmann's own miscarriages.

•

'No bed for Beatle John!' chants Yoko Ono, high and quavering, as though she's singing across a pillow. As indeed she is. In November 1968 Ono was admitted to Queen Charlotte's Hospital in London, five months pregnant and experiencing complications. Her partner John Lennon slept by her bedside throughout and as she recuperated, the couple recorded themselves singing news coverage of this most private experience, including a quote from a Beatles press spokesman: 'There is a good chance for the baby's survival.' A week after Ono and Lennon made this recording, Ono suffered a miscarriage. The B-side of their experimental sound work *Unfinished Music No.2: Life With The Lions* (1969) is a monument to this event. The album's cover shows Ono in her hospital bed, with Lennon on the floor **116**. *No Bed for Beatle John* is followed by a recording of the baby's heartbeat made while Ono was in hospital – a few seconds looped over five minutes – and then by two minutes silence, the traditional period observed for episodes of public mourning. In the final track – 'Radio Play' – whiplashes of crackling sound produced by strobing a radio on and off are laid over a withdrawn soundscape of phone calls, rustling clothing and casual conversation. Ono is a conceptual and sound artist, was part of the international Fluxus art movement, and the track is usually appraised formally in that context. Mocked at the time of its release, it was later seen as daringly experimental. To me, though, *Radio Play* feels like being trapped in a jagged sonic cage that interrupts apprehension of the everyday. It reminds me of the experience of being isolated inside pain and unbearable preoccupation, and the apparently insurmountable effort required to reach beyond and engage with the mundanity of the everyday again. It feels, in other words, like a sound work about the painful and isolating experience of late-stage miscarriage.

•

Embroidered into the surface of Su Richardson's *Heartstrings* (2022) **117** are a first birthday card and bib stitched with the name Kennedy. Both were passed to Richardson by a friend who had become pregnant aged sixteen, as a schoolgirl still living with her parents. This was in 1967, the year before the UK's Abortion Act came into effect. As an unwed teenager, she was placed in a 'mother and baby home' with twenty-five other girls, and her baby daughter was adopted ten weeks after birth. Legally, she was forbidden from tracking her daughter down or contacting her. The

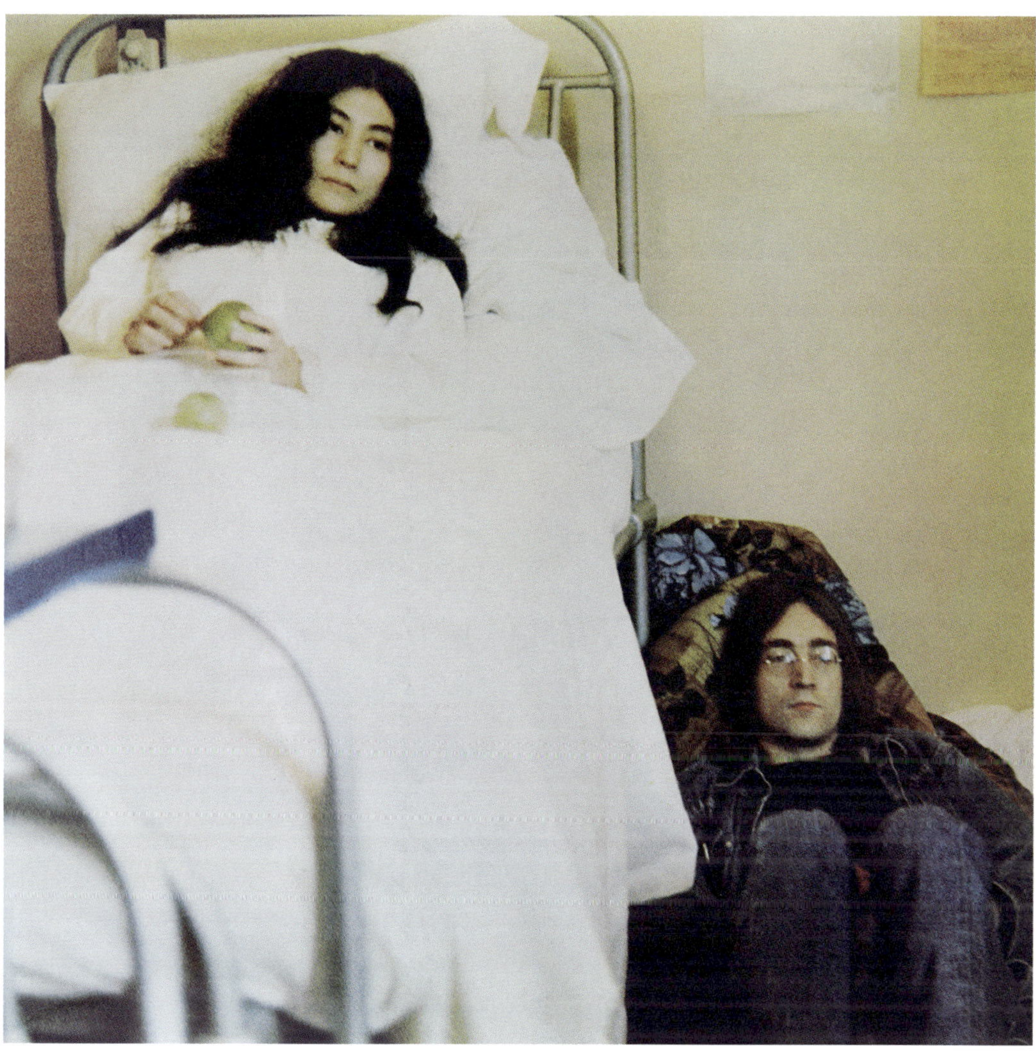

116

116.
Yoko Ono and John
Lennon, *Unfinished
Music No.2: Life
With The Lions*,
1969

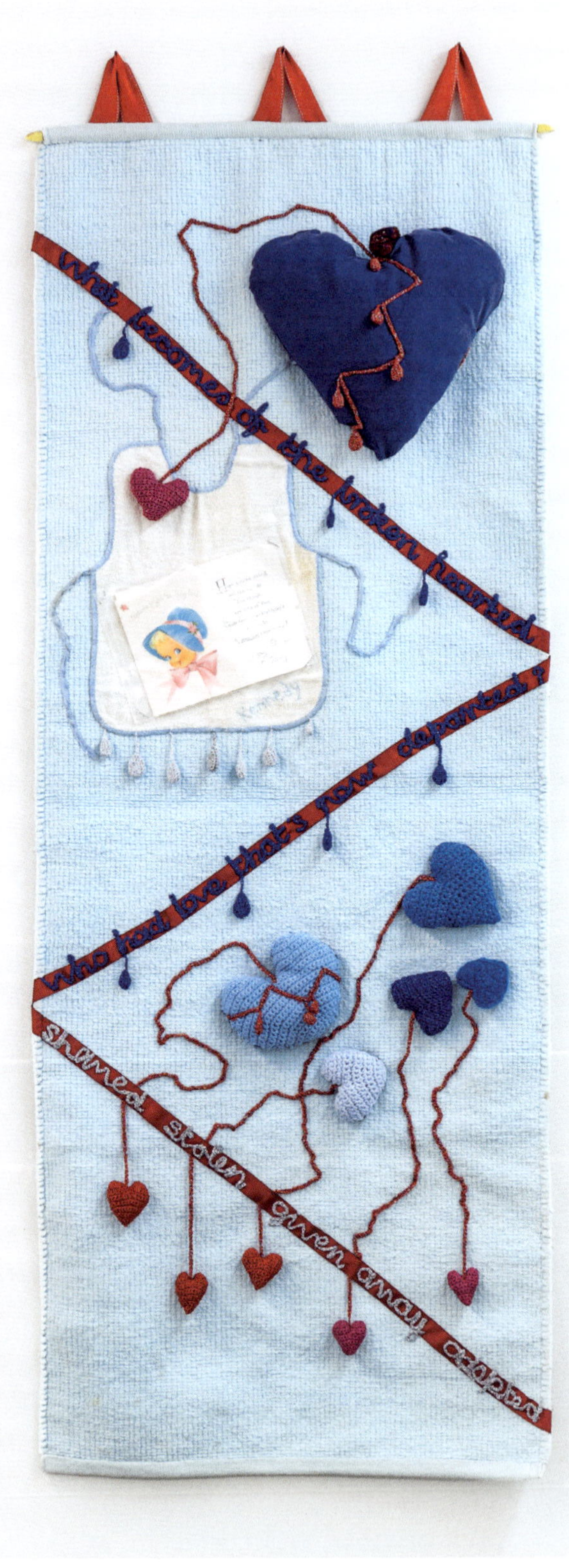

card stitched into *Heartstrings* fifty-five years later was written without hope of being sent – 'to my daughter Kennedy, on your first birthday, wherever you are.' In ribbons of text crisscrossing the piece, Richardson has embroidered the lyrics to Jimmy Ruffin's 'What becomes of the broken hearted?', a popular hit played on the radio while her friend was in the mother and baby home. Around them bob crocheted hearts – blue for the mothers, red for the babies – and teardrops, marking her friend's experience out as one story among thousands.

This was not a 'forced' adoption – but it was impelled. There was little choice available to unmarried girls in the UK unable or unwilling to seek a dangerous illegal abortion. There is a subtle sliding scale between social pressure, coercion and the forced removal of babies. Some 185,000 infants were forcibly taken for adoption between 1949 and 1976. This is not only a story of the recent past, but of our own time. A report from 2014 suggested that some 2,500 children – around half the number adopted in the previous year – had been given new homes without their parents' consent. [11] 'If you look at the kids being adopted, they're much more likely to be from single mums, disabled mums, mums of colour, mums who were in care themselves, young mums and victims of domestic violence,' Anne Neale of the campaign group Support not Separation told the news journal *Prospect* in 2022.[12] A cycle of trauma emerges. Of those children taken from their mothers and placed in care, over forty percent have a parent who has been in care themselves.

Kennedy would be her mother's only child. Newly married, Richardson's friend was told she had been left infertile by an infection. 'She was given a lecture when they found out – about how if she hadn't had a baby at that age, and hadn't been "doing things", she would never have caught the infection,' Richardson tells me. 'That was probably just as bad an experience. To find out then that she and her husband couldn't have children.'[13]

•

In 1990 Nancy Willis was appointed artist-in-residence at Hammersmith Hospital, London. In her first months, she made tender portraits of babies in the Neonatal ICU. I wonder at the emotional bridge she crossed to draw these newborns. Two years earlier Willis had made an etching – *Self Portrait with Lost Baby* (1988) **118**. In the lower corner a tiny girl is curled as though in utero – vegetal tentacles and leaves spring from her

117.
Su Richardson,
*Heartstrings (What
Becomes of the Broken
Hearted?)*, 2022

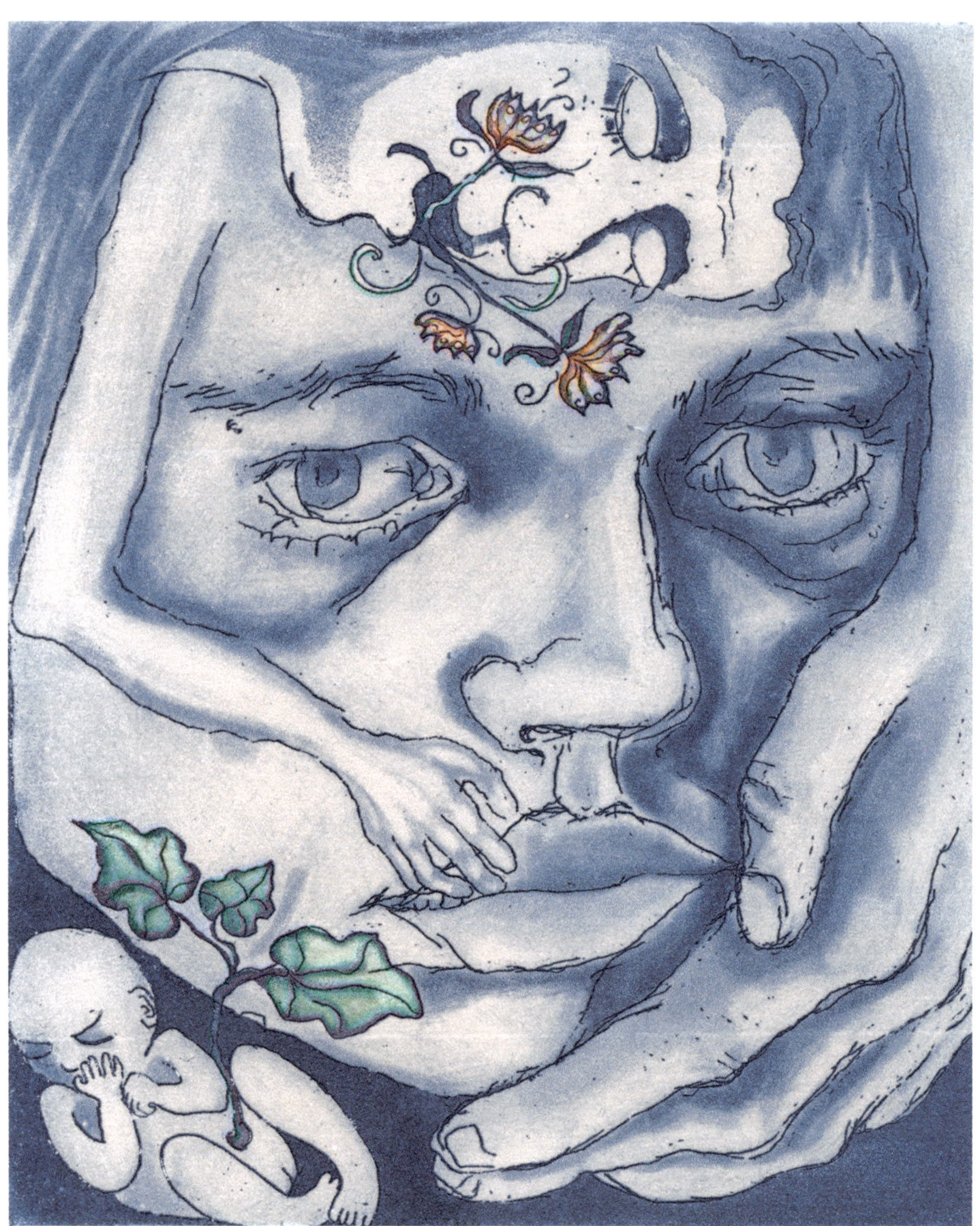

navel, connecting to a young woman's face, sad eyed and wide mouthed. Another woman cradles the face as flowers bloom from her mouth – Willis, embracing her younger self. During her childhood Willis was diagnosed with muscular dystrophy and as her disability progressed was placed in a residential 'special' school run according to strict rules to which she refused to comply. Her liberation was art college – a foundation course and then degree at North East London Polytechnic in the early 1970s. She qualified as a teacher in 1981. During the 1980s she embarked on a series of looser, more abstracted self-portraits that reimaged how a figure in a wheelchair might be pictured. She became involved in the Disability Arts Movement, organizing and participating in exhibitions and workshops. The life Willis has lived was unimaginable to her as a young woman. As a child she had been told she would die young. In 1972 at the age of nineteen she had her first sexual experience and became pregnant by accident. In a later animation based on this etching, Willis explains that she wasn't going to live long enough to look after a baby. 'What would happen if it was disabled? There would be nobody to love it and look after it.' She decided to get a termination. The doctor responsible for the procedure offered 'in that cheery doctorish way' to perform a sterilisation at the same time. Believing she would never live long enough to bring up a child, Willis accepted. 'And then – carried on being alive.'[14] Ten years later, Willis was given a new prognosis and life expectancy. She fought to have the sterilization reversed, but by then too much damage had been done to her fallopian tubes. In 1988 she finally felt able to address the trauma in an artwork. In the animation she explains that she 'didn't know it was ok to hope.' Space for hope would have allowed her to imagine she would live long enough to raise a child: space for hope would have allowed her to imagine she might feel differently were she to become pregnant again. She imagines a young girl coming to her for advice and telling her not to allow the doctors to carry out a sterilization – 'Don't let them do it. Don't bar the door. Don't seal the windows. Leave a little room.'

118.
Nancy Willis,
*Self-Portrait with
Lost Baby*, 1988

assassins of the people

In 2022, the US Supreme Court reversed *Roe v. Wade*, overturning a federal right to legal abortion in place since 1973. Monumental in the moment, this is just the latest in a long history of affronts to women's reproductive rights, from Chile to China. Whether imposed in the name of religion or nationalist politics, these are laws of population control: to expand the soldiery and workforce, to contain the number of mouths to feed, to manipulate in favour of a preferred social type or ethnic group. Under such laws, a woman's body becomes a vessel for a higher national purpose, her rights of individual personhood diminished. When I write of reproductive rights, I refer to personal choice regarding reproduction per se. Not only access to contraception and to legal abortion, but also to maternal care, the right to choose to have a child, and to raise it in safety. The myriad affronts to women's reproductive rights over the last century have included (but are by no means limited to) birth control campaigns in the 1920s and 1930s funded by eugenicists who feared the 'racial deterioration' that would result from the abundant fertility of immigrant races (in the US) and the poor and ignorant (in the UK)[15]. In the same period, the promotion of ethnically selective natalism by fascist regimes in Germany and Italy[16]. The abuse and fatal neglect of tens of thousands of unwed women and their children taking refuge in mother and baby homes run by the Church in Ireland from the 1920s to the 1990s, and the removal of their infants for the supply of foreign and domestic adoption markets.[17] The compulsory or coerced sterilization of some 70,000 Native Americans of childbearing age – as well as lower income Black, Latinx and women with disabilities – in the US over the course of the 20th century.[18,19] The forced sterilization of over 250,000 women of indigenous heritage in Peru between 1996 and 2001.[20] In our own moment, the shackling during labour and denial of medical care to women giving birth in the US prison system.[21]

Loss, in relation to abortion, can be understood in various ways. There is the loss of a possible child. There is the loss of the imagined future with that child. There is also the loss of the future that had been imagined without a child – this is the loss perpetuated by state bans on abortion.

Tracey Emin's video *How It Feels* (1996) **119** is technically simple, but emotionally complex. A friend with a Hi8 camera follows Emin as she walks between locations around London's Euston Road dressed in peak 1990s style, a chalk-striped suit jacket and sunglasses with pink lenses. Her vision is anything but rose tinted. Starting outside her doctor's office – a clinic housed in a neoclassical church – she launches into the story of an abortion received six years earlier. Believing herself infertile after an STI, Emin finds herself pregnant, penniless and unmarried, and faces the loss of all she has fought for. 'Where I grew up, by the time you were seventeen you had one or two kids,' she tells us. She

119.
Tracey Emin,
How It Feels, 1996

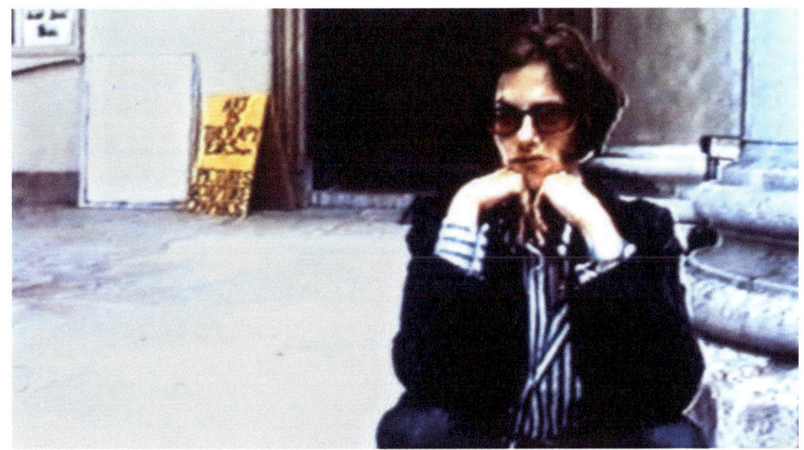

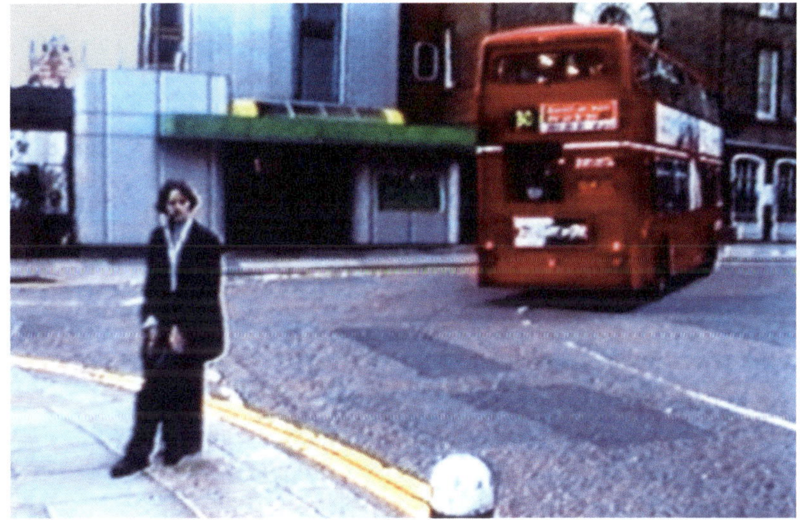

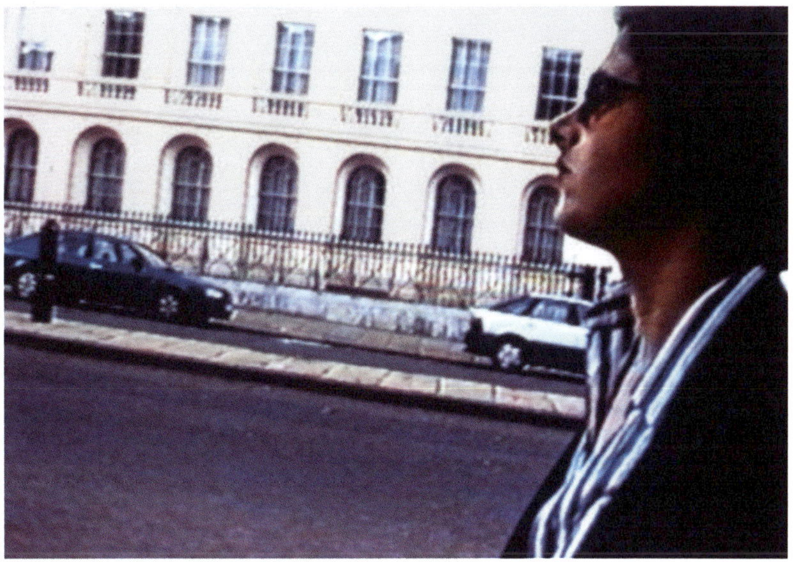

119

had wanted something more, and grafted her way to art college, a first class degree and an MA. She tells the doctor she wants an abortion. He tells her she'll be a great mum and procrastinates, dangerously, for six weeks. The late termination leaves Emin sick and delirious. She tells doctors that something is wrong – that she feels the baby is still inside her – but they brush her off ('what do you expect after you've had an abortion? Do you expect to feel good?'). A week later, yellow and swollen, she is taken to the emergency department where she haemorrhages and the abortion is revealed to have been botched. *How It Feels* is an account of obstetric violence: the obstruction of access to abortion, and the paternalistic condescension of doctors who do not consider a young woman a trustworthy judge of her own body and its pain. To not understand how it feels.

Behind the horror of its telling *How It Feels* provides a rationale for safe and legal access to abortion. Emin was twenty-six when she became pregnant, still a struggling artist with no means of supporting herself, let alone a child. 'When you are pregnant, you don't make your mind up that you want to have an abortion: you make your mind up that you can't have a child, which is a very different thing', she explains. In the balance hangs that whole glorious, troubled future – the artist we have come to know over three decades of work. The abortion was both trial and liberation. At the end of the film she identifies the trauma – of physical suffering, of being patronized and coerced, of giving up what might be her only chance of motherhood – as transformative. She realized that if she was going to make art, it had to be authentic, emotional, important. 'If I couldn't fill the world up with something I could love for ever and ever and ever,' she decides, there was no way she should be filling the world up with trivial things. Her art had to occupy the space of the child she couldn't have.

120.
Paula Rego,
Untitled No.4, 1998,
from the *Abortion*
Series, 1998–99

•

Paula Rego's *Abortion* series **120** was made in fury following a failed referendum to legalize abortion in Portugal (her mother country) in 1998. Over two decades after creating these works, Rego spoke of seeking a 'back street' abortion as an art student: 'When I was at London's Slade School of Art in the 1950s, abortion was illegal in England, and a lot of girls got pregnant,' she recalled. 'The referendum brought back all the pain.'[22] Rego shows women of various ages and social positions in makeshift

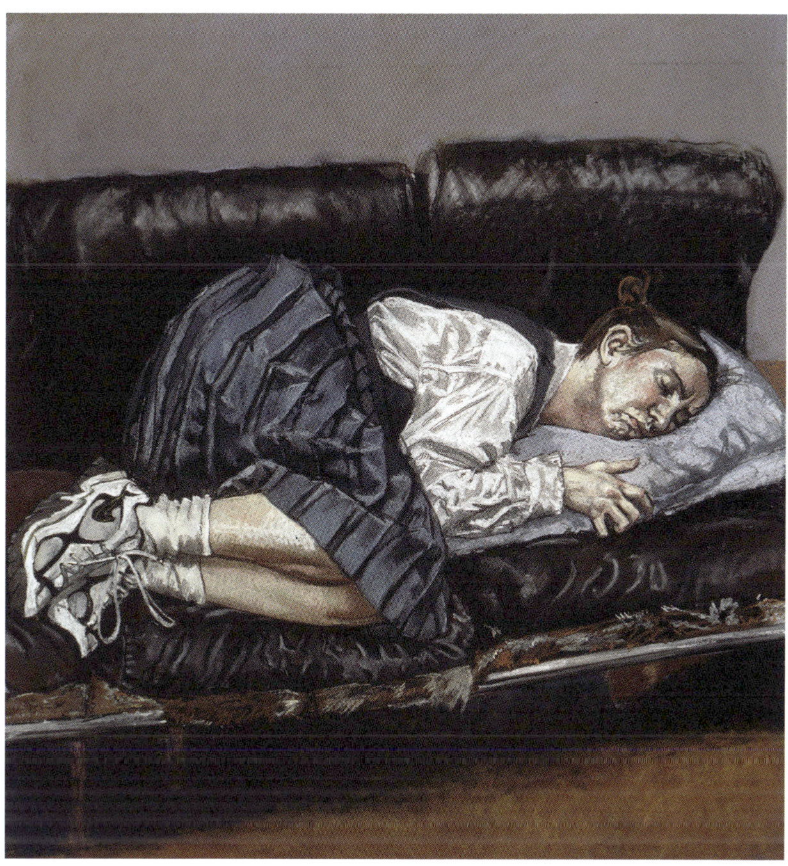

120

clinics waiting for, or recovering from, a termination. Wearing an elegant red dress, a woman with eyes as sharp as a bird perches on a plastic-covered table, legs splayed over folding chairs, waiting for intrusion. A schoolgirl curls agonized on a leather sofa, her knuckles gripped tense and white. Another squats over a plastic bucket, pleated skirt hitched above her hips. These great pastel works and the etchings that followed are claustrophobic, adrenal, heavy-bodied, charged, almost erotic. The story they tell is not of laws, votes and paperwork, but of the physical and psychological experience of abortion. There is pain here, but also relief, weariness, resignation, urgency. The works were shown in Portugal and prints widely circulated. Rego described how they provided a gathering point for women to recall and share their own experiences. She spoke of the grim normalization of women dying after home abortions in Portugal, but also of her own abortion, without which she would have had to quit art school and return home. A second referendum in 2007 legalized abortion in Portugal. Rego's work was considered a contributing factor, encouraging honest conversation around a subject so common and yet still so taboo.

•

The first chapter of Catalan artist Laia Abril's project *A History of Misogyny* is a travelling exhibition and book of new and archival photographs, and terse, devastating interviews **121**. *On Abortion and the Repercussions of Lack of Access* (2018) surveys the means by which women have attempted to induce abortion – which include knitting needles, hot baths, heavy stones and poisonous herbs as well as back street clinics – and the harms done in the process. She tells us that each year 47,000 women around the world die following botched abortions. The book included a black-and-white photograph of the court files of seventeen Salvadorian women charged with homicide after miscarrying. A significant section is dedicated to the experiences of women in Poland, one of only a few countries (the others being El Salvador, Nicaragua and the US) around the world to have rolled back abortion laws. The accounts detail violent reactions to abortion pills illegally obtained online, and a woman who went blind after being denied an abortion that could have saved her sight. Published just ahead of the 2018 vote to repeal the prohibition on abortion in Ireland, it also includes an Irish widower's testimony of a fatal refusal to provide his wife with either an abortion or the chemotherapy that would keep her alive. There are blurred photographs of others who died because they were denied a termination – in the Dominican Republic, Ireland, US and Argentina. It is elegant and nasty. Burning with fury. An accumulation of evidence. Otherwise innocuous objects – a rock, a stick, a coat hanger – take on nauseating significance.

keep your rosaries off my ovaries

The Artists' Campaign to Repeal the 8th Amendment – a 1983 clause in the Irish constitution that essentially gave the foetus the same right to life as its mother – was formed in 2015 by Cecily Brennan, Alice Maher, Eithne Jordan, and the poet Paula Meehan. Touting bright stitched and painted banners ripe with symbolism and historic references, they formed a very visible component of protest marches leading up to the 2018 referendum **122**. 'A Day of Testimonies' at the Project Art Centre in Dublin in 2016 included the reading of anonymous first-hand

121.
Laia Abril,
*On Abortion:
Human incubator,
Hippocratic
Betrayal*, 2016

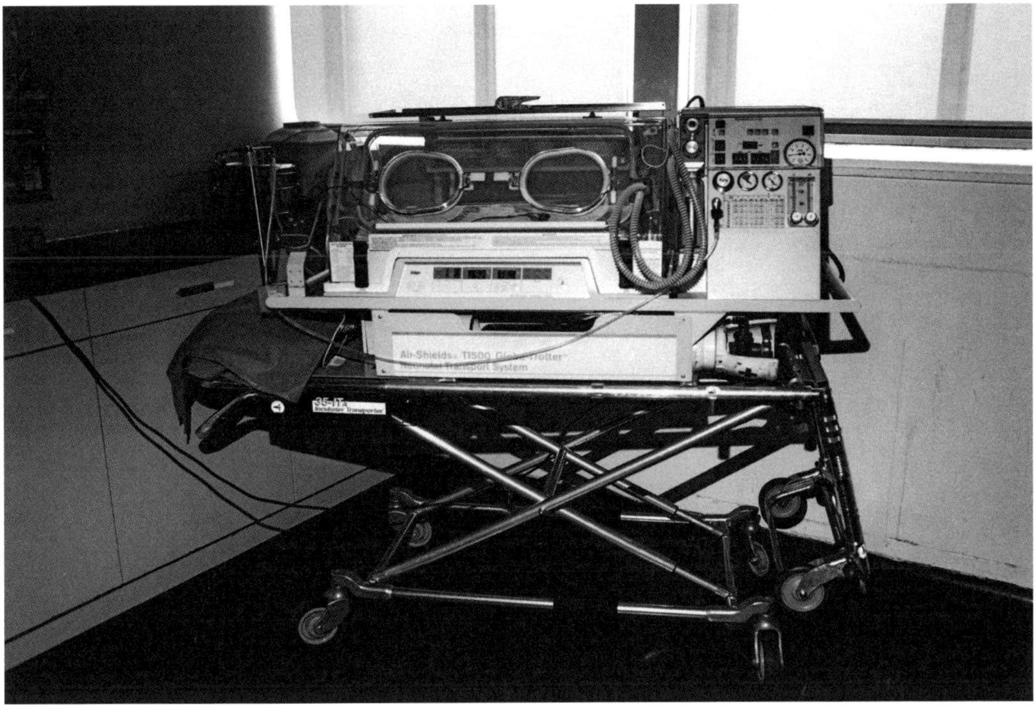

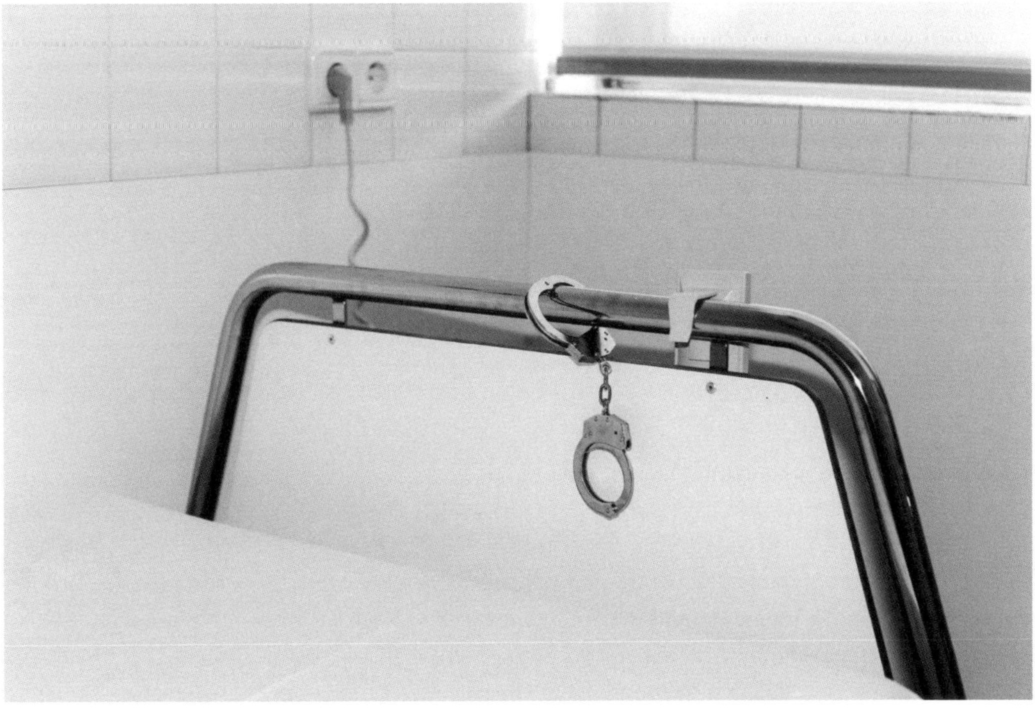

121

REPEAL NOW
Fortune
Favours
THE
BRA
ARTISTS' CAMPAIGN
TO REPEAL THE
EIGHTH AMENDMENT
REPEAL

122

TO ENSUR
HOPE
IS
OUR
ROLE
GRACE
UNDER
PRESSURE
UNDER
THE
LAW,
FREEDOM
TRUST
WOMEN
+
REPEAL
FORTITUDE
OVERCOMES
ALL
DIFFICULTY
TO US,
NOTHING
IS
IMPOSSIBLE

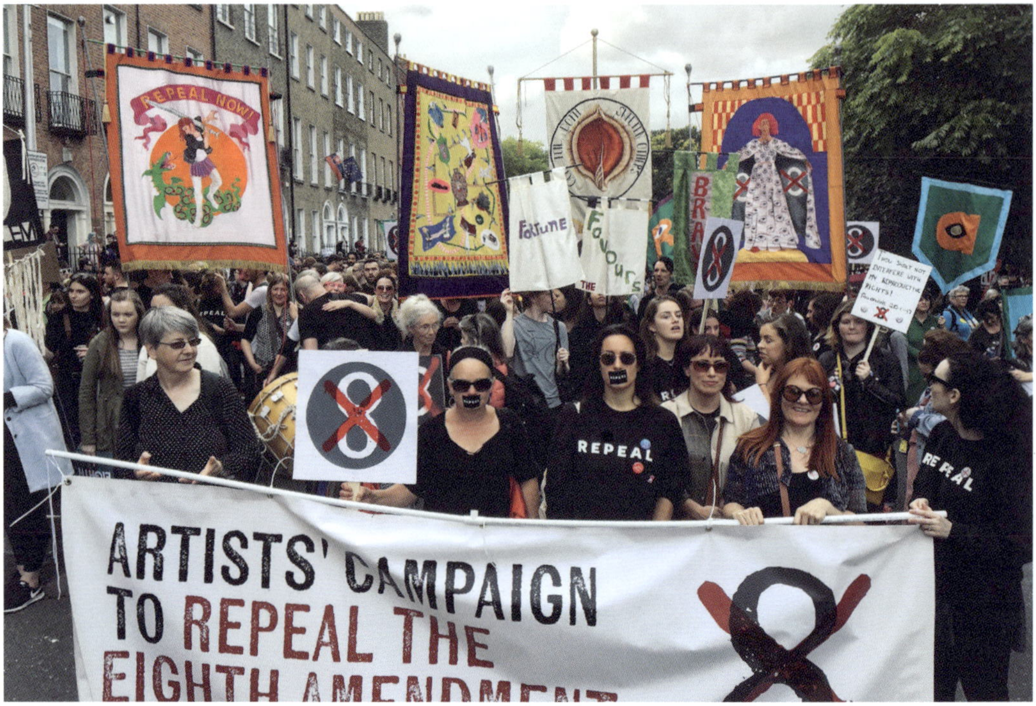

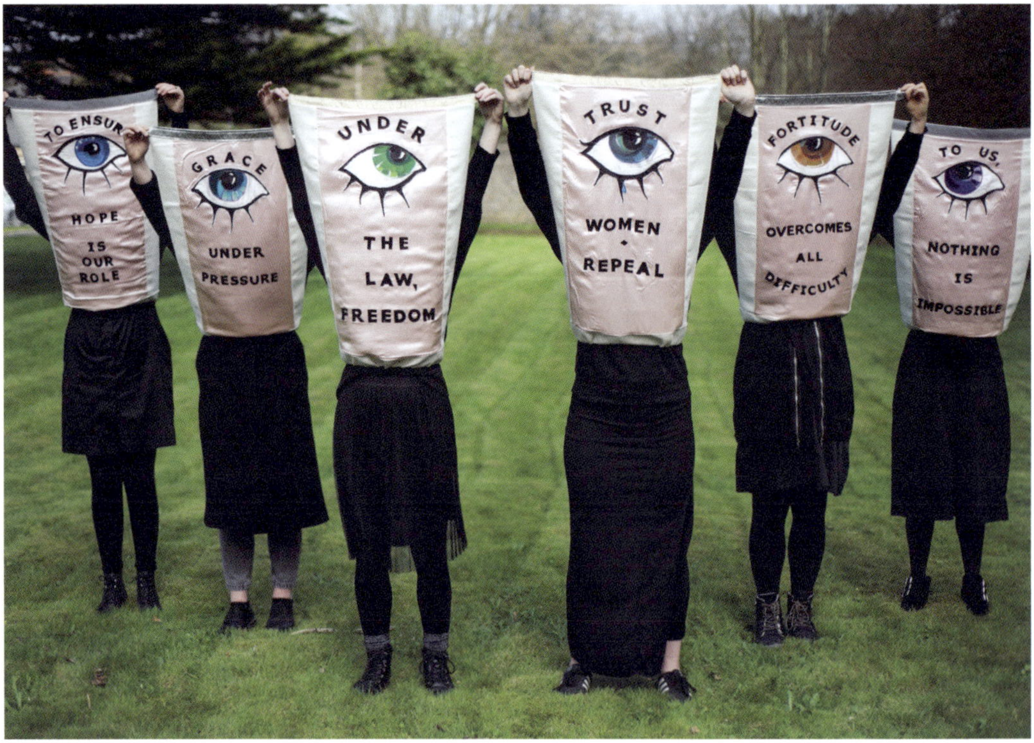

123

accounts of Irish women's abortion experiences. 'The arts at its best allows discussion, allows people to experience something, look at it, listen to it, consider it for their own selves,' Brennan told *The Guardian* a few weeks ahead of the referendum. 'It opens places that haven't been open for a long time. That was our experience about the debate about abortion – it had not been public. Art helped to bring it out in a different way.'[23] The Repeal! procession at EVA International Biennale in April 2018 gathered outside the city's art school. The building had once been Limerick's Magdalene Laundry, 'where pregnant women and girls were shamed, incarcerated and enslaved, and their children taken from them, brutalized and sold,' Alice Maher told the crowd. 'With this procession, we honour their memory today, and we carry them with us through the streets of the city from which they were barred. The 8th amendment is another attempt to stigmatize, brutalize and control women. And we reject it.' Within the procession, among dancers and musicians, walked a group of sombre women wearing Rachel Fallon's *Aprons of Power* **123**. Raising their aprons – in a gesture that recalls the rebellious self-exposure of the Celtic sheela-na-gigs – they revealed scrutinizing eyes and protest slogans stitched onto the underside: 'Under the Law Freedom'; 'Fortitude Overcomes All Difficulties'; 'Trust Women Repeal'. In the referendum of May 2018, Irish voters delivered an overwhelming 'Yes' vote, opening the route to safe and legal abortion in the country.

•

Interviewed by Caroline A. Miranda for the *Los Angeles Times* in April 2022, artist Barbara Kruger struck a cynical, if not weary note. 'It would be kind of good', she told Miranda, 'if my work became archaic.' Their conversation took place in the clenched and doomy pause between the revelation, in February of that year, that the Supreme Court had the majority opinion to overturn *Roe v. Wade* and the fulfilment of that threat in June. Already, Kruger's *Untitled (Your body is a battleground)* (1989) **124** was ubiquitous on social media. Nodding to US Army recruitment posters, the photocollage showed a mid-century beauty's face split negative/positive down the centre, with white text laid in red boxes over the top. Kruger's research let her to 'ideologically intense' parts of the Internet, she told Miranda, among them far right (which is to say racist, white supremacist, antisemitic, anti-Islamic, misogynist, and anti-LGBTQI+) imageboards on 4chan, and the

122.
The Artists'
Campaign To Repeal
The Eighth
Amendment Banners
at The ARC
(Abortion Rights
Campaign) 6th
Annual March for
Choice, 2017

123.
Rachel Fallon,
Aprons of Power
performance, 2018

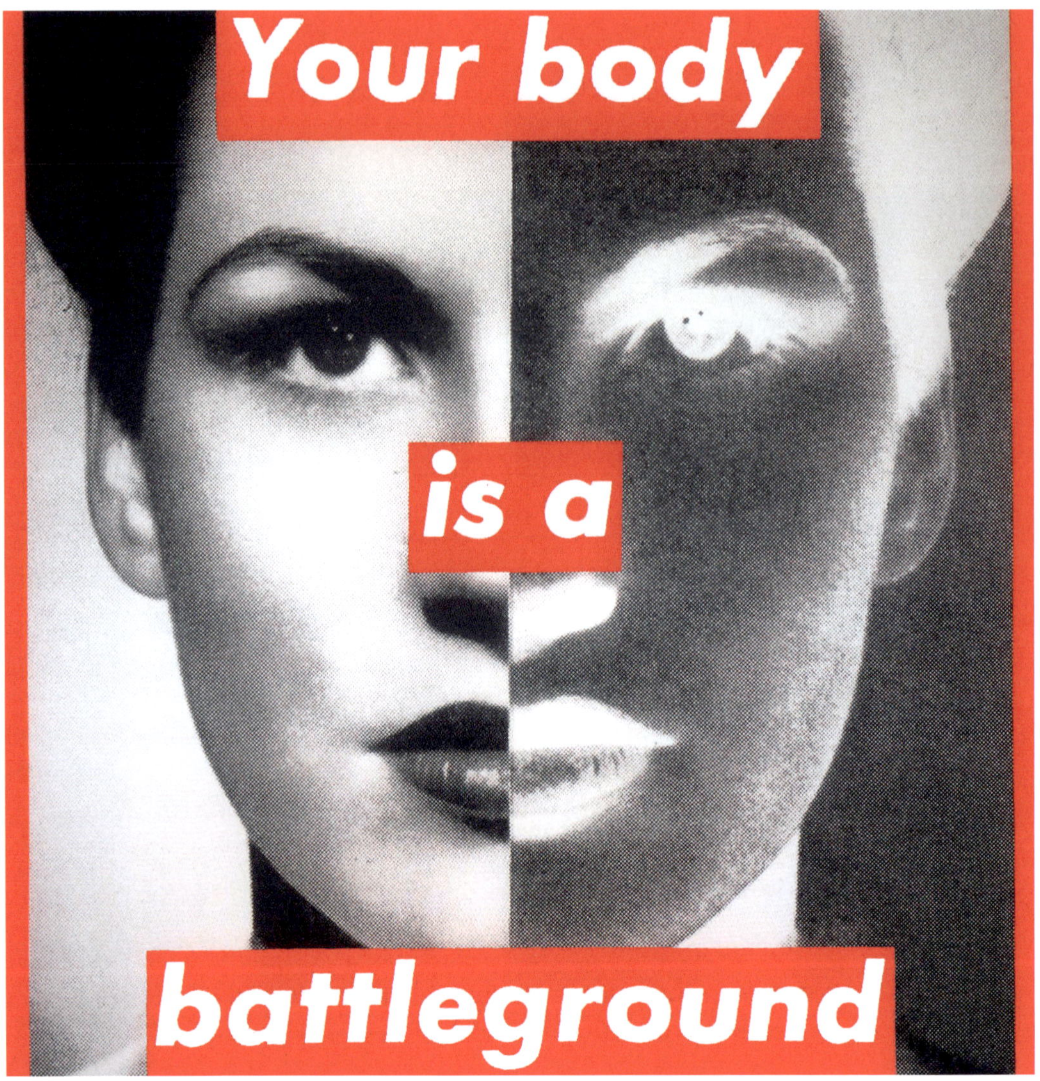

124

124.
Barbara Kruger,
*Untitled (Your body
is a battleground)*,
1989

neo-Nazi website Stormfront. The news about *Roe v. Wade* was not unexpected: 'Every time I hear people say they are shocked, I'm like…[shakes head]. It's that failure of imagination that has led us to today. None of this was a surprise.'[24] It is germane here to note that Kruger's original protest posters, in black and white, were made in response to an earlier threat to *Roe v. Wade* under President Bush in 1989. On 9 April of that year, over 300,000 protestors mustered in Washington. 'We are marching here to ask, is the Supreme Court going to affirm that women are full citizens and not property, or is the Supreme Court the captive of the extreme right wing?' feminist activist Gloria Steinem asked the crowd.[25]

•

As regards reproductive rights, as with many other things, the future is not a matter of inevitable progress. Events of recent years caution against complacency. Nevertheless, vigilance intact, the broader picture is hopeful. Journalist Siân Norris notes in her otherwise doom-laden account of the attack on reproductive rights in our time *Bodies Under Siege* (2023) that 'since 1973, a total of fifty-five countries have improved access to abortion. Only four [have] rolled back abortion rights.'[26] The 2020s have witnessed a green tide – the *Marea verde* – sweeping across Latin America. The united efforts of pro-choice demonstrators wearing green bandanas helped push through changes to the abortion laws in Argentina (2020), Colombia (2022) and Mexico (2023). As Nancy Willis reminds us, we should always leave space for hope.

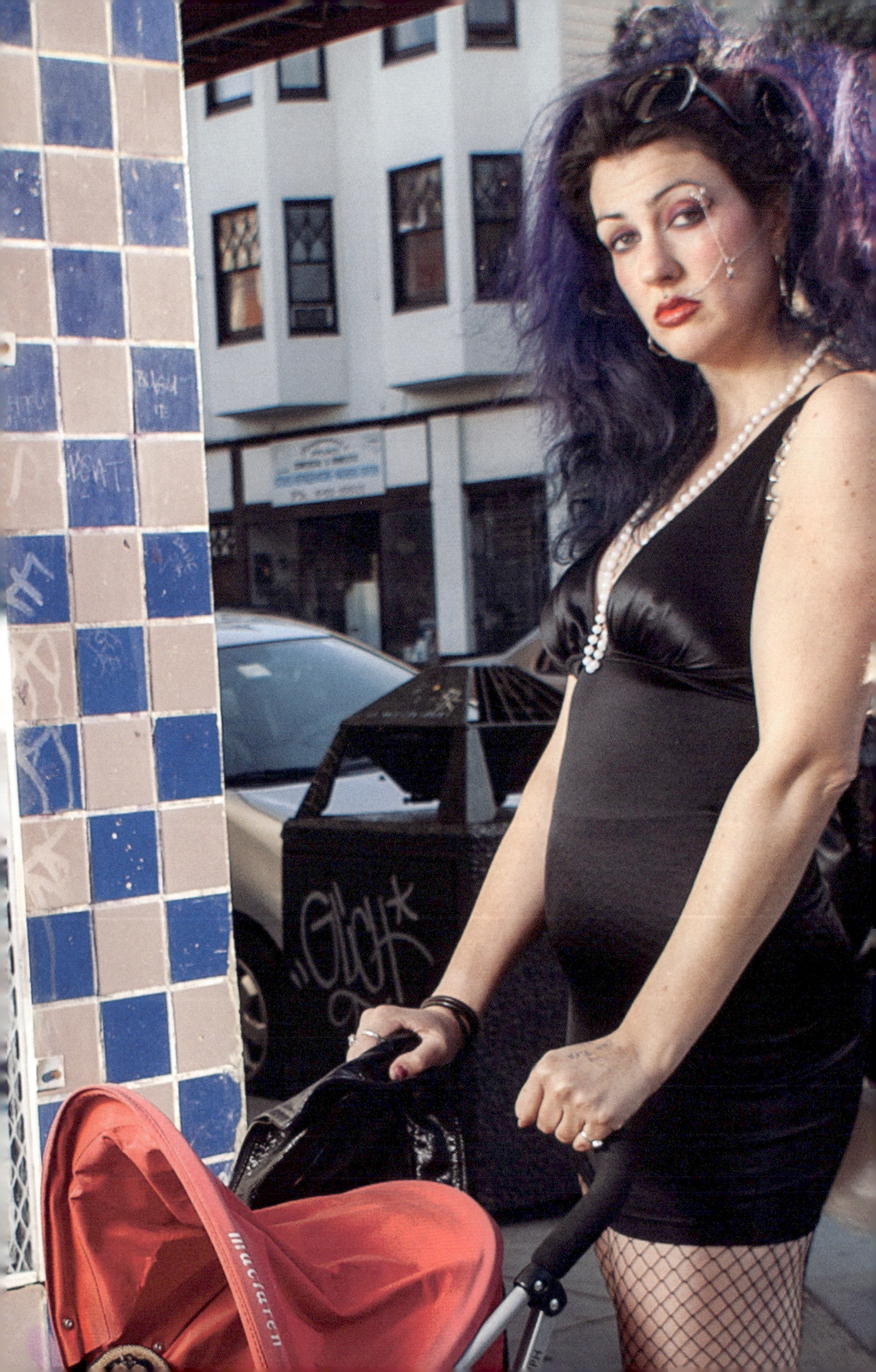

mothering: the family reborn

a queer collaboration with the future

'Motherhood' describes a relational state in a way 'childhood' does not. One can simply be a child. To be a mother denotes membership of a family – an elastic term that can encompass a single-parent/lone-child unit, a multigenerational sprawl and other archipelagos besides. I enjoy describing my own blended household as a bacterial family. Eating, washing, shitting in close quarters, our intimacy is metabolic. This kinship grouping extends to the dog and cat, and possibly also my partner's sourdough starter and the compost heap. I'm kind of joking but also kind of not.

Maggie Nelson's spare and sapid memoir of queer family-making *The Argonauts* (2015) offers a new paradigm for this ancient institution. In the febrile intensity of their early relationship, she sends her lover Harry Dodge a passage by Roland Barthes in which the French philosopher describes each profound utterance of love as a reinvention. How can 'I love you' be felt and understood afresh with each speaker? Barthes explores this using a paradox known as the 'Ship of Theseus'. If the Argonauts continuously repair and rebuild their boat, is it still the *Argo* by the end of the voyage? The *Argo* is something more than stuff: it's a name, a notion, a set of relations, a story, a site in time and space. Barthes uses it to explain the enduring potency of overfamiliar words. Nelson launches the *Argo* as a proposal for rebuilding the family. She, Harry and their kin become the Argonauts, pulling up the rotten boards, shaping this vessel – the family – according to their needs. While voyaging in these fresh waters, Nelson asserts the mother as a dynamic force: a provider of life and care, a sexual and intellectual being. Bullshit is hereby called on Tolstoy's famous opening to *Anna Karenina* – 'All happy families are alike'.

This vessel – the family – can carry us a long way, on a journey through various queer homesteads, to travel along networks of collectivized kinship and care, and beyond that to explore our relationship with the non-human. Along the way we might ask how transforming ideas of the family invites us to reflect on the mother as a figure, and motherhood as a state of being.

In her 2016 essay 'm/other ourselves' the writer and activist Alexis Pauline Gumbs reminds us that mother*hood* is a privilege reserved for those whose race, class, citizenship, sexuality, gender identity and health place their legal rights to their children beyond dispute. She is instead interested in the radical potential of mother*ing* as a form of expanded care, asking 'What would it mean for us to take the word 'mother' less as a gendered identity and more as a possible action, a technology of transformation'.[1] Gumbs reflects on the First National Third World Lesbian and Gay Conference, held in 1979, and Audre Lorde's keynote speech calling for those gathered to understand their collective responsibility toward the next generation as a collaboration with the future. Those present responded by claiming the labour of mothering as shared, and the responsibility for the children of all individual lesbians of colour as collective. Gumbs finds in this a powerful riposte to the legal and social pressure placed on queer families to assimilate to the prescribed shape of heterosexual marriage. She also imagines the transformation it might effect on the adult/child relationships, potentially 'transforming the parenting relationship from a property relationship to a partnership in practice'. For Gumbs, this call to queer collective parenting carries the potential not only for 'non-dominating relationships with our children, but…also makes visible and viable meaningful relationships between children and adults who do not have the legal or biological status of parenthood.'[2]

Reading Gumbs, I think of the urgency of Zanele Muholi's series *Being* (2007) – an intimate portrait of a Black lesbian community in South Africa. Muholi photographs their extended family in moments of private tenderness – entangled in bedsheets, washing in a tub, kissing in the kitchen – but also out in the world. Nomonde Mafunda and Tumi Ndweni are pictured at the door of a register office on the day of their civil union. Nomsa Mazibuko and Fondo are pictured with their toddler on a bench outside a gay church in Johannesburg on Good Friday **125**. Knowing Muholi's later poised and performative black-and-white work, what is particularly striking in this series is the mundanity of these scenes. When *Being* was first shown, Muholi remarked on the prior lack

125.
Zanele Muholi,
*Nomsa Mazibuko
and Fondo, outside
the Hope Unity
Metropolitan
Community Church,
a gay church, during
Good Friday. Mayfair,
Johannesburg,*
2007

of images of loving and affectionate relationships between Black women in South Africa. In addressing this absence, they emphasized their choice to create images of the community for the community, rather than to please the outside world – Muholi adopts a position of refusal as a creative choice. *Being* not only asserts presence: it is a gesture of survival for a community under attack. Queer relationships are stigmatized as 'un-African', Muholi writes.[3] Lesbians had been subjected to violent attacks and hate crimes that included 'corrective rape', leaving many infected with HIV. Two members of the community had died that year from AIDS-related illnesses. *Being* is a precursor to Muholi's ongoing *Faces and Phases* series, a collective portrait of Black lesbian and trans life in South Africa: a photographic monument that also charts a community growing up and moving through life.

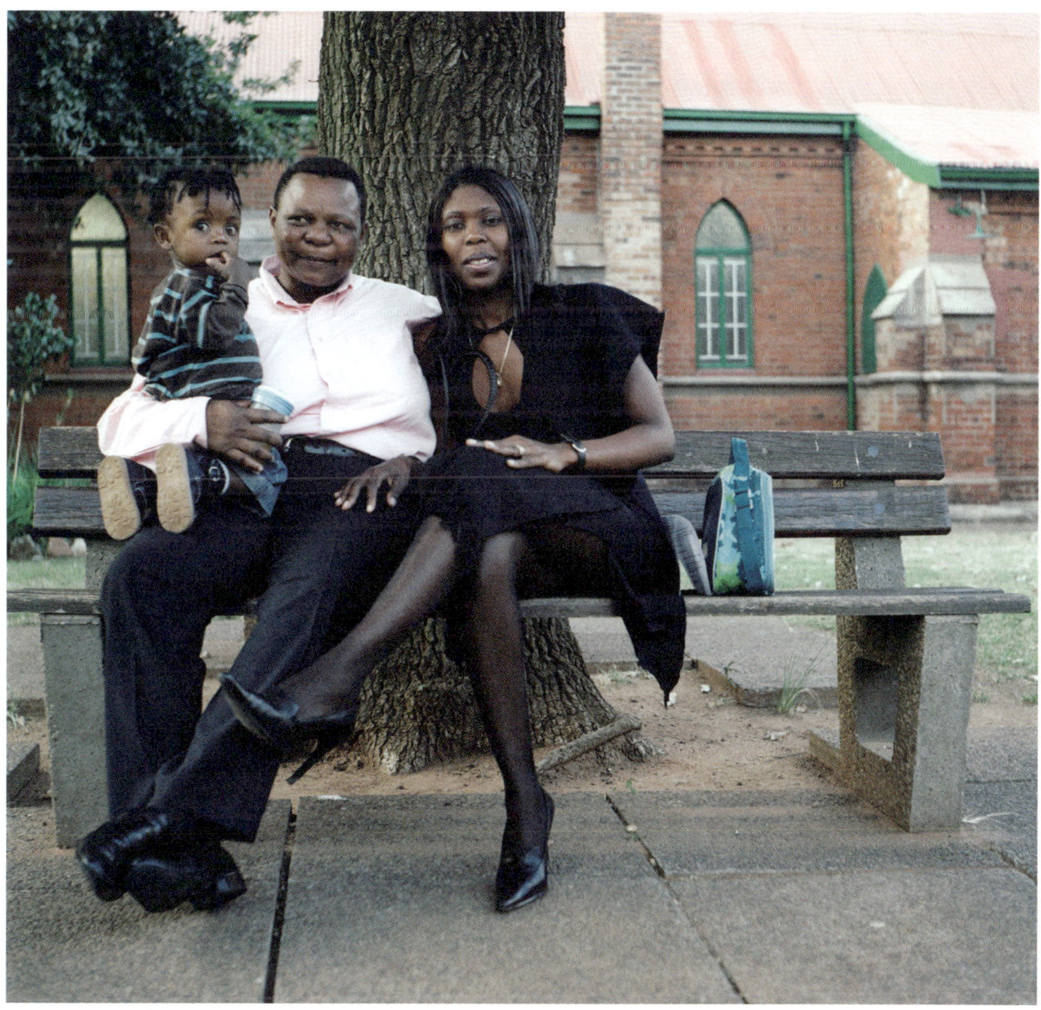

we love our gay parents

In 1973, Cathy Cade staged a photograph in the San Francisco apartment she was then sharing with two other women – her friend Pat and lover Kate – as well as Kate's young son Guthrie. **126** All wear overalls and gaze into the lens with 'yeah, what?' energy. Around them Cade has arranged the tools of their various enterprises. Guthrie has his toy truck, Kate has equipment from her car workshop, Pat – a sculptor – sits beside clay maquettes, including the figure of a pregnant woman. Scattered camera equipment and photos of civil rights and gay pride demonstrations indicate Pat and Cade's membership of a lesbian photography group. A quilt and woollen sock nod back to earlier traditions of female making. *Emerson Street Household, Berkeley, CA* (1973) is a portrait of an extended family group, but for the women involved it also recorded a moment of radical experimentation. Raised in the Midwest, Cade had spent much of the 1960s involved in the civil rights movement. Moving from Atlanta to San Francisco in 1970 she joined women's liberation groups, and in 1971 came out as a lesbian, and picked up a camera. Even in the civil rights movement, photography was something men did, and she assumed it was not a skill taught to women. The term 'artist', too, seemed elitist and a little scary. Watching women around her acquiring technical skills in other trades emboldened her. 'We had grown up in the '40s, '50s, and '60s, and women were supposed to be passive, not active,' Cade explained in 2015. 'They weren't supposed to develop a lot of skills – they weren't to be taken seriously. We were on the brink of changing this...and this photograph in part reflects that.'[4] Relations in Emerson Street were tangled. Kate's ex-husband still helped look after Guthrie, and her ex-girlfriend was his official second mother. Pat moved out after a couple of years. Kate started a relationship with another woman with kids and moved into the house next door. Cade's experience of collective mothering at Emerson Street brought her into contact with a lesbian mothers' support group. She started documenting lesbian families and decided to become a mother herself through donor insemination, giving birth to the first of her two sons in 1979. Cade had learned how empowering it was to share common experiences: 'It was very important to have a place where you could...learn that there are other people having similar problems or successes.' Her photographs felt like a way to pass on some of this sensibility, to show that a new shape of family was possible **127**. Through Cade's work we see episodes of domestic romance, days out at the beach, and a home birth performed amid a crowd of supportive women.

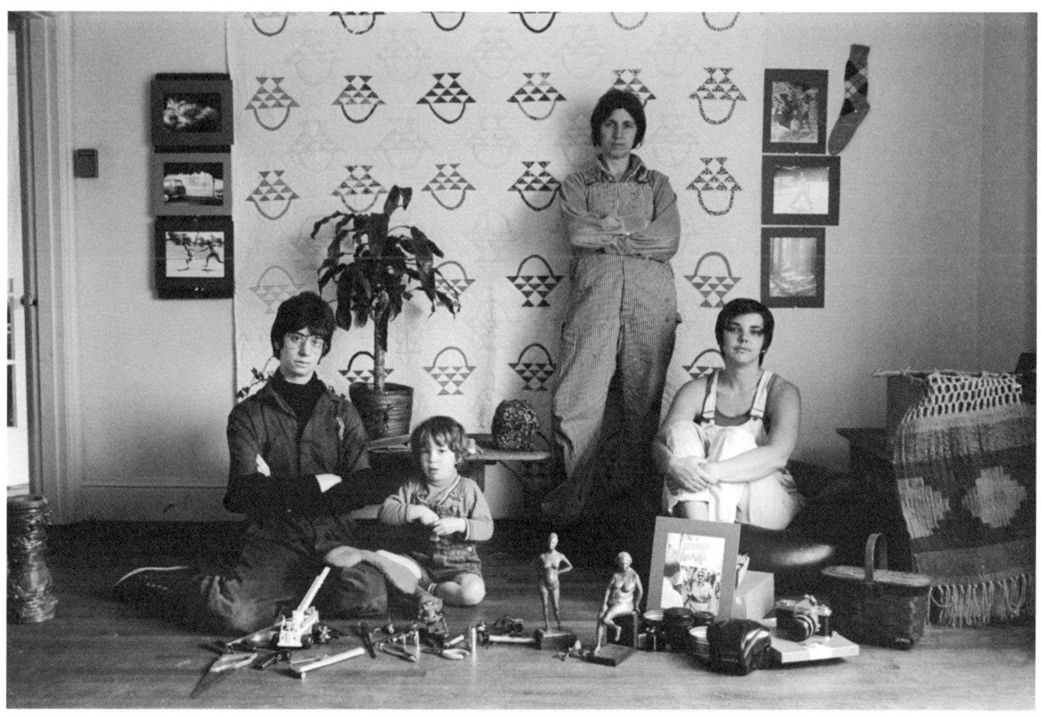

126.

Cathy Cade,
*Emerson Street
Household,*
Berkeley, CA,
1973

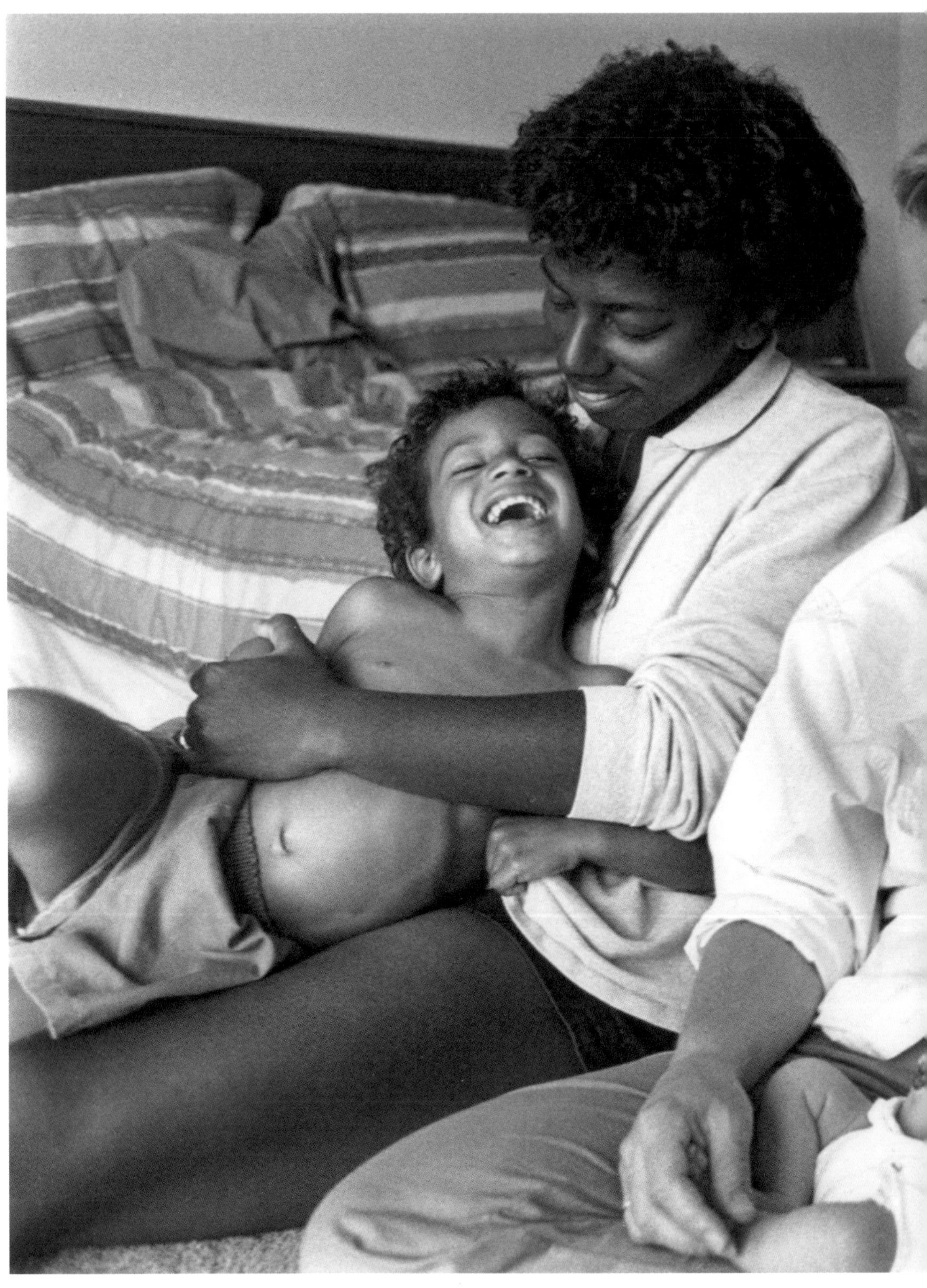

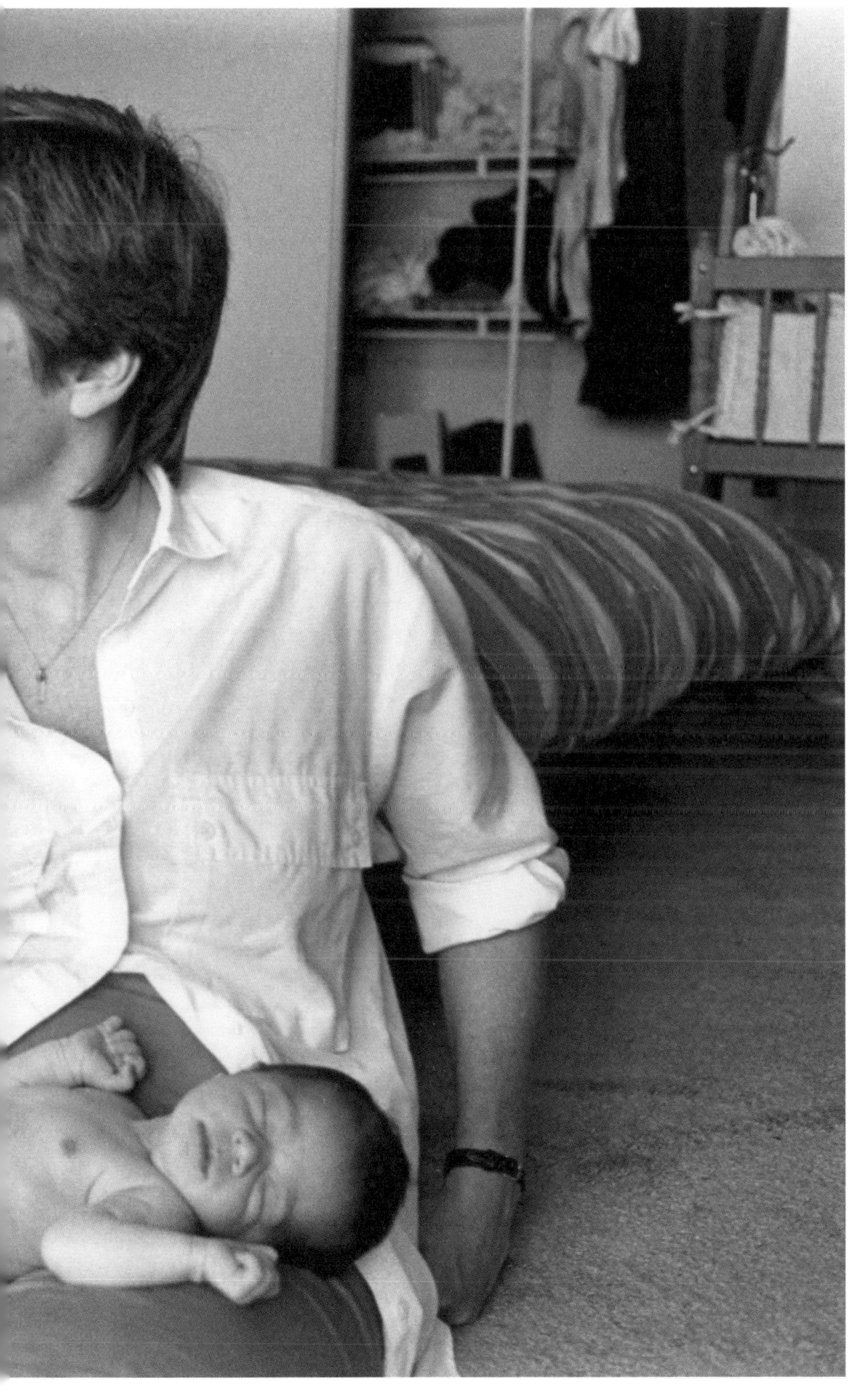

127.
Cathy Cade,
*Laurie Hauer
and Gusse II*,
1989

There were other sides to this story. Cade's 1977 photo *Rally for Jeanne Jullion* shows mothers and children holding placards on a San Francisco street. Figures in the crowd behind them include Harvey Milk. 'We're Proud, Not Stigmatized,' read the children's placards, 'We Love Our Gay Parents'. 1977 was a turbulent year for gay rights. The former beauty queen and Evangelical Christian Anita Bryant launched Save Our Children, Inc, promoting the idea that gay people were a threat to society and succeeded in having recent hard-won gay rights repealed in Dade County, Florida. She testified that children, homes, and schools were endangered, because 'homosexuals cannot reproduce – so they must recruit. And to freshen their ranks, they must recruit the youth of America.'[5] Following her success in Florida, Bryant launched a rolling opposition to gay rights. The implication for queer parents was catastrophic. A flyer circulated ahead of the San Francisco rally tells of how Jeanne Jullion, a lesbian mother, had lost custody of her four- and eight-year-old sons in a decision based on sexual orientation rather than parenting ability. On 23 May, her four-year-old had been forcibly removed from her by a group of men including his father, a lawyer and policemen. The child was not told where he was going or allowed to bid his mother farewell. 'This decision has ramifications far beyond the present case. The rights of all of us are in danger.'[6]

These are not just the problems of our yesterdays. In their video *Nel Nome Del Padre* (*In the Name of the Father*, 2018) Silvia Campidelli and Luna Coppola, who work together as Duae Collective, detail their fight with the Italian state to be recognized as the parents of their children. Italian by birth and based in Barcelona, the artists sit on their bed as their two children play around them – children who, for the first year of their life, were considered stateless persons. 'In Italy, the "natural" family is formed from a socially recognized and lasting union of a man with a woman and a child,' the couple explain in the video. Without the name of the father, it took a year of fighting to be officially recognized as legal parents of their own children. Five years later, the rights won by Campidelli and Coppola, and other queer families, were repealed. In 2023, the right-wing government of Giorgia Meloni demanded councils only register a child's biological parent, leaving hundreds of couples in a legally precarious situation, with unregistered parents unable to make medical decisions or take on care of their own children if a partner dies.[7]

a pretended family relationship

Britain's 'Anita Bryant' moment came in 1986, amid a wave of disinformation and homophobic hype whipped up over a sweet and well-observed storybook. Designed to help children understand that not all families took the same shape, *Jenny Lives with Eric and Martin* **128** was written by Danish children's author Susanne Bösche. Illustrated with photographs by Andreas Hansen, it follows a sunny weekend in the life of a little girl who lives with her dad and stepfather. Eric and Martin go through the everyday ups and downs of life: they visit the laundrette, navigate a tantrum, and get woken up too early on Saturday morning. There are also episodes that touch on the particularities of life with gay parents. We meet Jenny's mum Karen who lives nearby and joins them to organize a surprise birthday tea for Eric. They experience a homophobic response from a neighbour, and Eric gently helps Jenny process it. The book did not cause a scandal on publication in Denmark in 1981. In 1983 an English-language version was published by the Gay Men's Press, and in 1986 a copy was made available to teachers in a centre run by the Inner London Education Authority as part of a resource for staff who wanted to know more about same sex parents. True to form, the British press whipped up a scandal with misleading reports that the book was available to children in school libraries and that it was 'homosexual propaganda' with the implication that children were being 'recruited'. Bösche's book was a work of fiction. The figures in the photographs are the author's own daughter Louise and her actor neighbours Henrik and Lars. Bösche had no agenda to promote anything, she was a professional author who wanted to create a book that reflected the lives of children she knew in Denmark. Back in the UK, however, the furore over *Jenny Lives with Eric and Martin* contributed to the passing of Section 28 of the 1988 Local Government Act, a clause which forbade 'the teaching in any maintained school of the acceptability of homosexuality as a pretended family relationship.'

The language of this new legislation was picked up by Sunil Gupta for his work *'Pretended' Family Relationships* (1988) **129**. The series had started as an exploration of multiracial queer relationships: 'I was in one and it seemed to be quite the cool thing to do in London,' Gupta recalled.[8] Meanwhile Margaret Thatcher's government was pushing in the opposite direction, trying to place the everyday of gay experience out of sight. In each triptych Gupta offers a colour portrait of a couple in a suggested

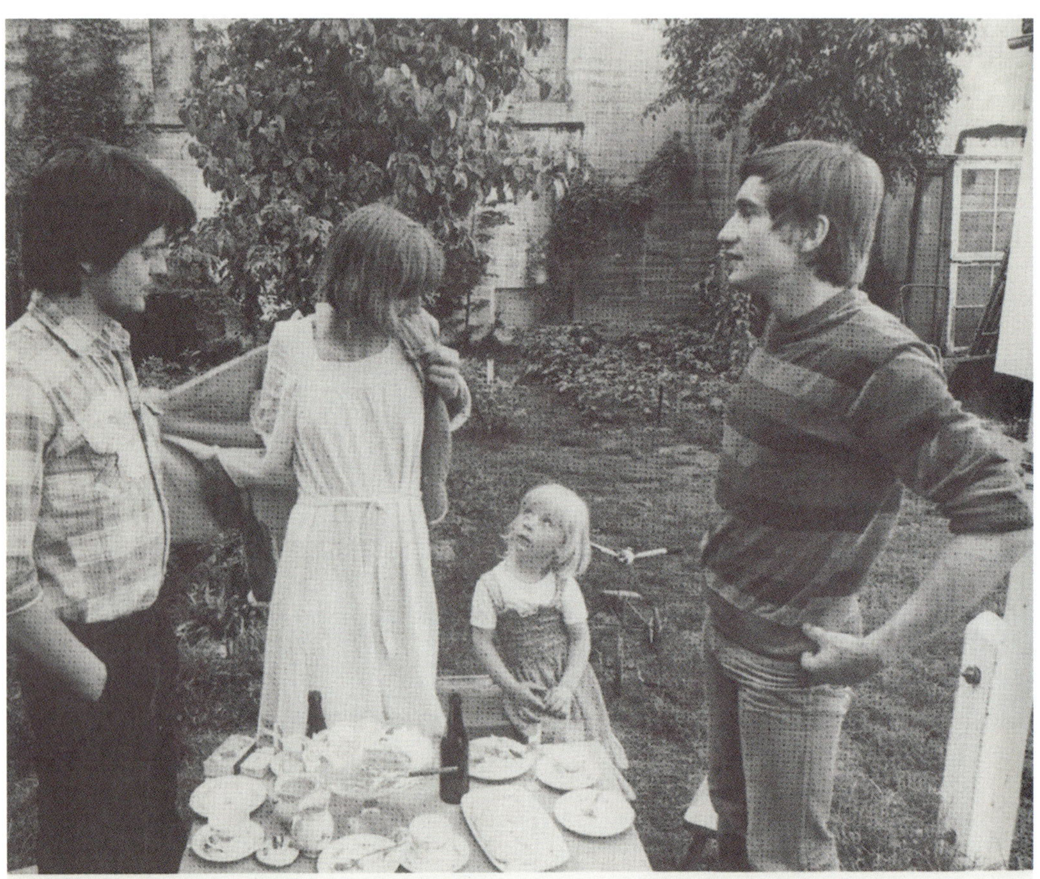

The time passes much too quickly.
Suddenly it is evening and Karen gets
up and puts on her jacket.
   "I must go now," she says.
"Thanks for a lovely party."
   "Oh, do you have to go so soon?"
Jenny asks sadly.

12

128.
Susanne Bösche
and Andreas Hansen,
*Jenny Lives With
Eric and Martin*,
1981/1983

129.
Sunil Gupta,
Untitled #9,
from the series
*'Pretended' Family
Relationships*,
1988–2021

romantic relationship. Most are pictured in a relaxed domestic setting – lounging in casual clothes on a bed or sofa, sharing tea and a cigarette on the roof – remarkable for the very ordinariness of their lives together.

To the right of each picture is a black-and-white strip showing documentation from an anti-Section 28 protest. We see snippets of protest banners, parents and kids, and helmeted police officers against a backdrop of London landmarks. The photographic panels are separated by a fragment of poetry by Gupta's then partner Stephen Dodd, which hints at complex inner lives and everyday struggles. In the midst of the AIDS epidemic, at a moment when gays and lesbians were portrayed as sinister and predatory by the British media, the affectionate domesticity of *'Pretended' Family Relationships* gave an alternative view. Section 28 had repercussions for those well beyond the school system, and hit those in the culture sector particularly hard, as Gupta notes, because 'productions across many art forms depended upon venues and funding from local authorities.'[9] These were the people that Section 28 sought to place out of sight.

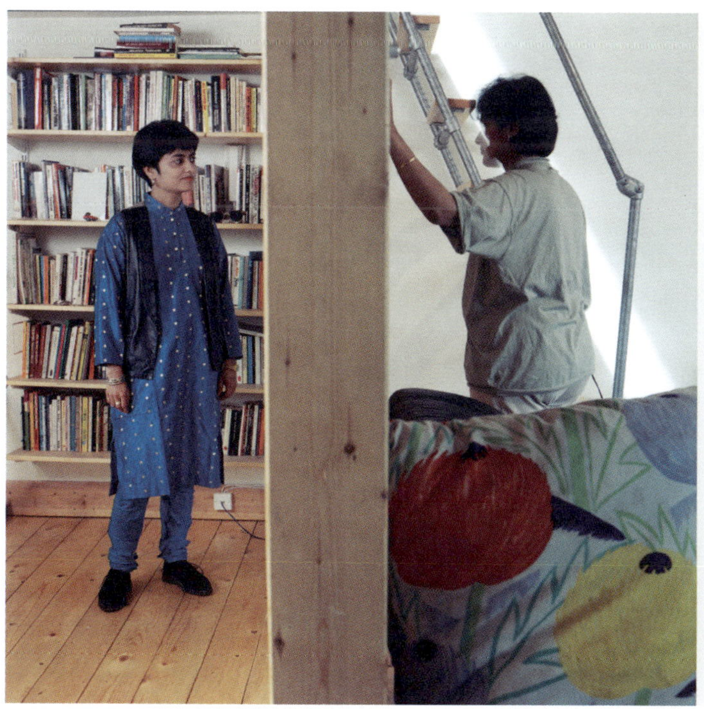

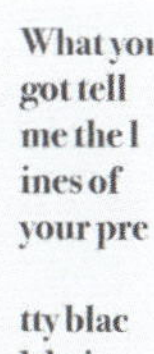

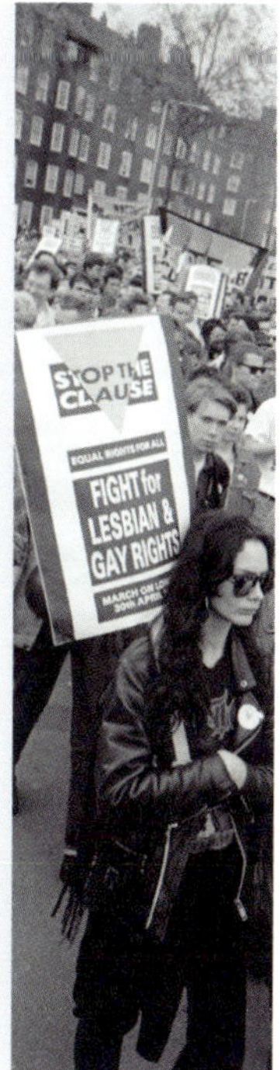

129

i feel like / a science experiment

In a 2017 short film made as part of her MA thesis, Candy Guinea's *Mariposa* **130** charts her partner Castro's journey to conceive, which commences with the question of how, as a lesbian couple, you get pregnant. The route is long. It takes two years to find a sperm donor. Many, many months down the line, the cute reveal moments that they perform over each pregnancy test become tense and dispiriting. Eventually they seek professional help. Two moments in the film touch on Castro's anxiety around her forthcoming pregnancy. As she sits in a barber's chair having her short back and sides neatened, we hear her worrying about feeling 'unsafe' in the face of people's reactions. Like Catherine Opie, who we met in Chapters 1 and 3, Castro does not conform to the stereotypical vision of femininity associated with the pregnant body. She worries about how public her pregnancy will be, and about having to share the news with her colleagues and students at school. 'For someone who is straight, cis-gendered, the question "oh, how did you get pregnant?" wouldn't come up in the classroom, because that would be a very inappropriate question to ask someone who's straight. For me that will be the question that would come, again and again and again.' The couple shop for baby equipment at a local second-hand store. Castro visibly tenses as Candy proposes maternity options. She usually rocks a sharp menswear style – what will she wear? Her impeccably constructed butch persona is under imminent threat from the visible condition of pregnancy.

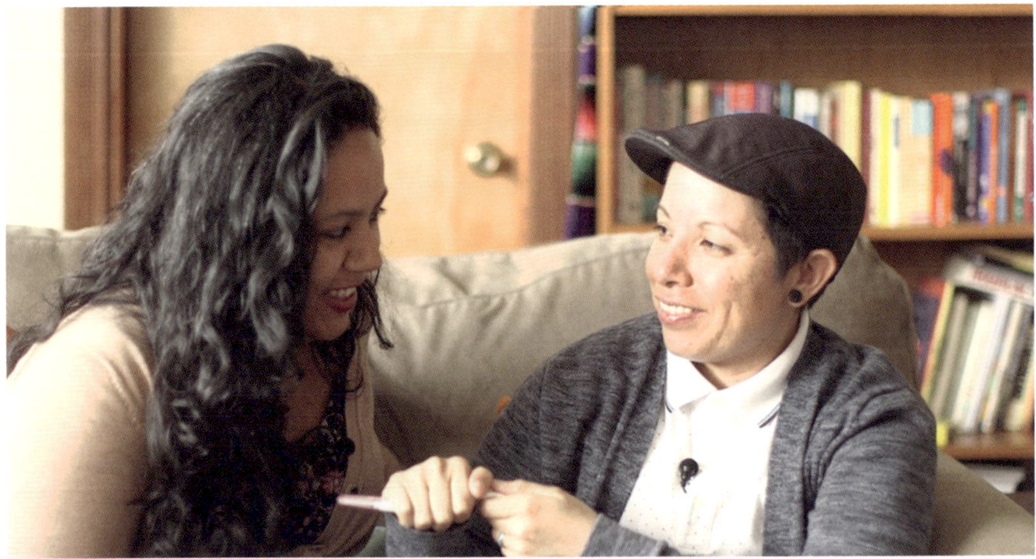

•

I first encountered the work of Del LaGrace Volcano through their spicy photographs of drag kings and leather-loving lesbian subcultures in the UK and US in the 1990s. Today they live in a small town in Sweden with their long-term partner with whom they parent outside of gender binaries **131**. Volcano goes by the name 'MaPa' and describes with delight their child Mika's thoughtful response when asked at school, aged five, whether they were a boy or girl: 'Well, MaPa, I say that I'm both, but I know I'm a boy. And I also say "that question – it's not important for us."' Volcano speaks of their great happiness in becoming a parent, but also notes that they have lost a lot of their 'queer capital' by engaging in the heterosexual-associated activity of raising children. 'How we construct our queer identities is often in a reactionary way. Whatever heterosexuals do, we don't do. Even though we do shit and eat and go to the movies and all those other things.' Volcano instead chooses to position family-making as an act of resistance 'because the world needs more good men, and who better to create them than me?'[10]

•

The *Queer Birth Project* (2021–26) is a five-year collaboration between artist Liss LaFleur and sociologist Katherine Sobering, at the heart of which is a database of personal testimonies gathered from across the US. The first part of this queer reimagining of Judy Chicago's *Birth Project* (1980–85) asked how it was to be pregnant in a femme, butch, trans or non-binary body. As LaFleur points out, if we don't openly discuss the specifics of queer birth, there is little hope of providing adequate healthcare and community support. Within suspended curtains of long yellow fringing, like a giant baby's mobile, interview fragments play out as a sing-song digitized lullaby in a sci-fi soundscape. 'I feel like/ a science experiment/ It is strange to take up so much space,' the digital voice tells us. 'Pregnancy helped to confirm what I knew from a very young age, which is that I'm not a woman.' Pregnancy and birth, apparently the very essence of womanly identity, is experienced from the converse perspective. Elsewhere, the voice describes pregnancy as a trans man as an experience of private pleasure and public anxiety: 'I hated/ the way people looked at me/ and/ tried to stay inside as much as possible'. There seems to be an ever-present chorus of whispers just out of earshot, questioning the interviewees' status as parents, struggling to reconcile markers of the masculine and feminine.

130.
Candy Guinea,
Mariposa, 2017

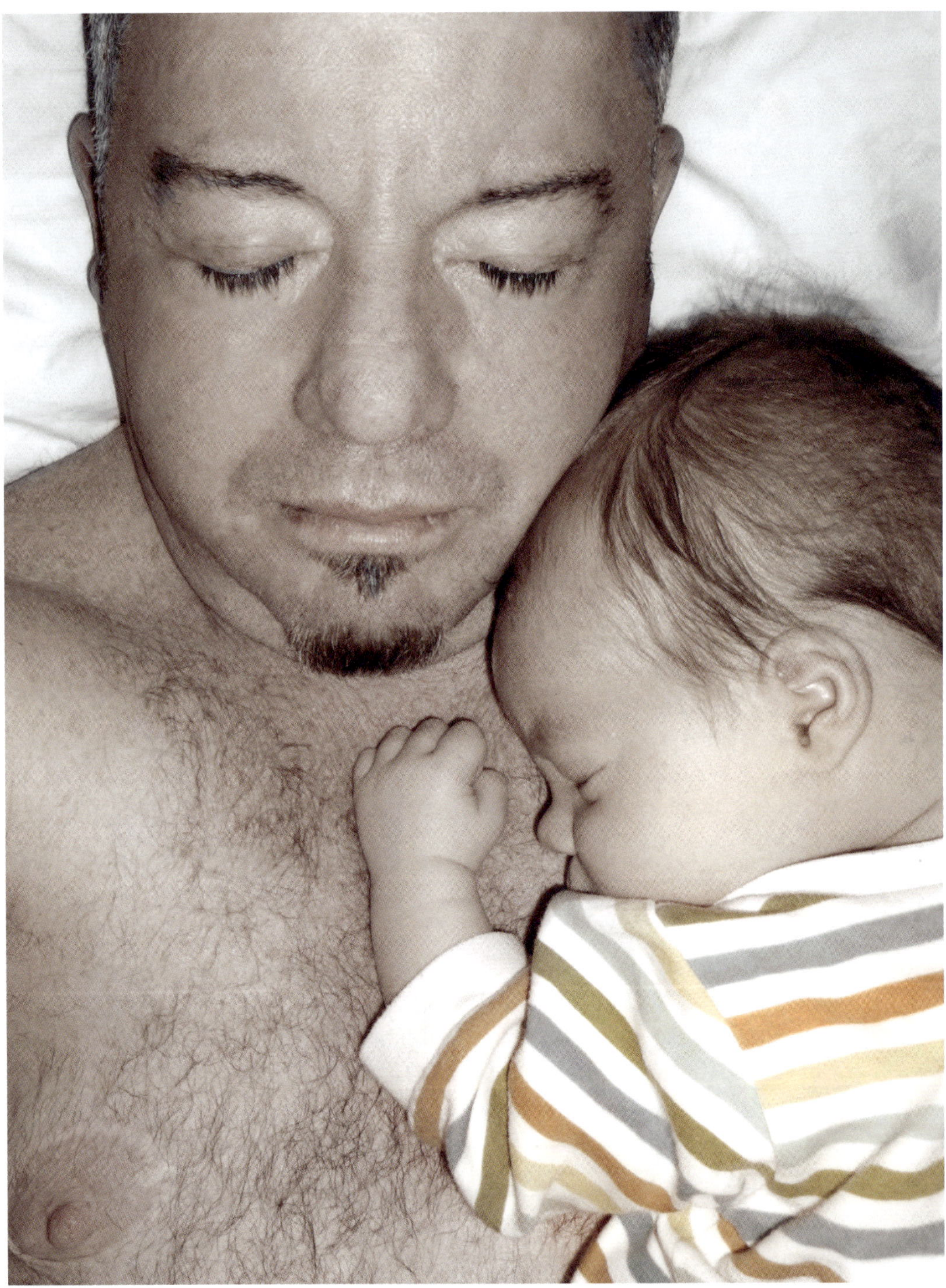

131

slack-poor life

Where are the kinship networks to support these new families in their new shapes? The consciousness-raising groups that transformed the lives of Cathy Cade and her contemporaries were a phenomenon of the 1970s and 1980s. In our current century the search for community more often happens online. Helen Benigson's film *Jude* (2020) **132** is the story of the eponymous wife of an orthodox rabbi who realizes they are queer and gender nonconforming. Jude tells their story, accompanied first by family photographs, then, aften an arranged marriage and move from Israel to a new community in London, by a waterfall of Facebook messages. As the rabbi's wife, Jude's Facebook 'friends' offer their approval of the wig with which they cover their natural hair, and of their repeated pregnancies. Jude has three babies in quick succession. Facebook tells them they look beautiful as a new mother. Inside they are consumed by anxiety and depression, and feel trapped. Another identity starts to emerge in the online messages: rainbow flags, questions about gender identity. After revealing their sexuality during a marriage counselling session, the couple get divorced and Jude faces a new life as a single parent, cut off from their husband's community, entirely alone. In a post, they celebrate five years as a queer single mother – the support they receive in return bears testament to a new community acquired online in the intervening years. Jude's life on social media goes unmentioned in the verbal narrative: it is held apart from the story of their life, and yet, Benigson suggests, it became an essential extension of their experience as a parent. A portal held in the palm of their hand.

131.
Del LaGrace Volcano,
*MaPa Del and Mika,
Örebro, Sweden*, 2011

132.
Helen Benigson,
Jude, 2020

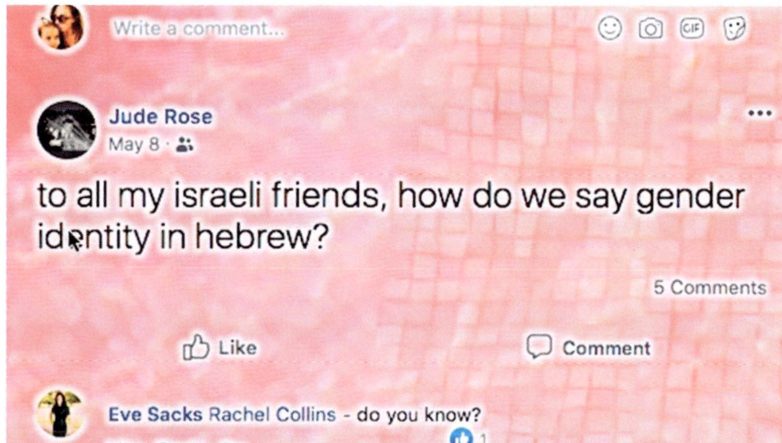

•

It's early morning and Sadie Lune is doing various mum things while talking to me from her home in Berlin. An artist, sex worker, and pleasure activist **133**, I first encountered Lune's work via a video she posted in 2011 initiating her project *Biological Clock*. In the video, Lune lounged on a velvet sofa in sperm-print shorts and red stilettos, a snake writhing around her, and announced her desire to have a child. The video solicited donations to help make it happen: 'because you know what's expensive? Children. And self-funded art projects.' The centrepiece of *Biological Clock* was an insemination performance at a San Francisco art gallery, during which Lune hoped to conceive surrounded by a loving and turned-on community of supportive queers. She describes it as a 'community ritual gangbang' albeit the 'banging' was of the queer hands, vibes and toys variety. The ritual was led by Lune's 'handmade-ins' who guided the group through chants and exercises, then provided erotic stimulation to Lune, and her inseminator elect Oberon. The payload was delivered by Oberon in private and delivered to the handmade-ins who manually insemi-nated Lune, while those gathered were invited to contribute to the erotic energy in the room. In performing conception as a public ritual, Lune gathered a community around herself and solicited their support in her coming life (pun absolutely intended) as a mother. The business of making and raising children is unpre-dictable. Which makes it tricky material for performance art, and for planning life in general. Lune didn't conceive during *Biological Clock* but through routine insemination some months later. She moved to Berlin heavily pregnant, and laboured with the support of queer friends, an experience she had imagined concluding in a beautiful home birth, but, over sixty hours later, ended with an emergency C-section. Lune's life as a mother – as a co-parent within an expanded unconventional family – had begun. Lune consciously provokes questions about who is allowed to be a mother, which people's pregnancies get to be celebrated, and how those living unconventional lives might construct new family constellations around themselves.

'I wanted a family made out of love and spirituality and deep intersectionally feminist political solidarity, but that is a fucking big ask in the world in which we live,' Lune told me. 'This is a group I feel so tender and protective of, but it's hard. I think it's hard with any new child to understand the levels of commit-ment and care you can expect or receive from any person in your world. If you are trying to architect something that is outside

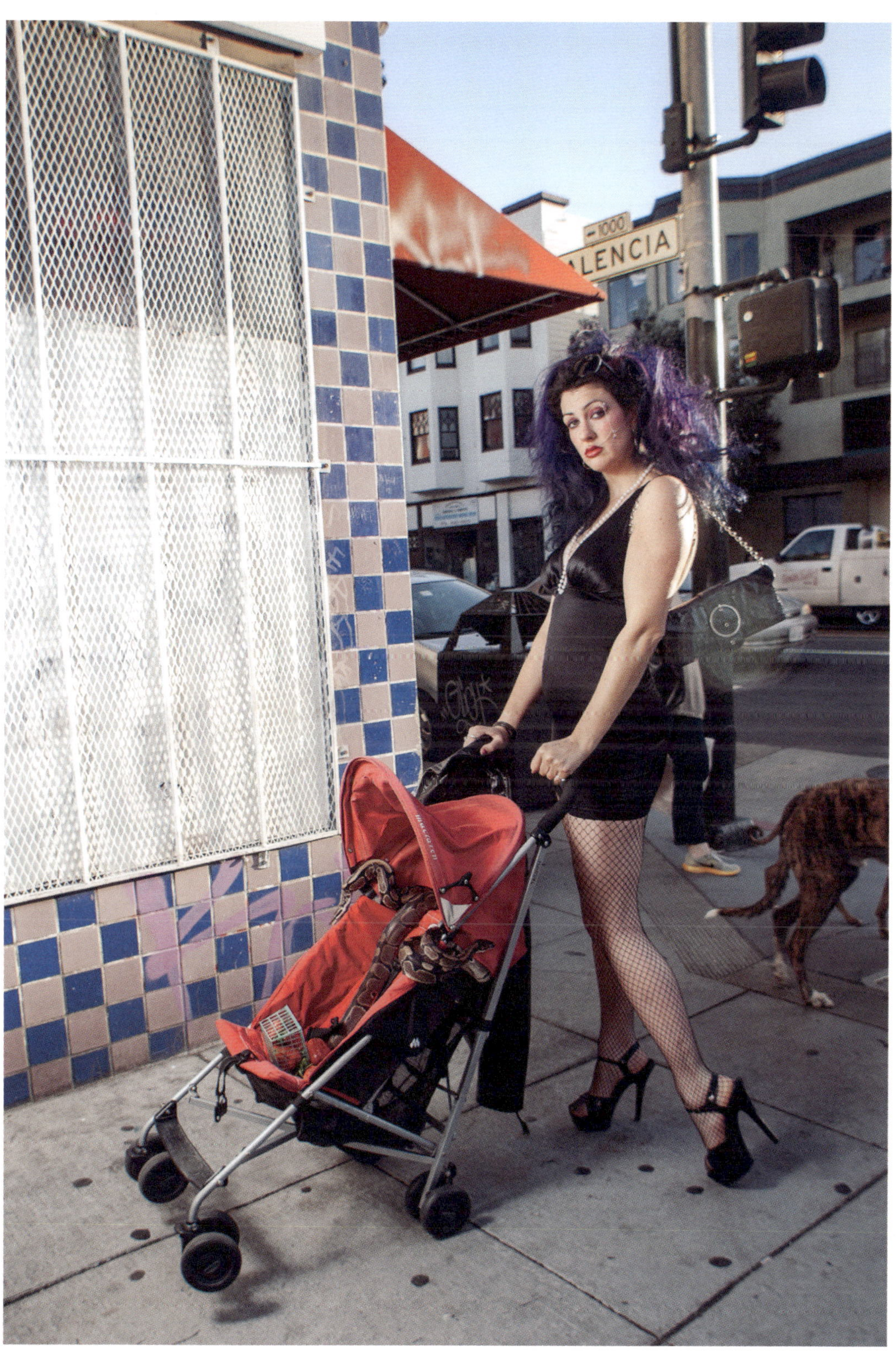
1000
ALENCIA

the well-worn paths, that is a lot of extra work. The community really has to rise up and give extra support to that constellation so they can see it thrive, but at the end of the day the birth parent is usually holding the baby.'[11]

Lune is a mother of two, and busies herself leaving the house while we talk – who has time for art chat on top of mothering and the general business of life? As she walks out of her door, she pauses to tell me about a 1970s parody religion called the Church of the Subgenius in which the quality of 'slack' was held sacred. 'I think about 1970s second wave feminists a lot, and the slack energy and time they had available that allowed people to organize,' she tells me, pointing out how slack-poor contemporary city life is, and the challenge that poses to collective parenting. 'When people need all the hours in the day to make money to support themselves or fulfil individual ambitions, it's hard to spend time helping your community.'

the bumptious fray

Back to my bacterial family. For it strikes me that the self-same impediments to collective parenting that Lune describes apply to engagement with the broader environment. Care requires time. The project of queer, collective and other forms of radical parenting shares much common ground with broader sustainable practice. Donna Haraway invites us to 'Make kin, not babies!' – to form communities of mutual support.[12] To extend the labour of mothering to non-human as well as human kin. I have had many conversations with young artists who feel they should not reproduce in a time of climate crisis. Thinking of mothering in this expanded sense and committing to networks of care in the full knowledge that this is a demanding and long-term relationship, is a way forward. As Lune pointed out to me, rather than proffering theories and engaging in utopian thinking, we need some positive models to show how such expansive kinship networks might be sustained long term, amid all the demands and challenges of real life.

•

Tabita Rezaire's *Amakaba* is not an artwork but a site in the Amazonian rainforest of French Guyana, imagined as a farm, a site of connection to ancestry, a spiritual retreat, and a birth centre. It is light years away from the sparkly high artifice of the digital realm for which Rezaire is known as an artist **134**, though absolutely congruent with the issues that inform her work, among them indigenous and ancient knowledge systems, and spiritual practice rooted in 'womb wisdom'. A doula whose grandmother was a celebrated midwife, Rezaire positions birth practice at the centre of her environmental project. '*Amakaba* is about birth on so many levels, from the birth of a plant, to a child, to another dimension of existence,' she has said. 'I literally see *Amakaba* as a womb that you can go into in order to be rebirthed – to cleanse.'[13] In her 2021 book *Womb Consciousness*, Rezaire locates her work with mothers and children in both spiritual and political terms. 'If we really want to serve the world we exist in, to participate in the struggle for decolonization and the birth of a decolonial reality, we must radically transform the way we support expectant mothers and caretakers. I plant the seeds for a future generation to come out of our wombs in tune with the earth, with all species, with themselves, and with spirit.'[14] As Rezaire points out, we often ask ourselves what kind of world we'll leave our children, but seldom what kind of children we'll leave our world.

•

Feral Domestic. I couldn't love that title more. It speaks of the home as a wild place, outside of rules and conventions. An untamed way of keeping house. It's the umbrella title to a trilogy of experimental films made by Dani and Sheilah ReStack – *Strangely Ordinary This Devotion* (2017) **135**, *Come Coyote* (2019) and *Future From Inside* (2022) – each of which is like a crazed family album melding the real and fantastical. The *Feral Domestic* is a homelife in which adults make art and do chores and play with the kids and process their disputes through creative acts and have sex and acknowledge the horrible parts of reality are alongside the delightful. There are injured animals in this visual world, but there are also flowers. The ReStack's chosen name is a step away from a 'patriarchal lineage of ownership' says Sheilah, and also a reference to their layered collaborative process.[15] In the eco-fantasy narrative that gently bubbles under the first film, a new generation of children adapted to live without water emerges 'as a result of lesbian activity in Ohio.' There are witchy goings on involving the burial of bloody objects and an incision being sliced into Dani's scalp, which I could not watch. From an early scene in which Sheilah inserts a rock into Dani's mouth, the mineral and biological are tightly bound. Just as there is little separation between the ReStacks' life and their art, so their separation from

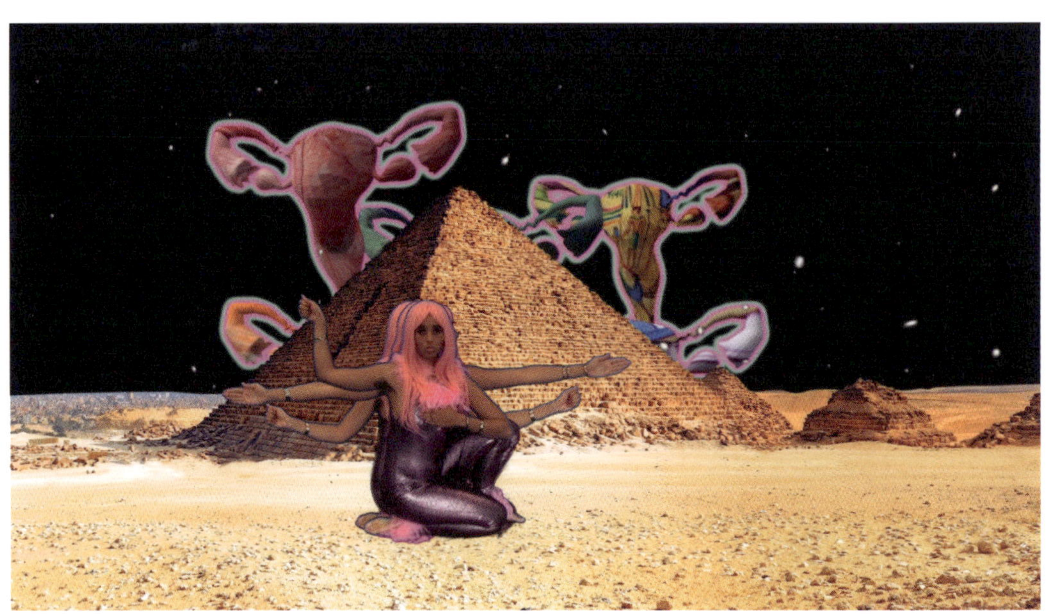

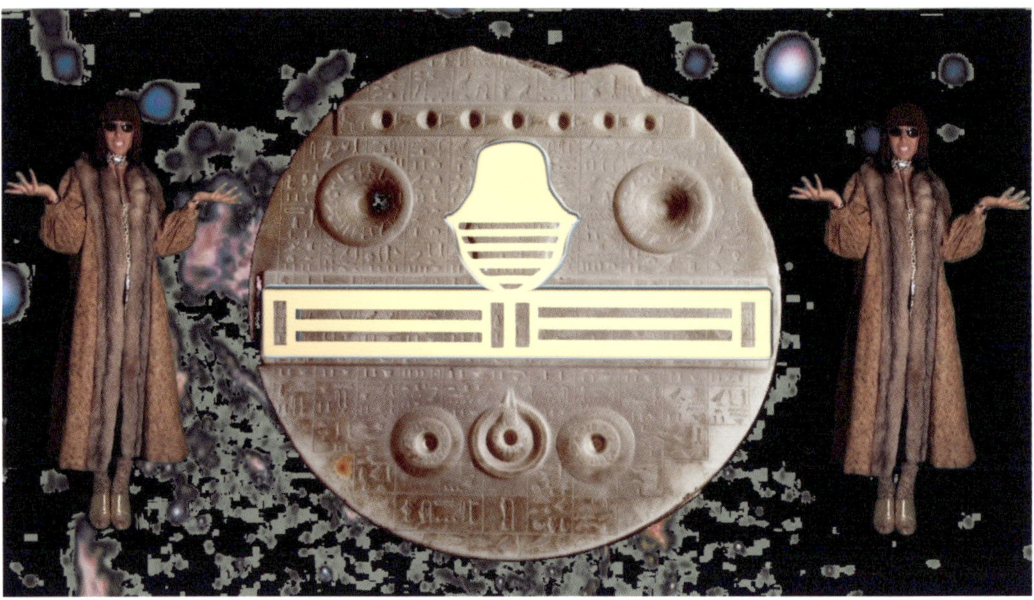

134

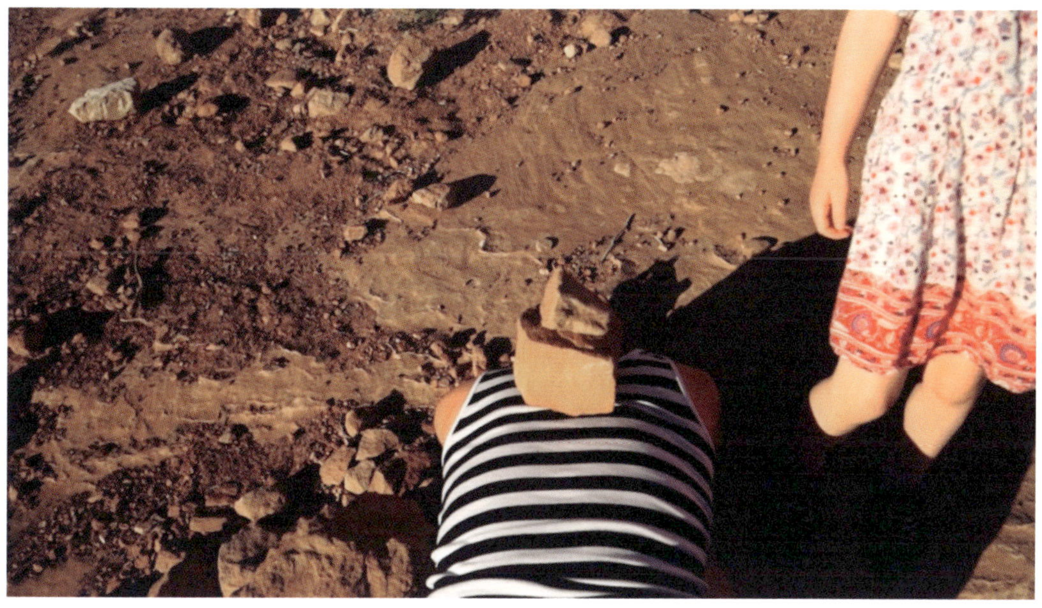

135

134.
Tabita Rezaire,
Hoetep Blessings,
2016

135.
Dani and Sheilah
ReStack, *Strangely
Ordinary This
Devotion*, 2017

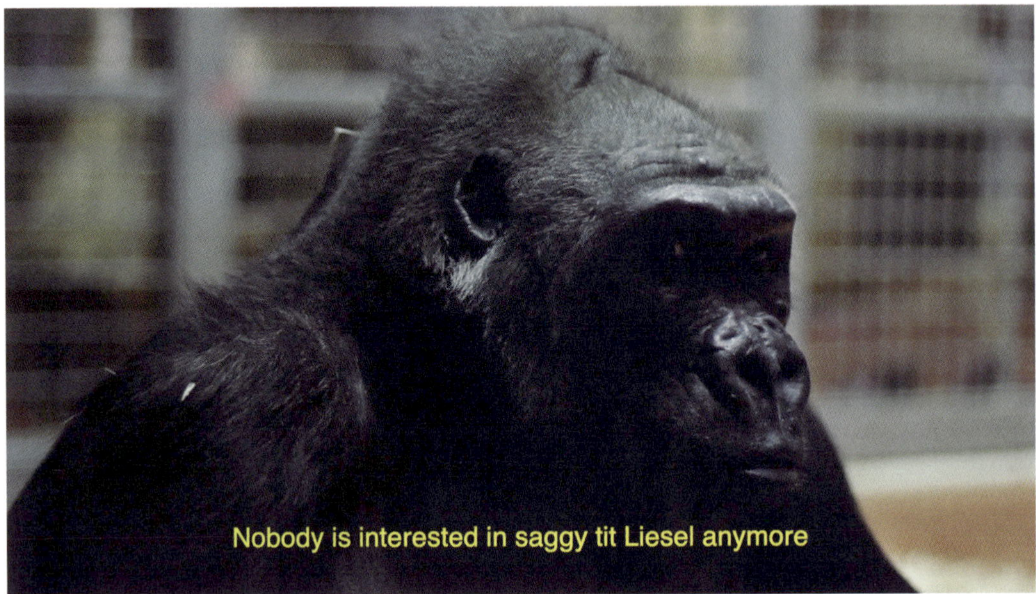

136

the wild landscape seems paper thin. The artists derive their seamless and often shocking shifts between different registers from watching their daughter Rose as a young girl, transported by flights of imagination while engaged in the most everyday tasks. *Future From Inside* is peppered with intense conversations about wanting and not wanting children, performed by female and non-binary couples who speak Dani and Sheilah's arguments about conceiving biological kin. Characters carry brimming pans of water, echoing the fragile weightiness of late pregnancy. Meanwhile, the lesbian witches of Ohio have expanded their powers, and are able to channel visions from the future. In its surreal and scrapbooky intimacy, *Feral Domestic* is a manifesto of sorts: a proposal that rural family life can also be radical.

baby animals

What about the animal herself as mother? In *Gorilla Milk* (2020) **136**, Liesel Burisch joins Csilla Frank, a hobby primatologist and YouTube vlogger, to observe an elderly primate with whom the artist shares a name. 'This is Liesel, she is 43 years old, lives in Budapest zoo and is miserable', Burisch types over footage of this hirsute matriarch. Frank enjoys telling gorilla Liesel how beautiful she is and shoots whimsical videos of her looking variously depressed or playful. Burisch is transfixed by the gorilla's empty, wrinkled breasts and her loss of status within the group following childbirth and the surgical removal of a suspected cancerous ovary. 'Because what is left of you when you are no longer either fertile or desirable?' Burisch asks, noting that the younger females get a better share of the food. 'Nobody is interested in saggy tit Liesel anymore.' The artist lists the things they share: their name, their vampire-like teeth, their eyes and their nipples. 'And Liesel takes what others consider trash, another thing we have in common.' Burisch is a birth worker and the author of *Queer Nursing* (2020), a tenderly empathetic guide to feeding and weaning for co-parents and allies. They are interested in the politics of interdependence and systems of care. *Gorilla Milk* offers the flip vision: an extreme metaphor for the maternal experience. A figure trapped in a literal cage, diminished by a social structure that does not value an elderly maternal figure.

•

Laure Prouvost's sticky and tentacular installation *MOOTHERR* (2021) **137** breathes in rasping swooshes and pulses with light. We are surrounded by the body of a fantastical octopus, with domed glass breasts drooping from her suckers, glistening, wet and abundant, dripping ink on the gallery floor. She seems to be waiting for something, or someone. Occasionally a voice echoes around the arching tentacles – 'Motherr!' – urgent and anxious. This writhing cyborg octopus is a nurturing, tactile pendant to Louise Bourgeois's hard and spiky spider mother. Prouvost describes the octopus as a malleable entity, thinking through touch. This is an ancient mother, which predates the human by some 300 million years. She only spawns once then she stops eating and wastes away, dying before the eggs hatch. Prouvost's hybrid entity is here to nurture her young and pass on knowledge, language and memories. We hear the whispered sounds of a French mother – perhaps Prouvost – talking to her children. For Prouvost the work is also about the 'extreme beauty of pure love' that can come with mothering: the joy and magic of being with a young creature, the pleasure of touching and being together.[16] In Prouvost's watery, milky world, breasts are imagined as fountains offering a never-ending abundance of nourishment, and the job of maternal nurture becomes a collective act in which the boundaries between mother and other, human and more-than-human soften and blur.

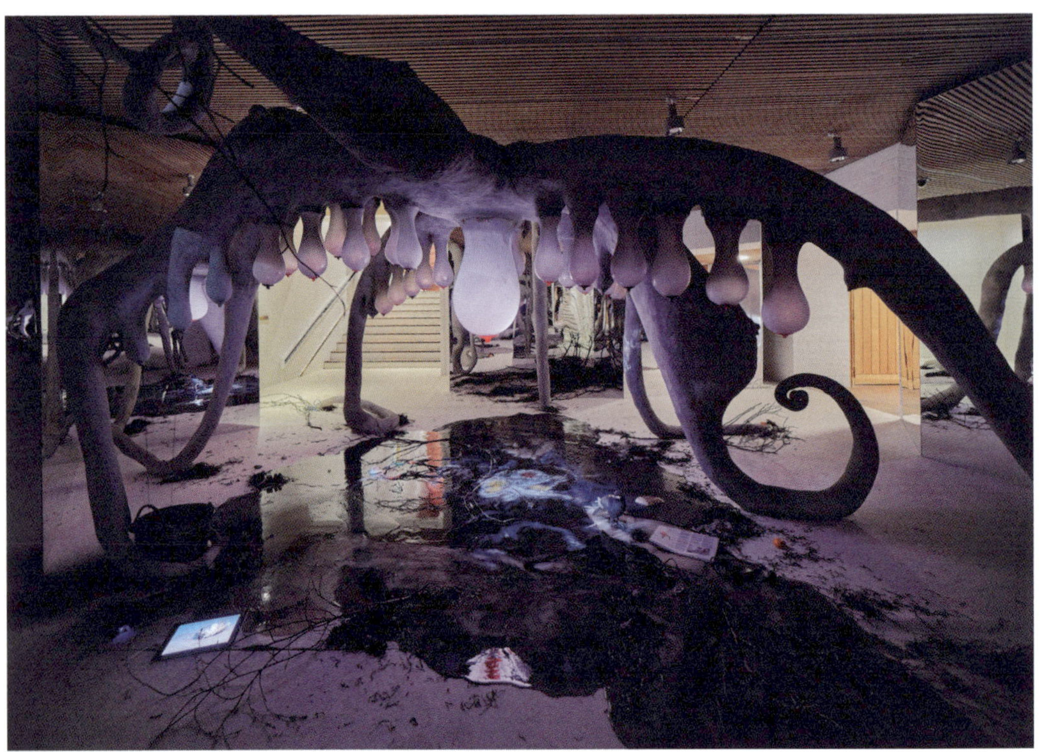

137

137.
Laure Prouvost,
MOOTHERR,
2021

mothering the more than human

The first chapter of this book opened with a painting of the Madonna breastfeeding her new-born son. I would like to end it with a *pietà* **138**. Kiki Smith portrays herself seated, barefoot, hair fuzzing around her head like a halo. Across her lap in place of the dead Christ lies her cat Ginzer. Much of Smith's work explores humans' cultural relationship to animals, and the myths and symbols that bind them. Ginzer was, she explains 'my primary relationship in major parts of my life…my cat was my solace.' She had first attempted a *pietà* with him while he was still alive:

> *I had a friend of mine take a picture of me holding the cat. I was big and heavy and voluptuous and the cat was just sort of sitting there, thinking, what are you doing to me?*
> *It had no meaning, it had no substance to it. It was totally not true.*[17]

That it took Ginzer's actual death for Smith to successfully make her *Pietà* with him two years later should not suggest she did so flippantly. This is a picture of true heartbreak. Smith's eyes are so swollen with weeping that she can barely raise the lids. Describing their relationship, she reaches for the language of family and mothering. 'I didn't live with anybody and the cat gave me a great deal of company and solace and pleasure and direction. It was good to look after something.'[18] The seriousness of Smith's *Pietà* makes me think of Ciara Healy's text 'Mother to the Other' (2021). With admirable frankness, Healy places her experience as a woman who has unexplained infertility in historic and cultural context. She receives judgment from some quarters where she might have expected support, and a distinct lack of sympathy from others. 'As the years passed, and the likelihood of conceiving, adopting or fostering a child became more and more unlikely, I became increasingly interested in finding a way of doing justice to the maternal intensity I treasured in my other non-human relationships,' she writes. 'These relationships allowed me to experience what I have come to call an enriched form of mothering the more than human world.'[19] Healy looks to the Scottish and Irish myth of the selkie, a seal-person who could set aside their skin and walk on land as human. In remote communities, a 'selkie baby' was an infant of mysterious parentage, considered to have mystical qualities: to have 'lain with the selkies' offered a veil of convenience for acts of adultery. For

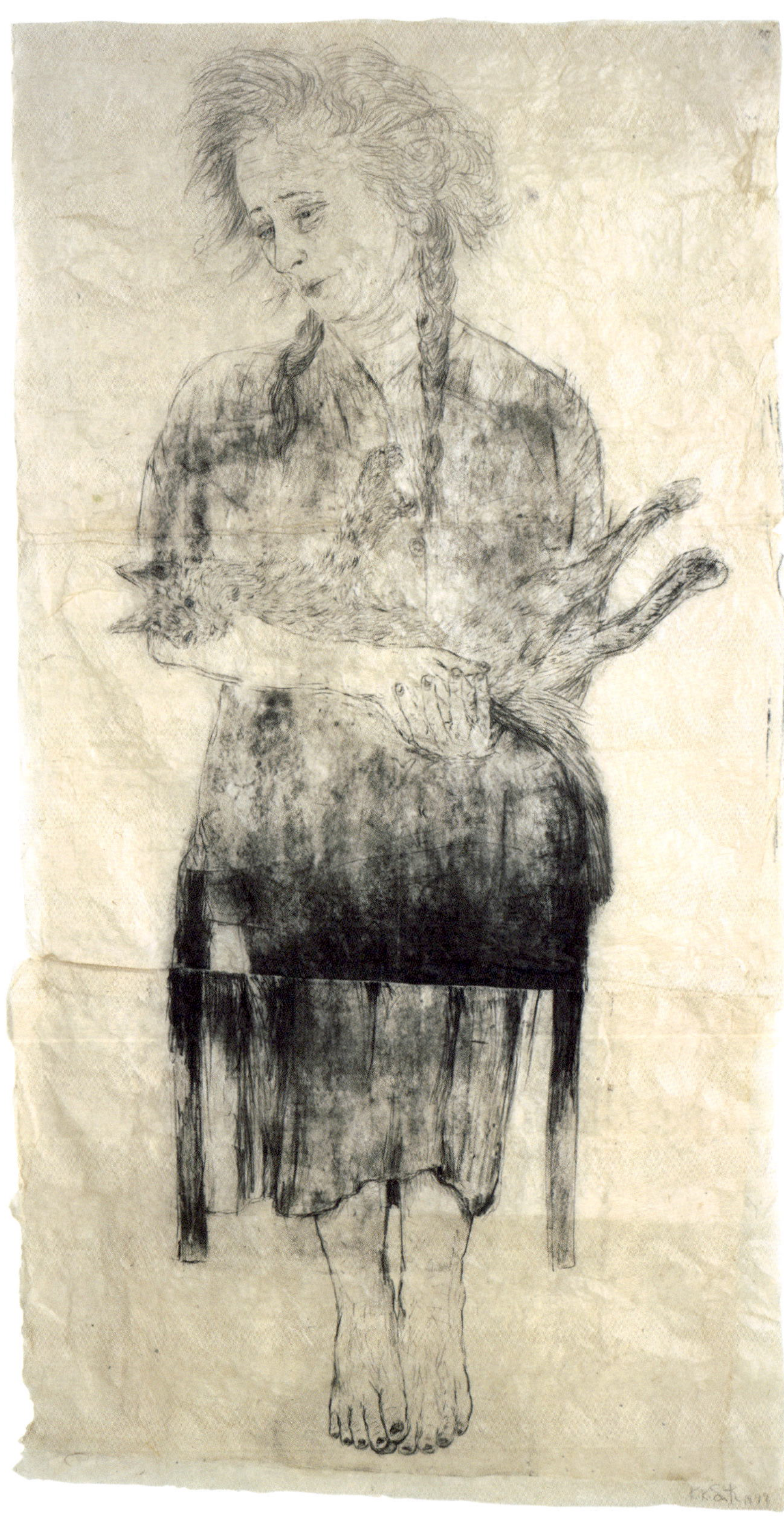

138.
Kiki Smith,
Pietà, 1999

Healy, the myth becomes a way to understand the relationship between the human and the more-than-human, and she comes to think of her little white dog as her own selkie baby. Mothering the 'other' becomes a way for Healy to articulate and frame her relationship to the world around her that becomes hypersensitized to the impact all objects and entities have on one another. 'While it remains an experience rarely articulated in art or in life, those of us who find ourselves involuntarily childless, might just be the ones who will reconsider and revision motherhood in this uncertain and fragile future.'

Pietà is most commonly taken to mean 'pity' or 'compassion', but it can also be understood as 'devotion'. It is in this spirit that I wish to read Smith's drawing. It is a picture of sorrow, an act of mourning, a memorial gesture. It is also a portrait of devotion. And that, it seems to me, is really the heart of the matter.

notes

introduction

1 Conversation with the author, November 2019.

2 Justine Kurland, 'Six Years on the Road, as an Artist and a Mother' *The New Yorker*, 21 October 2016 <www.newyorker.com/culture/photo-booth/six-years-on-the-road-as-an-artist-and-a-mother> [accessed 22 October 2023].

3 See Hettie Judah, 'Full, Messy and Beautiful', in Dr Kate McMillan (ed.) *Representation of Female Artists in Britain During 2019* (London: Freelands Foundation, 2020 pp. 14–19; Hettie Judah, *How Not to Exclude Artist Mothers (and other parents)* (London: Lund Humphries, 2022); and Hettie Judah et al. 'How Not to Exclude Artist Parents' <www.artist-parents.com> [accessed 22 October 2023].

4 Jérome Sans, 'The Screen of the Real: Interview with Lea Lublin', in Matthias Muhling and Stephanie Weber (eds) *Lea Lublin: Retrospective* (Cologne: Snoek, 2015) p. 201.

5 Conversation with the author, July 2023.

6 Hilary Robinson, 'The Body of the Mother: Paradoxes and Absences', in Angela Kingston (ed.) *Mothers* (Birmingham: Ikon Gallery, 1990) p. 7.

chapter 1

1 Commonly her older relative Elizabeth – mother to John the Baptist – and her own mother Anne. Both figures also experienced miraculous conceptions. St Marina the Monk makes very rare appearances clutching a baby.

2 Lennard J. David, 'Migrant Mother: Dorothea Lange and the Truth of Photography' *LA Review of Books*. March 2020 <lareviewofbooks.org/article/migrant-mother-dorothea-lange-truth-photography> [accessed 22 October 2023].

3 Dedication by Jim Cave, quoted in Anna Halprin, 'Planetary Dance' *TDR* (1988–), Vol. 33, No. 2, Summer 1989, p. 60.

4 Adriaan de Buck, *The Ancient Egyptian Coffin Texts* (Chicago: University of Chicago Press, 1935–61), quoted in Susan Tower Hollis, 'Women of Ancient Egypt and the Sky Goddess Nut' *The Journal of American Folklore*, Vol. 100, No. 398, Oct–Dec 1987, p. 497.

5 Quoted in Kaira M. Cabañas, 'Ana Mendieta: "Pain of Cuba, Body I Am"' *Woman's Art Journal*, Vol. 20, No. 1, Spring–Summer 1999, p. 12.

6 Ibid, p. 14.

7 Mutu titled one of her exhibitions 'Nguva na Nyoka' – 'Sirens and Serpents' in Kiswahili.

8 LeRoy McDermott, 'Self-Representation in Upper Paleolithic Female Figurines' *Current Anthropology*, Vol. 37, No. 2, April 1996, p. 231.

9 Ian Hodde, 'Women and Men at Çatalhöyük' *Scientific American*, 1 January 2005 <www.scientificamerican.com/article/women-and-men-at-atalhyk-2005-01> [accessed 22 October 2023].

10 Judy Chicago, *Birth Project* (New York: Doubleday, 1985) quoted at <throughtheflower.org/projects/birth-project> [accessed 22 October 2023].

11 Ibid.

12 Caroline Malone, 'Ritual Space and Structure – the context of Cult in Malta and Gozo' in Caroline Malone, David Barrowclough (eds) *Cult in Context: Reconsidering Ritual in Archaeology* (Oxford: Oxbow Books, 2010).

13 Cynthia Eller, *The Myth of Matriarchal Prehistory, Why an Invented Past Won't Give Women a Future* (Boston: Beacon Press, 2000) <www.nytimes.com/books/first/e/eller-myth.html> [accessed 22 October 2023].

14 Adrienne Rich, *Of Woman Born* (New York: Norton, 1976/86) pp. 84–109.

15 Jennie Klein, 'Goddess: Feminist Art and Spirituality in the 1970s' *Feminist Studies*, Vol. 35, No. 3, Fall 2009, p. 588.

16 Estate of Monica Sjöö <monicasjoo.co.uk/2014/03/28/god-giving-birth> [accessed 22 October 2023].

17 Amy Tobin, 'Monica Sjöö's Cosmic Feminism' *Monica Sjöö: The Great Cosmic Mother* (Stockholm: Moderna Museet/Oxford: Modern Art Oxford, 2023) p. 67.

18 Georgia Rhoades 'Decoding the Sheela-na-gig' *Feminist Formations*, Vol. 22, No. 2, Summer 2010, p. 168.

19 Ibid, p. 176.

20 Cecelia Klein, 'A New Interpretation of the Aztec Statue Called Coatlicue, "Snakes-Her-Skirt"' *Ethnohistory*, Vol. 55, Issue 2, Spring 2008, p. 245.

21 Enuma Elish from W.G. Lambert, *Mesopotamian Creation Stories* used under Creative Commons license from the <etana.org/node/581> quoted at <www.worldhistory.org/article/225/enuma-elish---the-babylonian-epic-of-creation---fu> [accessed 22 October 2023].

22 Shaktism is a goddess-centric denomination of Hinduism

23 Eddie Chambers, *Black Artists in British Art: A History since the 1950s* (London: I.B. Tauris, 2014), p. 153.

24 First published in 1981 by Routledge & Kegan Paul, London, *Old Mistresses: Women, Art and Ideology* was co-authored by Rozsika Parker and Griselda Pollock.

25 Pande estimates that 'For most of the surrogates' families, the money earned through surrogacy was equivalent to almost five years of total family income'. Amrita Pande, 'Commercial Surrogacy in India: Manufacturing a Perfect Mother-Worker' *Signs*, Vol. 35, No. 4, Summer 2010, p. 971.

chapter 2

1 I use 'Western' here as to acknowledge the partiality of the art history I am telling – which in itself echoes the structures of many art galleries in Europe and North America, though I am aware the term itself carries its own issues. See <www.theguardian.com/world/2016/nov/09/western-civilisation-appiah-reith-lecture> [accessed 22 October 2023].

2 Rosemary Betterton, *Maternal Bodies in the Visual Arts* (Manchester: Manchester University Press, 2014) p. 123.

3 Notebooks of Leonardo da Vinci, p. 797, quoted in P. M. Dunn, 'Leonardo Da Vinci (1452–1519) and reproductive anatomy' *Archives of Disease in Childhood – Fetal and Neonatal Edition*, Vol. 77, No. 3 November 1997, F249.

4 All notes on Leonardo's sketchbook derived from M. Clayton and R. Philo, *Leonardo da Vinci: Anatomist* (London: Royal Collection Trust, 2012) adapted and reproduced with the sketchbooks in facsimile <www.rct.uk/collection/themes/publications/leonardo-da-vinci-anatomist> [accessed 23 October 2023].

5 Quoted in Dunn.

6 Franz Hartmann, *The Life and the Doctrines of Paracelsus* (1887) facsimile <universaltheosophy.com/fh/the-life-and-the-doctrines-of-paracelsus> [accessed 23 October 2023].

7 Rebecca Kate Whiteley, *Picturing Pregnancy: A History of the Early Modern Birth Figure*, Ph.D thesis, UCL (London: University College London, 2018), p. 19.

8 Ibid, p. 56.

9 Matthew 19.13/14, King James Version

10 Christine Ozarowska Kibish. 'Lucas Cranach's Christ Blessing the Children: A Problem of Lutheran Iconography' *The Art Bulletin*, Vol. 37, No. 3, September 1955, pp. 196–203.

11 Denis Diderot, 'The Salon of 1765' *Diderot on Art: The Salon of 1765 and Notes on Painting* (New Haven: Yale University Press, 1995) p. 102.

12 Ibid, p. 106.

13 Kathleen Russo, 'A Comparison of Rousseau's "Julie" with the Heroines of Greuze and Fuseli' *Woman's Art Journal*, Vol. 8, No. 1, Spring–Summer 1987, p. 5.

14 Jutta Sperling, 'Book review of *Maternal Breast-Feeding and Its Substitutes in Nineteenth-Century French Art* by Gal Ventura' *Nineteenth-Century Art Worldwide*, Vol. 18, No. 2, Autumn 2019 <www.19thc-artworldwide.org/autumn19/sperling-reviews-maternal-breast-feeding-by-gal-ventura> [accessed 23 October 2023].

15 Mary Jacobus, *First things: The Maternal Imaginary in Literature, Art, and Psychoanalysis* (New York and London: Routledge, 1995) p. 122.

16 E. Claire Cage, 'The Sartorial Self: Neoclassical Fashion and Gender Identity in France, 1797–1804' *Eighteenth Century Studies*, Vol. 42, No. 2, Winter 2009, p. 197.

17 Gal Ventura, 'Breastfeeding, Ideology and Clothing in Nineteenth-Century France' in Shoshana-Rose Marzel and Guy D. Stiebel (eds), *Dress And Ideology: Fashioning Identity From Antiquity To The Present* (London: Bloomsbury Academic, 2014) p. 215.

18 Carol Duncan, 'Happy Mothers and Other New Ideas in French Art' *The Art Bulletin*, Vol. 55, No. 4, December 1973, p. 574.

19 Virginia Woolf, 'Professions For Women' (1931) <www.literaturecambridge.co.uk/news/professions-women> [accessed 22 October 2023].

20 Quoted in Jessica Webb, 'Why Women Fell: Representing the Sexual Lapse in Mid-Victorian Art (1850–65)' *eSharp*, Issue 9. Spring 2007, p. 11.

21 Margaret Reynolds, 'Fallen Women and the Great Social Evil in Victorian Literature and Culture' *The Fallen Woman* (London: The Foundling Museum, 2015) unpaginated.

22 Betterton, p. 106.

23 Jessica Webb, 'Why Women Fell: Representing the Sexual Lapse in Mid-Victorian Art (1850–65)' *eSharp*, Issue 9, Spring 2007, p. 7.

24 Lynda Nead, 'Fallen Women and Foundlings: Rethinking Victorian Sexuality' *History Workshop Journal*, No. 82, Autumn 2016, p. 180.

25 Victoria Mills, 'The Fallen Woman and the Foundling Hospital' *The Fallen Woman* (London: The Foundling Museum, 2015) unpaginated.

26 Nead, pp. 183, 184.

27 Griselda Pollock, *Mary Cassatt* (London: Jupiter Books, 1980) p. 12.

28 Letter from Mary Cassatt to Sara Hallowell, 1864, quoted in Linda Nochlin, 'Mary Cassatt's Modernity' (1999) in Maura Reilly (ed.), *The Linda Nochlin Reader* (London and New York: Thames & Hudson, 2015/2020) p. 218.

29 Wendy Slatkin, 'Maternity and Sexuality in the 1890s' *Woman's Art Journal*, Vol. 1, No. 1, Spring–Summer 1980, pp. 13–19.

30 See, for example, Rozsika Parker and Griselda Pollock, *Old Mistresses: Women, Art and Ideology* (London: Routledge & Kegan Paul, 1981) p. 121.

31 Andrea Pérez-Fernández, 'From compassion to distance. Hannah Höch's "Mother"' *European Journal of Women's Studies*, Vol. 29, Issue 1, February 2002, pp. 140–54.

32 Rachel Epp Buller, 'Pregnant Women and Rationalized Workers. Alice Lex's Anonymous Bodies' in Michael Cowen and Kai Marcel Sicks (eds). *Leibhaftige Moderne: Körper in Kunst und Massenmedien 1918 bis 1933* (Bielefeld: Transcript Verlag, 2005) p. 349.

33 Michelle Vangen, 'Left and Right: Politics and Images of Motherhood in Weimar Germany' *Woman's Art Journal*, Vol. 30, No. 2, Fall–Winter 2009, pp. 28–29.

34 Ibid, p. 29.

35 The National Association for the Advancement of Colored People (NAACP) estimate that 72% of lynching victims were Black. NAACP 'History of Lynching in America' <naacp.org/find-resources/history-explained/history-lynching-america> [accessed 22 October 2023].

36 Betty Lochrie Hoag, 'Oral history interview with Charles W. White, 1965 March 9' *Smithsonian Archives of American Art* <www.aaa.si.edu/collections/interviews/oral-history-interview-charles-w-white-11484> [accessed 22 October 2023].

37 Equal Justice Initiative (EHI), 'Remembering Black Veterans Targeted for Racial Terror Lynchings', 11 November 2019 <eji.org/news/remembering-black-veterans-and-racial-terror-lynchings> [accessed 22 October 2023].

38 NAACP, 'History Of Lynching In America' <naacp.org/find-resources/history-explained/history-lynching-america> [accessed 22 October 2023].

39 Op. cit. Lochrie Hoag.

40 Titus Kaphar, 'I Cannot Sell You This Painting' *TIME*, 15 June 2020 <time.com/5847487/George-floyd-time-cover-titus-kaphar> [accessed 22 October 2023].

41 Jennifer C. Nash, *Birthing Black Mothers* (Durham, NC: Duke University Press, 2021) p. 4.

42 Susan Bright, *Home Truths: Photography and Motherhood* (London: Art/Books, 2013) p. 15.

43 Ibid.

chapter 3

1 Jennifer Higgie, *The Mirror and the Palette: Rebellion, Revolution and Resilience: 500 Years of Women's Self-Portraits* (London: Weidenfeld & Nicholson, 2021) pp. 2, 3.

2 Rainer Maria Rilke, *Requiem for a Friend (In memoriam Paula Modersohn-Becker)* in *The Selected Poetry of Rainer Maria Rilke*, edited and translated by Stephen Mitchell(New York: Random House, 1982) p. 81.

3 Suzanne Bauman (dir.) *Spirit Catcher: The Art of Betye Saar* (New York: WNET, 1977).

4 Cindy Nemser, et al. *Feminist Art Journal*, Vol. 4, No. 4, December 1975, p. 22.

5 My search was conducted in 2020/21. At its reopening in 2023 the National Portrait Gallery announced a commitment to improving the gender balance of the collection. What bearing this has had on the visibility of artist motherhood remains to be seen.

6 Elizabeth Alice Honig, 'The Art of Being "Artistic": Dutch Women's Creative Practices in the 17th Century' *Woman's Art Journal*, Vol. 22, No. 2, Autumn 2001–Winter 2002, p. 33.

7 Helen Draper, 'Mary Beale and Art's Lost Laborers: Women Painter Stainers' *Early Modern Women*, Vol. 10, No. 1, Fall 2015, p. 144.

8 Whitney Chadwick, *Women, Art and Society* (London and New York: Thames & Hudson, 1990) p. 166.

9 Frima Fox Hofrichter, 'An Intimate Look at Baroque Women Artists: Births, Babies and Biography' in Rosalynn Voaden and Diane

Wolfthal (eds), *Framing the Family: Narrative and Representation in the Medieval and Early Modern Periods* (Tempe: Arizona Centre for Medieval and Renaissance Studies, 2005) pp. 139–160.

10 Letizia Treves, *Artemisia Gentileschi* (London: National Gallery, 2020) p. 130.

11 Quoted in Fox Hofrichter, p. 144.

12 Colin Crawford, 'Fresh Concerns over Thalidomide' *New Scientist*, Vol. 77, No. 1088, 2 February 1978, pp. 276–79.

13 Everlyn Nicodemus, *African modern art and black cultural trauma* (London: Middlesex University's Research Repository, 2012) p. 15.

14 Ibid, p. 38.

15 Ibid, p. 30.

16 Gal Ventura, 'Breastfeeding, Ideology and Clothing in 19th Century France' in Shoshana-Rose Marzel and Guy Stiebel (eds), *Dress & Ideology: Fashioning Identity from Antiquity to the Present* (London: Bloomsbury Academic Publishers, 2014), p. 217.

17 Linda Nochlin, 'Morisot's *Wet Nurse*: The Construction of Work and Leisure in Impressionist Painting' first published in *Women, Art and Power and Other Essays* (London: Routledge, 1988), reprinted in Maura Reilly (ed.), *Women Artists: The Linda Nochlin Reader* (London and New York: Thames & Hudson, 2015) p. 161.

18 André Utter and Garnet Rees, 'Maurice Utrillo and Suzanne Valadon' *Journal of the Royal Society of Arts*, Vol. 86, No. 4481, 7 October 1938, pp. 1125–27.

19 Gem Fletcher, 'The Radical Optimist: Catherine Opie on the Subversive Joy of Queer Domesticity' *Mother Tongue*, Issue No. 3, Fall/Winter 2022, p. 36.

20 Dorothy Roberts, *Killing the Black Body: Race, Reproduction and the Meaning of Liberty* (Vintage Books, NY, 1997/2017) p. 4.

21 All quotes from interview with the author, 19 July 2023.

22 Celia Paul, *Self-Portrait* (London: Vintage 2019/2022) p. 141.

23 All quotes from interview with the author, 24 July 2023, unless otherwise noted.

chapter 4

1 See Anne Middleton Wagner, *Mother Stone: The Vitality of Modern British Sculpture* (London: Paul Mellon Centre for Studies in British Art, 2005).

2 Nuffield Council on Bioethics,

Bioethics Briefing Note: Egg freezing in the UK, 30 September 2020 <www.nuffieldbioethics.org/ publications/egg-freezing-in-the-uk> [accessed 22 October 2023].

3 Amanda Mull, 'The New, Invasive Ways Women Are Encouraged to Freeze Their Eggs' *The Atlantic*, 4 March 2019 <theatlantic.com/ health/archive/2019/03/egg-freezing-instagram/584053> [accessed 22 October 2023].

4 Sophie Gallagher, 'I'm 32 years old – so why am I and all my friends so worried about fertility?' *The i*, 27 July 2023, pp. 36–37.

5 Melinda Wenner Moyer, 'Women Are Calling Out "Medical Gaslighting"' *New York Times*, 28 March 2022 <nytimes.com/2022/03/28/well/live/ gaslighting-doctors-patients-health. html> [accessed 22 October 2023].

6 Karen Hearn, *Picturing Pregnancy: From Holbein to Social Media* (London: Paul Holberton Publishing, 2020) p. 102.

7 Ibid, p. 34.

8 Piri Halasz, 'Alice Neel: "I have this obsession with life"' *ARTnews*, Vol. 73, No. 1, January 1974, p. 49.

9 Patricia Hills, *Alice Neel* (New York: Abrams, 1983) p. 77.

10 Elissa Auther, 'Interview with Senga Nengudi, 2013 July 9–11' *Smithsonian Archives of American Art* <www.aaa.si.edu/collections/ interviews/oral-history-interview-senga-nengudi-16131> [accessed 22 October 2023].

11 Lovia Gyarkye, 'An Artist's Continuing Exploration of the Human Form' *New York Times*, 9 November 2020 <nytimes.com/2020/11/09/t-magazine/senga-nengudi-art.html> [accessed 22 October 2023].

12 Op. cit. Auther.

13 Op. cit. Gyarkye

14 Op. cit. Auther.

15 Galerie Andere Zeichen-Frauen + Kunst.

16 Nina Mdivani, 'Interview with Annagret Soltau', *Whitehot Magazine*, February 2022 <whitehotmagazine.com/articles/ offensive-interview-with-annegret-soltau/5315> [accessed 22 October 2023].

17 Susan Hiller, 'Within and Against: women being artists' *Thinking about Art: Conversations with Susan Hiller* (Manchester: Manchester University Press, 1996) p. 50.

18 Ibid, p. 47.

19 Ibid, pp. 48–49.

20 Hermione Wiltshire was in conversation with the author on

various dates in 2022 and 2023.

21 Heather Spears <heatherspearsblog. wordpress.com/2017/12/02/ blog-11-special-care-nurseries-the-end-of-drawing> [accessed 22 October 2023].

22 Robin L Martinez, 'Tiny Dismantled Parts: An Interview with Heather Spears', 15 June 2015 <web.archive. org/web/20181202070524/https:// robinlmartinez.com/2015/06/15/ tiny-dismantled-parts-an-interview-with-heather-spears> [accessed 22 October 2023].

23 Melanie Jackson and Esther Leslie, *Deeper in the Pyramid* (London: Banner Repeater, 2018) p. 3.

24 Ibid, p. 67.

25 Catherine Elwes, *Video Loupe* (London: KT Press, 2000) p. 60.

26 Ibid, p. 12.

27 Silvia Federici, *Wages Against Housework* (Bristol and London: Power of Women Collective and Falling Wall Press, 1975), reprinted in *Revolution at Point Zero* (Oakland, CA: PM Press, 2012) p. 15.

28 Hélène Cixous, 'The Laugh of the Medusa' translated by Keith Cohen and Paula Cohen, *Signs*, Vol. 1, No. 4, Summer 1976, p. 890.

29 The reference is from Sylvia Plath's 'Morning Song', 1961.

30 'Mike Kelley: The Uncanny', Tate Liverpool and RIBA North, 20 February–3 May 2004.

chapter 5

1 Silvia Federici, *Wages Against Housework* (Bristol and London: Power of Women Collective and Falling Wall Press, 1975) reprinted in *Revolution at Point Zero* (Oakland, CA: PM Press, 2012) p. 16.

2 Tom Finkelpearl, 'Interview: Mierle Laderman Ukeles on Maintenance and Sanitation Art' *Dialogues in Public Art* (Cambridge MA: MIT Press, 2001), supplied to the author as a PDF.

3 Ernest Callenbach, 'Review: Schmeerguntz by Gunvor Nelson, Dorothy Wiley', *Film Quarterly*, Vol. 19, No. 4, Summer 1966, p. 67.

4 Brenda Richardson et al, 'Women, Wives, Film-Makers: An Interview with Gunvor Nelson and Dorothy Wiley', *Film Quarterly*, Vol. 25, No. 1, Autumn 1971, p. 36.

5 Betty Friedan, *The Feminine Mystique* (New York: Dell Publishing, 1963/1983) p. 226.

6 Interview with author, December 2019.

7 VALIE EXPORT, 'Women's Art:

A Manifesto' (1973) republished in Breanne Fahs (ed), *Burn It Down! Feminist Manifestos for the Revolution* (London and New York: Verso, 2020) p. 443.

8 David Herzberg, '"Will Wonder Drugs Never Cease!": A Prehistory of Direct-to-Consumer Advertising' *Pharmacy in History*, Vol. 51, No. 2, p. 49.

9 Reproduced in David Herzberg, '"The Pill You Love Can Turn on You": Feminism, Tranquilizers, and the Valium Panic of the 1970s' *American Quarterly*, Vol. 58, No. 1, March 2006, p. 91.

10 Susan Rubin Suleiman, *Subversive Intent: Gender, Politics and the Avant-Garde* (Cambridge, MA: Harvard University Press, 1990) p. 180.

11 Ibid.

12 Interview with author, 19 April 2021.

13 Ibid.

14 Susan Fraiman, *Cool Men and the Second Sex* (New York: Columbia University Press, 2003) p. xv.

15 Ibid, p. xii.

16 Audre Lorde, 'Uses of the Erotic: The Erotic as Power' *Sister Outsider* (London: Penguin, 1984/2007) p. 45.

17 Susan Thompson and Deana Lawson, 'Motherhood in The Work Of Deana Lawson. A conversation with the Artist' in Lesly Deschler Canossi and Zoraida Lopez-Diago (eds), *Black Matrilineage, Photography, and Representation: Another Way of Knowing* (Leuven: Leuven University Press, 2022) pp. 100–1.

18 bell hooks, 'Homeplace (a site of resistance)' *Yearning: Race, gender, and cultural politics* (Boston, MA: South End Press, 1990), reproduced in Joy Ritchie, Kate Ronald (eds), *Available Means: An Anthology of Women's Rhetoric(s)* (Pittsburgh: University of Pittsburgh Press, 2001) p. 385.

19 Ibid, p. 388.

20 bell hooks, 'Talking Art with Carrie Mae Weems' *Art on My Mind: Visual Politics* (New York: The New Press, 1995) p. 76.

21 Ibid, pp. 76–89.

22 Quoted in Michelle Moravec, 'Introduction' in Suzanne Siegel, Laura Silago and Deborah Krall, *Mother Art: A Collective of Women Artists* (Los Angeles: OTIS, 2011) p. 12.

23 *Los Angeles Times*, 12 June 1978, quoted in *Mother Art*, p. 40.

24 Interview with the author, 18 July 2023.

25 Amy Tobin, 'Breaking Down A Woman's Place' *14 Radnor Terrace: A Woman's Place* (London: Raven Row, 2017) p. 11.

26 Interview with the author, 18 July 2023.

27 Kathy Battista, *Renegotiating the Body: Feminist Art in 1970s London* (London: I. B. Tauris, 2013) p. 111.

28 Mónica Mayer, '¡MADRES!', in Myrel Chernick and Jenny Klein (eds), *The M Word: Real Mothers in Contemporary Art* (Toronto: Demeter Press, 2011) p. 167.

29 Ibid, p. 163.

30 Bethan Bell, 'Erin Pizzey: The woman who looked beyond the bruises' *BBC News*, 10 November 2021, <www.bbc.co.uk/news/uk-england-london-59064064> [accessed 22 October 2023].

31 Sandra Laville, 'Domestic violence: how the world's first women's refuge saved my life' *The Guardian*, Monday 28 April 2014 <www.theguardian.com/lifeandstyle/2014/apr/28/domestic-violence-first-womens-refuge-saved-my-life> [accessed 22 October 2023].

32 Maxwell Graham Gallery, New York, 8 September–15 October 2022.

33 A Katsiyannis, L.J. Rapa, D.K. Whitford and S.N. Scott, 'An Examination of US School Mass Shootings, 2017–2022: Findings and Implications' *Adv. Neurodev. Disord.*, Vol. 7, No. 1, 19 August 2022, pp. 66–76.

34 Cassie Arnold <www.cassiearnoldart.com/portfolio#/school-uniform-bulletproof-dress> [accessed 22 October 2023].

35 In the year ending 31 March 2022 there were 27.2 stop and searches for every 1,000 Black people, compared with 5.6 for every 1,000 white people. Gov.uk 'Stop and search' 10 August 2023 <www.ethnicity-facts-figures.service.gov.uk/crime-justice-and-the-law/policing/stop-and-search/latest> [accessed 22 October 2023].

36 Gov.uk, 'National statistics: Police powers and procedures: Stop and search and arrests, England and Wales, year ending 31 March 2022' 22 October 2022 <www.gov.uk/government/statistics/police-powers-and-procedures-stop-and-search-and-arrests-england-and-wales-year-ending-31-march-2022> [accessed 22 October 2023].

37 Eddie Chambers, 'It's a Bit Much' *Barbara Walker: Louder Than Words*, Unit 2, London Metropolitan University, 20 November–16 December 2006.

38 Jennifer C. Nash, *Birthing Black Mothers*, p. 4.

39 Hettie Judah, *How Not to Exclude Artist Mothers (and Other Parents)* (London: Lund Humphries 2022) pp. 44–45.

40 Sally Mann, *Hold Still: A Memoir with Photographs* (New York: Little, Brown & Company, 2015) quoted in Sarah Boxer, 'The Maternal Eye of Sally Mann' *The Atlantic*, July/August 2015 <www.theatlantic.com/magazine/archive/2015/07/sally-mann/395240> [accessed 22 October 2023].

41 Anna Grevenitis, *Regard*, artist statement, <https://annagrevenitis.me/new-cover-page> [accessed 22 October 2023].

42 Marlene Dumas, 'The perfect Lover, The absent Lover and the Daughter' originally published in *Marlene Dumas* (cat.), (London: Tate Gallery, 1996) <www.marlenedumas.nl/the-perfect-lover-the-absent-lover-and-the-daughter/> [accessed 23 October 2023].

43 Mirene Arsanios, *Notes on Mother Tongues: Colonialism, class, and giving what you don't have* (New York: Ugly Duckling Presse, 2020) p. 7.

44 Frantz Fanon, *Black Skin, White Masks* translated by Charles Lam Markmann (London: Pluto Press, 2008) p. 8.

45 Interview with the author, May 2022.

chapter 6

1 Centers for Disease Control and Prevention, 'Infant Mortality' <www.cdc.gov/reproductivehealth/maternalinfanthealth/infantmortality.htm#mortality> [accessed 22 October 2023].

2 Joan Didion, *Blue Nights* (London: Fourth Estate, 2011) p. 54.

3 Dorothy Price, '"Between us sleeps our child – art": Creativity, Identity, and the Maternal in the Works of Marianne von Werefkin and Her Contemporaries', in Tanja Malycheva and Isabel Wünsche (eds), *Marianne Werefkin and the Women Artists in Her Circle* (Leiden: Brill, 2017) p. 16.

4 Hans Kollwitz, *Käthe Kollwitz 1867–1945. Briefe der Freundschaft und Begegnungen* ('*Letters of Friendship and Encounters*') (Munich: List Verlag, 1966) quoted in the catalogue entry for *Woman with Dead Child*, Käthe Kollwitz Museum, Cologne < https://www.kollwitz.de/en/woman-with-dead-child-kn-81> [accessed 22 October 2023].

5   Denise Riley, *Time Lived, Without its Flow* (London: Picador, 2012) np.

6   Kelly Baum, 'Political Creatures' *Alice Neel: People Come First* (New York: The Metropolitan Museum of Art, 2021) p. 40.

7   Melanie Stidolph, *Endless Reproduction* (artist's book, 2022) p. 69.

8   Text by Elina Brotherus in Susan Bright (ed.), *Home Truths: Photography and Motherhood* (London: Art/Books Publishing, 2013) p. 90.

9   Louisa Hall, *Reproduction* (New York: Scribner, 2023) p. 26.

10   Quoted in Hall, p. 15.

11   Cherry Casey, 'The UK has a forced adopted problem' *Prospect*, 22 October 2022 www.prospectmagazine.co.uk/society/60185/the-uk-has-a-forced-adoption-problem [accessed 22 October 2023].

12   Ibid.

13   Interview with the author, 18 July 2023.

14   Nancy Willis, *Self Portrait* (2009).

15   Richard A. Soloway, 'The "Perfect Contraceptive": Eugenics and Birth Control Research in Britain and America in the Interwar Years' *Journal of Contemporary History*, Vol. 30, No. 4, October 1995, p. 639

16   Siân Norris, *Bodies Under Siege: How the Far-Right Attack on Reproductive Rights Went Global* (London: Verso, 2023) pp. 24–25.

17   Rory Carroll, 'Ireland publishes report on "appalling" abuse at mother and baby homes' *The Guardian*, 12 January 2021 <www.theguardian.com/world/2021/jan/12/ireland-report-appalling-abuse-mother-baby-homes> [accessed 22 October 2023].

18   'The Supreme Court Ruling That Led To 70,000 Forced Sterilizations' *NPR*, 7 March 2016, www.npr.org/sections/health-shots/2016/03/07/469478098/the-supreme-court-ruling-that-led-to-70-000-forced-sterilizations [accessed 22 October 2023].

19   Elizabeth O'Brien and Miriam Rich, 'Obstetric violence in historical perspective' *The Lancet*, Vol. 399, Issue 10342, 11 June 2022, p. 2183.

20   Ibid, p. 2189.

21   Sophie Hamacher, 'A Conversation with Priscilla Ocean' in Sophie Hamacher & Jessica Hankey (eds), *Supervision: On Motherhood and Surveillance* (Cambridge, MA: Orbis Editions, 2023) p. 164.

22   Paula Rego, 'Abortion will happen – Whatever the Law Says' *The Art Newspaper*, 31 May 2019 <www.theartnewspaper.com/2019/05/31/abortion-will-happenwhatever-the-law-says> [accessed 22 October 2023].

23   Emine Saner, 'The hateful Eighth: artists at the frontline of Ireland's abortion rights battle' *The Guardian*, 12 April 2018 <www.theguardian.com/artanddesign/2018/apr/12/the-hateful-eighth-artists-frontline-ireland-abortion-rights-battle-eighth-amendment> [accessed 22 October 2023].

24   Caroline A. Miranda, 'Barbara Kruger on remixing her own art and her visits to 4chan' *Los Angeles Times*, 4 April 2022 <www.latimes.com/entertainment-arts/story/2022-04-04/artist-barbara-kruger-lacma-show-remixes-her-she-talks-about-her-4chan-visits> accessed 22 October 2023].

25   Robin Toner, 'Right To Abortion Draws Thousands To Capital Rally' *New York Times*, 10 April 1989 www.nytimes.com/1989/04/10/us/right-to-abortion-draws-thousands-to-capital-rally.html> [accessed 22 October 2023].

26   Siân Norris, *Bodies Under Siege*, p. xiii.

chapter 7

1   Alexis Pauline Gumbs, 'm/other ourselves: a Black queer feminist genealogy for radical mothering', in Alexis Pauline Gumbs, China Martens and Mai'a Williams (eds,) *Revolutionary Mothering: Love on the Front Lines* (Oakland, CA: PM Press, 2016) pp. 22, 23.

2   Ibid, p. 29.

3   Quoted in Stevenson Gallery <archive.stevenson.info/exhibitions/muholi/being.htm> [accessed 22 October 2023].

4   Stephen Vider, 'Introduction and Interview with Cathy Cade' *Out History*, 2015 <outhistory.org/exhibits/show/cathy-cade/introduction-and-interview> [accessed 22 October 2023].

5   Gillian Frank, '"The Civil Rights of Parents": Race and Conservative Politics in Anita Bryant's Campaign against Gay Rights in 1970s Florida' *Journal of the History of Sexuality*, Vol. 22, No. 1, January 2013, p. 127.

6   'Lesbian Mother Jeanne Jullion Lost Her Children' California social, protest, and counterculture movement ephemera collection, California Historical Society, SOC MOV EPH, Box 1, Folder 13.

7   Ashifa Kassam, '"Orphaned by decree": Italy's same-sex parents react to losing their rights' *The Guardian*, 21 August 2023 <www.theguardian.com/world/2023/aug/21/orphaned-by-decree-italy-same-sex-parents-react-losing-rights> [accessed 22 October 2023].

8   Sunil Gupta, *Pictures From Here* (London: Autograph, 2003) p. 56.

9   Artist's text <www.sunilgupta.net/pretended-family-relationships.html> [accessed 22 October 2023].

10   Del LaGrace Volcano, 'Corpus Queer: Bodies of Resistance' *GenderFest Athens*, January 2017 <www.youtube.com/watch?v=nhHBVj5ZePU> [accessed 22 October 2023].

11   Interview with author, various dates, summer 2023.

12   Donna Haraway, *Staying with the Trouble: Making Kin in the Chthulucene* (Durham, NC: Duke University Press, 2016) p. 103.

13   Ravi Ghosh, 'Tabita Rezaire – How the artist created her Amazon forest project for the Serpentine' *Wepresent*, June 2021 <wepresent.wetransfer.com/stories/serpentine-groundwork-tabita-rezaire-amakaba> [accessed 22 October 2023].

14   Tabita Rezaire, *Womb Consciousness* (Dijon: Les Presse du Réel, 2021) p. 47.

15   Leeza Meksin, 'Feral Domesticity: Dani and Sheilah ReStack Interviewed' *BOMB*, 9 January 2023 <bombmagazine.org/articles/feral-domesticity-dani-and-sheilah-restack-interviewed> [accessed 22 October 2023].

16   'New Laure Prouvost installation MOOTHERR on view at Louisiana Museum' *Lisson Gallery News*, 19 February 2021 <www.lissongallery.com/news/new-laure-prouvost-installation-mootherr-on-view-at-louisiana-museum> [accessed 22 October 2023].

17   Christopher Lyon, 'An Interview with Kiki Smith 2017 July 20 and August 16' *Smithsonian Archives of American Art*, <www.aaa.si.edu/collections/interviews/oral-history-interview-kiki-smith-17502> [accessed 22 October 2023].

18   Ibid.

19   Ciara Healy-Muson, *Mother to the Other*, text supplied by artist.

Abril, Laia, *A History of Misogyny Chapter One: On Abortion and the Repercussions of Lack of Access* (Stockport: Dewi Lewis, 2018)

Abu ElDahab, Mai, *Why Call it Labor? On Motherhood and Art Work* (Berlin/Brussels: Mophradat and Archive Books, 2020)

Agarwal, Pragya, *(M)Otherhood: On the choices of being a woman* (Edinburgh: Canongate Books, 2021)

Allen, Felicity, *The Disoeuvre: an Argument in 4 Voices (WASL Table)* (London: Ma Bibliothèque, 2019)

Arsanios, Mirene, *Notes on Mother Tongues* (New York: Ugly Duckling Presse, 2020)

Bailer, Sascia, Magdalena Kallenberger and Maicyra Teles Leão e Silva (eds), *Maternal Fantasies - Re-Assembling Motherhood(s): On Radical Care and Collective Art as Feminist Practices* (Eindhoven: Onomatopee, 2021)

Barrett, Michèle, and Bobby Baker, *Bobby Baker: Redeeming Features of Daily Life* (Milton Park, Oxfordshire: Routledge, 2007)

Battista, Kathy, *Renegotiating the Body: Feminist Art in 1970s London* (London: I.B. Tauris, 2013)

Baum, Kelly, and Randall Griffey (eds), *Alice Neel: People Come First* (New Haven, Connecticut: Yale University Press, 2021)

Betterton, Rosemary, *Maternal Bodies in the Visual Arts* (Manchester: Manchester University Press, 2014)

Bright, Susan (ed), *Home Truths: Photography and Motherhood* (London: Art/Books, 2013)

Burisch, Liesel, *Queer Nursing (The Phasing System)* (Berlin: Gorilla Milk, 2020)

Care Collective, The, *The Care Manifesto: The Politics of Interdependence* (London/New York: Verso, 2020)

Chadwick, Whitney, *Women, Art, And Society* (London: Thames & Hudson, 1996)

Chernick, Myrel, and Jennie Klein, *The M Word: Real Mothers in Contemporary Art* (Ontario: Demeter Press, 2011)

Conway and Young, *Milk Report* (Bristol: Conway and Young, 2021)

Crerar, Belinda, *Feminine Power: The Divine to the Demonic* (London: The British Museum, 2022)

Dadzie, Stella, *A Kick in the Belly: Women, Slavery & Resistance* (London/New York: Verso, 2020)

Davey, Moyra, *Mother Reader: Essential Writings on Motherhood* (New York: Seven Stories Press, 2001)

Deschler Canossi, Lesly, and Zoraida Lopez-Diago, *Black Matrilineage, Photography, and Representation* (Leuven: Leuven University Press, 2022)

Didion, Joan, *Blue Nights* (Glasgow: Fourth Estate, 2011)

Elwes, Catherine, *Video Loupe* (London: KT Press, 2000)

Epp Buller, Rachel, and Charles Reeve (eds), *Inappropriate Bodies: Art, Design, and Maternity* (Ontario: Demeter Press, 2019)

Fahs, Breanne (ed), *Burn it Down! Feminist Manifestos for the Revolution* (London/New York: Verso, 2020)

Federici, Silvia, *Caliban and the Witch: Women, the Body and Primitive Accumulation* (London: Penguin Modern Classics, 2004)

—, *Revolution at Point Zero: Housework, Reproduction, and Feminist Struggle* (New York: PM Press, 2020)

Fournier, Lauren, *Autotheory as Feminist Practice in Art, Writing and Criticism* (Cambridge, Massachusetts: The MIT Press, 2021)

Fraiman, Susan, *Cool Men and the Second Sex* (New York: Columbia University Press, 2003)

Friedan, Betty, *The Feminine Mystique* (New York: W.W. Norton, 1963)

Gumbs, Alexis Pauline, China Martens and Mai'a Williams (eds), *Revolutionary Mothering: Love on the Front Lines* (New York: PM Press, 2016)

Hall, Louisa, *Reproduction* (New York: Scribner, 2023)

Hamacher, Sophie, and Jessica Hankey, *Supervision: On Motherhood and Surveillance* (Cambridge, Massachusetts: The MIT Press, 2023

Haraway, Donna J., *Staying With the Trouble: Making Kin in the Chthulucene* (Durham, North Carolina: Duke University Press, 2016)

Hartman, Saidiya, *Lose Your Mother: A Journey Along the Atlantic Slave Route* (New York: Farrar, Straus and Giroux, 2007)

Hearn, Karen, *Portraying Pregnancy: From Holbein to Social Media* (London: The Foundling Museum and Paul Holberton Publishing, 2020)

Higgie, Jennifer, *The Mirror and The Palette: 500 Years of Women's Portraits* (London: Orion, 2021)

Hiller, Susan, and Suzanne Treister (eds), *Monica Ross – Ethical Actions: A Critical Fine Art Practice* (London: Sternberg Press, 2016)

hooks, bell, *Art On My Mind: Visual Politics* (New York: The New Press, 1995)

Jackson, Melanie, and Esther Leslie, *Deeper in the Pyramid* (London: Banner Repeater, 2018)

—, *The Inextinguishable* (Limerick, Ireland: EVA International, 2020)

Jacobus, Mary, *First Things: The Maternal Imaginary in Literature, Art, and Psychoanalysis* (Abingdon, Oxford: Routledge, 1995)

Jones, Lucy, *Matrescence: On The Metamorphosis of Pregnancy, Childbirth and Motherhood* (London: Allen Lane, 2023)

Keegan, Claire, *Small Things Like These* (London: Faber, 2021)

Kingston, Angela (ed), *Mothers* (Birmingham: Ikon Gallery, 1990)

Kristeva, Julia, (trans. Leon S. Roudiez) *Powers of Horror: An Essay on Abjection* (New York: Columbia University Press, 1982)

Larratt-Smith, Philip, *Louise Bourgeois: The Return of the Repressed* (London: Violette Editions, 2012)

Lerner, Gerda, *The Creation of Patriarchy* (Oxford: Oxford University Press, 1986)

Lewis, Sophie, *Full Surrogacy Now: Feminism Against Family* (London/New York: Verso, 2019)

Lippard, Lucy, *From the Center: Feminist Essays on Women's Art* (New York: E.P. Dutton, 1976)

Long Chu, Andrea, *Females* (London/New York: Verso, 2019)

Lorde, Audre, *Sister Outsider* (London: Penguin Modern Classics, 2019)

McCormack, Catherine, *Women in the Picture: Women, Art and the Power of Looking* (London: Icon Books, 2021)

Millar-Fisher, Michelle, and Amber Winick, *Designing Motherhood: Things That Make and Break Our Births* (Cambridge, Massachusetts: The MIT Press, 2021)

Nash, Jennifer C., *Birthing Black Mothers* (Durham, North Carolina: Duke University Press, 2021)

Nelson, Maggie, *On Freedom: Four Songs of Care and Constraint* (London: Jonathan Cape, 2021)

—, *The Argonauts* (New Jersey: Melville House, 2015)

Norris, Sian, *Bodies Under Siege: How the Far-Right Attack on Reproductive Rights Went Global* (London/New York: Verso, 2023)

O'Donnell, Darren, *Haircuts by Children and Other Evidence for a New Social Contract* (Toronto: Coach House Books, 2018)

Offill, Jenny, *Dept. of Speculation* (London: Granta, 2014)

Parker, Rozsika, and Griselda Pollock, *Old Mistresses: Women, Art and Ideology* (New York: HarperCollins, 1981)

Paul, Celia, *Self-Portrait* (London: Vintage, 2019/2022)

Pollock, Griselda, *Mary Cassatt* (London: Jupiter Books, 1980)

—, *Vision & Difference: Femininity, Feminism and the Histories of Art* (Milton Park, Oxfordshire: Routledge, 1988)

Reddy, Maureen T., Martha Roth and Amy Sheldon (eds), *Mother Journeys: Feminists Write about Mothering* (Tallahassee, Florida: Spinsters Ink, 1994)

Reilly, Maura (ed), *Women Artists: The Linda Nochlin Reader* (London: Thames & Hudson, 2015)

Rezaire, Tabita, *Womb Consciousness* (Dijon: Le Presses du Réel, 2021)

Rich, Adrienne, *Of Woman Born: Motherhood as Experience and Institution* (New York: Norton, 1986)

Ridgway, Emma (ed), *Claudette Johnson: I Came to Dance* (Oxford: Modern Art Oxford, 2019)

Ringgold, Faith, *A Letter to My Daughter Michele Wallace* (California: CreateSpace, 2015)

Roberts, Dorothy, *Killing the Black Body: Race Reproduction and the Meaning of Liberty* (London: Vintage, 1997)

Rosenberg, Judith Pierce, *A Question of Balance: Artists and Writers on Motherhood* (California: Papier-Mache Press, 1995)

Rousseau, Jean-Jacque, *Emile, or On Education* (1762)

—, *Julie or the New Eloise* (1761)

Rydal Jørgensen, Lærke, Marie Laurberg and Kirsten Degel (eds), *Mother! Origin of Life* (Louisiana: Louisiana Museum of Modern Art, 2021)

Siegel, Suzanne, Laura Silagi and Deborah Krall, *Mother Art: A Collective of Women Artists* (Los Angeles: Otis, 2011)

Suleiman, Susan Rubin, *Subversive Intent: Gender, Politics, and the Avant-Garde* (Cambridge, Massachusetts: Harvard University Press, 1990)

Tobin, Amy, Amy Budd and Naomi Pearce (eds), *14 Radnor Terrace: A Woman's Place* (London: Raven Row, 2017)

Vigée Le Brun, Élisabeth Louise, *The Memoirs of Madame Vigée Lebrun* (1835)

Voaden, Rosalynn, and Diane Wolfthal (eds), *Framing the Family: Narrative and Representation in the Medieval and Early Modern Periods* (Arizona: Arizona Centre for Medieval and Renaissance Studies, 2005)

Wagner, Anne Middleton, *Mother Stone: The Vitality of Modern British Sculpture* (New Haven, Connecticut: Yale University Press, 2005)

Wallace, Michele, *Black Macho and the Myth of the Super Woman* (London/New York: Verso, 1978)

Warner, Marina, *Alone of All Her Sex: The Myth and The Cult of the Virgin Mary* (New York: Knopf, 1976)

Widoff, Jo, and Amy Budd, *Monica Sjöö: The Great Cosmic Mother* (Stockholm/Oxford/Cologne: Moderna Museet, Modern Art Oxford and Verlag der Buchhandlung Walther König, 2023)

Williams, Paul (ed), *The Lennon Tapes: John Lennon and Yoko Ono in Conversation with Andy Peebles 6 December 1980* (London: BBC, 1981)

Wolfarth, Joanna, *Milk: An Intimate History of Breastfeeding* (London: Weidenfeld & Nicolson, 2023)

Images are listed by illustration number

Dimensions are given in cm followed by inches, unless indicated otherwise

1   Marlene Dumas, *The Painter* (detail), 1994. Oil on canvas, 200 × 100 (78¾ × 39⅜). The Museum of Modern Art, New York. Fractional and promised gift of Martin and Rebecca Eisenberg. Photo Peter Cox, Eindhoven. © Marlene Dumas. Courtesy Studio Dumas

2   Frida Kahlo, *My Birth*, 1932. Oil on copper, 30.5 × 85 (12⅛ × 33½). Private collection, USA. Photo Jorge Contreras Chacel/Bridgeman Images. © Banco de México Diego Rivera Frida Kahlo Museums Trust, Mexico, D.F./DACS 2024

3   Justine Kurland, *Mama Baby, Ocean View*, 2006. C-print, 76.2 × 101.6 (30 × 40). Courtesy the artist and Higher Pictures Generation

4   Barbara Hepworth, *Mother and Child*, 1934. Pink Ancaster stone. Wakefield Permanent Council Art Collection (The Hepworth Wakefield). Photo Jerry Hardman-Jones. Barbara Hepworth © Bowness

5   Lea Lublin, *Mon Fils (My Son)*, 1968. Nine vintage gelatin silver prints, 24 × 18 (9½ × 7⅛). The Museum of Modern Art, New York. Acquired through the generosity of The Modern Women's Fund, the Latin American and Caribbean Fund, Estrellita Brodsky, and Mauro Herlitzka. Courtesy Nicolás Lublin and 1 Mira Madrid

6   Felicity Allen, *Baby II*, 1989. Black and white photo on paper, stretched on canvas, 203 × 142 (80 × 56). Photo Chris Dorley-Brown. Digital edit Henry Newcomb Jackson. Baby Louis Gibson. Baby's mother Sophie Gibson. © Felicity Allen

7   Miriam Schaer, *Babies (Not) On Board, The Last Prejudice? Number 2: Childless Women Lack an Essential Humanity*, 2013. Hand embroidery on Baby Dress. Photo Stephen DeSantis. Courtesy Miriam Schaer

8   Tommaso di Cristoforo Fini, known as Masolino, *Madonna of Humility*, *c.* 1415. Tempera on wood, gold base, 113 × 63 (44½ × 24⅞). The Uffizi Gallery, Florence

9   Winold Reiss, *The Brown Madonna*, 1925. Pastel on Board, 78.1 × 55.9 (30¾ × 22) Fisk University Galleries, Nashville, Tennessee. Gift of the artist

10 Dorothea Lange, *Migrant Mother, Nipomo, California, March*, 1936. Nitrate negative, 10 × 13 (4 × 5). Farm Security Administration/Office of War Information Black-and-White Negatives. Library of Congress Prints and Photographs Division Washington, DC, USA

11 Anna Halprin in '*Planetary Dance*', *c.* 1980s. Anna Halprin Digital Archive, Museum of Performance + Design, San Francisco. Courtesy Tamalpa Institute

12 Nut, from the *Book of the Dead of Henuttawy*, Third Intermediate Period (*c.* 1070–664 BCE). Frame 2. Papyrus, frame 74 × 22.8 (29¼ × 9). The British Museum, London. The Trustees of the British Museum

13 Ana Mendieta, *Untitled (Esculturas Rupestres) [Rupestrian Sculptures]*, 1981. Black and white photograph, 17.8 × 22.9 (7⅛ × 9⅛). © 2024 The Estate of Ana Mendieta Collection, LLC. Courtesy Galerie Lelong & Co./ Licensed by DACS

14 Wangechi Mutu, *Water Woman*, 2017. Bronze, 91.4 × 165.1 × 177.8 (36 × 65 × 70). The Contemporary Austin, Austin, Texas. Photo David Regen. © Wangechi Mutu. Courtesy the artist and Gladstone Gallery

15 Louise Bourgeois wearing her latex sculpture *Avenza* (1968–69) which later became part of *Confrontation* (1978), New York, 1975. Photo Mark Setteducati. © The Easton Foundation/VAGA at ARS, NY and DACS, London 2024

16 Venus of Hohle Fels, *c.* 35,000 BCE. Ivory, height 5.9 (2⅜). Prehistoric Museum of Blaubeuren, Germany. mauritius images GmbH/Alamy Stock Photo

17 Seated Woman of Çatalhöyük, *c.* 6,000 BCE. Clay, 17 × 11 (6¾ × 4⅜). Museum of Anatolian Civilizations, Turkey. Images & Stories/Alamy Stock Photo

18 Judy Chicago, *Birth*, from the *Birth Project*, 1984. Filet Crochet, Executed by Dolly Kaminski, 239 × 572 (94 × 225). Collection of the Albuquerque Museum, New Mexico. Photo Donald Woodman/ARS, NY. © Judy Chicago. ARS, NY and DACS, London 2024

19 Niki de Saint Phalle, From the exhibition *She – A Cathedral*, Moderna Museet, 1966. Installation, 23 × 6 m (75½ × 19⅔ ft). Moderna Museet, Stockholm. Photo HansHammarskiöld. © Hans Hammarskiöld Heritage. © Niki de Saint Phalle Charitable Art Foundation/ADAGP, Paris and DACS, London 2024

20 Monica Sjöö, *God Giving Birth*, 1968. Oil on board, 183 × 122 (72 × 48). Courtesy Museum Anna Nordlander. Photo Krister Hägglund. © Monica Sjöö Estate

21 Sheela na Gig: A carved stone corbel showing a sheela na gig, or fertility symbol, on the church of St Mary and St David, Kilpeck, Herefordshire, UK, built *c.* 1140. Alex Ramsay/Alamy Stock Photo

22 Mary Beth Edelson, *Zipper Sheela: Stepping Out*, 1973. Oil, pen and ink, wax crayon, collaged paper and glitter on gelatin silver print, 25.4 × 20.3 (10 × 8). Whitney Museum of American Art, New York. Purchase, with funds from the Drawing Committee. Estate of Mary Beth Edelson and David Lewis

23 Coatlicue, *c.* 1500. Basalt, height: 257 (101¼). National Museum of Anthropology and History, Mexico City, CDMX, Mexico. Pascopix/Alamy Stock Photo

24 *Battle between Marduk (Bel) and Tiamat.* Drawn from a bas-relief from the *Palace of Ashurbanipal, King of Assyria*, 885–860 BCE, at Nimrûd. Drawing by L. Gruner, from *Monuments of Nineveh, Second Series* plate 5, London, 1853. Publisher J. Murray, editor Austen Henry Layard. The New York Public Library

25 Sutapa Biswas, *Housewives with Steak-knives*, 1983–85. Oil, acrylic, pastel, pencil, collage, white tape, and house-paint on paper mounted onto stretched canvas, 245 × 222 (96½ × 87½). Collection of Cartwright Hall Gallery, Bradford Museums and Galleries, UK. Photo Andy Keate. © Sutapa Biswas. All rights reserved, DACS 2024

26 Nancy Spero, *The Great Mother*, 1960. Ink on paper, 41.6 × 55.9 (16½ × 22). Pennsylvania Academy of the Fine Arts, Philadelphia. John S. Phillips Fund Art. © The Nancy Spero and Leon Golub Foundation for the Arts/VAGA at ARS, NY and DACS, London 2024

27 Yashoda with the Infant Krishna, early 12th century. Copper alloy, 44.5 × 30 × 27.6 (17½ × 11⅞ × 10⅞). The Metropolitan Museum of Art, New York. Purchase, Lita Annenberg Hazen Charitable Trust Gift, in honor of Cynthia Hazen and Leon B. Polsky, 1982

28 Bharti Kher, *Angel*, 2004. Digital print on archival Hahnemuhle Photo Rag paper, 114.3 × 76.2 (45 × 30). © Bharti Kher. Courtesy the artist and Hauser & Wirth

29 Leonardo da Vinci, *The Fetus in the Womb, Sketches and Notes on Reproduction*, c. 1511. Red chalk and traces of black chalk, pen and ink, wash, 30.4 × 22 (12 × 8¾). Royal Collection Trust, London

30 Martin Caldenbach, woodcut illustrations for Eucharius Rösslin, *Der schwangeren Frauen und Hebammen Rosengarten (The Rose Garden of Pregnant Women and Midwives)*, 1528. Göttingen State and University Library, Germany

31 Titian, *Diana and Callisto*, c. 1556–59. Oil on canvas, 187 × 204.5 (73⅝ × 80⅝). The National Gallery, London

32 Francesco de Rossi, known as Salviati, *Charity*, c. 1545. Oil on panel, 156 × 122 (61½ × 48⅛). The Uffizi Gallery, Florence

33 Peter Paul Rubens, *Roman Charity*, c. 1612. Oil on canvas, 140.5 × 180.3 (55⅜ × 71). Hermitage Museum, Saint Petersburg, Russia

34 Lucas Cranach the Elder, *Christ Blessing the Children*, c. 1537–53. Oil on beech, 56.5 × 74 (22¼ × 29¼). Statens Museum for Kunst (SMK), Copenhagen

35 Pieter de Hooch, *A Mother's Duty*, c. 1660–61. Oil on canvas, 52.5 × 61 (20¾ × 24⅛). The Rijksmuseum, Amsterdam. On loan from the City of Amsterdam. A. van der Hoop Bequest

36 Jean-Baptiste Greuze, *La mére bienaimée (The Well-Loved Mother)*, 1775. Brush and grey ink wash with black chalk, 49 × 62.4 (19⅜ × 24⅝). Art Gallery of New South Wales, Australia. Gift of James Fairfax AC 1999. Art Gallery of New South Wales/Bridgeman Images

37 Jean Honoré Fragonard, *The Happy Family*, c. 1775. Oil on canvas, 53.9 × 65.1 (21¼ × 25⅝). National Gallery of Art, Washington, DC. Timken Collection

38 John Everett Millais, *Mrs Coventry Patmore*, 1851. Oil on wood, 19.7 × 20.3 (7⅞ × 8). The Fitzwilliam Museum, Cambridge, UK. Given by The Friends of the Fitzwilliam Museum, 1920

39 Ford Madox Brown, *Take Your Son, Sir*, c. 1851–92. Oil paint on canvas, 70.5 × 38.1 (27⅞ × 15). Tate, London. Presented by Miss Emily Sargent and Mrs Ormond in memory of their brother, John S. Sargent 1929

40 John Everett Millais, *The Woodman's Daughter*, 1851. Oil on canvas, 89 × 65 (35⅛ × 25⅝). Guildhall Art Gallery, London

41 Mary Cassatt, *Breakfast in Bed*, 1897. Oil on canvas, 58.4 × 73.7 (23 × 29). The Huntington Library, Art Museum, and Botanical Gardens. Gift of the Virginia Steele Scott Foundation

42 Giovanni Segantini, *The Evil Mothers*, 1894. Oil on canvas, 105 × 200 (41⅜ × 78¾). Belvedere Museum, Vienna

43 Paula Modersohn-Becker, *Kneeling Mother with Child at her Breast*, 1906. Oil and tempera on canvas, 113 × 74 (44½ × 29¼). State Museums in Berlin, Nationalgalerie

44 Käthe Kollwitz, *At the Doctor's*, sheet 3 of the series *Images of Misery*, 1908–9. Black crayon on Ingres paper, 55 × 35 (21¾ × 13⅞). Käthe Kollwitz Museum, Cologne

45 Paula Modersohn Becker, *Reclining Mother and Child II*, 1906. Oil on canvas, 82.5 × 124.7 (32½ × 49⅛). Museen Böttcherstraße, Paula Modersohn-Becker Museum, Bremen

46 Charles White, *Hope for the Future*, 1945. Lithograph, 33.5 × 27.2 (13¼ × 10¾). The Metropolitan Museum of Art, New York. Gift of Reba and Dave Williams, 1999. © The Charles White Archives

47 Titus Kaphar, *Analogous Colors*, 2020, featured on the cover of *Time*, 15 June 2020. © Titus Kaphar. Courtesy TIME

48 Paula Modersohn-Becker, *Self-Portrait with Two Flowers in her Raised Left Hand* (detail), 1907. Oil on canvas, 55.2 × 24.8 (21¾ × 9¾). The Metropolitan Museum of Art, New York. Jointly owned by The Museum of Modern Art, New York, Gift of Debra and Leon. Black, and Neue Galerie New York, Gift of Jo Carole and Ronald S. Lauder. Conservation was made possible by the Bank of America Art Conservation Project

49 Betye Saar, *Anticipation*, 1961. Serigraph, 45.7 × 36.2 (18 × 14⅜). Hammer Museum, California. Collection of Alvin and Jeffalyn Johnson. © Betye Saar. Courtesy the artist and Roberts Projects, Los Angeles

50 Frida Kahlo, *The Henry Ford Hospital*, 1932. Oil on metal, 30.5 × 38 (12⅛ × 15). Fundacion Dolores Olmedo, Mexico City, Mexico. Photo Schalkwijk/Art Resource/Scala, Florence. © 2024 Banco de México Diego Rivera Frida Kahlo Museums Trust, Mexico, D.F./Artists Rights Society (ARS), New York

51 Chantal Joffe, *Self-Portrait with Esme*, 2008. Oil on board, 305 × 153 (120 × 60¼). National Portrait Gallery, London. Given by Victoria Miro Gallery, 2015. © Chantal Joffe. Courtesy the artist and Victoria Miro

52 Mary Beale, *Self-Portrait*, 1666. Oil on canvas, 109.2 × 87.6 (43 × 34½). National Portrait Gallery, London. Purchased, 1912

53 Elisabeth Louise Vigée LeBrun, *Self-Portrait with her Daughter, Julie*, 1786. Oil on canvas, 105 × 84 (41⅜ × 33⅛). Musée du Louvre, Département des Peintures, Paris

54 Billie Zangewa, *Every Woman*, 2017. Hand-stitched silk collage, 136 × 98.5 (53⅝ × 38⅞). © Billie Zangewa. Courtesy the artist and Lehmann Maupin, New York, Hong Kong, Seoul, and London

55 Everlyn Nicodemus, *Min Stympade Mänsklighet (My Mutilated Humanity)*, 1982. Oil on canvas, 97.5 × 41 (38½ × 16¼). © Everlyn Nicodemus. Courtesy Richard Saltoun Gallery, London and Rome

56 Berthe Morisot, *The Wet Nurse Angele Feeding Julie Manet*, 1880. Oil on canvas, 50 × 61 (19¾ × 24⅛). Private Collection. Artefact/Alamy Stock Photo

57 Berthe Morisot, *Berthe Morisot Drawing with her Daughter*, 1889. Drypoint on wove paper, 19 × 13.9 (7½ × 5½). The Courtauld, London. Samuel Courtauld Trust

58 Clare Bottomley and Hermione Wiltshire, *...and another thing...*, from the series *The Birth of the Image*, 2020. Digital C-type photographic print, 68 × 80 (26⅞ × 31½). Courtesy the artists

59 Suzanne Valadon, *Family Portrait*, 1912. Oil on canvas, 97 × 73 (38¼ × 28¾). Georges Pompidou Center, Paris. Donation to the national museums by Mr. Cahen-Salvador as a souvenir from Madame Fontenelle-Pomaret, 1976. The Archives/Alamy Stock Photo

60 Ishbel Myerscough, *All*, 2016. Oil on canvas, 190 × 120 (74¾ × 47¼). © Ishbel Myerscough. Courtesy Flowers Gallery, London and New York

61 Leni Dothan, *Sleeping Madonna*, 2011. Performance to camera, mother, child, drawing on wall, 2 mins 46 secs looped video. Courtesy the artist

62 Catherine Opie, *Self Portrait/ Nursing*, 2004. C-type print, 101.6 × 76.2 (40 × 30). © Catherine Opie. Courtesy Regen Projects,

Los Angeles and Thomas Dane Gallery, London

63 Renee Cox, *THE YO MAMA*, 1993. Archival digital ink jet print on cotton rag, 121.9 × 213.4 (48 × 84). Courtesy the artist

64 Janine Antoni, *2038*, 2000. C-type photographic print, 50.8 × 50.8 (20 × 20). © Janine Antoni. Courtesy the artist and Luhring Augustine, New York

65 Jenny Saville, *Reproduction Drawing II (After the Leonardo Cartoon)*, 2009–10. Charcoal on paper, 233.5 × 144.5 (92 × 57). Photo Mike Bruce. Courtesy Gagosian. © Jenny Saville. All rights reserved, DACS 2024

66 Eileen Cooper, *Putting Down Roots*, 1985. Oil on canvas, 243.3 × 182.8 (95⅞ × 72). Arts Council Collection, Southbank Centre, London. © Eileen Cooper

67 Celia Paul, *Frank and Me*, 2011. Oil on canvas, 76.2 × 50.7 (30 × 20). © Celia Paul. Courtesy the artist and Victoria Miro

68 Lea Cetera, *You Can't Have It All*, 2022. Borosilicate glass, sand, 21 × 10.2 × 21.6 (8¼ × 4 × 8½). Photo Ben Westoby. © Courtesy the artist and Phillida Reid, London

69 Wangechi Mutu, *Fertility Heal IX*, 2018. Red soil, cow horn, acrylic heels, paper pulp, wood glue, wood, glass beads, 10 × 29 × 32 (4 × 11⅜ × 12⅝). Photo Flavio Karrer. © Wangechi Mutu. Courtesy the artist and Victoria Miro

70 Lindsey Mendick, *Hairy on the Inside*, 2021. Single-channel HD video, 16 mins 36 secs. Courtesy the artist

71 Jessa Fairbrother, *Role Play (Woman with Cushion)*, 2017. Hand perforated, painted photographs, on wooden baton, 120 × 120 (47¼ × 47¼). Courtesy the artist

72 Alice Neel, *Pregnant Maria*, 1964. Oil on canvas, 81.3 × 119.4 (32 × 47). © The Estate of Alice Neel. Courtesy the artist and Victoria Miro

73 Senga Nengudi, *R.S.V.P*, 1977/2003. Pantyhose and sand, 10 pieces. Overall dimensions variable. Senga Nengudi, Amistad Research Center, New Orleans, LA. © Senga Nengudi, 2024

74 Annegret Soltau, *Ausgeliefert (Vulnerable)*, 1978. Gelatin silver print with thread overstitched, 10.5 × 8.5 (4¼ × 3⅜). © Annegret Soltau. Courtesy Richard Saltoun Gallery London and Rome. © DACS 2024

75 Susan Hiller, *Ten Months*, 1977. 10 gelatin silver prints and 10 text panels, 203 × 518 (80 × 204). © The Estate of Susan Hiller, courtesy Lisson Gallery. All rights reserved, DACS, 2024. On the following spread: Susan Hiller in front of *Ten Months* at the Hayward Gallery, London, 1980. Photo Robin Klassnik. © The Estate of Susan Hiller, courtesy Lisson Gallery. All rights reserved, DACS, 2024

76 Louise Bourgeois, *DO NOT ABANDON ME*, 1999. Pink fabric and thread, 12 × 52 × 21.5 (4¾ × 20½ × 8½). Collection Ursula Hauser, Switzerland. Photo Christopher Burke. © The Easton Foundation/ VAGA at ARS, NY and DACS, London 2024

77 Hermione Wiltshire, *Preparing for Birth*, 2008. Black and white digital print, dimensions variable. Courtesy the artist, originally commissioned by Birth Rites Collection

78 Heather Spears, *Studies/Drawings of Labour/Childbirth, Rigshospitalet 26–27 January 1987*, 1987. Pencil on paper, 21 × 29.7 (8⅜ × 11¾). Courtesy Wellcome Collection, London. © Heather Spears. Wellcome Collection, London

79 Chantal Joffe, *Esme (First Painting)*, 2004. Oil on board, 29.2 × 21.8 (11½ × 8⅝). © Chantal Joffe. Courtesy the artist and Victoria Miro

80 Fani Parali, *Incubator/Flight*, 2022. Steel and graphite on paper, 118 × 104 × 44 (46½ × 41 × 17⅜). Photo Ben Deakin. © Fani Parali. Courtesy Cooke Latham

81 Rineke Dijkstra, *Julie, Den Haag, Netherlands, February 29 1994*, 1994. C-print, 62 × 52 × 4 (24⅜ x 20½ × 1⅝). Courtesy the artist and Marian Goodman Gallery

82 Claudette Johnson, *Afterbirth*, 1990. Pastel on paper, 118 × 83 (46½ × 32¾). Courtesy the artist and Hollybush Gardens, London. © Claudette Johnson. All rights reserved, DACS/Artimage. 2024

83 Catherine Elwes, *There is a Myth*, 1984. Film, 9 mins. Courtesy the artist and LUX

84 Caroline Walker, *Bottles and Pumps*, 2022, Oil on board, 36 × 30 (14⅛ × 11¾). Courtesy the artist and Stephen Friedman Gallery; GRIMM Amsterdam/New York/ London and Ingleby Gallery, Edinburgh. Photo Peter Mallet. © Caroline Walker. All rights reserved, DACS 2024.

85 Camille Henrot, *Wet Job*, 2019. Watercolor on heavy Somerset Velvet paper mounted on ALU, 88.9 × 118.7 (35 × 46¾). Courtesy the artist, Mennour (Paris) and Hauser & Wirth

86 Carmen Winant, *White Ink*, 2018. Ink, collaged images on paper (15 pages), dimensions variable. Courtesy the artist and PATRON Gallery, Chicago

87 Tabitha Soren, (clockwise from top left): *My Great American Novel, All 400 Photographs*, 2006–7/2021, *The Month the Baby Slept Through the Night*, 2007/2022, *The Night the Panic Attacks Started*, 2006/2022, *The Month I Could Walk Without Peeing on Myself*, 2007/2022 from the series *Motherload* (2006–7/2022. Archival pigment prints, 56 × 86 (22 × 34). © Tabitha Soren 2024. Courtesy Jackson Fine Art Gallery. © ARS, NY and DACS, London 2024

88 Dorothy Cross, *Amazon*, 1992. Cow skin, teat and tailor's dummy. Courtesy the artist and Frith Street Gallery, London

89 Cathy Pilkington, *Surrogate*, 2007. Wood, wire, wool, jesmonite, fur and paint, 57 × 30 × 30 (22½ × 11⅞ × 11⅞). © Cathie Pilkington. Courtesy The David and Indrė Roberts Collection

90 Mierle Laderman Ukeles, *Maintenance Art Tasks*, 1973. Excerpt from *Doing the Laundry* album with red cover and black & white photographs, chain and dust rag, album: 33.2 × 31.75 (13 × 12½). © Mierle Laderman Ukeles. Courtesy the artist and Ronald Feldman Gallery, New York

91 Gunvor Nelson and Dorothy Wiley, *Schmeerguntz*, 1966. 15 min. Filmform, Stockholm

92 VALIE EXPORT, *Die Geburtenmadonna (The Birth Madonna)*, 1976. Chromogenic colour print laid on chipboard, 152 × 126 × 2 (59⅞ × 49⅝ × ⅞). Courtesy Thaddaeus Ropac Gallery, London, Paris, Salzburg, Seoul. © VALIE EXPORT. © DACS, 2024.

93 Hackney Flashers, *Who's Holding the Baby?*, 1978. © Hackney Flashers. Courtesy Bishopsgate Institute

94 Bobby Baker, *Drawing on a Mother's Experience, ICA*, London, 1988. Photo Andrew Whittuck. © Bobby Baker. All rights reserved, DACS/Artimage 2024

95 Tala Madani, *Shit Mom (Remodel)*, 2019, from the series *Shit Moms* (2019–). Oil on linen, 182.9 × 182.9 × 3.2 (72 × 72 × 1¼). Courtesy the artist

and Pilar Corrias, London. Solomon R. Guggenheim Museum

96 Mary Kelly, *Post-Partum Document, Documentation VI: Pre-Writing Alphabet, Exerque and Diary/ Experimentum Mentis VI: (On the Insistence of the Letter)*, 1978–79. Slate and resin, 18 parts, each 36.5 × 29 × 4 (14⅜ × 11½ × 1⅝). Arts Council Collection, Southbank Centre, London. © Mary Kelly. © DACS 2024

97 Hannah Starkey, *Untitled, February 2013*, 2013. Framed c-type print mounted on aluminium, 122.4 × 163.6 (48¼ × 64½). © Hannah Starkey. Courtesy Maureen Paley, London

98 Carrie Mae Weems, *Untitled*, from *The Kitchen Table* series, 1990. Platinum print, 39 × 39 (15⅜ × 15⅜). Private Collection, London. © Carrie Mae Weems. Courtesy Jack Shainman Gallery, New York, 2024

99 The Mother Art Collective, *Laundry Works*, 1977. The Getty Research Institute. Special Collections. Mother Art records 2017. Courtesy Mother Art

100 *Feministo: Postal Art Event, 'A Portrait of the Artist as a Housewife'*, exhibition poster, 1977. Courtesy Monica Ross Archive

101 Polvo de Gallina Negra (Mónica Mayer and Maris Bustamante), *Madre por un día (Mother for a day)*, 1987. Video, color, sound, 17:27 min. Hammer Museum, California. Collection of Mónica Mayer and Víctor Lerma. Courtesy Archivo Pintomiraya

102 Christine Voge, *Untitled (Three Children and a Woman)*, 1978. Gelatin silver print, 29.8 × 20.3 (11¾ × 8). © Christine Voge

103 Cassie Arnold, *School Uniform (Bulletproof Dress)*, 2022. Hand knit Kevlar cord. Courtesy the artist

104 Barbara Walker, *Untitled* from the *Louder than Words* series, 2006. Mixed media on digital image, 114 × 85 (45 × 33½). Photo Gary Kirkham. Courtesy the artist and Cristea Roberts Gallery, London. © Barbara Walker. All rights reserved, DACS, 2024

105 Emma Talbot, *The Mountain, Time After Time*, 2016. Acrylic on silk, 309 × 155 (121⅝ × 61). Arts Council Collection, Southbank Centre, London. Photo Achim Kukulie. Courtesy the artist and Petra Rinck Galerie

106 Sally Mann, *Emmett's Bloody Nose*, 1985. Silver gelatin print, 50.8 × 61 (20 × 24). © Sally Mann. Courtesy Gagosian

107 Anna Grevenitis, *May 25 2015*, from the *Regard* series, 2015-ongoing. Photograph, dimensions variable. Courtesy the artist

108 Marlene Dumas in collaboration with her daughter Helena, *Underground*, 1994–95. Eight drawings, mixed media on paper, 62 × 50 (24½ × 19¾). Courtesy the artist

109 Zineb Sedira, *Mother Tongue*, 2002. 3 screen installation with headphones, 5 minutes each. Photo Tate, London. © Zineb Sedira

110 Daphne Wright, *I Know What It's Like*, 2021. Video projection, 6 mins. Courtesy the artist and Frith Street Gallery, London

111 Käthe Kollwitz, *Woman with Dead Child (Frau mit totem Kind)*, 1903. Etching with chine collé, 41.2 × 47.1 (16¼ × 18⅝). The Museum of Modern Art, New York. Acquired through the generosity of the Contemporary Drawing and Print Associates

112 Alice Neel, *After the Death of the Child*, 1927–28. Watercolour, gouache and graphite on paper 29.8 × 22.2 (11¾ × 8¾). Vassar College. Gift of Mrs. John Benson Brooks (Frances K. B. Jones, class of 1940). Photo Frances Lehman Loeb Art Center, Vassar College, Poughkeepsie, NY/Art Resource, NY. © The Estate of Alice Neel. Courtesy the artist and Victoria Miro

113 Alice Neel, *Futility of Effort*, 1930. Oil on canvas, 67.9 × 62.2 (26¼ × 24½). Collection of Anne McNamara, Dallas, Texas. © The Estate of Alice Neel. Courtesy the artist and Victoria Miro

114 Elina Brotherus, *Annonciation*, 2009–13. Pigment prints from digital originals, dimensions variable. Courtesy the artist

115 Renate Bertlmann, *Die Missgebildeten Menschen von Morgen (The Malformed Humans of Tomorrow)*, 1975. Pacifiers, needles, scalpel knife, glass and perspex, 55 × 62 × 10 (21¾ × 24½ × 4). © Renate Bertlmann. Courtesy Richard Saltoun Gallery, London and Rome

116 Yoko Ono and John Lennon, *Unfinished Music No. 2: Life with the Lions*, 1969. Zapple Records Album cover photograph © Susan Wood. © Yoko Ono

117 Su Richardson, *Heartstrings (What Becomes of the Broken Hearted?)*, 2022. Cotton woven mat, metallic and cotton yarn, recycled materials, birthday card, plastic and embroidered bib, 160 × 62 (63 × 24½). © Su Richardson. Courtesy Richard Saltoun Gallery

118 Nancy Willis, *Self-Portrait with Lost Baby*, 1988. Etching with hand colouring, 28 × 24 (11⅛ × 9½), edition of 27. Courtesy the artist

119 Tracey Emin, *How it Feels*, 1996. Single channel video (shot on Hi8), 22 min, 33 secs. © Tracey Emin. All rights reserved, DACS/Artimage 2024

120 Paula Rego, *Untitled No.4*, 1998, from the *Abortion Series*, 1998–99. Pastel on paper on aluminium, 110 × 100 (43⅜ × 39⅜). Photo Bridgeman Images. © Paula Rego. All rights reserved 2024

121 Laia Abril, *On Abortion: Human incubator, Hippocratic Betrayal*, 2016. *On Abortion*, 2016, Laia Abril/ Les Filles du Calvaire

122 The Artists' Campaign to Repeal the Eighth Amendment Banners at The ARC (Abortion Rights Campaign) 6th Annual March for Choice, 2017. Banners by Sarah Cullen, Rachel Fallon, Alice Maher, Breda Mayock and Áine Phillips. Photo Christian Kerskens

123 *Aprons of Power* performance as part of Repeal! Procession for The Artists' Campaign to Repeal the Eighth Amendment at EVA International Biennale, Limerick, 2018. Photo Darren Ryan. Courtesy the artists and Arts Council of Ireland

124 Barbara Kruger, *Untitled (Your body is a battleground)*, 1989. Photographic silkscreen on vinyl, 284.5 × 284.5 (112 × 112). The Broad Art Foundation, Los Angeles. Courtesy the artist, The Broad Art Foundation and Sprüth Magers

125 Zanele Muholi, *Nomsa Mazibuko and Fondo, outside the Hope Unity Metropolitan Community Church, a gay church, during Good Friday. Mayfair, Johannesburg*, 2007. Lambda print, 76.5 × 76.5 (30⅛ × 30⅛). © Zanele Muholi. Courtesy the artist and Yancey Richardson, New York

126 Cathy Cade, *Emerson Street Household, Berkeley, CA*, 1973. Cathy Cade photograph archive, Bancroft Library (BANC PIC 2012.054.R196.42.25--NEG, R196 #42, 25). © The Regents of the University of California. The Bancroft Library, University of California, Berkeley

127 Cathy Cade, *Laurie Hauer and Gusse II*, 1989. Cathy Cade photograph archive, Bancroft Library (BANC PIC 2012.054--AX

AX box 3, Folder 5). © The Regents of the University of California. The Bancroft Library, University of California, Berkeley

128 Susanne Bösche and Andreas Hansen, *Jenny Lives with Eric and Martin*, 1981/ 1983. Written by author Susanne Bösche. Photo Andreas Hansen. © 1981, 2022 Susanne Bösche and SAGA Egmont

129 Sunil Gupta, *Untitled #9*, from the series *'Pretended' Family Relationships*, 1988–2021. Archival inkjet print, 61 × 91.4 (24 × 36). © Sunil Gupta. All rights reserved, DACS 2024

130 Candy Guinea, *Mariposa*, 2017. Video, 18 min. Directed by Candy Guinea. © Candy Guinea

131 Del LaGrace Volcano, *MaPa Del and Mika, Örebro, Sweden*, 2011. Giclee print, dimensions variable. © Del LaGrace Volcano 2011. Courtesy the artist

132 Helen Benigson, *Jude* (still), 2020. HD video. © Helen Benigson

133 Sadie Lune, *Strolling*, from the series *Preparing for Motherhood*, 2010. Photo Mabel Jiménez

134 Tabita Rezaire, *Hoetep Blessings*, 2018. Copper installation and video, 12 min, 30 secs. Commissioned for Summer Happenings by The Broad Museum, LA, USA. Courtesy Tabita Rezaire and Goodman Gallery

135 Dani & Sheilah ReStack, video still from *Strangely Ordinary This Devotion*, 2017. First video in the trilogy called *Feral Domestic*. Courtesy Dani & Sheilah ReStack

136 Liesel Burisch, *Gorilla Milk*, 2021. Video, 9 min, 54 secs. Courtesy Liesel Burisch

137 Laure Prouvost, *MOOTHERR*, 2021. On display at the exhibition *MOTHER ! Origin of Life* at Louisiana Museum of Modern Art, January 28th – August 29th, 2021. Louisiana Museum of Art, Denmark. Photo Louisiana Museum of Modern Art/Anders Sune Berg. © Laure Prouvost

138 Kiki Smith, *Pietà*, 1999. Ink on Nepalese paper, 141 × 74.9 (55½ × 29½). Whitney Museum of American Art, New York. Purchase, with funds from the Drawing Committee. Photo G.R. Christmas. © Kiki Smith. Courtesy Pace Gallery

Chapter opener details, listed by page number

p.18 Sutapa Biswas, *Housewives with Steak-knives*, 1983–85 (detail of ill. 25)

46 Lucas Cranach the Elder, *Christ Blessing the Children*, c. 1537–53 (detail of ill. 34)

116 Jessa Fairbrother, *Role Play (Woman with Cushion)*, 2017 (detail of ill. 71)

158 Christine Voge, *Untitled (Three Children and a Woman)*, 1978 (detail of ill. 102)

198 Alice Neel, *After the Death of the Child*, 1927–28 (detail of ill. 112)

224 Sadie Lune, *Strolling*, from the series *Preparing for Motherhood*, 2010 (detail of ill. 133)

author's

acknowledgments

When I started this project some years ago, the subject of motherhood was distinctly unfashionable. It has taken many attempts and false starts to get *Acts of Creation: On Art and Motherhood* published. A few early supporters convinced me to keep going, among them Rebecca Morrill who returned to the project as copy editor and was as a fierce as I hoped she might be. Rebecca, thank you for the knowledge, sensitivity, insight and belief you brought this book. Gilly Fox of Hayward Gallery Touring encouraged me to turn my then-going-nowhere book idea into an exhibition. Gilly – it has been a delirious experience working with you and getting this show on the road.

Downcast, in 2022 I applied to the Society of Authors for a grant and then forgot about it. Months later I was so bewildered to receive an award notification that I almost deleted the email. That grant gave me a boost when I was losing hope and felt I'd never find a publisher. In 2022 I was also awarded a residency at the Villa Lena Foundation which gave me time and space to start shaping the book in earnest. The Villa's grand staircase provided a spectacular arena for my first public reading from Acts of Creation. Lena Evstafieva has become an extraordinary supporter of the book, allowing us to bring Rebecca on as copy editor, and Carol Montpart as designer. Lena, I am so grateful that you followed your instincts after seeing the images taped on my studio wall. I knew Carol Montpart could turn this book into something really special, and she has come up with a design that is at once sharp and approachable, inventive and inviting. If readers feel welcomed into this book it is due in large part to Carol's work.

In February 2023 the Danish Arts Foundation supported my visit to Copenhagen through their International Research Programme. There I met artists and curators, and visited what I think we can all agree is the BEST version of Lucas Cranach the Elder's *Christ Blessing the Children*, in the Statens Museum for Kunst.

Thanks to: Althea Greenan for identifying relevant material from the Women's Art Library archives at Goldsmiths. The Wellcome Collection for letting me look through the uncatalogued drawings of Heather Spears (Sorry for being so explosively rowdy – I was very excited!). Those who have offered recommendations and pointers over the years – they were noted and appreciated. All the artists who have given their time to talk, share images and archive material. I have been so touched by your willingness to discuss difficult and personal subjects.

I read the first full draft of *Acts of Creation* in public, chapter by chapter over the summer of 2023. It was a brutally exposing experience, but a valuable one, revealing flaws in my writing and keeping me on deadline. Thanks to: Cathie Pilkington and Jemima Fitzjohn for making the Keeper's Studio of the Royal Academy available for the readings; Kelsey Corbett and Unit London Gallery for hosting Chapter 2; Penelope Kupfer for making Kupfer Project Space available for a marathon weekend run-through of the whole book. My thanks too, to all who attended: you were so generous with your time, feedback and suggestions.

I am indebted to Brian Cass and all at Hayward Gallery Touring for championing the exhibition produced alongside this book, and for securing such fantastic touring partners. Charlotte Flint – you were such a positive and uplifting spirit during your time as co-curator. Cathy Cade's photographs are in this book because of you.

Fragments of the text on Caroline Walker first appeared in *The Place of Motherhood in the Art World* in Issue 229 of *Frieze* magazine. I am grateful to Andrew Durbin for permission to reprint them. Fragments of the text on Hannah Starkey first appeared in the catalogue for *In Real Life* (2022), republished with kind permission of Dr Abi Shapiro at The Hepworth Wakefield.

My agents Sarah Chalfant and Emma Smith gave this book a crucial final push. Thank you, not only for your tenacity, but also for being the first readers of the manuscript and offering such touching feedback.

I am grateful to Roger Thorp, Mohara Gill, picture researcher Anabel Navarro, production controller Sadie Butler and all at Thames & Hudson for giving this book a home and bringing it to the page.

Ben – this would not have been possible without your love, support and patience, right up to the 'year of great abandonment' (aka year of research, reading and residency trips). You have been the greatest co-pilot in this messy business of parenting.

I dedicate this book with so much love to Jacob and Isaac. You made me the mother I am.

acknowledgments

Our immense gratitude goes to all the individual collectors, institutions, galleries and participating artists who have made artworks available for publication and display. Without their generosity, neither the book nor the related exhibition would have been possible. Thanks also to the Villa Lena Foundation for their crucial support in the realization of this project.

An exhibition that tours to multiple museums and galleries is by its nature an exercise in transformation. We are very grateful to our colleagues and collaborators in each partner venue for their enthusiasm and commitment, with particular thanks to: Garry Topp, Gemma Brace and Keiko Higashi at Arnolfini, Bristol; Deborah Kermode and Roma Piotrowska at Midlands Arts Centre, Birmingham; Kirstie Hamilton and Alison Morton at Millennium Gallery, Sheffield; Beth Bath and Tiffany Boyle at Dundee Contemporary Arts.

A number of individuals on the Hayward Gallery Touring curatorial team contributed greatly to this project. We would like to thank Assistant Curator Gilly Fox, as well as former Assistant Curator Charlotte Flint, for their endless energy and imagination in developing the exhibition with Hettie Judah, ably supported by Philippa Douglas, Curatorial Assistant. We are also indebted to Stephanie Busson, Alison Maun, Kate Parrot, Jenny Hunter, Kate Sullivan and Marcia Ceppo for their tireless and skilful work.

We extend our thanks to the following individuals for their support: Kate Bradbury, Roberts Institute of Art; Gemma Lloyd, Daily Life Ltd; Chloe Carroll, Phillida Reid Gallery; Susan May, White Cube; Moira Lindsay, British Council; Sarah Rustin, Ropac; Christian Peake; Deborah Smith and Alona Pardo, Arts Council Collection; Gabriel Coxhead, Susan Hiller Archive; Nella Franco, Hollybush Gardens; Báirbre O'Brien, Pilar Corrias; James Ulph, Flowers Gallery; Kathy Stephenson, Victoria Miro; Sophie Lindo, Cristea Roberts; Hannah Robinson, Alison Jacques; Niamh Coghlan and Costanza Simonini, Richard Saltoun Gallery; Melanie Keen and Rowan DeSaulles, Wellcome Collection; Ali MacGilp, Frith Street; Maureen Paley and Naja Bak Rantorp, Maureen Paley; Tamsin Huxford, Stephen Friedman Gallery; Janey McAllester, Collection Manager; Victoria Mitchell, Lisson Gallery.

Hayward Gallery Touring

Page numbers in *italic* refer
to the illustrations

4chan 221

a

abortion 75, 112, 200, 211, 213–23
Abortion Act (UK, 1968) 208
'About Time' exhibition, London
    (1980) 146
Abril, Laia
    A History of Misogyny 218
        *On Abortion: Human incubator,
        Hippocratic Betrayal* 219
        *On Abortion and the Repercussions
        of Lack of Access* 218
Abstract Expressionists 168
Abzu 39
'Acts of Creation' exhibition,
    Bristol (2024) 14, 121
adoption 199, 208–11, 214
advertising 163–66
Africa 26, 96
Agent Provocateur 80
AIDS epidemic 227, 235
Algeria 196–97
Allen, Felicity, *Baby II 16*, 17
Alzheimer's disease 197
Ama Mawu 34
Amalthea 40
Amazon region 242
Amazons 153
Anabaptists 58
Andes 22
'Angel in the House' 64–65
Angelico, Fra, *Annunciation*
    fresco 204
animals
    mothering 249–51
    as mothers 246–47
Anne, St 109, 118
Annunciation 117–18, 121, 123
Antiope 153
Antoni, Janine
    2038 109, *110*
    Loving Care 108–109
Ardern, Jacinda 93
Argentina 218, 223
Aristotle 49
Arnold, Cassie, *School Uniform
    (Bulletproof Dress)* 184–85, *185*
Arnolfini, Bristol 121
Arsanios, Mirene, *Notes on Mother
    Tongues* 196
Art Front 204
Artists' Campaign to Repeal the 8th
    Amendment 218, *220*
Atlanta, Georgia 228
Aurignacian 'Venus' 28
Australia 29
Austria 164
Avallon 204
Aztecs 39

b

babies
    birth 128–38
    breastfeeding 55–57, 63, 95, 144,
        147–56
    childcare 159–63, 167–74, 176–96
    as foetuses 47–52, 218
    Neonatal Intensive Care Units 135,
        138–40
    selkies 249
baby monitors 184
Babylonians 39
Bachofen, Johann Jakob 32
Badlands (film) 173
Baker, Bobby, *Drawing on a Mother's
    Experience* 168, *169*, 171
Barcelona 232
Baroque art 22, 58, 99
Barthes, Roland 225
Battista, Kathy 180
Beale, Mary 102
    Self-Portrait 88–89, 91, *92*
Beat Generation 173
The Beatles 208
Beegan, Kathleen 133
Behn, Aphra 91
Benham, Pameli 197
Benigson, Helen, *Jude 239*, *239*
Berlin 126, 201, 240
Bertlmann, Renate 206–207
    *Die Missgebildeten Menschen von
    Morgen (The Malformed Humans
    of Tomorrow)* 207, *207*
    Pregnant Bride in a Wheelchair 207
Betterton, Rosemary 67
biological clock 118
birth 128–30, 141
    birth figures 51–52
    Goddess Movement and 32
    stillbirths 199, 206
birth control campaigns (1920s
    and '30s) 214
Birth Rites Collection 133
Biswas, Sutapa, *Housewives
    with Steak-knives* 40, *41*
Black people
    homespace 175–76
    lesbian families in South Africa
        226–27
    lynchings 77–9
    as mothers 105–108
    stop and search 185–87
#BlackLives Matter protests 79
blended families 225
Boccaccio, Giovanni, *De Mulieribus
    Claris (Famous Women)* 153
Book of the Dead (Egyptian) 24, *24*
Bösche, Susanne, *Jenny Lives with
    Eric and Martin* 233, *234*
Bottomley, Claire, *The Birth of the Image*
    99, *100*
Bourgeois, Louise 247
    Avenza 27, 28
    DO NOT ABANDON ME 128–33, *132*
Brando, Marlon 173
breast pumps 144, 146–7

breastfeeding 55–57, 63, 95, 144, 147–56
Brennan, Cecily 218, 221
Bretteville, Sheila Levrant de 29
Briffault, Robert 32
Bright, Susan 79
Bristol Cathedral 34
Britain 63–65
    'Angel in the House' 64–65
    anti-Section 28 protests 233–35
    medications for stress and
        depression 166
    pregnancy excluded from portraits 123
    sheela-na-gigs 34–36
    women's refuges 183–84
Brotherus, Elina
    Annunciation series 204–206, *205*
    Carpe Fucking Diem series 206
Brown, Ford Madox, *Take Your Son,
    Sir 66*, 67
Brown, Helen Gurley, *Having It All* 93
Brussels 204
Bryant, Anita 232, 233
Budapest 246
Burdett Coutts, Angela 67
Burisch, Liesel
    Gorilla Milk 246, 246–47
    Queer Nursing 247
Bush, George H. W. 223
Bustamente, Maris 180–83

c

Cade, Cathy 228–32, 239
    *Emerson Street Household, Berkeley,
    CA* 228, *229*
    Laurie Hauer and Gusse II 230–31, 232
    Rally for Jeanne Jullion 232
Caldenbach, Martin *50*, *51*
California 88
California Arts Council 178
Callenbach, Ernest 162
Callisto 52
Calvin, John 58
Cameron, Julia Margaret 189
Campaign for Nuclear Disarmament
    (CND) 180
Campidelli, Silvia, *Nel Nome Del Padre
    (In the Name of the Father)* 232
Canada 138
Capitoline Wolf 42
Caravaggio, *The Seven Acts of Mercy* 55
Caribbean 25
Cassatt, Mary 70–71, 74
    Breakfast in Bed 70, 71
Çatalhöyük 28–29, *30*
Catholic Church 48, 55, 57, 164, 214
Cats, Jacob 95
CCTV 184
Ceres 28
Cetera, Lea, *You Can't Have it All* 118, *119*
Cézanne, Paul 74
Chambers, Eddie 40, 187
Chamunda 40
Charity 55, 63, 80
Chicago 77
Chicago, Judy 29–31, 32
    Birth Project 10, 31, *31*, 237

The Dinner Party 29
In the Beginning 31
childbirth *see* birth
children
    adoption 199, 208–11, 214
    in artworks 188–89
    artworks by 192–96
    in care 211
    childcare 159–63, 167–74, 176–96
    loss of 199–223
    see also babies
Chile 213
China 213
Chiswick Women's Refuge *182*, 183–84
Chola bronzes 42
Christ 19, 44, 55, 57–58, 99, 109,
    164, 249
Christian art 117–18
Church of the Subgenius 242
Cimon 55–57
civil rights movement 228
Cixous, Hélène, 'The Laugh of
    the Medusa' 150, 153
climate crisis 242
clothing, *à la Grecque* 63, 91
Coast Miwok people 22
Coatlicue *38*, 39
collage 167
collective parenting 242–43
collectives 166–67, 176–83
Colombia 223
Communist Party (Germany) 75
Communist Party (US) 204
conception 117–18, 236–37, 240
consciousness-raising groups 176, 179,
    183, 239
consumerism 163–66
contraception 214
Conway and Young, *Milk Report* 147–50
Cooke Latham, London 120
Cooper, Eileen 112
    Putting Down Roots 112–14, *113*
Copenhagen 135–38
Coppola, Luna, *Nel Nome Del Padre
    (In the Name of the Father)* 232
Cornell, Joseph 88
Cosmopolitan 93
Council of Trent (1545) 55
Cox, Renee, *Yo Mama* series 105–108,
    108
Cranach, Lucas the Elder 83–84
    Christ Blessing the Children 56, 57
    The Feeding of the Five Thousand
    57–58
Crete 40
Cronos 40
Cross, Dorothy, *Amazon* 153, *156*
Cuba 24–25, 112, 203

d
Dade County, Florida 232
Day of Testimonies, Dublin (2016)
    218–21
Dean, James 173
death 199–223
Degas, Edgar 102

Demeter 28
Denis, Maurice 72
Denmark 47, 135–38, 233
depression 166, 167
Der Weg der Frau 75
Detroit 84–85
Diana 52
Diana of Ephesus 28
Dickens, Charles 67
Diderot, Denis 60–61
Didion, Joan, *Blue Nights* 199
Dijkstra, Rineke 141
    *Julie, Den Haag, Netherlands,
    February 29 1994* 141, *142*
Disability Arts Movement 213
Dix, Otto 75
Dodd, Stephen 235
Dodge, Harry 225
domestic abuse 183
Dominican Republic 218
Dothan, Leni
    Playing Dead/Pietà 105
    Sleeping Madonna 104–105, *106*
Draper, Helen 91
drugs 164–65, 167
Duae Collective, *Nel Nome Del Padre
    (In the Name of the Father)* 232
Dublin 218–21
Duia, Pietro di Niccoló 42
Dumas, Helena 193–96
Dumas, Marlene
    Models 193
    The Painter 8, 9, 193
    Underground 193, *194*
Dunne, Quintana Roo 199
Dürer, Albrecht 51
Durga 40
Dutch art 58, 89–91

e
Earth Mother 22–26, 39
Edelson, Mary Beth 32
    Trickster series 36
    Zipper Sheela Stepping Out 36, *37*
Egg, Augustus Leopold, *Past and
    Present* 67
eggs, freezing 118
Egypt, ancient 23–24, 32
El Salvador 218
Elizabeth I, Queen 123
Eller, Cynthia 32
Elwes, Catherine, *There is a Myth*
    144–46
Emin, Tracey, *How It Feels* 214–16, *215*
Enlightenment 63
Enriquez, Carlos 203
Enuma Elish 39
Epstein, Jacob 13
    Matter 117
Erizku, Awol 80
Ethiopia 96
Etruscans 42
eugenics 214
EVA Internationale Biennale, Limerick
    (2018) 221
Eve 121–23

EXPORT, VALIE
    The Birth Madonna 164, *165*
    Women's Art: A Manifesto 164
Eyck, Hubert van 121
Eyck, Jan van
    The Arnolfini Portrait 121
    Ghent altarpiece 121–23

f
Facebook 239
Fairbrother, Jessa, *Role Play
    (Woman with Cushion)* 121, *122*
'fallen women' 47, 65–69
Fallon, Rachel, *Aprons of Power 220*, 221
families, queer 225–46
Fanon, Frantz 196
fascism 214
Fayum mummy portraits 83
Federici, Silvia 147, 159
feminism 29, 32–33, 72–74, 133, 159,
    166–67, 176, 180, 242
Feminist Studio Workshop 176
Feministo: Postal Art Event, 'A Portrait
    of the Artist as a Housewife', London
    (1977) 14, 179–80, *179*
fertility 118–21
fertility figures 28–29, *29*, *30*
fertility treatments 204–206
First World War 201
Florence 28, 42, 55, 95
Fluxus 208
foetuses 47–52, 218
    see also babies
Ford Motor Company 85
formula milk 144
Foundling Hospital, London 67, 69
Fragonard, Jean-Honoré, *The Happy
    Family* 62–63, *62*
Fraiman, Susan, *Cool Men and the
    Second Sex* 173, *174*
France 60–63, 91–93, 98–99
Frank, Csilla 246
'Frauen in Not', Germany 75
French Guyana 242
French Revolution 63, 93
Friedan, Betty 167
    The Feminine Mystique 163–64,
    166

g
Gabriel, Angel 44, 117–18
Gaia 24
Gauguin, Paul 72
Gay Men's Press 233
gay rights 232
Geb 23
Genesis 29
Gentileschi, Artemisia 55, 96, 102
    Judith Beheading Holofernes 40
    Madonna and Child 94–95
Germany 28, 51, 72–75, 214
Gimbutas, Marija 29, 32
Goddess Movement 29–33
goddesses 7, 22–24, 39–40, 47
Golub, Leon 42
Great Depression 21

Great Goddess 33
Greece, ancient 24, 28, 40
Greenberg, Clement 168
Greenham Common Women's Peace
    Camp 180
Greuze, Jean-Baptiste 60–61
    *La mére bienaimée (The Well-Loved
        Mother)* 60, 61, 64, 93
Greuze, Madame (Gabrielle
    Babuti) 61
Grevenitis, Anna, *Regard* series 189–92,
    192
The Guardian 221
Guildhall, St Ives 33
Guinea, Candy, *Mariposa* 236, *236*
Gumbs, Alexis Pauline, 'm/other
    ourselves' 226
Gupta, Sunil, *'Pretended' Family
    Relationships* series 233–36, *235*
Gutai art group 125

h
Hackney, London 173
The Hackney Flashers 166–67
    Who's Holding the Baby? series
        166, 167
    Women and Work 167
Hall, Louisa, *Reproduction* 206
Halprin, Anna, *Planetary Dance* 22–23,
    23
Hammersmith Hospital, London 211
Hansen, Andreas 233
Hapi 32
Haraway, Donna 242
Harlem Renaissance 21
Harlow, Harry 153–56
Hassinger, Maren 125
Hawai'i 22
Healy, Ciara, *Mother to the Other* 249–51
Hearn, Karen 123
Helsinki 204
Henrot, Camille, *Wet Job* 147, *149*
Hepworth, Barbara 14
    Mother and Child 12, 13
Heresies 32
Higgie, Jennifer, *The Mirror and
    the Palette* 83
Hiller, Susan, *Ten Months* 126–28,
    129–31
Hinduism 40
HIV 227
Höch, Hannah 75
Hofrichter, Frima Fox 95
Hohle Fels cave 28, *29*
Holy Spirit 117–18, 121
Hooch, Pieter de, *A Mother's Duty*
    58–60
hooks, bell 176
    'Homeplace' 175
Horus 23
housework 159, 163–64
Huitzilopochtli 39
humour 167–68
Hunt, William Holman, *The Awakening
    Conscience* 67

i
ICA, London 171, 180
Ikon Gallery, Birmingham 17
'Images of Womanpower' exhibition,
    London (1973) 34
immigration 214
Impressionists 70, 98
India 40, 42–44
infant mortality rates 95–96, 199
infertility 199
Inner London Education Authority 233
insemination, artificial 240
Instagram 80
Internet 221–23
Ireland 34–35, 214, 218–21, 249
Isis 23
Islam 118
Israel 239
Istanbul 199
Italy 214, 232–33
IVF treatment 120, 199, 204–206

j
Jackson, Melanie, *Deeper in the
    Pyramid* 141–44
Japan 125
'Jim Crow' laws 88
Joffe, Chantal
    Self-Portrait with Esme 89, *90*
    Esme (First Painting) 139
Johannesburg 226
John, St 99
John the Baptist 109, 118
Johnson, Claudette, *Afterbirth* 141, *143*
Jordaens, Jacob 40
Jordan, Eithne 218
Jullion, Jeanne 232
Jupiter 52
Just Above Midtown gallery,
    New York 125

k
Kahlo, Frida 84–85, 112
    Fulang Chang and I 21–22
    The Henry Ford Hospital 84–85,
        86–87
    My Birth 10, *10*
Kali 40
Kamsa, king of Mathura 42
Kaphar, Titus, *Analagous Colors*
    77–79, *81*
Kelly, Mary 146
    Post-Partum Document 171–73, *172*
Kent, Sarah 112
Kenya 25–26
Kher, Bharti
    Angel 44, *45*
    Hybrid series 44
Kienle, Else 75
King, Martin Luther 88
Klein, Jennie 33
Klimt, Gustav 72
Knowles-Carter, Beyoncé 80
Kollwitz, Hans 201
Kollwitz, Karl 201
Kollwitz, Käthe 77

At the Doctor's 76
*Frau mit Totem Kind (Woman with
    Dead Child)* 200–201, *200*
Images of Misery series 75
Peasants' War cycle 200
Kollwitz, Peter 200–201
Krishna 42–44, *43*
Kruger, Barbara, *Untitled (Your body is a
    battleground)* 221–23, *222*
Kurland, Justine, *Mama Babies*
    series 11–13, *11*

l
labour *see* birth
LaFleur, Liss, *Queer Birth Project* 237–39
Lampedo 153
Lange, Dorothea, *Migrant Mother*
    series 21, *21*
languages 196–97
Latin America 223
laughter 167
Lauper, Cyndi, *Time after Time* 187–88
Lawson, Deana, *Baby Sleep* 174–75
League for the Protection of Mothers
    and Sexual Reform 74, 75
Lebanon 40–42
Leeds University 40
Leibovitz, Annie 79
Lely, Peter 91
Lendvai-Dircksen, Erna, Das deutsche
    Volksgesicht 74
Lennon, John, *Unfinished Music No.2:
    Life With The Lions* 208, *209*
Leonardo da Vinci 48–49, 51
    'Burlington House Cartoon' 109
    The Fetus in the Womb 48, 49
lesbian families 223–33
Leslie, Esther, *Deeper in the Pyramid*
    141–44
Leung, Ghislaine, 'Balances' exhibition,
    New York (2022) 184
Levasseur, Thérèse 61–62
Lex-Nerlinger, Alice 75
Lexington, Virginia 189
Leyster, Judith 95–96
Liebig, Justus von 144
Limerick 221
Lippard, Lucy 32
Local Government Act (UK, 1988)
    233–36
Locke, Alain, *The New Negro* 19–21, 77
London 167, 173, 239
Lorde, Audre 226
    'Uses of the Erotic' 175
Los Angeles 124, 168, 176
Los Angeles Times 178, 221
loss 199–233
Luba people 26
Lublin, Lea, *Mon Fils (My Son)* 14, *15*
Lune, Sadie 240–42
    Biological Clock 240
    Preparing for Motherhood series
        241, 242
Luther, Martin 57, 58

m

McDermott, LeRoy 28
Madani, Tala, *Shit Moms* 168–71, *170*
Madonna *see* Mary, Virgin
Mafunda, Nomonde 226
Magdalene Laundry, Limerick 221
Mahadevi 40
Maher, Alice 218, 221
Malta 32
Mami Wata 26
Mann, Emma, *Emmett's Bloody Nose*
     189, *190–91*
Mann, Sally 188–89
   Damaged Child 189
   Family Pictures 189
Mantegna, Andrea, *Lamentation
     over the Dead Christ* 99
Marduk *38*, 39
Marea verde 223
Marie Antoinette, Queen of France
     91–93
Marina the Monk 40–42
Marpesia 153
Mars 42
Mary, Virgin (Madonna) 39, 42, 52,
     55, 188
   Annunciation 117–18, 123, 204
   and the Crucifixion 99
   iconography 80, 104
   Madonna and Child paintings 6,
       19, 22, 44, 108–109, 164
Mary Magdalene 99
Masolino (Tommaso di Cristoforo Fini),
     Madonna of Humility 20
Maswell Graham Gallery,
     New York 184
Mathura 42
matriarchy 32
Matthew, St 58
Mayer, Mónica 180–83
Mazibuko, Nomsa 226–27
Medicaid 105
medications 164–66, 167
Medieval art 19
Mediterranean 28, 29
Meehan, Paula 218
Meloni, Giorgia 232–33
memento mori 83–84
Memmi, Lippo 117–18
Mendick, Lindsey, *Hairy on the
     Inside* 120, *121*
Mendieta, Ana 24–25
   Siluetas 24
   *Untitled (Esculturas Rupestres)
     [Rupestrian Sculptures]* 25, *25*
Metropolitan Museum of Art,
     New York 42
Mexico 39, 84, 180–81, 223
Mexico City 77
Michelangelo, *Pietà* 164
midwives 51–52
milk 141–44, 150
   breastfeeding 55–57, 63, 95, 144,
       147–56
Milk, Harvey 232
Millais, John Everett

Mrs Coventry Patmore 64, 65, *65*
   The Violet's Message 64
   The Woodsman's Daughter 68–69, *68*
Miranda, Caroline A. 221
miscarriages 84–85, 199, 206–208
Mississippi 77
Mrs. America (TV drama) 167
Moderna Museet, Stockholm 33
Modersohn-Becker, Paula 72–74
   *Kneeling Mother with Child at her
     Breast* 72, *73*
   Reclining Mother and Child II 75, *76*
   *Self-Portrait with Two Flowers in
     her Raised Left Hand* 82, 83–84
Moore, Demi 79
Moore, Henry 13
Morisot, Berthe
   *Berthe Morisot Drawing with her
     Daughter* 99, *100*
   *The Wet Nurse Angele Feeding Julie
     Manet* 98–99
Mother Art 176, 180
   Laundry Works 176–78, *178*
   Mother Art Cleans Up 178
   Rainbow Playground 176
Mother Nature 22–26
motherhood 225–51
mothering 159–97, 226
'Mothers' exhibition, Birmingham
     (1990) 17
Mount Dicte 40
Mount Tamalpais 22
Muholi, Zanele
   Being series 226–27, *227*
   Faces and Phases series 227
Munch, Edvard 75
Museum of Modern Art, Oxford
     144–46
Museum of Modern Art, New York
     150
Mutu, Wangechi 25
   Fertility Heal 118–20, *119*
   Water Woman 25–26, *26*
Myerscough, Ishbel, *All 103*, 104

n

Nagel, Otto 75
Nash, Jennifer 187
   Birthing Black Mothers 79
natalism 214
National Childbirth Trust (NCT)
     133–35
National Gallery, London 121
National Museum of Anthropology and
     History, Mexico City 39
National Portrait Gallery,
     London 88
National Society for Women's Service 64
National Third World Lesbian and Gay
     Conference, First (1979)
     226
Native Americans 214
Nazis 74, 75, 164
Ndweni, Tumi 226
Nead, Lynda 68–69
Neale, Anne 211

Neel, Alice 123–24
   After the Death of the Child 201–203,
     202
   Futility of Effort 203–204, *203*
   Pregnant Maria 123–24, *124*
Nelson, Gunvor, *Schmeerguntz* 162–63,
     162
Nelson, Maggie, *The Argonauts* 225
Nengudi, Senga 124–26
   R.S.V.P. 125–26, *125*
neo-Nazis 221
Neolithic figures 28–29
Neonatal Intensive Care Units (NICU)
     135, 138–40
Nephthys 23
Netherlands 58, 89–91, 95–96, 123
'new woman' 72, 74–75
New York 123, 201–203, 204
New York Sanitation Department
     160
New Zealand 29, 93
Nicaragua 218
Nicodemus, Everlyn
   My Mutilated Humanity 96, *97*
   Woman in the World 96–98
Nile River 32
Nineveh 39
Nochlin, Linda 98–99
Nolde, Emil 75
Norris, Siân, *Bodies Under Siege* 223
North East London Polytechnic 213
nudes 123–28
Nuestro Mundo (TV show) 180
Nut 23–24, *24*

o

obstetric violence 199, 216
Ochoa, Guillermo 180
Ohio 244, 246
Oliver, Guy 120
Ono, Yoko 208
   No Bed for Beatle John 208, *209*
   'Radio Play' (album track) 208
   *Unfinished Music No.2: Life With
     The Lions* 208, *209*
Opie, Catherine 236
   Self-Portrait/Cutting 105
   Self-Portrait/Nursing 22,
     105, *107*
orgasm 60–61
Orothyia 153
Osiris 23
Ovid, *Metamorphoses* 52, 55
Oxford 144–46

p

Pachamama 22
Palaeolithic figures 28
Palazzo Grassi, Venice 193
Pande, Amrita 42–44
Paracelsus 49–51
Parali, Fani
   Early Universe series 140
   Incubator/Flight 140, *140*
Paris 14, 70, 74
Paris Salon 60–61, 93

Parvati 40
Patmore, Coventry, *The Angel
in the House* 64, 68–69
Patmore, Emily Augusta 64, 65, *65*
Patmore, Tennyson 64
patriarchy 24, 32, 164, 243
Paul, Celia
Frank and Me 114, *115*
Self-Portrait 114
Paula Modersohn-Becker Haus,
Bremen 75
Pele 22
Pero 55
Persephone 28
Peru 214
Philadelphia General Hospital 203
Pilkington, Cathy, *Surrogate* 156, *157*
Pizzey, Erin 183
Plath, Sylvia 153
play 167–68
Poland 218
police, stop and search 185–87
Pollock, Griselda 70
Old Mistresses 40
Polvo de Gallina Negra
Madre por un dia (Mother for a day)
180–83, *180*
¡MADRES! 180–83
polycystic ovarian syndrome
(PCOS) 120
Pool, Juriaen 91
Poole, Mason 80
Portugal 216–18
Postal Art Event (1975–77) 179–80
Poussin, Nicolas 40
Pre-Raphaelite Brotherhood 64
pregnancy 47–55, 105, 109–12
abortion 75, 112, 200, 211, 213–23
lesbian couples 236–39
miscarriages 84–85, 199, 206–208
naked bodies 123–28
photographs of 79–80
self-portraits 83–88
stillbirths 199, 206
as taboo in paintings 121–23
trans people 237–39
Price, Dorothy 201
Project Art Centre, Dublin 218–21
Prospect 211
Protestantism 58
Prouvost, Laure, *MOOTHERR* 247, *248*
Puvis de Chavannes, Pierre 102

q

Queen Charlotte's Hospital,
London 208
queer families 225–46

r

Ra 24
Raven, Arlene 29
Reagan, Ronald 178
Rees, Jeremy and Annabel 121
Reformation 55, 58
Refuge 183
Rego, Paula, *Abortion* series 216–18, *217*

Reiss, Winold, *The Brown Madonna*
19–21, *20*
Renaissance art 19, 42, 55, 99, 105
Renoir, Auguste 102
reproductive rights 213–23
ReStack, Dani and Sheilah
Come Coyote 243
Feral Domestic 243–46
Future From Inside 243, 246
Strangely Ordinary This Devotion
243, *245*
Rezaire, Tabita
Amakaba 242–43
Hoetep Blessings 244
Womb Consciousness 243
Rhea 40
Rhea Silvia 42
Rich, Adrienne, *Of Woman Born*
32–33
Richardson, Su 14–17, 178, 179–80
Burnt Breakfast 180
Heartstrings 208–11, *210*
Rigshospitalet, Copenhagen 135–38
Riley, Denise, *Time Lived, Without
its Flow* 201
Rilke, Rainer Maria, *Requiem for
a Friend* 84
Rivera, Diego 77, 84
Robb Elementary School, Uvalde,
Texas 184–85
Roberts, Dorothy, *Killing the Black
Body* 105–106
Robinson, Hilary 17
Roe v. Wade 213, 221–23
Roman Charity 55–57
Romans 28, 42, 52–55
Rome 95
Romulus and Remus 42
Roselius, Ludwig 75
Ross, Monica 178, 179
Rösslin, Eucharius
*Der schwangeren Frauen und
Hebammen Rosengarten (The Rose
Garden of Pregnant Women and
Midwives)* 50, 51
Rousseau, Jean-Jacques 61–62
Emile, or On Education 61, 62
Julie or the New Eloise 62, 64
'Roussel Law' 63
Royal College of Art, London 99
Rubens, Peter Paul, *Roman Charity*
55–57, *56*
Ruffin, Jimmy, 'What becomes of the
broken hearted?' (song) 211
Ruskin, John 64
Ruysch, Rachel 89–91
Rymsdyk, Jan van 49

s

Saar, Betye 33, 85–88
Anticipation 85–88, *85*
St Ives, Cornwall 33
St Mary and St David, Kilpeck *36*
Saint Phalle, Niki de
Nana sculptures 33
She – A Cathedral 33, *34*

Salon de Mai, Paris (1968) 14
Salviati (Francesco de Rossi),
Charity 54, 55
Samoa 26
San Francisco 228, 232, 240
Sandy Hook school shooting
(2012) 184
Santería 24
Saturn 147
Save Our Children, Inc 232
Saville, Jenny, *Reproduction Drawings
(after the Leonardo Cartoon)*
109, *111*
Saxony 55
Schaer, Miriam, *Babies (Not) On Board:
The Last Prejudice? 16*, 17
Schneemann, Carolee, *Anti-Demeter*
109–12
school shootings 184–85
Scotland 249
Sebastian, St 55
Section 28, Local Government Act
(1988) 233–35
Sedira, Zineb, *Mother Tongue 195*,
196–97
Segantini, Giovanni 72
The Evil Mothers 71, 72
The Punishment of Lust 72
self-portraits 83–114
selkies 249
semen 49–51
Seth 23
sexuality 174–75
Shaktism 40
sheela-na-gigs 34–36, *36*, 221
Sheen, Martin 173
Shelley, Mary, *Frankenstein* 206
'Ship of Theseus' 225
shit 168–71
Silagi, Laura 176
Simone Martini 117–18
Siqueiros, David 77
Sjöö, Monica, *God Giving Birth*
33–34, *35*
Slade School of Art, London
146, 216
Smith, Jenny 183–84
Smith, Kiki, *Pietà* 249, *250*, 249–51
Sobering, Katherine, *Queer Birth
Project* 237–39
social media 239–40
Soltau, Annegret 126
*Auf dem Geburtstisch I (On The Birth
Table I)* 126
Ausgeliefert (Vulnerable) 126, *127*
Schwanger (Pregnant) 126
Soren, Tabitha, *Motherload* 150–53,
154–55
South Africa 226–27
Spanish Harlem, New York 123, 201–203
Spears, Heather, 135–38
*Studies/Drawings of Labour/
Childbirth* (1987) *136–37*
Spence, Jo, *Beyond The Family
Album* 189
sperm donors 236

Spero, Nancy 33
   Codex Artaud 24
   The Great Mother 42, *43*
Spice Girls 79
spirituality 33–34
Starkey, Hannah, *Untitled, February
   2013* 173–74, *174*
Steinem, Gloria 223
Stephen Friedman Gallery,
   London 146
sterilization 213, 214
Stidolph, Melanie 204
stillbirths 199, 206
Stoker, Bram, *Dracula* 72
stop and search 185–87
Stormfront 221
Stuttgart 75
suffrage 72
Suleiman, Susan 167–68
Support not Separation 211
surrogate mothers 42–44
surveillance 184
Sweden 109, 237
Symbolism 72

t

Taino people 25
Talbot, Emma, *The Mountain,
   Time after Time* 187–88, *188*
Tanzania 96
Tate gallery, London 193
terminations *see* abortion
thalidomide 96
Thames, River 67
Thatcher, Margaret 233
Thompson, Florence Owens 21
Tiamat *38*, 39
Tiber, River 42
Time magazine 79, *81*
Time Out 112
Tintoretto 144
Titans 24
Titian, *Diana and Callisto* 52–55, *53*
Tokyo 125
Tolstoy, Leo, *Anna Karenina* 225
Torre, Marcantonio della 48
Toulouse-Lautrec, Henri de 102
tranquillizers 166, 167
trans people 227, 237–39
Turkey 28–29

u

Ukeles, Mierle Laderman 163
   Maintenance Art Tasks 160, *161*
   Manifesto for Maintenance Art 160
   Mikva Dreams 32
   Touch Sanitation 160–62
Ullman, Tracey 167
United Nations General
   Assembly 93
United States of America
   abortion rights 213–14, 218,
     221–23
   consumer advertising 163–64
   infant mortality 199
   school shootings 184–85

violence against Black men
   77–79
unmarried mothers 52, 65–69, 208–11,
   214, 221
Urania Cottage, Shepherd's Bush 67
US Army 221
US Supreme Court 213, 221–23
Utrillo, Maurice 102–104
Utter, André 102–104
Uvalde, Texas 184–85

v

Valadon, Madeleine 102, 104
Valadon, Suzanne 102–104
   Family Portrait 101, 102, 104
Valerius Maximus 55
Vanity Fair 79
Venus 80, 201
'Venus' figures 28, *29*, *30*
'Venus of Willendorf' 28
Vesalius, Andreas 51
Vestal Virgins 42
Victoria, Queen 64
Vienna 164, 206
Vietnam War (1954–75) 24
Vigée Le Brun, Élisabeth Louise
   Marie Antoinette and Her Children 93
   *Self-Portrait with her Daughter
     Julie* 91–93, *92*
violence
   against Black people 77–79
   domestic abuse 183
   obstetric violence 199, 216
   school shootings 184–85
Virgin Mary *see* Mary, Virgin
Voge, Christine, *Untitled (Three Children
   and a Woman)* (1978)
   182, 183
Volcano, Del LaGrace, *MaPa Del
   and Mika* 237, *238*

w

Wadsworth Atheneum,
   Connecticut 160
Walker, Barbara, *Louder Than
   Words* series 185–87, *186*
Walker, Caroline, *Bottles and
   Pumps* 146–47, *148*
Walker, Kate 178
   Death of a Housewife 178–79
Wall, Jeff 13
Washington 223
Watt, George Fiddes, *Found
   Drowned* 67, 69
Watts Riots (1965) 125
Watts Towers Art Center,
   Los Angeles 124
Weems, Carrie Mae, *Kitchen
   Table Series* 175–76, *177*
Der Weg der Frau (The Woman's Way)
   75
Weimar Republic 75
Wellcome Collection, London 135
wet nurses 61–63, 95, 98–99, 109
White, Charles, *Hope for the Future*
   77, *78*

Whitely, Rebecca 51
Wiley, Dorothy, *Schmeerguntz*
   162–63, *162*
Willis, Nancy 211, 223
   Self Portrait with Lost Baby
     211–13, *212*
Wiltshire, Hermione 133–35
   The Birth of the Image 99–102, *100*
   Nicola Preparing for Birth 133–35
   Preparing For Birth series
     133–35, *134*
Winant, Carmen
   My Birth 150–53, *152*
   White Ink 150, *151*
witch hunts 34
Wolf, Friedrich 75
A Woman's Place, London (1974)
   178–79
Women's Art History Conference,
   London (1975) 178
The Women's Building, Los Angeles 29,
   33, 176, 180
Women's Images of Men, London
   (1980) 146
women's liberation movement
   164, 228
Women's Movement 88, 124,
   175, 176
Woolf, Virginia 64
World War I 74
Worpswede, Germany 72, 74
Wright, Daphne, *I Know What It's
   Like 195*, 197

y

Yashoda 42–44, *43*
YouTube 247
Yugoslavia 32

z

Zangewa, Billie, *Every Woman*
   93–94, *94*
Zeus 40